# THREE LANGUAGE FORMULA
## An Educational Problem

# THREE LANGUAGE FORMULA

## An Educational Problem

Santosh Aggarwal

With a Foreword by

**Prof. Satish Chandra**

GYAN

GYAN PUBLISHING HOUSE

New Delhi 110 002

**GIAN PUBLISHING HOUSE**
**4-C, Ansari Road, Daryaganj**
**New Delhi-110 002**



ISBN-81-212-0336-8

Consultant : Dr. D.P. Pattanayak

This publication is financially supported by the ICSSR. The responsibility for the facts stated, opinions expressed or conclusions reached, is entirely that of the author and that the ICSSR accepts no responsibility for them.

PRINTED IN INDIA

Published by Mrs. Gayatri Garg for Gian Publishing House, New Delhi-110002.
Laser type set by Ocean Laser Prints, Delhi-51.
Printed at Goyal Offset Works, Delhi.

# Foreword

The question of language, specially at the school level, is important for any people in any country. In a country such as India where nationalism is still in the process of development and which is unique in having 14 major national languages, the question of language becomes even more important.

From the second half of the 19th century when the national struggle for freedom started in India it was recognised that a common language was necessary for communication all over India. The point at issue was whether it would be Hindi or Urdu or a mixture of two called Hindustani. This issue was resolved after 1947 when the Constituent Assembly took a decision in favour of Hindi. However, bearing in mind the concrete situation, a formula called the 'three-language formula' was hammered out.

The spirit of this formula was that every one would learn Hindi in addition to English and the regional language. This implied that in the Hindi speaking state, a third language, preferably a southern language, would be taught.

The implementation of this formula has faced many problems. One of the concrete problem being that people do not learn languages for themselves but for some advantage. Where people live in areas adjacent to two language groups it is not difficult to persuade them to learn both the languages. In other cases, people learn languages which bring them some economic or cultural benefit.

Dr. Santosh Aggarwal has examined the entire complex set of issues with special reference to the matter of its implementation in the school curriculum. Since the three-language formula and attendant problems are likely to face us for a considerable period, I am quite sure that Dr. Santosh Aggarwal's research in the topic would be found both useful and timely.

Jawaharlal Nehru University
New Delhi-110067.

Satish Chandra

# Preface

The present work is a research study done on the three language policy of the Government of India. This study includes a historical survey of the languages used and learnt. The present work is a humble effort in this direction. I have tried to substantiate my treatment of the subject with the help of field work, and the opinion of the students as well as the cross section of society. I have incorporated a comparative study of the language policy of some of the foreign countries like the U.S.S.R., Africa and several others.

The present work was submitted for the Ph.D. thesis from Delhi University. This opportunity was availed of by me under the Teacher Fellowship scheme but for which it would not have been possible for me to pursue my research study and as such I owe my heartiest thanks to Professor Satish Chandra—the Ex-Chairman of U.G.C.

I wish to express my heartfelt thanks to the Principals of schools and men of eminence in public life who helped me in providing information related to my research work in a number of ways.

My thanks are also due to the staff of several renowned libraries, centres of advanced studies and several university centres for permitting me to consult books and personnel from time to time.

I express my sincere thanks to the Education Attachese of the Embassies/High Commissions of the U.S.S.R., Indonesia, Tanzania and Nigeria.

I am extremely grateful and obliged to my guide Prof. (Miss) K. Bose, till recently Dean, Faculty of Education, University of Delhi, who has all along been a source of inspiration to me. It is only due to her able guidance and constant advice that I could pursue my research work.

I shall be failing in my duty if I do not acknowledge the immense assistance I got from my friend Dr. (Miss) Savitri Saxena, of the Department of Skt. D.S.C., University of Delhi, who helped me in no mean measure. In any case, a brief mention in preface is a small repayment for the debt of gratitude that I owe to her.

It will be unjustified if I do not recognise the help given by my brother Dr. R.K. Agrawal, Deputy C.M.O., Northern Railway who in spite of many hurdles has always been a source of encouragement in the completion of my work.

I owe my thanks to Prof. S. Shukla, former Head and Dean of the Faculty of Education, University of Delhi, for his constant inspiration in the completion of my research study.

My deep gratitudes to Babuji—late Shri Ram Richpal Saxena (my friend Dr. Savitri Saxena's father) who had always been a source of inspiration for taking up this research work.

I also owe my heartfelt thanks to the late Principal, S.S. Kothari and the then Secretary of the Management Committee of my college, who were kind enough to sanction me study leave for this work.

I am extremely grateful and obliged to those persons and acquaintances especially to Dr. N.K. Mishra, Prof. and Head, Department of Physiology, Himachal Pradesh University, Simla, who, in some or the other way have been helping me in the completion of my work.

I am also thankful to my typist Shri R. Padmanabhan for his late night sitting and excellent timely work. Last but not the least I am thankful to M/s Gian Publishing House who have taken up this work for publication.

Santosh Aggarwal

# Contents

## *Abbreviations*

| | | |
|---|---|---|
| Ar | = | Arabic |
| B | = | Bengali |
| G | = | Gujrati |
| Ger | = | German |
| H | = | Hindi |
| K | = | Konkani |
| Mar | = | Marathi |
| M.T. | = | Mother Tongue |
| N. | = | Nepali |
| Per | = | Persian |
| Pu | = | Punjabi |
| RL | = | Regional Language |
| Skt | = | Sanskrit |
| Si | = | Sindhi |
| Ur | = | Urdu |

# List of Tables

# List of Tables

| Table | Title | Page |
|---|---|---|

# 1 Rationale of the Study

"The ideal language situation is one where a single accepted norm of pronunciation, grammar and vocabulary is used for all levels of speaking and writing", says Ferguson.[1] But the arrivals of new communities and different alien Governments in India have made it impossible to have this situation because, the foreigners had captured not only the central seat of the Government of the country but had uprooted its indigenous system of education and the cultural set up also. With the result, people became bilinguals or even trilinguals, as they stuck to their vernaculars and were compelled to learn and use the language of the rulers. As language is an important means of communication, the political and economic participation during the last several centuries in this land have given rise to the awakening of the existence of one's own language and culture on the one hand and the national consciousness, on the other. Consequently, the former is creating the problem of the use of more than one language, for, 'within a political community, emotionally, as a rallying point of group consciousness, language serves as a very frequent badge or symbol'.[2] In fact, it is the latter i.e. 'the national consciousness, which is tending towards the removal of the societal language barrier'.[3] While discussing the issue of national consciousness, Alexandra Pierre writes, 'It is the consciousness of unity or community and the will to live together, although a *common language,* common origin, common customs and a common territory are the preconditions of the former',[4] broadly speaking, nationalism is referred to as a political movement or a process of growing self-consciousness based on a feeling of common ethnicity. Of the several criteria of common ethnicity, a common language has often been the paramount one, with religion coming in the second place,[5] because, 'Language has often been regarded as the matrix of a national state and the real expression of the character of a nation, as the emanation of the national spirit.[6,7] It is an important element in the consciousness of nationhood, although it may not always be a decisive factor. "Language in its relationship to nationality with reference to the 'National State' has now come to be the prototype of political organisation in the modern world."[8] Linguistically, nationalism may be defined as 'a symptom of the rise to power of new economic and social classes in place of the old'.[9] Although the connection between language and nationality seems to be essentially modern, the most important factor in modern nationalism is language.[10] 'Every self respecting nation has to have a language as 'nation' and 'language' have become inextricably intertwined.'[11]

As language is the sole instrument of intercommunication in a civilised society, the modern governments face a problem of a linguistic medium in a country's governmental organisation. Haugen thinks, that, 'A nation feels handicapped if it is required to make use of more than one language for official purposes, unless the language borders are stable as in Switzerland.[12] Secondly, a single linguistic medium is needed in the day to day dealing with citizens by administrative agencies in the dispensation of justice, in the conduct of legislative bodies, in education, trade and commerce, etc. Thirdly, as language is the only medium for social intercourse, the need of one single linguistic medium becomes more essential for the mutual understanding and communication. Hence, it is not always emotionally, that, people demand a language, which can be symbolised as the 'National Language' of a particular nation. It is a language, which, can be used as a common means of communication. It is in fact a medium of inter-communication to overcome the diversity of different mother tongues. "Undoubtedly, consideration on national self-respect is not without relevance in respect of language which, touches the entire national life of a people so intimately and which is besides such a sensitive point of honour in the field of international contacts."[13] Though the problems of the languages of minorities generally occur in a large number of countries like U.S.S.R., France and Switzerland yet, the problem is unique in India, because, the language issue is generally related in this country, to the religious faiths of its citizens. Moreover, the use of one language at the national level extends some of the loyalties of the family of the neighbourhood or the clan to the whole nation. 'In a society, that is essentially familiar or tribal or regional, it stimulates a loyalty beyond the primary-groups. Hence, a common linguistic medium to be recognised as the common or national language becomes essential and the decision has to be taken while keeping in mind the interests of minority linguistic groups, so that, they can retain as well as develop their separate languages and can also intelligibly communicate with each other in almost all the fields of life. In India, where 1,652 languages are recognised as the mother tongues,[14] a common language is required for wider communication, e.g., for the daily business of the Government, Commerce and especially for Education. 'Functionally, it is a *sine-qua non* for rapid development of an undeveloped language which has not been used in all the functions that a language can perform in a society, larger than that of the local tribe or peasant village.'[15] "National Languages" observed Haugen, "have offered membership in the nation, an identity that gives one entry into a new kind of group, which is not just kinship, or government, or religion, but a novel and peculiarly modern brew of all three."[16] Though 'the ideal of national language is internal cohesion, external distinction yet, it discourages any conflicting loyalty to other nations' says Haugen. Besides, the recognition of 'National language' is an indication of not only self-pride, but, it also raises the social status of its users in the eyes of the other nations. "It is primarily symbolic, a matter of prestige (or lack of it) that attaches to specific forms or varieties of language by virtue of identifying the social status of their users."[17]

The most important reason for developing a national language is for checking the tendencies of narrow patriotism, which, may arise in a democratic country like India, where freedom is granted in the Constitution for maintaining the educational institutions on the basis of both language and religion. "All minorities, whether based on *religion* or *language* shall have the right to establish and administer educational institutions of their choice."[18] Not only that, the State Government too, cannot discriminate while granting aid to such educational institutions which are based on the basis of religion or language. "The State shall not, in granting aid to educational institutions, discriminate against any educational institution on the ground that it is under the management of a minority, whether *based on religion or language*."[19] However, on the desirability of having a common language for intercommunication within the country, Thirtha holds, "A common linguistic medium helps in checking the tendencies of regional exclusivism, nativism and revivalism."[20] It becomes politically more respectable to speak one language than several, as our country (India) believes in 'Federal Nationalism' where unity is sought in diversity. People may insist on having a 'national language', because where there is a language, there must be a nation, or, where there is a nation, there must be a national language. In the words of Hayes, 'The language of a free people ought to be one and the same for all.'[21] In words of Pattanayak, 'To build bridges of understanding among the masses of people, a communication language is an essential necessity.'[22] Still, in the midst of multilingual environment, that the framers of the Indian Constitution decided to accommodate the varied languages and religions, was amazingly an indication of great wisdom on their part.

Though the demand for a common language in India was made long ago in pre-independence period yet, nothing substantial could be done in this direction as India was not politically free. Tilak, Gandhi and other national leaders laid much emphasis on the need of having a common language. In December 1905, Bal Gangadhar Tilak expressed his views in a Conference of the Nagri Pracharini Sabha at Banaras, 'If you want to draw a nation together, there is no force more powerful than common language for all.'[23] In 1937, when the provincial autonomy was granted, the demand for a common language became stronger and after the achievement of freedom in 1947 the demand for a common language as the medium of instruction and administration came to the forefront. On December 21st, 1947, Maulana Azad, while delivering the Convocation address, to the Patna University remarked, "Today, we find ourselves in the unenviable predicament of offering explanations. The rest of the world naturally wants to know why we are without a national language in spite of our independence."[24] In the 15th meeting of 1949, the C.A.B.E.[25] also raised a question as to what language was going to be the 'national language' of the country.

On this issue of 'national language' *four different types* of opinions were expressed by the intellectuals. First are those, who recognise the importance and practical superiority of English as a medium of inter-ethnic communication, of trade, of intellectual life and of contact with the rest of India and the world. Radhakrishnan, more a scholar than a statesman, held, 'whatever the advantage of English and the immediate risks in a change-over, the balance of advantage on a long view of the matter lies in the change.'[26] Besides, according to the census of 1971 English in terms of native speakers, is the mother tongue of 191,579 persons only, in this country, populated by 548,159,652 persons.[27] Though, English has been the language of the Government, administration and education for nearly 250 years, it is understood by 1% of population only.[28] Furthermore, English is associated with a segment of the dominant social minority. Swami Dayanand, Mahatma Gandhi, Subhash Chandra Bose, Mrs. Annie Beasant and other national leaders refuted the argument in favour of English, because, it can never be the language of the masses.[29] 'Those who want to retain English for a further indefinite period vote for the stagnation of our language for a further indefinite period, says Kanhaiya Lal Bhaeru Lal,[30] and in a continuation of the status-quo in respect of language inflicts loss of self-respect on the masses of our people.[31] Earlier, Mahatma Gandhi (in *Young India*, 1921), asserted, that, 'to get rid of the infatuation for English is one of the essentials of Swaraj' (Freedom). Till September, 1947, Mahatma Gandhi had pressed for "banishing English as a cultural usurper as we successfully banished the political rule of the English usurper.[32] But to quote him again on the role of English, "rich English language will ever retain its natural place as the international speech of commerce and diplomacy", one admires the foresight of the man. From here one deduces certain points. The basic aim of hunting information for the position of language as accepted by the Constitution of India (Articles 343 to 351, Part XVII) is to gain some accurate factual data on the role of various Indian languages for different purposes in this country. At the turn of every debate containing fiery sentiments from the renowned Indians from the four corners of the country, there appears a sane consideration regarding total banishing or not, of any language, Indian or English which happens to be the foreign language. After quoting Mahatma Gandhi's views on acceptance of Hindi as the language of the Union of India (1921, 1947) the Official Language Commission could not take courage to recommend displacement of English for all purposes. "While . . . it is essential to displace English as the medium of administration at the All India level by the Union Language, as the medium of administration at state levels by the respective regional languages and as the medium of higher education in universities by some suitable Indian language or languages, it would still be necessary that English is taught well in the educational system to those who have reasons for learning it. We also believe that a reorientation in the teaching of English is called for in view of the different role that it will hereafter play in the country's educational structure. English should be taught hereafter more as a 'language of comprehension' than as a 'literary language'. (p. 36 OLC 1956). It is quite clear that the controversy about the position of a language is there if only a partial view of a language is unnecessarily overstressed. The role of languages is to be seen in proper perspective in respect of their utility, intelligibility, currency, feasibility of learning and practice, and the wider as well as the varied spheres for which they are very much relied upon. A common man uses his language, may be the only one, in all spheres. An educated man might be using his mother tongue at home, a regional language for interpersonal communication, a classical language for the satisfaction of his scholarly pursuit or religious readings and one or more foreign languages when he can manage. His command over each variety of language will depend on the purposes for which he uses his tool of communication and his competence for one or more languages will be determined by the level he has acquired. Opportunities need to be made available at the school stage for learning--more than one language and that is what the Indian Constitution holds out to the people of India.

In a Convention held in September 1949, Hindi was accepted as the official language for the Union of India. The linguist, Suniti Kumar Chatterjee, the historian Neelkanth Shastri, the great Sanskrit scholar Raghavan, Keshav Chandra Sen, Gopalaswamy Ayangar and other renowned persons wanted that English should be replaced by Hindi within ten years.[33] Otherwise says the economist Ashoka Mehta, 'Only a handful of men who know English will be able to operate effectively in political and administrative matters.'[34] In another Convention of Hindi Sammelan held in Karnataka at all-India level, a resolution with regard to English language to be recognised constitutionally was passed as follows : 'The convention is of the opinion that to give in the Constitution, an official status to a foreign language is below the self-respect of any nation. Therefore, the Convention earnestly urges upon the government to give up their efforts to make English an associate official language for an unspecified period.[35] Suniti Kumar Chatterjee expressed his opinion, at a date much later than the Official Language Commission's Report (1957): 'We cannot make English the official language of a free-India,' that would hurt our national sensitivity make us look small before other people with national languages of their own (1963)'.[36] Hence, the suggestion for making English as the official language of India was resented in different quarters.

The second group held the view that all the constitutionally recognised languages should be given equal status at the central level. This, if accepted, would present practical problems, for instance, this would lead to high cost and inefficiency of administration. The mere cost of translating and printing the official documents in 15 languages and of simultaneously translating legislative debates would be prohibitive for a none-too-affluent country.[37] Consequently, although all the 15 languages were given the same status in the Indian Constitution, Hindi was chosen as the official language and English as an associate official language.

The third group constituted some of those intellectuals who suggested that Sanskrit be recognised as the 'national language' of India. It had been a common medium of communication in the different regions/linguistic group in the remote past.[38] At present also, it is being suggested as the best pan-Indian medium of communication,[39] since it is the parent language of almost all the Indian languages. In fact, at some stage Suniti Kumar Chatterjee the Indologist suggested a simplified form of Sanskrit as the most suitable and most universally accepted national language for India.[40] He further strengthened his suggestion by quoting eminent scientists like C.V. Raman, a humanist like Radhakrishnan and the other educationists from all parts of India. Even some of the European admirers of Sanskrit like F.W. Thomas of Oxford and others advocated that only Sanskrit was the suitable language for modern India. Regarding the difficult structure of the Sanskrit language, MacDonell in 1913 observed that, 'It not only represents all the sounds of Sanskrit but is arranged on a thoroughly scientific method, the simple vowels (short and long) coming first, then diphthongs and lastly the consonants in uniform groups according to the organs of speech with which they are pronounced.'[41] But the suggestion could not be finalised for, Sanskrit is neither the mother tongue of any section of society, nor it is spoken by even 1000 persons.[42]

The fourth is the largest group holding the view in favour of 'Hindi' as the language of the Union and the language for the Inter-State Communication.

"The point to remember is that Hindi has been adopted in the Constitution for the official business of the Union and for purposes of Inter-state-communication not because it is better developed than the other regional languages are; not because a greater or more varied wealth of literary output is available in it; nor because it has presently a larger availability of books in the sciences and in different other branches of modern knowledge. It is chosen for performing the job of the official language medium and spoken, amongst the regional languages by the largest number of people. Apart from the 42 per cent people of the total population . . . it is understood to a considerable extent in areas outside Hindi speaking areas . . . where persons hailing from different regions of India and not knowing English have occasion to converse." (p. 37. OLCR – Official Language Commission Report 1956).

Even earlier in 1928, the Motilal Nehru Report had advocated the adoption of such a language at the national level of the country which could be understood by the masses, so that they could participate in the business and politics of the country.[43] Regarding its vast use in the country Rajendra Lal Mitra in 1864 stated that, 'Hindi has been in use from the Eastern boundary of Bihar to the foot of the Soleman range and from the Vindhya to the Tarai. The Gorkhas have carried it to Kumaon and Nepal and as a lingua franca, it is intelligible everywhere from the Kohistan to Cape Comorin'.[44] Kellog in 1875 had mentioned, 'Of the two hundred and fifty million inhabitants of India, speaking a score or more of different languages, fully one fourth or between 60 and 70 million, own Hindi as their vernacular,[45] while another author Cust says, 'This estimate is probably too low. The Hindi speaking population of India cannot fall short of 80 millions.'[46] He further stated that 'If Persianised Hindi called Urdu or Hindustani be reckoned as, by most people, a dialect of Hindi, then Hindi must be counted as the vernacular of over one hundred millions of Indian population, and is spoken by more of our race than any language except the Chinese.'[47] To be precise, in the words of Kellog himself, 'In short, throughout an area of more than 248,000 square miles, Hindi is the language of the great mass of population.'[48]

Chatterjee further pointed out, that in a vast country like India, it is the language used by the large, civilized groups, that matter,[49] and among these languages, it is Hindi which is most widely used.[50] "In practice, Hindi is already largely in use as a 'link language' for the country," [51,52] because 'This great "Palavar speech" is also understood by a good number of people in the bigger towns.'[53] As a result, Hindi acts as 'the most natural inter provincial link' among the speakers of the different Aryan languages.[54] In Orissa, Bombay, Andaman and Nicobar Islands in the Bay of Bengal, Hindi is the medium of communication among the different language groups.

In 1949, the CABE decided that the language most commonly understood and spoken by the people in this great country should become the language of entire nation.[55] The eminent philosopher Radhakrishnan stated that, "there is no other alternative, but, to choose a language spoken by a high percentage of the people of India, to give it the status of 'state-language', and to develop it for the chosen, task . . . the language designated Hindi or Hindustani has to fulfil this destiny."[56] Nehru, the then Prime Minister had also realised that, 'We cannot communicate with the masses in English, of course, Hindi will be the National Language.' Bankim said, 'without Hindi, we can not proceed.' Even the world known poet Rabindranath Tagore realised that Hindi was the suitable language for being given the recognition of the national language of the country. Grierson may be recalled here, while stating about Hindi at the turn of the century, that "In themselves, without any extraneous help whatever the dialects from which it is sprung are, and for 500 years have been capable of expressing with crystal clearness any idea which the mind of man can conceive. It has an enormous native vocabulary and a complete apparatus for the expression of abstract terms. Its old literature contains some of the highest flights of poetry and some of the most eloquent expressions of religious devotion which have found their birth in Asia. Treatises, on philosophy and rhetoric are found in it, in which the subject is handled with all the subtlety of the great Sanskrit writers and this with hardly the use of a Sanskrit word."[57]

If a common language is required at the national level a common script is also required so that the different linguistic groups can comprehend mutually whatever is written by them. Therefore, another issue was raised regarding a single script to be adopted for writing the 'national language'. For maintaining the homogeneity of the script on the national level, either of the two, such as the Roman or the Devanagari scripts were suggested. A section of the people raised their voice in favour of Roman scripts on the ground, that it is more scientific and that the non-Hindi speaking states would not have to make special efforts for learning the Devanagari script, which was less scientific and more laborious for learning. Besides, equal amount of burden will be shared by all the states for learning this script. The script of Devanagari, therefore, should be replaced by the Roman script. Ultimately, it was decided, that the Hindi written in Devanagari script would be used at the national level.

Regarding the other 14 languages namely, Assamese, Bengali, Gujarati, Kannada, Kashmiri, Malayalam, Marathi, Oriya, Punjabi, Sanskrit, Tamil, Telugu, Urdu placed with Hindi, the Prime Minister Nehru said, that 'all our Indian languages are our national languages, Hindi as defined in Article 351, of the Constitution of India will have the distinction of being used for inter-state and all India inter-course, as it is known to the largest bulk of our people.'[58]

Hence, after a great deal of arguments in the Constituent Assembly debates ending in a thoughtful discussion, and on the basis of different surveys undertaken by the linguists, and government officials, decision was taken in favour of Hindi written in Devanagari script.

One has to examine closely the Constitutional directives enshrined in Articles 343 to 351 (Part XVII) wherein Status of Languages — for Official, Administrative and Education purposes, had been very clearly enunciated. These articles are being examined here for the benefit of clear understanding on Status of Languages in India.

Article 343.

1. "The Official Language of the Union shall be Hindi in Devanagari script.
2. Notwithstanding anything in Clause (1), for a period of fifteen years from the commencement of this Constitution, the English language shall continue to be used for all the official purposes of the Union for which it was being used immediately before such commencement . . . .
3. Notwithstanding anything in the article, Parliament may by law provide for the use, after the said period of fifteen years, of—
   (a) the English language, or
   (b) the Devanagari form of numerals,
   for such purposes as may be specified in the law."

So very logically the above lines were formulated that they strengthened the national consciousness for the acceptance of Hindi, one of the 14 languages, to be the language for official use for the Union. They also permitted the use of English for a maximum period of 15 years for official purposes or even the period might be extended by an Act of Parliament if the chosen Representatives of the People of India so desire. A concern, — underlying that the country's development must not be hampered at any cost — because of language problem of any kind — was imperative at that time which was the 'teething period' of a newly independent country. But given a chance, the liberty to use English indefinitely might be misused. Hence followed Article 344, which stated that within 5 + 10 (15) years, the President shall by order constitute a Commission with a Cháirman, and members of the different language groups as specified in the Eighth Schedule. The Commission shall recommend to the President as to :

(a) the progressive use of the Hindi language for the official purposes of the union;
(b) restrictions on the use of the English language for all or any of the official purposes of the Union;
(c) the language to be used for all or any of the purposes mentioned in Article 348;
(d) .........
(e) any other matter referred to the Commission by the President as regard the official language of the Union and the language for communication between the Union and a State or between one State and another and their use.

Article 348, now needs a close scrutiny. Comments are also offered alongside. This Article appeared to be both protective and promotive. It states that all authoritative texts relating to Bills and Acts in Parliament and in State Legislatures "shall be in the English language." Interests of law enforcement in the early years of Indian democracy when change of language already in use from pre-independence days might jeopardise the entire purpose of legal activity were kept in mind, it appears. The Article further extends its scope to the promotive aspect. It states (Article 348(2)) that "the Governor of a State *may with the previous consent of the President,* authorise the use of the Hindi language, or any other language used for any official purpose of the state, in proceedings in the High Court having its principal seat in the State." It is interesting to note how the Constitution framers provided the *flexibility* for the use of Indian languages but with the due consent of the President of India. What follows in Article 349, was a further provision with a warning such as, "no bill or amendment making provision for the language to be used for any of the purposes mentioned in clause (1) of Article 348 shall be introduced or moved in either House of Parliament without the previous sanction of the President and the President *shall not give* his sanction to the introduction of any such Bill. . . ." The inferences from the above Articles in the Constitution are several — (1) The Administration adopted Hindi as the language for the official use of the Union, (2) For a period of 15 years English, however, should be used and if necessary, by Act of Parliament the period of its use should be extended. (3) The President, by order, shall constitute a Language Commission comprising representatives of all major regional language groups to devise progressive use of Hindi language, gradual restrictive use of English language and advise the President on the official language of the Union and the language for inter-state and State-Centre communication. One wonders with what clearheadedness these issues, relating to the proper use of proper language/languages for particular purposes of nation's life, were made. A determination to install Hindi as an Official language, to be transformed into a decision for all practical purposes was weighed against all utility and caution as not to either overdo or underdo the language issue. There was no concept of imposition of Hindi; there was full consideration shown for the use of and placement of Indian regional languages; there was concern expressed in case English is overused. The President's comments at various points of conflict and indecision alongwith the Constitutional bindings on the President himself as not to interfere, if not warranted with lessening the period of use of English for 15 years for official purposes — were all matters of wisdom that the framers of the Constitution showed. But there was no period of relaxation, no chance of any misunderstanding to creep in. During these 15 years the setting up of Language Commission was decided upon. The Commission was to deliberate thoroughly with the varied language groups about the future status of language that the country should have. Astonishingly, it was not missed sight of that besides choosing the official language for the Union, considerations — "industrial, cultural and scientific advancement of India and the interests of persons belonging to the non-Hindi speaking areas in regard to the public services" (344(3)) should have due attention from the Official Language Commission. Perhaps nothing more reasonable than these features regarding the position of languages could have emerged than what was realised by these provisions with Constitution in a multilingual country like India.

Against such a background after the expiry of three decades and a half it would be worthwhile to examine the people's side on this language issue. No major amendment on Language question has come through in these years. Hindi as the official language is gaining in use year after year, with expansion of its scope and development on all sides. English, has occupied in the educational sphere, the position of a Compulsory second language in most States. Regional languages are gaining in richness as medium of the people of different States, language of culture, language for wider social contact and the language of one's faith and worship. For inter-state communication Hindi, English and Regional languages are coming to help from time to time. The question to be judged from the academic standpoint should weigh these varied considerations — past, present and future. The generation of students in schools who are concerned with the learning of languages set out in their school curriculum, might have also something to say in this regard about the status of languages as they view it. The veterans, statesmen, academicians, judiciary and people of some other walks of life had their viewpoints to express on the language issue when they were approached by the researcher for the above purpose.

Hence the study is planned on "Three Language Formula : An Educational Problem".

## Notes and References

1. Ferguson, Charles A., in *Language Problems of Developing Nations* edited by Fishman, Ferguson and Jyotindra Dass Gupta. London : John Wiley, 1968.
2. Report of the Official Language Commission, 1956. p. 10.
3. Gumperz John J. in *Language Problems of Developing Nations* edited by Ferguson *et al.* New York : John Wiley. 1968. p. 151.
4. *Ibid.*
5. *Ibid.*
6. Summerfelt, A. *Linguistic Problems of Eurpoean Diachronian and Synchronic Aspects of Language.* 1953.
7. (Quoted by) Perren, G.E. and F. Michael Holloway. *Language and Communication in the Commonwealth.* London : Her Majesty's Stationery Office. 1965. Ch. I.
8. Report of the Official Language Commission. 1956. p. 10.
9. Perren, G.E. and F. Michael Holloway. *op. cit.*
10. Boehm, Mexthalderburt. Nationalism Theoretical Aspects. *Encyclopaedia of Social Science.* XI (1937). p. 235.
11. Haughen, E. Dialect, Language and Nation : *American Anthropologist.* Vol. 68; 1966. pp. 922-35.

(Quoted and Edited by) Pride and Holmes. Sociolinguistics. England : Penguin Books Ltd. 1976. p. 103.

12. Pride and Holmes. *op. cit.* p. 104.
13. Report of the Official Language Commission, 1956. p. 33.
14. Census Report of 1971, Language Handbook on Mother tongues in Census, XVI, New Delhi : Ministry of Home Affairs. 1972. Report of 1981 not yet published.
15. (Edited by) Pride and Holmes. *op. cit.* p. 103.
16. Haugen, E. "Dialect, Language and Nation". Quoted by Pride and Holmes. *op. cit.*
17. *Ibid.*
18. Article 30(1). *The Constitution of India.* New Delhi : Government of India, Ministry of Law, Justice and Public Affairs (Amended form) 1980.
19. Article 30(2). *Ibid.*
20. Thirtha, N.V. 'Babal'. Madras : M. Seshachalam & Co. 1962. p. 34.
21. Francis, John De. *Nationalism and Language Reform in China.* Princeton : Princeton University Press. 1950. Ch. 13.
22. Pattanayak, D.P. *Language Policy and Programmes.* New Delhi : Ministry of Education and Youth Services, Government of India. p. 3.
23. Ram Gopal. *Linguistic Affairs of India.* Bombay : Asia Publishing House. 1966 p. 175.
24. *Speeches of Maulana Azad,* 1947-75. New Delhi : Publications Division.
25. Central Advisory Board of Education.
26. Report of the University Education Commission 1948-49. New Delhi : Govt. of India Press. 1950. p. 317.
27. Census of 1971. *op. cit.* Appendix II. p. 333.
28. Seth, Govind Das. *Raj Bhasha Hindi.* Prayag : Hindi Sahitya Sammelan. 1965 p. 15.
29. *Ibid.* p. 5-6.
30. Kanhaiya Lal Bahaeru Lal, Malvia, M.P. *Hindi --- 'The National Language'.* New Delhi : Malvia Prakashan. 1958 p. 6.
31. Desai, Maganbhai 'Explanatory Note' in the Report of the Official Language Commission 1956. New Delhi : Govt. of India Press. 1957. p. 396.
32. Cited in the Report of the Official Language Commission 1956. pp. 35-36.
33. Seth, Govind Dass. *op. cit.* p. 18.
34. Mehta, Ashoka. Group Prejudices in India, Bombay, 1953. Quoted by Shankar Ghosh. *Socialism, Democracy and Nationalism in India.* Ch. VI. Bombay : Allied Publishers. 1973. pp. 200-205.
35. Seth, Govind Das. *op. cit.* p. 36.
36. Chatterji, Suniti Kumar. *Language and Literatures of Modern India.* Calcutta : Bengal Publishers Pvt. Ltd. 1963. pp. 4-5.
37. Fishman, Ferguson and Jyotindra Das Gupta (ed.) *Language Problems of Developing Nations.* London : John Wiley. 1968. p. 222.
38. Report of the Official Language Commission, 1956. p. 38.
39. *Ibid.*
40. *Ibid.*
41. Chatterjee, Suniti Kumar. *op. cit.* p. 59.
42. *Ibid.* p. 47.
43. Gandhi, M.K. Thought on National Language. cited by Shankar Ghosh. *Socialism, Democracy and Nationalism in India.* Bombay : Allied Publishers. 1973. p. 199.
44. Mitra, Rajendra Lal. "Indian School in 1864". *Journal of the Asiatic Society of Bengal.* Quoted by Kanhaiya Lal Bheru Lal Malvia. *op. cit.*

45. Kellog, S.H. *A Grammar of Hindi Language.* London : Routledge and Kegan Paul Ltd. 1875 p. xi.
46. Kellog, S.H. *Modern Languages of East India. op. cit.* p. 46.
47. *Ibid.* p. v.
48. *Ibid.* p. xii.
49. Chatterji, Suniti Kumar. *op. cit.*, p. 6.
50. Report of the Official Language Commission, 1956. p. 39.
51. Report of the Committee of Members of Parliament on Education (1967). p. 4.
52. Pattanayak, D.P. *op. cit.* p. 3.
53. Chatterji, Suniti Kumar. *op. cit.*, p. 7.
54. *Ibid.* p. 6.
55. "Report of the Central Advisory Board of Education (onwards it would be referred as CABE) Silver Jubilee Souvenir" 1960. New Delhi : Ministry of Education, Government of India. 1960. p. 206.
56. Report of University Education Commission 1948-49. p. 319.
57. Nair, Baldevraj. *National Communication, Link Language and National Policy.* New York : Frederick A Praeger Publishers 1969.
58. Quoted by Desai, M.P. *The Problem of English.* Ahmedabad : Navjivan Publishing House 1964. p. 48.

# 2 Nature and Importance of Language

Language, in the Indian context has a sacred sanctity. Word is equated with 'Brahma'. The purpose behind the creation of this universe in the opinion of Indian seers is to see Existence in manifestation as a Reality. The wonder that is in Being and in Existence expressed itself in explicit form that is in word which was reverberated in sound. This complex matrix around the origin of the language thereafter got itself into one of the most important human activities -- such as articulation of Sound, of Word, and then of Speech, leading on to myriad Meaning that was fundamental for human civilization.

Language is indispensable for development of thought. As is given in *Chandogya Upanishada*,

यद्वै वाङ्ग नाभविष्यन्न धर्मो ना व्यज्ञा पयिष्मन्न
सत्यं नानृनं ना साधु न ह्रदयज्ञो नाह्रदयज्ञो
वागेर्वेतत्सर्व विज्ञापयति वाचमुपास्स्वैति । ।१ । ।[1]

(If there had been no speech neither virtue nor vice could be known, neither the true, nor the false, neither the good, nor the bad, neither the pleasant nor the unpleasant. Speech alone make known all this. Meditate upon speech.)

The importance of language in the life of a man, therefore, deserves an exclusive mention. Such a realisation of the early seers highlights the noble function of this unique endowment that man has been gifted with. Down the ages there had been scholars all over the world who contributed in specifying the functions of language in general terms. In any thesis pertaining to the position of languages in a national perspective a good understanding of all aspects concerning language/languages is essential.

**Functions of Language**

As language is present in every human activity, the functions it performs are many, because the human activities are multifarious. The opinion regarding the functions of language, though differ, yet the scholars do agree that language serves all the functions described by the linguists. The difference can be noticed in the degree of emphasis laid down by a particular school of thought.

Communication is the primary function of language so was thought by Saussure, Delacroix and Laguna (20th century). They argue that language develop more by the need of communication than by any other factor and this need encompasses all the aspects of language. Hockett and Malinowski (20th century) also lay emphasis on this point when they state that 'the conceptual use of words arises out of communal needs in dealing with environment.'[1] Language is a system by which the thoughts are conveyed, says Hughes the linguist. "Language is a system of arbitrary vocal symbols, by which, thought is being conveyed from one human to another."[2] The main and important function of language is to carry on the business of the society. Francis says, "A language is an arbitrary system of articulated sounds, made use of, by a group of humans as a means of carrying on the affairs of their society."[3,4] In Fraenkal's words, 'Language is a learned arbitrary system of vocal symbols with which people can communicate within a culture.'[5]

The other function of the language is the expression which is considered to be the most important but, common to man and animal both. Wundt, Sweet, Whitney, Buhler Schrist and others belong to this school of thought. Language functions as the 'medium for the expression of images and ideas', so says Wundt. Sweet opined that the function of the language is 'the expression of thought by means of speech sounds.'[6,7] While Whitney thinks that language serves both the communicative as well as expressive functions, because, 'language is considered as an expression for the sake of communication.'

The scholars have further described four different types of functions of language which are signified as — (i) referential, (ii) representative, (iii) evocative and (iv) emotive. Stout, Dewey and Whitehead insist upon the referential function of language. For Whitehead the essential character of language is the symbolic referential which is a process of functioning in which a transition is made from symbol to meaning, as, while uttering sentences, special words or symbols are used for specific meanings, whereas Stout thinks that "In language we make use of the special behaviour of speech instead of more immediate intercourse with things." Dewey is of the opinion that language serves as the means of organizing our thoughts about things. Edward Sapir (20th century) says, that 'Language is a perfect symbolic system in a perfectly homogeneous medium for the handling of all reference and meanings."[8]

Since language is the vehicle of thought, all the records of our experience are hidden in its repository and as such language functions in giving us a notion of the beliefs, civilization, and culture of a particular community. "Each community is formed by the activity of language; speech-utterances give us the most direct insight into its workings and play in everything that is done."[9] Hence, the representative function of language is all the more important because language represents culture. It expresses fancies, emotions and even nonsense. "Every language is a model of culture and its adjustment to the world."[10]

Dewey further writes that the evocative and the emotive-function of language go hand in hand. It is through language, that, 'human nature itself may be played on to evoke not only every act of which man is capable but every emotion and sentiment as well.' It becomes a means of environmental control including animate and inanimate things both. Markey, Larimer, De-laguna, Cassirer, Delacroix and a few others believe that language is an instrument and as such evocative and emotive are important functions of language.

There are some other functions also; like language helps the individual to store his experiences in the form of memory which again assists him in recalling these experiences. 'Memory, itself develops through speech.[11,12] All abstract thinking is possible only through language. It is language which 'makes possible the type of thinking known as 'discursive thinking or reason' and to evolve the optimum level in thinking, it is necessary to emphasize the utility of language in (the field of) education. Dewey believed that education is a process of living and that it is the fundamental method of social progress and reform. Leonard explained, that education means the knowledge of the linguistic skills i.e., reading and writing which can possibly be developed in the schools only. Without learning a language, one cannot get the knowledge of the ongoing culture, history etc.; which in his opinion is the most sacred fact."[13] Hence, language constitutes an essential component of the school-curriculum.

**The role of language in education**

Bernstein says, 'Those who are good in language are good in all other subjects and those who fail in language fail in every other subject.'[14] Language instruction is, therefore, a basic requirement for all types of education. For the attainment of different levels of education, language plays its important role. Even for differentiating a man from another, linguistic competence is the only criterion and as such, language becomes the most vital factor for determining the level of education a man has reached, because, all education is language education. "The total instructional-process in a formal educational system is more a linguistic-interaction between the teacher and the taught than anything else. Therefore, the degree of fluency in the language used in teaching, which is largely determined by socio-cultural factors has a considerable Influence on educational achievement."[15,16,17]

'In olden days, language instruction has usually been regarded synonymous with more or less total education.'[18] Though in modern times, 'education' is not restricted to the knowledge of languages alone yet, the importance of language instruction cannot be less than what it has been before, for even now, it is the language or languages which are the chief media of all education from beginning to end. Hence, importance of language instruction is self-evident as there can be no formal education in its absence. Desheriyev, the famous Russian linguist and educationist says that language is the content as well as the medium of primary education.[19] Teaching of language as such can be regarded as a pre-condition of all formal-education. Even for informal education, the language instruction is a *sine-qua-non,* although it may be a language different from the language codified in certain symbols or signs.

As a medium of communication, language enters almost 'ubiquitously' all processes of imparting knowledge of whatever subject it may be.[20] Without learning language, a man cannot grow intellectually, socially and emotionally. It is, therefore, essential that language should be learnt properly, correctly and extensively, so that whatever is taught to them, may be grasped by them. As language is the sole instrument of communication also at the state and central level, in the conduct of legislative bodies, in the day-to-day dealings with citizens by administrative agencies in the judiciary, commerce and industry and in education etc., its learning automatically plays an important role in the total existence of an individual.

For understanding the human nature of a particular society, it is essential, that, its literature should be studied. In the words of 'Sapir', "Our cultures, references and meanings are all hoarded in language, which are transferred from generation to generation by teaching the ancient languages." (Sapir Edward 1949). Even to understand the poetry and other cultivated styles, a profound knowledge of language is essential to understand their underlying meaning. The abstract ideas hidden in them will not be understood by a person, if he does not know that language thoroughly in which the ideas are expressed. Even 'creativity' finds no expression, if there is no language. As a painter uses colour and brush for his work, similarly says 'Hockett, that, literary writer uses some language to express his thoughts.[21] Hence, for a clear understanding of his work, it is necessary, that one should have a good command over language.

Without language, human beings will remain mute. It is in terms of language, that men do their thinking and convey their thoughts to others. Though the highest level of thinking is possible only in language yet, it does not mean, that there was no intellectual activity prior to verbal activity. If thinking can go on without verbal activity as is evident in the cases of deaf and dumb children or in animals even, mental development can also go on to a certain extent in the absence of verbal medium. But, the highest mental development can never take place to its fullest capacity without the aid of language. "Although language is the agency of a number of articulated and symbolic signs appearing in a variety of significant combinations, language is the medium by which thoughts are formulated and thinking is ordered." [22]

For establishing a meaningful relation between the word and its meaning, it is essential that the students should be taught all the four linguistic skills i.e. understanding, speaking, reading and writing properly; so that, whatever is being expressed, can be communicated in the same sense. Most of the 'Intelligence-tests' involve language skills. 'Each language-skill also has been found to be co-related to intelligence in these tests.'[23] Burt writes, 'Linguistic ability and linguistic attainment exert upon the Binet-Simon tests a special and positive influence of their own.'[24] Hence, teaching of correct sentence-formation and the functional use of various words with different meanings becomes an essential part of education. A good education, therefore, is apt to devote more time for teaching grammar, so that, the students may not only understand the style of a particular language, but can also get rid off certain arbitrary inconsistencies which are shown in every language, such as, 'I don't want any water' or I don't want some water.'[25] The interdependence of language skills and mathematical skills has been underlined by the UNESCO report on 'Interactions' between linguistics and mathematical education (1974).[26] When a child is asked to distinguish between red and blue balls out of a whole lot, he is confronted with the ambiguity of language. The knowledge whether in that lot some are blue and some red is necessary for defining 'set'. The child, therefore, must understand the inaccuracy, the ambiguity and the social acceptability of a language in use. In other words he comes to know the use of that language. Besides, the languages are likely to change. 'Since all languages are constantly undergoing changes in pronunciation, in grammar and in vocabulary,[27] they remain unintelligible to learning unless that form of language is taught to them.

It is language which teaches a man logic, law, astronomy, science and technology etc. For instance, the historian learns a language because the information he wants is available only in the historical document that is the written record of the past experiences. The philosopher learns languages, because, he cannot learn logic without learning language. Even for teaching 'ethics', language is needed. Since higher forms of psychic-thinking are bound up with language, the queries like 'who am I' and 'from where have I come' will remain unanswered in the absence of language. For understanding political manifestos, speeches of the political parties, language of propaganda and advertisements, knowledge of language is a must.

Since literacy is an indispensable necessity for each individual and for all sorts of development, knowledge of language is pre-requisite. Due to scientific and technological advancements, material equipment of living is so highly specialised that modern communities require a high degree of information and skills for their operation. The only means is the literacy for acquiring such information and developing skills for their operation. It is through literacy that such information can be acquired and skills can be developed. For the progress of a country, the masses are to be informed about technological advancements which is possible only through the medium of language, for literacy is not only an indicative of the material progress and higher living standard, but, for keeping them informed as to what is happening around them and for their intellectual development in the modern times, educationists have concerned themselves mostly with the psychological, sociological and philosophical foundations of curriculum.[28,29] They have neglected its linguistic foundation in the formal educational system.

For creating the universal brotherhood and integrating the different states and the union territories, it is the use of language which become basic for all. "Whenever agreement or assent is arrived at in human-affairs, it is reached by linguistic process or else, it is not reached."[30] All the agreements of the world trade and policies are always made in language. Next to religion, language is the most powerful cementing force. It can be destructive also. "Language is one of the decisive elements in the complex of forces, material, psychological and spiritual, by which the destinies of nations are being shaped at the present time,"[31] and in the words of Hockett, 'The more we understand a language, the more we understand ourselves and our place in the universe.[32] Language is not only inevitable practically for all interpersonal relations and social interactions but is also the medium through which all intrapersonal and interpersonal experiences of the people are structured, levelled and manipulated.[33] Similarly, in the context of formal educational system, language can be thought of as a 'structured instrumental activity', which is carried on in a society and "our society deals with linguistic matters through the school system," [34] as 'the problem is not one of linguistic-structure but of practical application.'[35] Hence, all education begins with language and continues till end through language or languages. Research has shown that the language competence is cumulative and that any weakness in the early childhood language experience shows up in the higher stages of education.[36]

**Significance of the study**

The position of languages in India as laid down in the Constitution is that all the languages have been recognised as of equal status and value.[37] Article 29 reads — 'Any section of the citizens residing in the territory of India or any part thereof having a distinct language, script or culture of its own shall have the right to conserve the same[38] and as such, they shall have the right to establish and administer educational institutions of their choice.[39] The official language of the union was to be Hindi in Devanagari script with numerals in Roman Script for the official purposes of the Union.[40] It was envisaged, that, for a period of 15 years from the commencement of the Constitution the English language shall continue to be used for all the official purposes of the Union for which it was being used immediately before such commencement,[41] and the same will continue to be used for communication between one state and another state and between a state and the Union.[42] The Article 345[43] reads, that "the legislation of a state may, by law, adopt anyone or more of the languages in use in the State or Hindi as the language or languages to be used for all or any of the official. Article 348(1) deals with the language to be used in the Supreme Court, High Courts, etc. (a) all proceedings in the Supreme Court and in every High Court, (b) the authoritative texts — (i) of all Bills to be introduced or amendments thereto be moved in either House of Parliament or in the House or either House of the Legislature of a State (ii) of all Acts passed by Parliament or the Legislature of a State and of all Ordinances promulgated by the President or the Governor. . . . of a state, and (iii) of all orders, rules, regulations and bye-laws issued under this Constitution or under any law made by Parliament or the Legislature of a State shall be in the English language[44] though the language to be used in representations for redress of grievances shall be any language used in the Union or in the State.[45] Article 120 reads, that business in Parliament shall be transacted in Hindi or in English with the condition that the Chairman of the Council of States or Speaker of the House of the People may permit any member who cannot adequately express himself in Hindi or in English to address the House in his mother tongue.[46] Though the use of English is emphasised in all the important spheres of life and country, Article 351 lays down[47] that it shall be the duty of the Union to promote the spread of Hindi language to develop it so that it may serve as a medium of expression for all the elements of the composite culture of India and to secure its enrichment by assimilating without interfering with its genius, the forms, styles and expressions used in Hindustani and in other languages of India specified in the Eighth Schedule and by drawing wherever necessary or desirable for its vocabulary, primarily on Sanskrit and secondarily on other languages.[48]

If the Constitutional provisions regarding the use of the language are analysed, one sees, that the retention of English as a medium for communication, declaration of Hindi as the official language, dependence on Sanskrit for enriching the vocabulary of languages, and the grant of liberty to the States to use any language, all created a situation wherein the study of more than one language became indispensable.

**Nature of Indian Languages**

Bloomfield, the German philologist believed that it was in India first, wherc a complete and accurate description of languages was given and that, it was based on observation and not upon theory.[49] It explained that, language to this day, has been so powerfully described that it has revolutionised the European ideas about languages.[50] Hence, it will not be out of place to consider the views of Indian scholars who had treated the facts related to language and its development long back, as early as compilation of the Rigvedic hymns, centuries before the work started in Western countries.

In *Rigveda* itself, (centuries before the birth of Christ) the Suktas सूक्त are found describing the origin and developing of speech. When the language of the Vedic hymns ceased to be spoken, attempts were made to preserve and understand the Vedic language. Since then, the study of linguistic phenomena emerged in India, although the thoughtful description of language and philological discussions have been a tradition from the times of the Vedas, in which, the language is explained keeping into consideration its biological, psychological, structural and functional aspects. The sage devoted their time in pondering over the subtlest problems of language. They thought over not only on the origin of speech but, on the linking of sound in roots and on the norm of the development of a 'Standard-language' Apart from this, they established the "eternality of the word". Sentences like,

'चत्वारि वाक् परिमिता पदानि:
'तुरीयं वाचो मनुष्या वदन्ति' and
'तां (वाचं) विश्वरुपा : पशवो वदन्ति' [51, 52].

taken from the *Vedas* are explained in *Srutis* श्रुति that there are 4 stages of speech; and it is the 4th stage, under which only a human being passes and it is this stage which differentiates him from an animal, as no animal, but, man commands an articulate language because no dog or elephant has one word for bread, another for meat and another for water, yet, while dreaming, their dream is accompanied by a mental image of the thing, that is dreamed of, much like what we experienced in dreams ourselves,[53] and as such it is only the 4th stage through which a human being alone can pass and that is the linguistic embodiment given to a definite but significant idea. While explaining the four stages, it is said, that, first is the desire to speak, second is the psychical process, passing through which the speaker tries to identify the words with the objects and vice-versa and after identifying the words with the objects, the speech organs play their role in producing the sound, but, it is the human being alone who is capable of giving it the linguistic-embodiment. Bhartrihari (5th cent. A.D.) described these stages as परा, पश्यन्ति मध्यमा and बैखरी Later on Nagesh Bhatt (in 1685 A.D.) also considered it likewise. The Mantra (मंत्र) ता विश्वरुपा पशवो वदन्ति describes the nature of the पशु who speaks the language i.e. animal, but rational, पश्यति इति पशु i.e. the one who is capable of speculating, can produce articulate sounds. It is also explained in the so-called seven (7) organs of speech (larynx etc.) act like servants, ordered by intellect or to carry the coherant ideas to the lips :—

यज्ञेन वाचः पदवीमायन् तामन्वविन्दन् ऋषिषु प्रविष्टाम्
तामाभृत्या : व्यदधुः पुरत्रा तां सप्तरेमाः अभिसंनवन्ते ।[54]

The conception of language, therefore, is based upon the articulate sounds produced by the speech organs as well as upon our thoughts and emotions. Hence, we have no other resort but, to accept the language as a fully formed functional system within man's psychic or 'spiritual' constitution, although the psychophysical basis is essential for its functioning, and in this process, the impulse to speak is main. The language is no language, unless, it conveys the coherent ideas to some other intelligent being and in this functioning, the important role is played not only by the speaker's desire to speak but by the listener's desire to listen, to understand it-

अक्षवन्तः कर्णवन्तः सखायो मनोजवेष्वसमाबभूवुः ।
ह्रदातष्टेषुमनसाजवेषु । ।[55]

i.e. though the human beings possess the organs of hearing (ears), yet, the language spoken by the speaker does not reach their ears, because they do not have the desire to listen. While to the other person who has got the desire of listening to language it becomes clear, rather opens all its secrets to the listener, like a wife to her husband :-

उत त्वः पश्यन्न ददर्शवाचम्
उत त्वः श्रृण्वन्न श्रृणोत्येनाम्
उतोत्वस्मै तत्वं विसस्रे जायेव पत्य उशती सुवासाः[56]

In *Atharv Veda* too, emphasis is laid on the perception of mind संश्रुतेव गमेमहि मा श्रुतेन विराधिषुः i.e. whatever we listen to, should be, heard carefully, because, the nature of the words counts for nothing. It is the gist of the matter which should be in perfect harmony between the sayer and the sayee to the extent that the significance associated with the language is communicated perfectly. Since the words, as explained in that Mantra (मंत्र) in the form singular, dual and plural are omnipresent —

ये त्रिषप्ताः परियन्ति विश्वरुपाणिः

the transfer of meaning is conveyed only when the hearer's auditory perceptions are translated into the appropriate thoughts conveyed to him.

**The relation between the word and the meaning :**

In 1000 B.C. Jaimini and Shabar discussed the relation between the word and its meaning. Like Naturalists, they established the fact that this relationship between the word and its meaning is natural because whenever, a word is used, it always carries some meaning. The words as symbols are agreed upon and understood by both the speaker and the listener as being associated with the particular ideas in question. Hence, the 3 grammarians — Panini, Katyayan and Patanjali (500, 350 and 200 B.C. respectively) called the relationship between the word and its meaning not only natural but eternal also :—

नित्ये शब्दार्थ सम्बन्धे लोकतोऽर्थ प्रयुक्ते ।

i.e. the essence cf the matter lies in a mutual 'covenant'.

**The importance of the word :**

Odumbarayana (1000 B.C.) has significantly considered the importance of a word and even of a single letter. If it can convey any sense —

एकः शब्दः सप्रयुक्ते सम्यग्ज्ञातः स्वगैलोके कामधुगभवति ।[57]

The nature of the word was further explained by Vyaddi (850 B.C.) who opined, that, the nature of the word is to become distorted— शब्द प्रकृतिरपभ्रंशः [58] : because it is used by the masses. The philosopher linguist Bhartrihari (5th century A. D.) explained it further by saying, that the words used by masses may not remain grammatically correct, but, their root words, would certainly have existed sometime in the past in their original forms, as, 'the words are traceable to roots and that inflections were originally independent words, which were joined on to other words to modify their sense', (Humboldt 1765-1835), since, a word never dies :—

अनादिनिधनं ब्रहम शब्दतत्वं यदक्षरम् ।
विवर्त्ततेऽर्थभावेन प्रक्रिया जगतो यतः । ।१ । ।[59]

i.e. the nature of the word is like Brahman (ब्रहमन् —God), who is Eternal. As God has personified Himself into different forms of human beings, similarly, the word expands itself in many new words, which, for the time being may appear carrying different meanings. The change occurs in the meaning due to its use in various contexts, but the word remains the same — निमित्तमे दाः सर्वत्र साधुत्वं च व्यवस्थितम् i.e. the word is the same, it is different (in meaning) because the context differs. The nature of the word is to retained, to expand and to revive again in its natural form, for, the word is Brahman (ब्रहमन्) or Aksharam (अक्षरम्)

**Difference between the written and spoken language :**

By differentiating the Vedic and Classical Sanskrit, a distinction is made between the written and spoken language as early as 950 B.C. The etymologists, Yask and the grammarians — Panini, Katyayana and Patanjali, also have accepted the remarkable difference between the written and spoken language and on the basis of this distinction the Munitraya मुनेत्रय the three grammarians Panini, Katyayana and Patanjali have determined the Standard — form of language, which, according to these sages can be determined by observing the use of a language among the cultural and educated people and not by its use among the masses :-

शिष्टप्रयोगममिसमीक्ष्य प्रकृतिरुहितव्या प्रत्ययश्च ।[60]

**Language and Dialect :**

But the words used by the masses are not less significant as they only help in the enrichment of a language, because some new forms of certain words emerge and gradually become common in use. Sometimes, even new words are coined to meet the present requirements. Since the human race cannot live and grow in segregated manner, the races mix together and as such, their languages also mix. No language can remain utterly uninfluenced by the surroundings. Panini calls such form of the language 'Dialect' and not language न वेतिभाषा विभाषा But according to Bhartrihari, the dialect, may not remain dialect in the long run and as such, it has its importance as the 'linguafranca, or लौकिकीभाषा. From the above discussion, it follows that the sociological aspect of language has also been considered, because, the sociology of language is concerned and language varieties as targets, as obstacles and as facilitators and the users and uses of language varieties as aspects of more encompassing social patterns or processes.[61]

On the basis of the Suktas (सूक्त)[S] available on the nature of language, it can be concluded that 'linguistics' as a science, has been a subject of inherent consideration : long back in our country the first treatises on Phonetics is available in Pratishakhyas (प्रातिशाख्या)[S] which are placed in 800 B.C.

The ostensible purposes of these treatises was to teach how to chant the Vedas, which in general reflects the importance of phonetics in language. The next great landmark in the history of linguistic studies in India is the great etymologist in Yask who explained the words scientifically by establishing the fact that all words are ultimately to be traced to their roots, without which, the nature of the semantics cannot be decided. After Yask, we find Apisali and Kasakrtsna as the founders of grammatical school. Katyayana is being mentioned as the Ist grammarian in Tattriyasamhita (तैत्तरीयसंहिता)[62] (vii,47) but it was Panini who is known as the greatest grammarian of India. Taraporewala calls him the greatest grammarian, of the world,[63] whereas Bloomfield calls his grammar 'one of the greatest monuments of human intelligentsia.'[64] It explained the fundamental conception of roots, which are a set of monosyllabic constants and that, each concept expresses an action. In the opinion of Bloomfield the grammar describes with the minutest detail every inflection, derivation and composition and every syntactic usage.[65] He held the view that the fundamental principle is, that 'the sentence is the unit of language'. The great grammarian Patanjali in his *Mahabhasya* (महाभाष्य) and the philosopher linguist Bhartrihari in his *Vakyapediya* describes the language from philosophical points of views as "the philosophy of language concerned with the evaluation of language as a bearer of meanings, as a medium of communication and as a sign or symbol of reality." A similar view is expressed by the Western scholars.[66] Bhartrihari propounded that the words are already present in the mind as has been suggested by the German philologist Humboldt (1765-1835); 'Language is not a thing created but, is an energy found in human beings.' He also held that the words are traceable to roots. It is the proper identification of the words with the objects, which, when uttered developed into language.[67] No speech can exist without the two elements i.e. the physiological and psychological. The physiological aspect of a language can be detected but, it is the psychological aspect of a language which is mainly responsible for the irregularities in language.

The German philologist Leonard Bloomfield was so much impressed by the insight in the linguistic structure explained by the Indian sages, that, he had to accept that, even, 'the Greek scholars did not clearly set off the features of each language.'[68] He further said, that 'the Hindu grammar taught European to analyze speech forms; when one compared the constituent parts, the resemblances, which hitherto had been vaguely recognised, could be set forth with certainty and precision.'[69]

In the context of formal educational system, the language instruction could certainly be thought of as a structured instructional activity, but it cannot be compared with the teaching and learning of any other subject or discipline including creative literature in the language. But because the educationists have usually equated language teaching with the teaching of any other subject or discipline like creative literature or history or physics, it has usually been treated as a curricular area, and not a foundation of total curriculum. It is evident that the linguistic interaction between the teacher and the taught in a class-room situation is the very base on which the total curriculum operates, through teaching and learning actions or behaviour of the teacher and the taught respectively. The language, therefore, is not a curriculum area, but, the foundation of the total curriculum, particularly when the language to be taught is also used as a medium of instruction for all the curricular areas i.e. subjects. But this significant distinction of the language to be taught as medium of total education and a language to be taught for any other purpose has usually been not made while planning the educational system and the language instruction therein.[70]

## Sanskrit — The Indian Classical Language

Since one of the important aims of education is to pass on the cultural heritage to the individual and society, it becomes essential, that, provision should be made to give its knowledge. India's vast literature in science, humanities and arts is available in Sanskrit language. In the opinion of Max Muller, India's literature is vast, if compared to Greek and Latin put together. 'Indian life and thought and Indian literature in ancient, medieval and modern times (until very recently) have remained embedded in the *Ramayana*, the *Mahabharat*, the *Puranas*, the Vedanta and the Yoga and Bhakti,[71] says Chatterji. Since they are available in Sanskrit, the learning of the language becomes necessary, as "Translation into the native language is bound to mislead the learner, because the semantic units of different languages, do not match."[72] Besides, in a vast country like India, where not only multiple languages are spoken and multiple religions are also followed, Sanskrit is the language which has brought and preserved the oneness and unity in the country.' 'The real integration of India into one 'Single Unity' in spite of some basic and fundamental racial, linguistic and cultural diversities has taken place through the world of the Epics and the Puranas and the philosophical literature of Sanskrit,'[73] 'It has been a common means of communication between the different regional groups of India.'[74] Chatterji, the renowned Indologist and linguist, holds the view, that, 'The classical Sanskrit was really the spoken language, the popular (Laukika) speech of the North Western and Northern Punjab and probably also current in Eastern Punjab and the Upper gangetic Doab in the time of Panini (5th cent. B.C.). It was also current in the Brahman Schools of the time everywhere in North India. But, in the Midland (Madhya Desh) it was specially cultivated too. Midland influences gave to Sanskrit its all India character.[75] Almost all the Sanskrit books have been translated in English and other languages of the world. 'There is hardly a part of the world or a language today in which the Upanishads and the Gita cannot be found translated'. These Sanskrit texts have already passed into the great common heritage of the whole world.[76] Hence, one might advocate the teaching of Sanskrit in all Indo-European schools, because, Sanskrit by its origin and basic character links us to the lands of Asia as well as to the West.

Sanskrit is our great mental and spiritual link with the Indo-European and Aryan speaking world to the West of India with Iran with Armenia, with Europe. Sanskrit is the elder sister of Greek and Latin, of Gothic and Old Irish, and of Old Slav. The Modern North Indo-Aryan languages and the Indo-European languages outside India—Hindi, Bengali, Marathi and the rest on the one hand, and the English, French, Russian and the rest on the other are cousins. The very large and indispensable Sanskrit element in the cultivated Dravidian languages of South India, Telugu, Kannada, Tamil and Malayalam, is a cultural link of great value between these and the Indo-European language of Europe.

Sanskrit, the oldest, Indo-European language with a vast literature, has a unique importance even for the people of Indo-European speech outside India. On a study of Sanskrit, and its sister languages, the basic unity of the Indo-European people has been to some extent established.[77]

Sanskrit by its origin and its basic character links us to the West. But it has been no less a potent bond of union for India with the lands of Asia - with Serindia or Central Asia of ancient and medieval times where the cultures of China and India had a common meeting ground; with Tibet : with China and its lands within the orbit of Chinese civilization - Korea and Japan and Vietnam; and above all, with the lands of Farther India, Burma and Siam, Pathet Lao and Combodia, and Cochin China or Champa and the area of Malaya and Indonesia. Ceylon is of course a historical and cultural projection of India. In all these lands, Sanskrit found a home for itself as the vehicle of Indian thought and civilisation which flowed out into them as a peaceful cultural extension, from the closing ceremonies of the first thousand years before Christ. It found also a place of honour in the culture of a great and civilised people like the Chinese and following the Chinese, the Koreans, the Japanese and the Vietnamese; and also the Tibetans, and the Turks of Central Asia and the Mongols and the Manchus.

The possession of Sanskrit by India thus makes India's position unique, as a sort of a link and synthesis of the various ramifications of the human race and society. It is thus easy to see that Sanskrit preserves the entire culture of India in the past (a culture) which went on developing for at least 4,000 years with the worlds of Europe and Asia. Hence, continues Warner, that '.... a knowledge of the common origins of our ways of thought is a desirable thing to have in a world which must unite or perish.[78,79] Hence the knowledge of a language which reflects the ancient culture and beliefs, becomes essential, if we want to know the attitudes and beliefs of a particular country, for, "Language is the loom, on which cultural patterns are woven,"[80] Mahatma Gandhi said that, 'A language is an exact reflection, of the character and growth of its speaker.'[81,82] The Sanskrit Commission comments that, Sanskrit literature helps into building up character and in making the faculties of mind more receptive and donative.[83]

Although Sanskrit has ceased to develop at a very early period, the literature, the culture and religion it enshrined, gave it a unique position among the languages of India. 'A knowledge of Sanskrit was essential for any pretension of learning and culture, because wherever in Aryan or non-Aryan Dravidian languages any abstract or higher idea had to be expressed, it had to be done by means of Sanskrit words with well known and long established connotations, even when pure dialect words were available. It is because of this reason, that the words in modern Indo Aryan languages are classified as तत्सम, तद्भव and देशज . Thus it has established its supremacy both as a building and lending language of speech.[85] Therefore, it will not be an exaggeration to say that all the Indian languages depend on varying degrees on its reservoir of vocabulary for their requirement.[86] If one wishes to know the Indian philosophy and the life before and after death, one has to study Sanskrit.[87,88] Even today when Sanskrit is no more a spoken language, all the Indian languages, which have retained and are still borrowing from its reservoir of rich vocabulary. The conception that the languages are different and divergent in character is, therefore erratic Amongst the Indian languages, there are in varying degree, large elements of identity and similarity and practically all of them draw upon a common literary tradition in Sanskrit and a common background of thought and experience which may generally be called, the Indian way of life and in their scripts and alphabet, all except Urdu, are variant expression of a common Indian Phonetic System.'[89] In the words of Pattnayak, "Almost all the languages of India irrespective of their family affiliation, have drawn on Sanskrit for nourishment over the past years."[90]

Sanskrit language is known not only for its flexibility, but, for its scientific philological implications also. The Indian grammatical tradition continues to inspire the modern linguists of both India and Europe. Leonard Bloomfield, Herman Paul and others have all realised, that it is the linguistic description of Sanskrit language which has enhanced the chances of exploring a language, which has been the common source of not only Sanskrit, Greek and Latin, but of Gothic, Celtic and older Persian also. Long back in 1786, William Jones, the first great European scholar stated that, Sanskrit bears a resemblance to Greek and Latin, which is too close to be due to chance, but shows rather that all three have sprung from some common source which perhaps no longer exists[91] and Gothic (that is Germanic) and Celtic probably had the same origin[92,93] and the Older Persian, observes Pattnayak might be added to the same family.[94]

Obviously, for continuing research in this field, the Sanskrit knowing scholars are required and scholars cannot be acquired unless the language i.e., Sanskrit is taught in the formal institutions. In 1854, the Wood's Despatch suggested the institution in the universities, of professorship for among other subjects Sanskrit, Arabic and Persian. It says, "A knowledge of the Sanskrit language, the root of the vernaculars of the great part of India is more especially necessary to those who are engaged in the work of composition in these languages."[95] Keeping into consideration this unique and specific character of the Sanskrit language, the Government of India introduced Article 351 in the Constitution and advised the linguists and educationists to develop and enrich all the Indian languages including the official language Hindi, by drawing primarily on Sanskrit. This places a responsibility on the States also to take necessary steps and to devise special means to encourage and promote the study of Sanskrit "by making secure the place of Sanskrit in the curricula of studies in schools and colleges."[96] In 1840, Captain Candy, the Superintendent of Education observed in his report on the Poona Sanskrit College (1840): "Sanskrit, I conceive to be the grand reservoir from which strength and beauty may be drawn for the vernacular languages."[97] He further stated that, "I look on every native who possesses a good knowledge of his own mother tongue, of Sanskrit and of English to possess the power of rendering incalculable benefit to his country men"[98] Long back in 1786, Sir William Jones had observed, that "The Sanskrit language whatever be its antiquity, is of wonderful structure, more perfect than the Greek, more copious than the Latin and more exquisitely refined than either."[99,100] Since it is the language of Hindu scriptures, a natural urge is there in the minds of the people to learn Sanskrit. There are instances, where people holding higher executive posts, have started learning Sanskrit in their advanced age just only to read the scriptures. For instance some people, although having technical degree, have joined courses in Sanskrit, simply to satisfy their desire to read their religious books. Even foreigners are inclined to Sanskrit just to know the rich heritage and culture of India. In the United Kingdom many Englishmen have been the Sanskrit scholars and are still fond of Sanskrit literature. The Chairs in Sanskrit have been established in Cambridge, Oxford and Manchester Universities. In Edinburgh, Sanskrit works are being translated. In London, the School of Oriental and African Studies and the Royal Asiatic Society of Great Britain have been promoting Sanskrit studies. In

France, Austria, Czechoslovakia, Holland, Denmark, Norway, Sweden, Switzerland and Italy, Chairs for Sanskrit have been established. In Germany, a fair number of professorship have been established in Sanskrit. The University of Bonn may be called Varanasi of Germany. At Keil, Hamburg, Marburge, Wurzbrug, Munich, Berlin, Sanskrit scholars are busy either in translating Sanskrit works or in deciphering certain manuscripts in Sanskrit. In the United States of America, the study of Sanskrit is still continuing in several universities such as Yale, Tohne Hopkins, Columbia, Harvard (Cambridge), Indonesia, Iran, Laos, Nepal, Thailand, Burma, Japan, and China have kept the study of Sanskrit alive outside India. Religious messages of India are carried even to Turkestan.[101] Besides, there have been Sanskrit scholars like Whitney, Edgerton, Lanman, Maurice Bloomfield, Norman Brown, Barat, Murray, Louis, H. Gray, Schuyler, Hoas, Nariman Mayura, Emeneau, Max Muller, Macdonell, Winternitz, Tunrner T. Burrow, Colebrook, Serebrykot, Quackenbos and others.[102,103] They are not only interested in knowing Modern India, but also in knowing the Ancient India, because even today, much of our present beliefs, customs and social structures are basically the same. Moreover, in the present circumstances, while overweightage is given to science and technology, the humanities in Sanskrit will prove greatly helpful in restoring the proper balance in studies. An example may be cited of Oppenheimer the great American atomic scientist, who used to spend considerable time in reading Sanskrit and Pali.[104] Study of Sanskrit therefore, is a compelling necessity even for the understanding of modern India with its multifarious facets of life and culture.[105] It is not confined to one particular country or to the region or state of the country, because its importance is great as the Sanskrit language and its literary tradition were not confined to the limits of the sub-continent, but, became a vehicle for the transmission of the ancient Indian culture into many other lands."[106] Being the source of most of the Indian language it is also recognised as the symbol of national unity. Various scholars have suggested to accept Sanskrit as the official language of the country, if not in the present form, then in some simplified form.[107] Taking into consideration these factors, Sanskrit has been placed as one of the 15 languages in the Constitution of India.[108] The Government had also appointed a Sanskrit Commission in 1956, to suggest the ways and means for promoting its study in the country because, many have deplored the fact that the Classical language — Sanskrit is being completely ignored.[109] Consequently, "the number of persons that take to classical studies is diminishing rapidly and if this continues it is felt that the study of the classics, which is of such immense value may eventually be neglected."[110] As "language are carrier of literature, literature in turn are embodiments of the national history of the peoples who produced them. Literatures are to a society what individual memory is to each one of us."[111,112] The knowledge of literature of a country obviously becomes important, if the society wants to inculcate her ideals and values in her citizens. As Cassirer puts it "All culture consists in the creation of certain intellectual symbol and by these symbolic forms, life is lifted from the plane of natural processes to that of conscious processes. The individual internalises the cultural norms and emotions expressed in arts, mythology and literature,"[113] and in India, the ancient literature and mythological stories are available in Sanskrit language. Even Pt. Nehru, the then Prime Minister, realising the value of Sanskrit stated "the Sanskrit language and literature is a magnificent inheritance and as long as this endures and influences the life of our people, so long the basic genius of India will continue."[114] The Sanskrit Commission, therefore, suggested that, the study of Sanskrit should be declared compulsory under the three language formula. But, the Government laying more emphasis on the study of science, technology and equally on the cultural heritage of India embodied in Sanskrit the parent language, declared it as one of the optional languages in the school curriculum from VIII onwards,[115] whereas, under the three language formula, it was supposed to be taught as a part of the composite course in Hindi or mother tongue from VI onwards.[116] As it was suggested, that it may be taught as forming a part of composite course of either mother tongue or regional language.[117] Pattnayak says, that "It is only through the study of Sanskrit, that one can reach a commanding height."[118] If the aim of the three language formula is to bring national integrity and solidarity, then, the study of Sanskrit also becomes essential, because, Sanskrit is not only a repository of our cultural heritage, but also an instrument in achieving national unity. Almost all the Indian languages have drawn upon Sanskrit language for their vocabulary and in some of the languages the percentage of Sanskrit words is very high. The importance of Sanskrit language, therefore, has very well been recognised. Unfortunately, Sanskrit not being a bread and butter subject, the average individual is prone to become less and less alive to its intellectual and spiritual values, but it is for these thinkers and administrators, who want to build up a balanced scheme of education and foster national solidarity,[119] that the study of Sanskrit should be boosted.

In faci, an academic discussion of the question regarding the justification and possibilities of the language studies is long overdue. Here, an attempt is being made to unravel the situation that existed in the past and the urgency to have an impartial search into the retention or otherwise of the three language formula.

**Other Studies**

Since language is the most vital issue, studies had continuously been done on this subject. Generally, they were concerned with the philosophical implications, pedagogy of languages, and their use as the media and the contents of language syllabi at different levels of school education. A few studies had also been conducted on the Government policy of teaching languages and their places in the school curricula. As language is the basis of all knowledge, it attracted attention of almost all the academicians in some way or the other. Linguisticians, psychologists, politicians and educationists by their studies were always busy in making efforts to solve the language problem.

Although such studies were not less in number they had yet to cope with the ratio, the language problem had grown. However, some works related to the present study and which needed close scrutiny were as follows :

**1. Babel-Thirtha[120]**

The book was presented in two parts :

(i) the problem of the study of language and

(ii) the problem of the medium of instruction. In the first part of the study, the author exposed the language dilemma in Indian schools by describing that in certain cases, the students learnt even more than three languages. For instance, if the child's parents belonged to two different linguistic groups, he/she had to learn both the parents' mother tongues. In addition he/she had to learn regional language in case it was different from the former two languages; Hindi - the Official language of the country, English as the foreign library language, and Sanskrit as a language of our cultural heritage in a composite course of mother tongue RL. The author discussed which languages and to what extent they were studied in the schools. In the other part of the study the three languages viz. Hindi, English and RL were mentioned being in use as media of education. Although different problems were analysed in using all the three media, no suggestion was made for using any particular language as the medium.

**2. The Language Controversy and the Minorities**
**Shrivastava, Gopi Nath[121]**

As indicated by the title, the author in the book focussed the issue of the language controversy and the implications of minorities. Having discussed the language pattern under the Constitution perspectives. He, not only mentioned the different dialects of Hindi language, but, also discussed the origin and nature of Hindi, Urdu and Hindustani.

**3. The Language Controversy in Indian Education**
**A Historical Study - Kanungo[122]**

In this book, the author drew a historical picture of the language controversy in Indian education since the beginning of 19th century upto 1960. The author pointed out that the number of languages to be learnt differed from person to person. The students in India, in certain cases had to learn the CL and the language of the Union, Hindi in addition to MT, RL and English.

**4. The Position of Languages in School -- Curriculum in India**
**Chaturvedi, M.G. and B.V. Mohale[123]**

The book dealt with the position of language instruction in the country. Efforts were made to highlight the languages taught and used as media at different levels of school education in all the states and the Union Territories of India. The authors also pointed out to the multilingual character of the country and as such according to the authors of the book weightage was given to the teaching of more than one languages. Having collected data on language instruction in the schools, the authors, concluded by saying that language instruction demanded a serious planning, for, it was the language through which all sciences, humanities and technology were taught and as such, the language teachers were in need of a new orientation programme of language pedagogy. Some salient features of this book were found to be the following :

1. the exact and names of the languages studied in different states and the Union Territories at different stages of school education;
2. the number and the names of the languages used a media of

instruction in India;
3. the weightage assigned to different languages in the school;
4. the objectives for which different languages were taught;
5. the tools used for pupil's evaluation in languages;
6. the qualifications of language teachers and inservice training programmes for them;
7. the position of supervision and guidance for language teachers.

This study was mainly based on the information available in school syllabi of different states and Union Territories. Besides, some supplementary information was also collected through a questionnaire and personal interviews with the officers of education department of each and every state and Union Territory of India.

**5.Education and Language Policy**
**V.V. John**[124]

As is clear by the title, the author discussed the language policy in its educational perspectives. The author emphasised the fact that the local languages and dialects could not be possibly ignored. Their impact could be observed in the people's cultural behaviour and as such they were bound to play an important role in all the domains of a community. Obviously the needs of learning RL/MT, Hindi as a link language and English as an international language were essential. The author further emphasised that the methodology of teaching languages should be improved so that after twelve years of schooling, the study of any language(s) might not be considered compulsory.

**6.National Communication and Language Policy in India**
**Nayar, Baldev Raj.**[125]

The book to some extent was related to the present study as it dealt with the language policy of our country. Besides, it revealed the languages being used in communication at the national level. The study also gave a picture of historical development of the language policy at secondary and university stages of education since the British period. For achieving these purposes, the library was used as the main source, though some fieldwork was also conducted by the investigator.

**7.The Language Problem. Vinoba**

This was a small brochure in which Acharya Vinoba Bhave expressed his views on the language problem of the country. Although the writer gave some of his suggestions to solve it, nothing was mentioned about the implementation programme of the language policy of the Indian Government.

**8. Translations of Indian Institutions of Advanced Study Vol. 8. Language and Society in India. Proceedings of a Seminar. Indian Institute of Advanced Study, Simla. 1969.**

In this volume, 57 papers were presented which were presented at seminar on "Language and Society in India", held at Indian Institute of Advanced Study, Simla from Monday, October 6 to Friday, October 27, 1967. In these lectures, the different lecturers, readers and writers discussed the importance of different languages in the society.

**9. A critical study of the language policy of India in relation to the educational needs and aspirations of the different linguistic communities of India - Usha Chaudhri.[126]**

The research had been made to study the language policy accepted by the Government of India in relation to educational needs and aspirations of the different linguistic communities staying in Southern and Northern part of Delhi. The investigator found a significant difference between the two groups belonging to South and North linguistic communities. Both these groups had expressed the desire that the teaching of three languages should not only be limited to the lower secondary level i.e. from VI to VIII class; but should also be continued till senior secondary level of school education i.e. upto XII standard. Though South and North both favoured Hindi and English as the two compulsory languages to be learnt yet they differed on the issue of the third language to be studied in the schools. South favoured mother tongue with the combination of Hindi and English whereas North favoured RL in addition to Hindi and English.

Regarding the official work of the country, South and North both agreed to the use of English language. But for the internal purposes of the country South preferred the use of English whereas North the use of Hindi also in addition to English.

Regarding the medium of instruction it was discovered that the said two groups favoured mother tongue till secondary stage of school education. These groups opined that at the senior secondary stage of school education it should be replaced by English medium, although two languages can also be adopted as media of instruction at the lower secondary and senior secondary levels of school education.

Besides the library material, the study was conducted through a questionnaire administered to the linguistic groups of south and north of Delhi. The questionnaire was also administered to the school teachers, principals, college lecturers, students, housewives and the like.

The few studies, that existed such as these, dealt either with the formulation of the language policy and its historical aspect or little more than the policy-oriented pronouncements. Operative relationships between the policy in theory and policy in practice in the field of school education largely remained a neglected and unexplored area of study. The Centre of Advanced Study in Education of the Maharaja Sayajirao University of Baroda made a survey of doctoral studies done in 'Education' in Indian Universities upto 1978. The Educational Research Survey listed some 343 + 806 (1149) studies and reviews respectively.

Besides, the Association of Indian Universities has made a bibliography of Doctoral Dissertations from 1979 to 1984. The number of such studies was found to be 931.[127] That means the number of the studies including the reviews, appeared to reach the number (numerically) 2080 (1149 + 931) but none of these was found to be on the three language formula-Its status in the school-curriculum. There however, was an immediate reason for the meagerness of research attention paid to the execution of the three language formula in the school-curriculum. A full fledged language policy of the government was in operation in this country only since the seventies. No assessment of the actual working of the language policy in the school curriculum could perhaps be meaningfully undertaken before the policy had operated for some time. The present study is a very modest effort to fill the gap in this area of study.

## LANGUAGE POLICIES IN SOME OTHER COUNTRIES OF THE WORLD

At this stage, it may not be futile to turn to some other multilingual countries in the world and cost a glance at the language policies implemented at the level of school education. This might assist in some way or the other in solving the language problem faced by India. The countries taken into consideration are the U.S.S.R., Indonesia and some of the countries in Africa. The choice hardly needs any explanation, as, they are all multiferous countries, having a number of languages, culture and followers of different faiths. Moreover, in India and U.S.S.R. not all the languages have developed into 'Standard language', some of them having neither a literature nor a script.[128, 129] The same is true in case of some of the languages of Indonesia[130] and Africa.[131] Besides the language policies at the official and educational levels both, are identical in India and U.S.S.R.[132] The latter has tackled her language problem in the light of a workable solution for carrying on administration, integrating various linguistic groups, facilitating inter-provincial communication and for people's education at different levels.

The Soviet Russia is a multilingual country having 200 languages and dialects spoken by various linguistic and national groups.[133] Out of 130 nations, only 20 had written languages at varying degrees of advancement,[134] but, only 16 of them have been considered important languages in which the laws passed by the Supreme Soviet of the USSR are published. Even the Gazettee of the Supreme Soviet is issued in these sixteen languages, which have now become means of everyday contacts and are used in Governmental Work, the press culture, science, education and other aspects of social life. For the Constitution of U.S.S.R. lays down the right of soviet people to use their mother tongues.[135] Though, in the pre-revolutionary period, V.I. Lenin professed full equality of all people and their languages,[136], [137] yet, the vital necessity of having a single means of common medium of contact with other Soviet nations, was pointed out by him. Hence he further said, that attempts to impose one or another language upon others or coercion in any form were inadmissible.[138]

The regional languages in U.S.S.R. find a great deal of scope. All local administration is carried on at the Republic level in the language of the concerned Republic, although in the pre-revolutionary period it used to be Russian. These days, the language of all law courts is the language of the region. "Judicial proceedings shall be conducted in the language of the Union Republic, Autonomous Republics, Autonomous Region or Autonomous Area or in the language spoken by the majority of the people in the locality. Persons participating in court proceedings, who do not know the language in which, they are being conducted, shall be ensured the right to become fully acquainted with the materials in the case, the services of an interpreter during the proceedings and the right to address the court in their language".[139] Sometimes the judgements and decisions are delivered at all levels upto the Supreme Court of the Union Republic in the RL, provided their official translations are available in the Russian language,[140] which normally is found to be convenient to use. In Moscow, in the Central Government, all instructions and decisions of State and Judicial bodies, departments and Ministries are issued in the Russian Language, but, it has not yet assumed the status of the obligatory official language, because, it implies compulsion and imposition. Legally it has no advantage over any other tongue.[141]

In U.S.S.R. after the October Revolution, the Declaration of Rights of Nationalities of 3rd Nov. 1917, proclaimed the equality of all races, creeds and languages and as such, the right to education through the medium of the native language/MT is given constitutional recognition.[142] Consequently, the provision is made for teaching the school students not only in 47 National languages,[143] but, even in those languages, which are not fully developed. Some of them are also used as the media of education upto 8th, 4th or 2nd form, but that depends on the stage of development of the 'Native language.' Beyond that stage, instruction is given through the Russian language,[144] which is compulsory in all the schools throughout the Union.[145] In the non-Russian Republics, where the local language is the medium of instruction, Russian being the official language of the Union is taught as the 2nd language from Class II, and in Russian speaking Republics, the 'Native language is taught from class II. In fact the national groups voluntarily learn and use the language of a neighbouring ethnic community.[146]

At the secondary level (Grades V to X) in the USSR, two languages were taught. One of them was Russian and the other was a foreign language, (either English/French/German) which was introduced in the V grade of School. The stated policy governing the teaching of a foreign language in the USSR, was that every pupil must begin to study other than his own language in the 5th grade of school[147] and continue till the end of the secondary school, i.e. upto the 10th grade.[148] However, in the Union Republics with languages other than Russian, three languages were learnt in practice, native language/MT was taught as the first language, Russian was introduced as the second language in class II and one of the 'Foreign languages' was also added as the third language from class V onwards. Almost the same policy was adopted in the non-Russian speaking Republics. In case of the linguistic minorities, in a Republic, the study of the 4th languages was also found necessary if they wanted to learn their MT, as well as, the language of the Republic. In such Republics like Lativia, Estonia and Lithuania for example, the total school course was a year longer to accommodate the time needed for extra language teaching. Thus at the Secondary level in the U.S.S.R. two language, three language and even four language policies operated in different Republics.[149]

In the 'Special Language Schools' known as the 'Foreign Language Schools', tne foreign language usually English/German/French is introduced in the second grade or even earlier. In the higher grades of these schools, teaching of some of the subjects was conducted through the medium of the foreign languages.[150] At the 'University level', pupils were expected to continue to study the foreign language taken up at school.[151] No second language is taught in the higher institutes. Since the knowledge of Russian is sound, "No difficulty of medium of instruction arises at universities or institutes of higher learning owing to the mother tongue of professor and students being different.[152] Although the Constitutional right of taking education in the native language at secondary level of school education was granted to all language groups, an accelerating trend is viewed by some critics of increasing education of non-Russian students through the Russian medium[153;154] which is adopted at the higher level of education also,[155] for Russian being the most widely, spoken language, has occupied the most outstanding position among all the languages of USSR.[156] Even under the Czars, it has been the language of administration and higher education throughout Russia. All the Republics of the Union have accepted the 'Russian script'. All the local languages are typed in Russian script with minor changes in the keyboard, although from 1929, the Roman script had been in use, which was soon discovered confusing, as the students had to learn Latin (Roman) and Cyrillic script both. With the result, the former was abandoned and in 1940, the Cyrillic script was adopted in place of Roman script. Obviously learning of different languages became easier, as the script to write in was one only, except with a few diacritical marks, but, the Russian did not abolish all the scripts. It must be pointed out at the same time that all the languages current in the U.S.S.R. have not switched over to the Russian or Cyrillic script. The Republics of Lativia, Estonia and Lithuania continue to use the Latin script. Armenia and Georgia have their own scripts which are neither Latin nor Cyrillic. The current literary output in these languages is not written even today in the Russian Script.[157]

The national minorities in U.S.S.R. are as a rule bilingual. Linguistically an interconnected bilateral process is going on in the U.S.S.R. today. On the one hand, national languages have been progressing in every way. On the other hand Russian as the language of international contacts, chosen by all nations and nationalities of the U.S.S.R. has been comprehensively developing in strength, scope and function.

Indicative of this is the rapid progress of nation wide bilingualism in the U.S.S.R.,[158] where linguistic conflicts, tensions and discords have been forestalled because for the development of a language, encouragement is given to every language as as part of the cultural inheritance. Hence, no linguistic controversy arises. According to Myrdal, the observed gap between enacted legislation and implementation in India exists, because, India is, what he calls a 'Soft State.'[159,160] For Myrdal, a 'Soft State' is one in which the rulers are "unwilling to impose obligations on the governed", and there is a "corresponding unwillingness on their part to obey rules laid down by democratic procedures."[161]

**Conclusion**

1. Out of 200 spoken languages and dialects, 16 were considered to be the languages of administration, education, culture and judiciary although the number of languages to be recognised as the national languages exceeded 16. There were 47 fully developed languages recognised as national languages. It is significant to note that the provision was made to teach the school students not only in these 47 languages but in those also which were not developed but were considered to be the native/MT of the students.
2. In U.S.S.R. the 3 languages were learnt by the school students. As the first language native language/MT was taught, Russian as the second and one of the foreign languages viz. English/French/German used to be taught as the third languages.
3. At the primary level of education, two languages were being taught in Russian as well as non-Russian Republics. In the former Republics, Russian was taught as the first language and native language was taught as the second language from class 2 onwards. In non-Russian Republics, native language was taught as the first language and Russian was taught as the second language from class 2 onwards. The native language/MT was used as the medium of education. But in case it was found to be undeveloped, Russian was adopted as the medium of instruction at the primary level of school education. It is significant to note that in Russian Republics, the national groups voluntarily learnt and used the language of a neighbouring ethnic community.

At the secondary level of education (from class V to X) two language, three language, and four language policies operated. In Russian Republics Russian was taught in addition to foreign language (English,

French, German) which was introduced in class V and continued till X. In non-Russian Republic three language policy operated. In addition to native language and Russian one of the foreign languages (English, French and German) was learnt from 2nd to 10th. In case of the linguistic minorities the four language policy operated. The students had to learn their MT, the RL, Russian and one of the said foreign languages. It may not be out of place to mention here that in such cases where four languages were being learnt like in Lativia, Estonia etc. the total school course was a year longer to accommodate the time needed for extra language teaching.

In special language schools known as the foreign language schools one of the foreign languages (English, French and German) was introduced in 2nd grade and some times even earlier. In the higher grades of these schools, these foreign languages were even used as the media of education.

At the higher level of education, only Russian was taught which remained medium of their education.

It is very significant to note that all the Republics of the Union had accepted the Russian script. All the local languages were typed in Russian script with minor changes in the key-board though the Republics of Lativia, Estonia and Lithuania continued to use the Latin script. Armenia and Georgia had their own scripts which were neither Latin nor Cyrillic.

By the above mentioned facts it can be concluded that at the primary level two languages were compulsory and at the secondary level, three languages were compulsory and at the senior secondary level of education, three language policies continued. One of them was two language policy, the other was the three language policy and the third was the four language policy which was to be implemented for the linguistic minorities. The total school course in such cases was a year longer to accommodate the language burden.

The special language schools known as the 'Foreign Language Schools' were also being run where the Foreign languages - English, German and French were to be introduced in class II or even earlier. In the higher grades in these schools, the medium of instruction used to be the foreign language.

## INDONESIA

In Indonesia, which is the largest archipelago consisting 13,677 islets,[162] 200 languages and dialects are spoken.[163] Two of them have been considered as the 'Standard languages' known as 'Bhasha Malesia' and 'Bhasha Indonesia' spoken in Malaysia and Indonesia respectively. Their parent language Malaya has been the lingua franca in both the regions for centuries.

Indonesia like so many other countries, was ruled by different political powers of the world. History unfolds, that there were Buddhists, Hindus, Dutch and Muslim rulers, who through mutual communication not only helped in enriching their languages, but also gave them various scripts. It may be significant to note, that the first script in which the Indonesians used to codify their language was the Brahmi script as the Indonesians came into contact with the Indians by the end of Ist Century A.D. Till the end of 15th century A.D. Sanskrit and Pali remained two main languages in Indonesia with the result that some of their words are still found in their language. Since Dutch ruled afterwards for 300 years, they also influenced their language and dialects. Quite a fair numbers of words picked up and amalgamated in the languages, which in due course of time developed into a dialect language and developed its own script. In 20th century, the Indonesians decided to use the Malaya language, which was spoken mostly in the ports and in 1945, after independence, they gave a new nomenclature to Malaya language. Since then, it is known as the Bhasha-Indonesia, which is compulsory for all senior High School state i.e. till XII class, though, it is introduced in class III only.[164;165]

The school course in Indonesia consists of 12 years, which is divided into 'Primary' and 'Secondary' stage of six classes each. The latter is again divided equally into a duration of 3 years, into junior and senior high school stage. It is at this stage of senior high school, that, the students can opt for different subjects. Regarding the languages to be learnt, it is the local language which is taught from class Ist and a second language - Bhasha Indonesia, is introduced in class 3rd and thereafter becomes the medium of instruction.[166] Thus at the primary level of education only 2 languages local and Bhasha Indonesia are taught to all the students. At the Junior high school stage one more language i.e. English is also added to the aforesaid two languages.[167]

At the stage of senior high school, the course is divided into A, B and C three different streams referring to language 'Mathematics and Commercial Streams respectively. The students can opt any of them according to their choice. Since the stream A devotes more time to language teaching, three languages were compulsory for the students placed under A stream, but in XII class, they learn only two language for the local language is dropped in XII class. However, it is not taught in any of the classes of the Mathematics and Commerce students at the senior high school stage. Provision is made to teach either German or French to Commerce students at the senior high school stage. To be precise the three languages are compulsory even at the senior high school stage, but only for language and commerce students i.e. A & C streams respectively. Mathematics students placed under B stream have to learn only two languages i.e. Bhasha Indonesia and English.[168;169] Keeping into consideration, all these facts, it can be concluded that the Bhasha Indonesia which is the language of administration has got the primary status followed by the local language and English. Since they have accepted the Roman script for writing down all the languages and dialects, they have no such problem of language load or learning, of multiple number of languages.[170]

**Conclusions**

1. At the primary stage of education (consisting of six classes) two languages - local language and Bhasha Indonesia were taught. It was the local language which was taught from class 1 onwards. Bhasha Indonesia, though introduced in class III, it replaced the local language as the medium thereafter.
2. At the junior high school stage (VII, VIII, IX) one more language (English) was added to the former group of two languages being learnt at the primary level of school education. Out of these three languages, first was the local language. Bhasha Indonesia continued to be the second and English was introduced as the third language. Bhasha Indonesia maintained its status as the medium language.
3. At the stage of senior high school stage (X, XI, XII) the course was divided into A, B, C three different streams referring to language, mathematics and commercial streams respectively. Out of these three streams for A and C streams i.e. language and commerce streams, provisions was made for teaching three languages that is, local language, Bhasha Indonesia and English continued to be learnt by the students of Language stream even at the senior high school stage. The local language was dropped in class XII.

The students in commerce stream (C stream) also learnt three languages but in lieu of local language they learnt German or French as one of the foreign language.

For the students in B stream known as Mathematics stream, provision was made for teaching two languages only - Bhasha Indonesia and English.

## AFRICAN COUNTRIES
## TANZANIA

Tanzania is one of the several countries in Africa, where nearly a 1000 languages were spoken.[171] If the dialects were also added, this number might exceed even 1000. Many of the Africans were able to speak their mother tongue/first language as well as six other languages. In Nigeria, the people were multilinguals as they moved from one place to another and thus picked up their language by communicating with each other. Kiswahili (Swahili) Hansa and Kongo were some of the important lingua francas. Because they were spoken among the speakers of different language groups, therefore they had developed some of the characteristics of 'Pidgins'. But there were such 90 groups of African languages, which had no distinct relationship in them. Where, there was no sufficiently wide spread lingua franca, the European languages of the former colonial powers were used as the official languages.[172] In some of the African countries, like Kenya and Zambia, the European languages were replacing local languages as the language of instruction.[173]

There were 130 vernaculars which were usually known as the Tribal languages in Tanzania. It was significant to note, that in grade 1 and 2 facilities for learning the respective MT were given to them by the Germans who ruled this island till 1960, but, after getting the independence in 1961, these facilities were discontinued as the Tanzanians realised that, for integrating the different nationals (speech communities) the easiest way was to speak and use one language. They, therefore, accepted Kiswahili because it was the MT of more than a million people and was used as the second language by about nine million others, whose MT was not Kiswahili.[174] Though the Tanzanian Government had taken a decision against the teaching of vernaculars and classical languages,[175] yet the attempts were made to teach the different MT particularly in the rural areas.

In Tanzania, school education continued for 13 years, which was divided into primary, secondary and form five respectively for seven years, four years and two years course. Kiswahili was the only language taught in grades 1 and 2. English is introduced in Grade 3. Upto the primary level of education i.e. grade 7, Kiswahili was retained as the subject and medium both, whereas English was taught as the subject only.

At the level of secondary education, Kiswahili was discontinued as the medium due to the practical reasons e.g. dearth of text-books and reference books etc. With the result, English was used as the medium of education and Kiswahili remained to be taught as the subject only. But, for teaching political science, especially socialism, Kiswahili was used as the medium language, as the training/education in socialism,[176] had to be given in the language, most commonly spoken. In the last two years of secondary course, the aforesaid two languages (Kiswahili and English) were continued to be taught. English was retained as the subject and medium both while Kiswahili was continued as the subject only.

At the higher level of education, only English was taught. The other language i.e. Kiswahili was dropped, but, those who had a taste for it, were given facilities to learn it at the advanced level.[177] Keeping in mind the aim of national integration, the Tanzanians had started to write down the Kiswahili their official national language in Roman script, although it was used to be written in Arabic script.

It is significant to note, that, in Tanzania, Hindi films were found to be more popular than the films in English, although no provision was made for teaching Hindi language at any level of education. A few films were made in Kiswahili, for the people of rural areas. The newspapers were also published in this language for maintaining the literacy of those who had taken adult-education. One major daily was used to be published in English.

In Tanzania the primary status was given to Swahili which was used at the official level of the country but, an equal status was given to English also for, the Roman script of English language had been unanimously accepted for writing down the Kiswahili language which was also the national language of Tanzania.

**Conclusion**

The school education was divided into three levels viz. Primary, secondary, and form 5. The duration of these three forms of school education was found to be 7, 4 and 2 years respectively. At the primary level two languages were taught Swahili and English. The former started from the first whereas the latter i.e. English was introduced in class three. Swahili was not only taught as a subject but was also continued as the medium of education.

At the secondary level of education 2 languages continued - Swahili and English. But instead of Swahili, English was used as the medium although for teaching political science and social studies. It was the Swahili which was used as the medium language. At form 5 also the same pattern continued.

## NIGERIA

One of the otherRepublics/in Africa is Nigeria, where, more than 100 languages were spoken. Though Hansa was the main spoken language yet it was not used at the official level. Ibo and Yonuba were the two their languages which were very popular in Nigeria, but no serious plans are made for teaching them as the compulsory languages beyond the primary level of education.

The school education in Nigeria, is divided into two stages, primary and secondary which were divided equally into a period of 6 years each. At the stage of primary education, two languages MT and English were taught from class 1 and were continued till the primary stage was over i.e. till class VI. The language spoken by the majority in the locality to which the child belongs, was used as the medium language, English was also used as the medium of instruction at this level, but in those schools only which were known as the special schools or University primary schools, where, due to the higher rate of fee, charged by the school authorities all the children were unable to seek admission.

At the level of secondary education provision is made to teach not only the MT and English, but French also. English is retained as the only compulsory language while the others are continued as the optional subjects. Normally, the students opt for their respective MT, because, passing in their MTs is compulsory while they appear for West African Examination which is held before seeking admission in the universities.[178] The status of English is raised as it is used as the medium of instructions at the level of secondary education.

At the level of higher education, English continues to be the medium. Though English does not continue as one of the subjects in the University, yet, the students have to pass a course in English the duration of which is one year only.

The primary status is given to English which is used at the official level of the country. The news from television centres and radios are broadcast in English followed by news in vernaculars. Films are made in English and vernacular, both.[179]

**Conclusion**

1. At the primary stage, two languages were taught, one of them was the MT and the other was English. In most of the schools MT was used as the medium of instruction, but in special schools known as university primary schools English was adopted as the medium of education.
2. At the secondary level, provision was made for teaching three languages - MT, English and French. English was found to be compulsory, while the other two languages i.e. MT and French were placed as optional subjects. The information collected from the Education Attache from Nigeria High Commission revealed that generally the students opted for MT also as passing in it was compulsory before the students sought admission in Universities. English remained the medium of education.

Since India is a multilingual country, it was thought proper that the language policies implemented in some of the foreign multilingual countries should also be studied. Indonesia, U.S.S.R. and a few African countries were considered for exploring the language situation. It was found that the language policies and the different levels of school-education at which they were implemented were not different from those of India. Some of the important features were as follows :

1. Minimum three languages viz. officials language, RL and one of the foreign languages were found to be taught at the school stage.
2. Native language/MT used to be the first well as the medium language at the primary level of school-education.
3. Though a number of languages were raised to the level of national languages, yet, the status of the official language was given to only one of them.
4. The children were exposed to two languages even at the primary level of education.
5. The three language policy was being implemented after the primary school stage.

## Notes and References


1. *Chandogya Upanisada,* VII. 2.1. Gorakhpur : Geeta Press. V.S. 2028 (1971).
1a. Lewis, M.M. *Infant Speech.* London : Kegan Paul French Trubner & Co. Ltd. 1936.
2. Hughes. "The Science of Language 1962", cited by Fraenkel, G. *Language.* Boston, Massachusetts : Ginn & Co. 1965, p. 17.
3. Francis, John De. *Nationalism and Language Reform.* Princeton, New Jersey : Princeton University Press, 1950.
4. Cited by Fraenkel, G. *Structure of America.* Boston, Massachusetts : Ginn & Co. 1954, pp. 16-17.
5. *Ibid.*
6. Sweet. "History of Language (1900)". Cited by Laguna, C.A. (1920) *Speech - Its function and Development.* New Haven : Yale University Press, 1920.
7. Cited by Bernard and George, L. Trager. *Linguistic Society of America.* Baltimore : Mount Royal & Gait for Avenues, 1942.
8. Sapir, E. *Language.* New York : Harcourt, Brace & World Inc., 1921.
9. Cited by Bernard and George L. Trager. *op. cit.*
10. Fraenkel, G. Language. *op. cit.* p. 18.
11. Laguna, C.A. *Speech - Its function and development.* New Haven : Yale University Press, 1927.
12. Olson, W.C. *Child Development.* London : D.C. Heath & Co., 1959.
13. Leonard, B. George. *Education and Ecstasy.* New York : Del Publishing Company Inc., 1968, p. 16.
14. Bernstein, B.A. "Socio-Linguistic Approach to Socialization". in *Direction in Socio-Linguistics.* by Gumperz and Hymes (ed). New York : Holt, Reinehart and Winston. 1970.
15. The Ayo Bamgbose (Ed). M.T. Education in the Western African Experience. Paris. The Unesco Press, 1976. p. 7.
16. Chaturvedi and Mohalo. *Position of languages in school curriculum in India.* New Delhi : National Council of Educational Research and Training, 1976, p. 8.
17. Chaturvedi and Sing. "Third All India Educational Survey - Languages and Media of Instruction in Indian Schools." New Delhi : N.C.E.R.T., 1981.
18. *Ibid.* p. 7.
19. Quoted by Pattnayak, D.P. "Role of Language in the Radicalisation of Education". Presidential Address given in the 7th All India Linguistic Conference. 28-30 Dec. 1977. Muzaffarnagar. p. 3.
20. Report of the Official Language Commission. 1956. p. 10.
21. Hockett, C.F. *A Course in Modern Linguistics.* New York : The Macmillan Company, 1958, pp. 5-6.
22. Reniez. "Origin and Prehistory of Language (Originally written in German Language, 1946)." Cited in *Language* (English Translation 1956) by Fraenkel, G. *op. cit.* 1965.
23. Burt. (Quoted in) "Bilingualism Bureau of Education" by West, M. New Delhi : Government of India. 1926.
24. *Ibid.*
25. Hockett, C.F. *op. cit.* p. 9.
26. Cited by Pattnayak, D.P. *op. cit.* p. 3.
27. Hockett, C.F. *op. cit.,* p. 9.
28. Florence, B. Stratemeyer and others (eds). *Developing a Curriculum for Modern*

*Living.* New York : Bureau of Publications, Teachers College Columbia University. 1957. p. 22.

29. Chaturvedi and Singh. *op. cit.* p. 26.
30. Benjamin, K.W. Quoted by Hayakawa, S.I. *Language in Thought and Action.* New York : Harcourt Brace and World Inc. 1939. p. 5.
31. Ministry of Education. "Language : A report by Her Majesty's Stationery Office", London. 1954. p. 13.
32. Hockett, C.F. *op. cit.* p. 4.
33. Chaturvedi and Mohale. *op. cit.* p. 7.
34. Bloomfield, L. *Language.* New York : Henry Holt and Company 1954. p. 499.
35. *Ibid.*
36. Pattnayak, D.P. *op. cit.* p. 3.
37. *The Constitution of India.* New Delhi : Government of India Press. 1980. p. 352.
38. *Ibid.* Article. 29.
39. *Ibid.* Article. 30.
40. *Ibid.* Article. 343(1).
41. *Ibid.* Article. 343(2).
42. *Ibid.* Article. 346.
43. *Ibid.*
44. *Ibid.* Article. 348(1).
45. *Ibid.* Article. 350.
46. *Ibid.*
47. *Ibid.*
48. *Ibid.* Article. 351.
49. Bloomfield. L. *op. cit.*, pp. 10-11.
50. *Ibid.*
51. *Rgveda.* 1.164.45. Varanasi : Chowkhamba Sanskrit Series. 1966.
52. *Atharvaveda.* 9.10.27.
53. Butler Samuel, Max Block and Max Muller (eds). London : Cornell Paperback. 1962. Cited by Varma, S. In *Vakyapadiya.* Delhi : Bhartiya Prakashan. 1968. p. 15.
54. *Rgveda.* 10.71.3.
55. *Ibid.* 10.71.8.
56. *Ibid.*
57. Patanjali. *Mahabhashya.* Patna : Motilal Banarsidas. 1966. (प्रथम आहिन्क)
58. Quoted in Haritika Vakyapadiya. 1.148 (cited by) Varma, S. *op. cit.*
59. Bhartrihari. *Vakyapadiya.* 1.1 Varanasi : Saraswati Bhawan Granthmala (91). 1976.
60. Bhartrihari. *Tripaditeeka.* 1.1.1 Cited by Varma, S. *op. cit.*
61. Fishman, Joshua (ed). *Advances in the Sociology of Languages.* Paris : Mouton The Hague. Vol. I., 1971, p. 9.
62. Bulvelkar. "System of Sanskrit Grammar". Cited by Varma, S. *op. cit.*
63. Taraporewala. *Elements of the Science of Language.* Calcutta : Calcutta University, 1962, pp. 424-25.
64. Bloomfield, L. *op. cit.* p. 11.
65. *Ibid.* p. 10.
66. Urban, W.M. Language and Reality. London : Macmillan & Co. 1939. Ch. 'The Philosophy of Language and the Principles of Symbolism'. Cited in *Readings in Psychology of Language,* by Leona, J. and Murrays (eds). New Jersey : Prentice-Hall. 1967. p. 11.

67. Bhartrihari. *Vakyapadiya*. Cited by Varma, S. *op. cit.*
68. Bloomfield, L. *op. cit.*, p. 27.
69. *Ibid.* p. 28.
70. Chaturvedi and Mohale. *op. cit.* p. 8.
71. Chatterji, S.K. *op. cit.* p. xiv.
72. Bloomfield, L. *op. cit.* p. 502.
73. Chatterji, S.K. *op. cit.* p. xxx.
74. Report of the Official Language Commission. 1956. p. 28.
75. Chatterji, S.K. *op. cit.* p. 49.
76. Report of the Sanskrit Commission. 1956-57. p. 76.
77. cf. Rex Warner. *Cult of Power* (London 1946) "... a knowledge of the common origins of our ways of thought is a desirable thing to have in a world which must unite or perish .... One might on similar grounds advocate the teaching of Sanskrit in all Indo-European Schools." (p. 151).
78. *Ibid.* p. 151.
79. Report of the Sanskrit Commission 1956-57.
80. Report of the Official Language Commission 1956. p. 53.
81. *Ibid.* p. 91.
82. Mahatma Gandhi in *Young India*. 5.7.1928.
83. Report of the Sanskrit Commission 1956-57. p. 83.
84. Taraporewala. *op. cit.*, p. 253.
85. Report of the Official Language Commission 1956. p. 38.
86. *Ibid.* pp. 38-39.
87. Sanskrit paper III, Lesson No. 27. 'Sanskrit Studies in the West' produced by the School of Correspondence - Academic Session 1974-75. Delhi University. Delhi.
88. Pattnayak, D.P. "Role of language in the radicalisation of Education" *op. cit.*, p. 13.
89. Report of the Official Language Commission 1956. p. 28.
90. Pattnayak, D.P. "Language Policy and Programmes." *op. cit.* p. 9.
91. Bloomfield, L. *op. cit.*, pp. 11-12.
92. *Ibid.*
93. Pattnayak, D.P. Role of "Language in the Radicalisation of Education". *op. cit.*, p. 13.
94. *Ibid.* p. 14.
95. Report of the Sanskrit Commission 1956-57. p. 20.
96. Report of the Sanskrit Commission 1956-57. p. 91.
97. *Ibid.* p. 18.
98. *Ibid.*
99. Raghvan, V. *The Indian Heritage - An Anthology of Sanskrit Literature.* Bangalore : The Indian Institute of World Culture, 1956, p. 1.
100. Cited by Taraporewala. *op. cit.* p. 447.
101. Report of the Official Language Commission, 1956. p. 21.
102. Pattnayak, D.P. "Role of language in the Radicalisation of Education". *op. cit.* p. 14.
103. Sanskrit Paper III. Lesson No. 27. Sanskrit Studies in the West. *op. cit.*
104. Report of the Sanskrit Commission 1956-57. p. 76.
105. Pattnayak, D.P. Role of Language in the Radicalisation of Education. *op. cit.*
106. Report of the Official Language Commission. 1956. p. 21.
107. *Ibid.* p. 38.
108. The *Constitution of India*, Eighth Schedule. Languages. p. 352.

109. The Report of the Secondary Education Commission 1952-54. p. 63.
110. *Ibid.*
111. Judd. Cited by Arsenian. *Bilingualism and Mental Development*. New York : Columbia : Teachers' College Bureau of Publications, 1937.
112. Report of the Sanskrit Commission 1956-57.
113. *Ibid.*
114. *Ibid.* p. 72.
115. Report of the Official Language Commission 1956.
116. Report of the Kothari Commission 1964-66.
117. *Ibid.*
118. Pattnayak, D.P. Language Policy and Programme. *op. cit.*, p. 9.
119. Report of the Sanskrit Commission. 1956-57. p. 91.
120. Thirtha, N.V. Babel, Masulipatinam : Seshachalam & Co. 1962.
121. Shrivastva, Gopi Nath. The Language Controversy and the Minorities. Delhi : Atma Ram & Sons. 1970.
122. Kanungo, Gostha Behari. The Language Controversy in Indian Education - A Historical Study. Chicago : Comparative Education Centre, University of Chicago. 1962.
123. Chaturvedi, M.G. and Mohale, B.V. *op. cit.*
124. John, V.V. Education and Language - Language Policy. Bombay : Nachiketa Publications. 1969.
125. Published in Cooperation with the Centre for Development Area Studies. New Delhi : McGill University Fredrick A. Prayer Publishers. 1969.
126. Chaudhri, Usha. "A Critical Study of the Language Policy of India in relation to the Educational needs and aspirations of the different linguistic communities of India." Unpublished Ph.D. Thesis. Maharaja Sayaji Rao University of Baroda. 1978.
127. Bibliography of Doctoral Dissertations 1983-'84. Social Sciences and Humanities. New Delhi. Association of Indian Universities. 1987.
128. Report of the Official Language Commission 1956. p. 13.
129. Karawalla, J.Gulistan. Language Problems and Policies in India and the USSR (A Comparative Approach). New Delhi : National Council of Educational Research and Training. 1979. p.2.
130. Indonesia 1979. An Official Hand book. New Delhi : Department of Information, Republic of Indonesia.
131. Information gathered from the Education Attache in the High Commissions of Uganda, Tanzania and Nigeria. New Delhi.
132. Kerawalla, J. Golistan. *op.cit.*, p.2.
133. Report of the Official Language Commission 1956. p.13.
134. Ibid.

     Vladimir Makarenko, Cand. Sc. (Philology) Solution of Linguistic Problem and Development of Socio-Linguistics Language Problem. 28th March 1978.
135. Article 36. Constitution (Fundamental Law) of the Union of Soviet Socialist Republics. Moscow : Novosti Press Agency Publishing House. 1985.
136. Karawalla J. Gulistan. *op. cit.*
137. Prof. Magomet Isayer, Institute of Oriental Studies. U.S.S.R. Academy of Sciences. New Delhi : Embassy of U.S.S.R. 1987.
138. Ibid.

     Prof. Magidov (Doctor of History) Soviet National Languages Today. New Delhi : Embassy of U.S.S.R. 28th July 1980.
139. Article 159. The Constitution of USSR National Languages of Soviet People.

140. Report of the Official Language Commission 1956. pp.482-85.
141. Ibid.
142. Article 45. The Constitution of USSR. *op. cit.*
143. National Languages of Soviet People, Soviet Affairs. New Delhi : Embassy of USSR. Bulletin-News and Views from the Soviet Union. 24th Sep. 1981.
144. Karawalla J. Gulistan. *op. cit.,* p.4.
145. Ibid. p.5.
146. Vladimir Makarenko. *op. cit.*
147. (Quoted by) Karawalla J. Gulistan. *op. cit.,* p.43.
148. R.S.F.S.R. Ministry of Education. 'Curriculum and Syllabuses for the 8th year and secondary school,' reprinted in Soviet Education. Vol. VII no. 1 (1968) p.18.
149. Ibid. p.44.
150. Ibid. p.4.
151. Ibid.
152. Report of the Official Language Commission 1956. p.490.
153. Kolasky, J. Education in the Soviet Ukraine. Ontario : Peter Martin. 1968. p. 41.
154. Cited by Karawalla J. Gulistan. *op. cit.,* p.39.
155. Ibid.
156. Census Report of 1979. Issued by the Information Department of the Embassy of U.S.S.R. in New Delhi.
157. Report of the Official Language Commission. 1956. p.490.
158. Prof. Sh. Magidov (Doctor of History) *op. cit.*
159. Myrdal, G. Asian Drama. New York : Pantheon. 1968. p.277.
160. Karawalla J. Gulistan. *op. cit.,* p.52.
161. Ibid.
162. Indonesia 1979. *op. cit.*
163. Ibid. Eduational Reforms. p.246.
164. The Report of Kothari Commission 1964-66.
165. Indonesia 1979. *op. cit.*
166. Ibid.
167. Ibid.
168. The Report of Kothari Commission 1964-66.
169. Indonesia. 1979. *op. cit.*
170. *Ibid.*
171. African Encyclopadia. Oxford University Press. 1974. p.43.
172. Ibid.
173. Ibid.
174. Ibid. p.494.
175. Arabic, Percian and Greek.
176. Tanzania is a Socialistic State. Information gathered from the Education Attachee: High Commission of Tanzania. New Delhi.
177. Ibid.
178. Information gathered from the Education Attachee. New Delhi : High Commission of Nigeria.
179. Ibid.

# 3 Methodology

An adequate study of the three language formula as has been implemented in the schools, requires an integrated approach of investigation upon several aspects of the policy of teaching languages. The educationists, the education ministers and the various local bodies authorised to introduce it in the school-curriculum have been insisting upon the inter-relationship of Centre and State, the policy-makers and those, who are responsible for its active implementation in the secondary schools. But, before the total impact of the policy is visualised, it is imperative to study not only the policy in the past as well as in the present, but also the views of the students, the language teachers, the intellectuals belonging to the cross-section of people of the society, who have directly or indirectly been affected by the national policy of teaching languages.

An educational problem like the three language formula and finding out its place in the school curriculum is open to investigators through various methods. Among these the ones most commonly used in education and similar fields involve large scale field studies aided by especially devised data-gathering tools. For the present research study, help of two research methods was sought namely historical method and descriptive method.

The study by its nature fell into two parts :

In the first part of the study an attempt was made to determine the language situation in the different historical periods in India comprising Vedic Medieval, British and Indian independent era. The methodology used for data collection was one of historical-documentary study leading on to analysis, discussion and relevant observation. The treatment of the data met with the requirement of the two objectives of the study laid down in Chapter 1.

The second part of the study related itself to the present position of language teaching and learning in schools and hence aimed at finding out the position of languages in some of the schools of Delhi. For this, the descriptive research methodology was used and the following procedure was adopted for data collection :

a) School visits.
b) Use of questionnaire for pupils of some selected senior secondary schools studying in class X.
c) Use of questionnaire to the language teachers to find out their views on teaching languages.
d) Use of interview technique for some leading public men with a view to seeking their opinion regarding the present policy of teaching languages.

**Historical Method**

Since a need was felt to find out the present situation as to what impelled the Indian leaders to adopt this policy for teaching three languages compulsorily at the school level, in the first part of the study, the historical method was employed to unravel the past events.[1] A quite similar view was expressed by Good, Barr and Scates. "The historical research is to examine the evidence and experience of the past as an aid in analysing and interpreting the present situation."[2]

The following were the objectives for applying the historical method :

1. To find out the linguistic character of the country down the ages.
2. To find out the different policies of languages if any, formulated by the different governments in India before independence.
3. To find out the number and varieties of languages taught in the schools in the pre and post independence era leading on to the emergence of the language policy.

While applying the historical method the different source books and documents available from primary and secondary sources were consulted. It is rightly said, "The thinking process requires at every stage of progress added increments of evidence in order that inferences, hypotheses or theories tentatively held may be identified as valid, verified as correct or rejected as untenable.... In fact data have to be collected," [3,4] because, data are the things we think with.[5]

**The Sources Tapped**

As the data base of the study, the *primary sources* consisted mainly of reports. Primary sources are eye-witness accounts. They are reported by an actual observer or participant in the event.[6] The most important among these were:

1. The Reports of the Constituent Assembly.
2. The Reports of the Lok Sabha Debates.
3. The Reports of the Rajya Sabha Debates.
4. The documents available in the National Archives of India, New Delhi.

For the language policy in Indian Republic, adequate provisions were made in the Constitution of India. To the primary sources may also be added some archival material that were used, particularly in the preparation of the historical chapter. The relevant historical documents were largely available in published forms. Subsequently the various Education Commissions set up by the Government submitted their reports to the Government and they were also consulted. The investigator consulted the Education Attaches in the Embassies of the U.S.S.R., Indonesia and in the High Commissions of some of the African countries like Tanzania and Nigeria.

It is known that, "Secondary Sources are documents of an event that were not actually witnessed by the reporter. He or she may have talked with an actual observer or read an account by an observer,but, his or her testimony is not that of an actual participant or observer.... They are used when primary data are not available."[7] The secondary data for the present study were collected from the published sources. Vedic literature, books on ancient history of education including Buddha and Mughal period works were consulted. Views of Charles Grant, Macaulay's Minutes, Wood's Despatch, Report of Sadler's Commission, Indian Act of Education 1935 and Delhi Gazetteers for, getting information about the educational set-up in the British period proved useful. Besides, reports on the policies of education adopted by Lord Curzon and on Wardha Scheme of Education, furnished background for the present study.

The investigator had also been to the Indian Institute of Advanced Studies, Simla and Maharaja Sayaji Rao University, Baroda, for collection of information.

**Descriptive Method**

After having a knowledge of different language policies which kept on changing from time to time, in the past, an attempt was made to collect information regarding the present situation of language teaching in the schools. The technique for identifying the schools for the study was based on the 'languages' used as media of instruction so that the status of the three language formula in practice might be explored. For the said purpose, schools, teaching through minority languages or mother tongues were taken for the study.

The schools chosen were primarily:

i) to establish the background information;

ii) to ascertain the language teaching programme for the groups under study; and

iii) to establish in detail the language learning positions of a section of students studying in class X.

**The Scope and delimitation of the Study**

It would have been in the fitness of things that a study of the language position in different Union Territories/States was made but for certain reasons the study was limited to the Union Territory of Delhi.

Education has been placed in the concurrent list and the different states are free to make changes in the educational policies according to their own needs and inclinations. Since the three language formula was mainly Central Government policy and its implementation was naturally to be seen in the schools of the Union Territory of Delhi, the study was limited to Delhi.

Out of all the Union Territories, Delhi was especially chosen as

1. In all the Union Territories, Delhi occupies a unique place for various reasons. It is the capital of Indian Republic. As a result, it has become a political, industrial, commercial and educational centre of great importance.
2. It provides numerous occupational opportunities. With the result, people from all the parts of the country came and settled down here. With them, they bring not only different cultures but different languages as well. Not only the languages mentioned in the VIII Schedule of the Constitution of India, other languages like Nepali, Dogri and dialects like Maithile, Brij, Bhojpuri *etc.* are spoken by them. In short, the Union Territory of Delhi is the multilingual city in the country.
3. Even those, who are well settled in different professions in other places, want to migrate to Delhi for better prospects.
4. In pre-independent era, during the British rule, English was mainly used at Government and educational levels. Its study was

naturally important. Even after India gained freedom the framers of the Constitution realising its importance in the national and international fields, did not eliminate it at a stroke. After much pondering, they set the limit for the gradual switch over to Mother tongue and Hindi. On the basis of the Census Reports in India, Hindi was given the status of 'Official Language' of the country because, the number of the people speaking Hindi was the largest. Fourteen Modern Indian Languages[8] were enumerated in the Constitution keeping in view the number of their users and speakers. Later on one more language 'Sindhi' was also included in the VIII Schedule of the Constitution of India. For the enrichment, promotion and preservation of different languages and cultures, it was thought necessary to give them their due place in the educational curricula. Besides this, since the MT is most natural and easiest medium for instruction, it was given primary status in the language policy of the country.

Naturally, besides Hindi and English, the largest number of MIL[9] was found in vogue in the Union Territory of Delhi. The use of such a large number of languages is bound to bring certain changes in the attitude of the people towards using and learning different languages.

5. Although the Centre is responsible for Co-ordination and determination of standards in institutions for higher education, or research and scientific and technical institutions,[10] the Union may also make its presence felt in secondary education, through powers developing in it, for the secondary schools are the only means to feed up the Universities. Hence, it was considered that in the areas put under the jurisdiction of the Union Government, the three language formula would be implemented fully.
6. Population of the literates is higher in the Union Territory of Delhi, because of its being the capital of India and secondly it is most densely populated of all the Union Territories.
7. Delhi is not only a national city or central place, but, internationally oriented. It is a host to Asiad games, International film festivals and NAM. Obviously, people in Delhi are more drawn to English. All the more 'Bhot', one of the Tribal languages, was also used as the medium in one of the schools of the Union Territories of Delhi.[11]

8. Travelling to other States and Union Territories was abandoned because of physical and financial constraints.
9. The investigator was a student of Delhi University in the Department of Education which is established in the Campus itself. Therefore, keeping into consideration all the facts mentioned above, it was decided to take the Union Territory under purview.

Since multiple number of languages were found in use, provision was also made for teaching the largest number of languages in the schools, where, it was found that the students had opted ten Modern Indian Languages[12] out of the 15 mentioned in the VIII Schedule of the Indian Constitution. Besides, they had opted Sanskrit, Arabic and Persian Languages also. Although the facilities were provided for teaching English, French, German, Russian, Polish, Japanese, Chinese, Hungarian, Bulgarian, and Portuguese at the different centres of teaching Foreign languages in the University of Delhi, the first 6 were being taught at the school level too.[13] Regarding the medium of instruction, there were ten[14] out of those languages mentioned above, which were used as the media of instruction.[15]

Hence, some of the institutions teaching through MT at the school level in the Union Territory of Delhi were taken for the study.

**Tools**

The following tools for research were used :

i) A questionnaire on language for X class students of senior secondary schools was constructed and administered.
ii) A closed form opinionnaire was constructed and administered to the language teachers in schools.
iii) A structured interview schedule for interviewing different public men was also designed.

**i) The Questionnaire**

The questionnaire is an instrument to be used for collecting data, "to obtain facts about the current conditions, practices and to make enquiries concerning attitudes and opinions."[16] According to Barr, Davis and Johnson, questionnaire may be defined as "a systematic compilation of questions that are submitted to a sampling of population from which information is desired."[17] Therefore a questionnaire[18] was constructed and administered to the students of class X to gather information from them.

The questionnaire fell into several broad issues on which the various tabular presentation was developed later to facilitate analyses. The issues discussed were as under:

1. Information regarding the MT of the students, the region they belonged to and the language(s) generally used by their parents. (Table-1)
2. Information regarding parents education and occupation (Table-2)
3. Information regarding the financial background of the families of the students. (Table-3)
4. Information regarding language(s) learnt by students at different levels and languages used by them as media. (Table-4)
5. Information regarding attainment in languages in reference to the four skills viz. understanding, speaking, reading and writing. (Table-5)
6. Information regarding languages difficult to learn. (Table-6)
7. Information regarding languages the students spoke at home. (Table-7)
8. Information regarding language(s) they used in different situation inside and outside home. (Table-8)
9. Information regarding language(s) used for writing for different purposes. (Table-9)
10. Information regarding the effect of learning three languages on other subjects. (Table-10)

**ii) The Opinionnaire**

As the participation of the teachers in the educational process is most important, their views were sought on this issue. An opinionnaire[19] was similarly constructed comprising ten statements on the three language formula. The opinionnaire was intended to be used to study reactions of language teachers. Such reactions were sought in the form of rating. The ten statements referred to ten different situations. Reactions sought were on a five point rating. It was considered a proper tool for use in the situations as it was accepted. "Rating is a term applied to expression of opinion or judgement regarding some situation, object or character. Opinions are usually expressed on a scale of values. Rating techniques are devices by which such judgements may be quantified."[20] Each situation was framed in the form of a statement. Thereupon the respondents (teachers) were asked to record their opinion in terms of the rating scheme offered to them. An example below should clarify the point.

**Teaching all the subjects through the medium of English language will determine the standard of education.**
**You can record your view under any one of the following category. (Put a cross (X) on any number).**

| 5 | 4 | 3 | 2 | 1 |
|---|---|---|---|---|
| Agree | Slightly Agree | Neutral | Slightly disagree | Disagree |

**iii) Interview**

Since the technique of interviewing is a major tool for gathering evidence in the field, it was used for collecting data[21] directly through dialogue, because, in a face to face meeting, the investigator could constantly encourage subjects and help them probe more deeply into a problem, which impinges on both cognitive and sentimental plane.[22] Since the planning of languages for learning is a complicated issue, the mental and social frame of mind of the people should be considered as best as possible.

An effort, therefore, was made to gather opinions of some important men in public on the language policy of the country. Being a collective product,[23] public opinion was supposed to represent the views of the entire public. An English political author regarded the free expression of public opinion as the chief safeguard against misrule and the characteristic mark of a democratic state.[24] Hobbes declared, that in a sense, the world was governed by opinion[25] and according to Hume, if self-governments were based upon opinions, why not their policies too? "Supporters of democracy had always provided public opinion, as the voice of enlightened middle-class as a safeguard against misrule and as an agent of progress."[26] The multitude should be supreme, said Aristotle. "Hence", he continues, "the many are better judges than a single man." The most prevalent method used for knowing public-opinion is that of survey, which can be done in two ways: (i) either by administering questionnaire or (ii) by interviewing the people from different categories.

An interview schedule[27] was drawn and interview was conducted to find out the views of the people belonging to a cross section of society. Secondly, in some cases, the people wanted to remain anonymous due to certain reasons. Subjects sometimes refrained from expressing their views freely and honestly in a group. Therefore, individual interviews were conducted. Though the thoughts were freely expressed while conducting unstructured interviews, due to the physical limitations and for having varied viewpoints on the same questions, the interview-schedule had only few suggestive guidelines to provoke the interviewee to express his ideas.

Following the interview schedule guidelines interviews were personally conducted by the investigator on people belonging to different professional and vocational groups. They were one hundred in all and each session continued for an hour or so. The group consisted of academicians, journalists, jurists, politicians, religious heads, practitioners of different medical systems and others. Altogether it had taken more than 150 hours as the investigator had to adjust to the busy time schedule of the important personalities whose opinion on the language issue was considered very significant by the investigator.

The data regarding the condition of language teaching in vogue in schools were collected from a number of visits paid by the investigator to different centres of Education Directorate, Delhi. The following institutions were approached to seek the varied information as required for a study on such a current problem:

1. The Directorate of Education, Old Secretariat, Delhi.
2. New Delhi Municipal Committee.
3. Municipal Corporation of Delhi.
4. Delhi Cantonment Board.
5. The Central Board of Secondary Education. (CBSE).
6. The Office of the Kendriya Vidyalaya Sangathan (K.V.S.).
7. The Office of the Delhi Administration.
8. All the four districts of School Education in the Union Territory of Delhi.
9. All India Radio.
10. The Television Centre.
11. The Centre of Audio-Visual Education, Daryaganj, Delhi.

**School Sample**

In descriptive survey research, generally the queries raised are concerned with groups or a large number of units, which, possibly can not be treated individually. A large sample always consumes more time, energy and money, which, the investigator was unable to afford. In view of the administrative difficulties and other physical constraints generally a small sample was preferred for a critical and analytical study. The school population, first of all was divided into different strata on the basis of some characteristics visible in a particular class of the people and then the survey was conducted. It was expected, that the possibilities of different views regarding the language-policy and different trends to learn different languages in the present society could be discovered in the scheduled time.

In the present study, the purposive[28] sampling was adopted for selection of schools on which data collection for the research was based. The school sample was selected in the following way.

First of all, all the schools in the Union Territory of Delhi which were scattered in 28 zones were considered. These zones were grouped under four districts, each under the charge of a Deputy Director of Education as follows:

Districts and Zones

| District | Zones |
|---|---|
| North | 1 to 7 |
| East | 8 to 15 |
| South | 16 to 21 |
| West | 22 to 28 [29] |

The approximate number of schools in all these Districts of Delhi was :

| | | |
|---|---|---|
| 1. | Primary schools | 1639 [30] |
| 2. | Unaided Primary schools | 65 |
| 3. | Middle, Secondary and Senior Secondary schools | 1030 |
| | | 2734 [31] |

Delhi Schools in Zones

| *Districts* | *Middle schools* | *Secondary Schools* | *Senior Secondary Schools* | *Total* |
|---|---|---|---|---|
| North | 92 | 44 | 114 | 250 |
| East | 93 | 58 | 136 | 287 |
| South | 68 | 41 | 127 | 236 |
| West | 75 | 60 | 122 | 257 |
| Total | 328 | 203 | 499 | 1030 |

These schools catered to the needs of both rural and urban population. The three language formula with which the investigator was concerned was applicable to both rural as well as urban areas. The schools established in rural areas were no more different from the schools established in urban areas. Hindi was the medium of instruction in all the rural schools except in the following two schools, where, English was used as the medium of instruction :

i) Central Secondary School, Zharoda Kalan.

ii) Salwan Public Senior Secondary School, Chhattarpur.[32]

The languages taught in all the rural schools were Hindi, English and Sanskrit. As there was no provision to opt for other RL[33] and Hindi, English and Sanskrit were used in all schools, the rural schools were therefore not included in the sample.

**The Middle Schools**

The schools where the three languages were taught from VI to VIII classes, were also excluded from the survey, because :

i) The students were in the process of learning three languages and as such, they were not in a position to use properly the three languages in different domains and situations of life.

ii) There was no provision for teaching more than three languages by the school authorities in such schools.

iii) As the linguistic-skills of the students were not supposedly developed satisfactorily while learning three languages, they might not find themselves capable enough to take any decision in favour or against any of the languages.

Keeping all these factors in mind, the levels of upper primary classes (i.e. till VIII class) even though they were in the senior secondary schools were abandoned for the present study.

**Secondary Schools**

The schools imparting education from I to X class were known as the secondary schools, where language variations were limited compared to senior secondary schools. Moreover, the study was based on MT[34] media concept and thereby wanted to identify schools where MT(s) were being used as medium of instruction up to the senior secondary stage. Hence class X of the secondary schools were not included in the study.

**Senior Secondary Schools**

These schools impart education upto XII class. According to statistical data provided by the Directorate of Education they were 499 in number.[35] As the Union Territory of Delhi was divided into four districts, the Senior Secondary Schools were scattered all over these districts. The district-wise and agency-wise distribution of schools, is shown in the table below.[36]

**District-wise Senior Secondary Schools**

| *Districts* | *Govt.* | *Aided* | *Unaided* | *Central* | *N.D.M.C.* | *Total* |
|---|---|---|---|---|---|---|
| North | 87 | 22 | 4 | 1 | - | 114 |
| East | 67 | 59 | 6 | 1 | 3 | 136 |
| South | 74 | 22 | 24 | 6 | 1 | 127 |
| West | 82 | 21 | 14 | 5 | - | 122 |
| Total: 4 Dists. | 310 | 124 | 48 | 13 | 4 | 499 |

While selecting the schools for the survey/study, preference was given to the schools teaching minority languages not only as the subject, but using them as the media also, because, the students who learnt through MT showed a better grasp of the subject and developed a healthier intellect than those who studied through languages other than the MT. It received the approval of the United Nations Educational Scientific and Cultural Organisation also.[37,38] The Government of India Resolution of 1913, stated, that, "There is much evidence to the effect, that scholars, who have been through a complete vernacular course are exceptionally efficient mentally."[39] A Resolution of the General Assembly supported the position "Every child is born into a cultural environment, the language is a part and an expression of that environment,"[40,41] because he can express better in the language of his environment.

The present study was confined to the three language formula in which the MT, one of the MIL and English were essential to be learnt and the medium of instruction had to be the MT of the students till senior secondary level of school education. Hence, such schools as adopted the MT medium were considered appropriate for the study.

Though a large number of languages were considered for teaching to the school-students yet, all of them were not used as the media of education. In certain cases, they were not even taught through the languages concerned.

The data gathered from the Directorate of Education revealed that, there were 51 senior secondary schools using minority languages[42] as the media of instruction in the Union Territory of Delhi. Numerically, these languages were found eight in number viz., Punjabi, Urdu, Bengali, Sindhi, Gujarati, Tamil, Telugu, and Malayalam. The latter four i.e. Gujarati, Tamil, Telugu and Malayalam were being continued as media till primary level in 13 senior secondary schools.[43, 44] Consequently, the number of minority languages being used as media beyond primary level of education remained four[45] and the schools having them as media - were found onlv 38 in number. Among these 38 schools, there were 21 Urdu medium, 8 Bengali medium, 7 Punjabi medium and 2 Sindhi medium senior secondary schools. Surprisingly, it was discovered that, in these schools too, the above mentioned minority languages were not used as media till senior secondary level in all the 38 schools as could be seen in the table below :

**Minority Languages used as media**

| *Minority languages being used as media of education* | *Till Lower primary level only* | *Till Upper primary level i.e. VIII class only* | *Upto X class only* | *Upto Sr. Sec. level i.e. XII Class* | *Total number of Schools* |
|---|---|---|---|---|---|
| Urdu | Nil | 7 | 7 | 7 | 21 |
| Bengali | 2 | Nil | 2 | 4 | 8 |
| Punjabi | 1 | 3 | Nil | 3 | 7 |
| Sindhi | 1 | Nil | Nil | 1 | 2 |
| Total No. of languages 4 | 4 | 10 | 9 | 15 | 38 |

Keeping into consideration the zonal division at the level of school education in the Union Territory of Delhi, it was found that among the minority languages, Urdu was used as the medium in no other district but East only. Punjabi was not used as the medium in District North, whereas, Bengali did not continue as the medium till senior secondary level in district West. Sindhi was followed as medium in district South only. See the table below :

**Minority Languages as Media till Senior Secondary Level (Zone-wise)**

| *Language* | *North* | *West* | *East* | *South* |
|---|---|---|---|---|
| Urdu | Nil | Nil | 7 | Nil |
| Bengali | 1 | Nil | 1 | 2 |
| Punjabi | Nil | 1 | 1 | 1 |
| Sindhi | Nil | Nil | Nil | 1 |

**Minority Languages, Four Zones, Schools Administration**

| *Language* | *Zones* | | | | | | | |
|---|---|---|---|---|---|---|---|---|
| *Minority Languages* | *North* | | *West* | | *East* | | *South* | |
| | *Govt. Sch.* | *Aided Sch.* | *Govt. Sch.* | *Aided Sch.* | *Govt. Sch.* | *Aided Sch.* | *Govt. Sch.* | *Aided Sch.* |
| Urdu | - | - | - | - | 4 | 3 | - | - |
| Bengali | - | 1 | - | - | - | 1 | - | 2 |
| Punjabi | - | - | - | 1 | - | 1 | - | 1 |
| Sindhi | - | - | - | - | - | - | - | 1 |

Out of these four districts, two districts East and South had been selected for the survey for the following reasons :

1. The language variation in districts East and South was not limited to that of North and West. As had already been stated, the languages taught in North and in the West were less in number in comparison to the languages taught in East and South where the languages provided for teaching were ten, while in North and West they were seven and six respectively. Similarly, languages used as media were more in number in districts East and South.
2. Urdu and Sindhi were taught in none of the schools in North and West.
3. Although the most popular foreign language English was taught in all the four districts, the other foreign languages like French, Russian, German, Polish and Japanese were being taught in addition to English in district South.

## Conclusion

In district North, besides Hindi and English only one more language, Bengali was used as the medium. Similarly, in district West, besides Hindi and English only Punjabi was used as the medium. Whereas in district East five languages were used as the media, namely Hindi, English, Urdu, Bengali and Punjabi and in district south, the number of languages used as media was also five viz. Hindi, English, Bengali, Punjabi and Sindhi, c.f. table below.[46]

**Delhi Districts: Number and Name of Languages as Media**

| *District* | *Number of Languages used as media* | *Languages used as media* |
|---|---|---|
| North | 3 | Hindi, English and Bengali |
| West | 3 | Hindi, English and Punjabi |
| East | 5 | Hindi, English, Urdu, Bengali and Punjabi |
| South | 5 | Hindi, English, Bengali, Punjabi and Sindhi |

On the basis of this data it was considered more appropriate to administer the questionnaire in senior secondary schools situated in East, and South districts of the Union Territory of Delhi.

The CBSE in its syllabi made provision for teaching of five more languages - Manipuri, Nepali, Tibetan, Arabic and Persian[47] besides the 15 languages (excluding Kashmiri) enumerated in the Constitution of India. Besides English, option was given for learning five more foreign languages - French, German, Polish, Russian and Japanese.[48] But, the data collected from the Examination Cell of CBSE revealed the fact, that, in the Union Territory of Delhi, the students opted for ten modern Indian languages,[49] three classical[50] and six foreign languages[51] out of 24 languages listed in the syllabus of CBSE. Though the option was provided to choose a particular language out of a fair number of them, yet, the medium of instruction was limited to Hindi and English. Obviously, these schools were kept out of purview of the study.

The schools in general were government, aided, unaided, Central and N.D.M.C. schools.[52] The languages taught in the Government schools were more than the languages used as media. Hindi, English, Urdu, Punjabi, Sindhi, Sanskrit, Arabic and Persian were taught as the subjects, whereas only Hindi and Urdu were being used as the media. Besides, in one or two sections English was also used as medium, but, for science subjects only. The number of languages taught as subjects and used as media in Government Schools was found to be less than those in aided and unaided schools. Hence, the Government schools were eliminated from the list of the schools taken for the study.

In Central schools, the languages taught were only Hindi, English and Sanskrit. Surprisingly enough in one of the Central Schools, situated in Janak Puri, Delhi, all the subjects were taught through the medium of 'Bhot language.'[53] Usually, the languages were taught through the media of concerned languages, but, in this school, even the languages were taught through the medium of Bhot language.[54] The said school was not considered, for, the study was related to the languages mentioned in the VIII Schedule of the Constitution of India where Bhot (language) was not included.

In N.D.M.C. schools only four languages Hindi, Urdu, Sanskrit and English were being taught and only Hindi was used as the medium of instruction. Therefore, these two varieties of schools viz. Central and N.D.M.C. schools were also not considered for the study on the ground that the number of the languages taught was limited to three only which were Hindi, Sanskrit and English, while the media languages were Hindi and English.

In aided-schools, the number of languages taught was 14 viz. Hindi, Bengali, Punjabi, Sindhi, Urdu, Gujarati, Tamil, Telugu, Kannada, Malayalam, Sanskrit, Arabic, Persian and English while provision for teaching for 24 languages[55] was given, if the demand was sufficient. But the languages used as media were six only viz. Hindi, English, Urdu, Punjabi, Bengali and Sindhi.

A number of denominational schools[56] were also included in the category of aided schools. The four languages - Hindi, Sanskrit, Urdu and English were being taught but, Hindi was the main medium of education. A few sections were following English medium.[57] These schools were given minority status,[58] as they were established and administered by a minority community having the right to do so under clause 1 of Article 30 of the Constitution of India.

There were certain unaided schools being run in the Union Territory of Delhi. They were usually categorised as the Public schools. Some of these schools which were affiliated to the Body of Public School Organization, followed their own syllabus, while the others which were not affiliated to this organization were free to follow either of the two syllabi laid down by the Public school organization or the CBSE.

In unaided schools the number of languages was of course the same as in aided schools, but instead of teaching RL like Gujarati, Sindhi, and Kannada (taught in aided schools) five more foreign languages i.e.

French, Russian, German, Polish and Japanese were offered. Regarding the languages being used as media, English only was followed as the medium of instruction.

While selecting the schools for the case study, preference had been given to the schools, teaching maximum number of languages and also using the maximum number of languages as media of instruction, so that it could be explored whether the status assigned to the three language formula in the school curriculum was the same in practice as it was assigned by the policy-makers.

It was found, that in these two districts viz. East and South, Urdu medium schools were seven, Bengali and Punjabi media schools were three each and Sindhi medium school was one only for which the investigator had no alternative, but, to include it in the sample. Regarding the Urdu, Bengali and Punjabi media schools a random sample within that parameter was taken by lottery system. This technique of stratified or quota-sampling was desired to ensure representativeness and avoid bias by use of a modified random sampling method. As Hindi and English were used as media of instruction in a number of schools in both East and South districts, a random sample should have been taken by lottery system.

In stratified random sampling the population is first divided into two or more strata (classes) as then from each stratum is taken a predetermined number of observations (sample) at random, because this scheme (of stratified random sampling) is applicable when the population is composed of sub-groups or strata of different sizes, so that a representative sample must contain individuals drawn from each category or stratum in accordance with the sizes of the sub-groups. Hence, the schools in districts East and South were first divided into the schools teaching through minority languages.

Instead, for conducting the survey in Hindi and English media schools under the technique of purposive sampling, Nutan Marathi Senior Secondary School in East, teaching through Hindi medium and Delhi Public School in South, teaching through English medium were considered. The following were the reasons for selecting the Nutun Marathi Senior Secondary (Co-educational) School in Paharganj (Deshbandhu Gupta Road) :-

1. Nutan Marathi School by its very name gave an impression, that Marathi must be one of the language, being taught in this school. On the contrary, Marathi found no place in the school curriculum, although three languages namely, Hindi, English and Sanskrit

were taught under the three language formula. Hindi was the main medium of instructions with English medium for science subjects in a few section.

2. Though Marathi was not taught in the school, the number of children studying in this school might be larger from Marathi speaking families, which in turn might influence through communication the languages spoken by non-Marathi students and vice-versa.
3. Marathi would be one more additional language known to the students which might create the positive attitude towards learning more languages or which would throw light on the positive and negative inclination towards learning more languages.
4. Although Marathi was not taught here, it could be surmised or it could be used primarily in practice because of the linguistic background of Marathi and the respective MT..

Another school studied under the technique of purposive sampling in District South was the Delhi Public School (Co-educational) at Mathura Road, New Delhi. It was surveyed because :

1. In no other school of the Union Territory of Delhi, as many as 8 languages were taught. Out of them, 4 were the foreign languages including the most popular language English, one classical language i.e. Sanskrit and the remaining 3 were the MIL i.e. Hindi, Urdu and Punjabi.
2. English continued to be the medium of instruction from the Ist Standard.
3. The school had maintained a 'Language Laboratory' in which the phonetics in all the 4 foreign languages mentioned above were improved.
4. Since it was an English medium school, charging higher school fee from the students, the socio-economic status of the students/their parents would naturally be higher and as such, the students would have developed interest in learning more languages.

Sindhi was used as medium beyond primary level of education in a school in District South only. The investigator had no choice but to consider S.E.S. Baba Nabhraj Senior Secondary School for survey, because, this was the only school teaching through Sindhi medium. Finally, following were the schools considered for the study :-

1. Nutan Marathi Senior Secondary School (Co-ed), Deshbandhu Gupta Road, Paharganj, New Delhi.
2. Delhi Public School (Co-ed), Mathura Road, New Delhi.
3. Fatehpuri Muslim Senior Secondary School, Fatehpuri, Chandni Chowk, Delhi.
4. Siri Guru Tegh Bahadur Senior Secondary School, Gurudwara Sis Ganj, Chandni Chowk, Delhi.
5. Raiseena Bengali Senior Secondary School (Co-ed) New Delhi.
6. S.E.S. Baba Nabhraj Senior Secondary School, Lodhi Colony, New Delhi.

These schools provided the facilities to the students for teaching the maximum number of languages listed in the VIII Schedule of the Constitution of India. Besides, all the languages, taught in the above mentioned schools, covered the maximum number of the MT spoken in the Union Territory of Delhi. Apart from this the schools, teaching different MIL to the students, could possibly indicate the attitude of the students towards Hindi, the official language of the country, MT/RL and English. Similarly, the attitude of those, learning Hindi, English and Sanskrit towards MIL was also necessary to know.

The questionnaire was administered to the students of Class X. The following were the reasons :

1. Since the school authorities did not allow the investigator to administer the questionnaire to XI and XII class students on the ground that, that would hamper their studies, she had no alternative but to administer it to the students of Class X. Moreover, the Senior Secondary students of XI were not required to study more than two languages and in XII class, students generally did not learn more than one language.[59]
2. Since the students of class VIII belonged to lower age-group who were still learning three languages, they were unable to express their views explicitly about the three language formula.
3. Generally they were not sufficiently grown up as to reach at certain conclusions regarding the efficacy, merit and demerits of the three language formula.

Of the six schools, sample each of fifty students, was taken for data collection through the students' questionnaire. The nature, background, parental education, occupation, approximate income of the family and the language they speak, were all tabulated and presented. This information would be treated at the time of analysis of the student's questionnaire.

**Pilot Study**

The questionnaire used for the school students was constructed after administering it to a number of students of class X. It was desirable to tryout a few copies of schedule.[60] The number of the students of class X was fifteen who were included for try-out purpose of the tool. On such a trial, it was found that some of the questions (included in the questionnaire) needed modification. All such questions were suitably modified for the use of class X students. It took an hour of each student to answer each questionnaire.

**Sample for Opinionnaire**

The opinionnaire was administered to the teachers teaching languages in the senior secondary schools. It was also sent to those educationists and intellectuals and administrators, whom the investigator could not contact personally.

**Sample for Interview**

Though "The interview is both a challenge and an opportunity for the use of tact,"[61] it was impracticable and impossible to seek opinion from every person on language problem for collecting data from the people directly. An endeavour was made for selecting the sample of persons in such a way, that, the resulting opinion of a limited number of people could be used to infer the reaction of majority of the people. Since the development of democratic processes has widened the public opinions which in reality count a sample consisting a number of people representing different walks of life[62] was taken with a view to obtaining their different interests, purposes and views regarding the language policy of the country. Thus, the evidence gathered not only would hint at current trends and the new tendencies taking shape but, also would establish the relationship between the public opinion and the language policy.[63] The sections of the people were categorised into the following strata :

1. Academicians
2. Journalists (Editors also)
3. Practitioners of different medical faith
4. Businessmen
5. Librarians of different well-known libraries
6. Government officers (Directors of Mass Communication Media)
7. Judiciary
8. Politicians

9. Religious heads
10. Administrative Officers
11. Chartered Accountants
12. Various Chiefs of Police, Vigilance and C.B.I.
13. Sportsmen
14. Cartoonists
15. Defence
16. Engineers

## Notes and References

1. "The process involved investigating, recording, and analysing and interpreting the events for the purpose of discovering generalisations that were helpful in understanding the past, understanding the present and to a limited extent in anticipating the future."
Best, John W. *Research in Education*. New Delhi; Prentice Hall of India Pvt. Ltd., 1977, p. 15.
2. Good, Barr and Scates. *Methodology of Educational Research*. New York: Appleton Century Crafts Inc., 1941, p. 223.
3. Monroe, W. S. and M. D. Engelhart. *Collecting the Data signified by a Problem Basic Technique*. New York: The Macmillan Co., 1936, pp. 3-26.
4. Cited by Whitney, F.L. *The Elements of Research*. New York: Prentice Hall. Inc., 1937, p. 131.
5. *Ibid.*
6. Best, John W. *Research in Education*. New Delhi: Prentice Hall of India Pvt. Ltd., 1982, p, 139.
7. *Ibid.*
8. Assamese, Bengali, Gujarati, Hindi, Kannada, Kashmiri, Malayalam, Marathi, Oriya, Punjabi, Sanskrit, Tamil, Telugu and Urdu.
9. Bengali, Urdu, Punjabi, Gujarati, Marathi, Sindhi, Malayalam, Tamil, Telugu and Kannada.
10. *The Constitution of India*. 1950. Union List. I; 66.
11. Planning Branch. Directorate of Education: Old Secretariat, Delhi.
12. Hindi, Urdu, Punjabi, Sindhi, Bengali, Gujarati, Malayalam Telugu, Kannada and Tamil; Planning Branch, Directorate of Education, Old secretariat, Delhi.
13. Planning Branch, Directorate of Education. Old Secretariat, Delhi.
14. Hindi, Punjabi, Urdu, Bengali, Gujarati, Sindhi, Malayalam, Telugu, Tamil, and English.
15. Planning Branch, Directorate of Education, Old Secretariat ,Delhi.
16. Dalen an Meyer. *Understanding Educational Research*. New York: McGrew Hill Book Co. Inc., 1962, p. 254.
17. Barr, A.S. Robert A. Davis and Palmer Johnson. *Educational Research and Appraisal*. Chicago: J.B. Lippin Cott Company., 1953, p. 65.
18. Vide Appendix. I
19. Vide Appendix. II
20. Barr, A.S., Robert A. Davis and Palmer Johnson., *op. cit.* p. 74.
21. "Data are the things we think with. They serve as a basic material for further and higher thinking."

Whitney, F.L. *The Elements of Research.* New York: Prentice Hall Inc., 1937, Ch. VI.

22. Dalen and Meyer. *op. cit*. p. 259
23. Public opinion should be viewed as "Collective-Product". Bernard and Janowitz (eds.) Herbert Blumer in *Public Opinion and Communication*. Illinois: The Free Press. 1950. p. 47.
24. *Ibid*. p.8.
25. *Ibid*. p.1
26. Jerrny Benthan. Theory of Public Opinion. (Edited by ) Berelson, B. and M. Janowitz. *Public Opinion and Communication*. Illinois: The free Press, 1950, Ch. I.
27. Vide Appendix III.
28. "The principle of selecting individuals for the sample according to a certain criteria known as controls". *Purposive Selection.* Goods and Scates. *Methods of Research:* New York: Appleton Century crafts. 1954.p. 598.
29. Booklet. Delhi: Delhi Administration. Reforms Branch, Old Secretariat., 1980-81. p. 1.
30. Information gathered form the Directorate of Education. Old Secretariat. Delhi
31. Data supplied by Delhi Administration (Education Department) Administrative Reforms Branch. Old Secretariat. Delhi. 1982-1983.
32. Information sought from the Directorate of Education, Old Secretariat, Delhi.
33. RL would always be referred to Regional Language.
34. MT would always be referred to Mother Tongue.
35. The Directorate of Education, Old Secretariat, Delhi.
36. List of the Senior Secondary, Secondary and Middle Schools. 1980-81. Delhi: Directorate of Education, Old Secretariat.
37. Emerson, R. *From Empire to Nation*. Cambridge: Harvard University Press, 1960, pp. 146-47.
38. La Page; p. 21 (cited by) Nair, Baldev Raj. *National Communication and Language Policy in India*. New York: Frederick A. Praeger, 1969, pp. 13-14.
39. (Cited by) Nag, D.S. Medium of Instruction. The Proceedings of the mother tongue medium conference held at Wardha on the 9th of Aug., 1946, p. VI.
40. *Ibid*.
41. *Ibid*.
42. Vide Appendix I.
43. Data gathered from the Directorate of Education. Delhi: Old Secretariat.
44. Booklet published by the Directorate of Education, Delhi : Old Secretariat. 1980-81.
45. Punjabi, Urdu, Bengali, and Sindhi.
46. *Educational Statistics 1980-81*. Booklet published by the Directorate of Education. Old Secretariat, Delhi.
47. Vide C.B.S.E. Syllabus.
48. *Ibid*.
49. Hindi, Urdu, Bengali, Punjabi. Sindhi, Gujarati, Malayalam, Kannada, Tamil and Telugu.
50. Sanskrit, Arabic and Persian.
51. English, French, Russian, German, Polish and Japanese.
52. N.D.M.C. Schools i.e. the schools run by New Delhi Municipal Committee.
53. One of the Tribal languages spoken near Ladakh.
54. Information given by the Office of the Kendriya Vidyalaya Sangathan, Bahadurshah Zafar Marg. New Delhi.

55. Vide Syllabus, C.B.S.E.
56. Opened by different societies like Arya Samaj, Jain Samaj, etc.
57. Information provided by the Directorate of Education, Old Secretariat, Delhi.
58. Booklet p. 1 published in 1980-81. Delhi. Administrative Reforms Branch, Old Secretariat, Delhi Administration.
59. Information provided by the Directorate of Education. Old Secretariat, Delhi.
60. Good and Scates *op. cit*, p. 622.
61. Good and Scates *op. cit.* p. 644.
62. "Value of cross-section of society and trend studies is established for tracing population trends." Good and Scates. *op. cit.*, p. 555
63. Berelson and M. Janou'tz (eds.) *op. cit.*, p. 1.

# 4 The Position of Languages in India

## Historical Perspective

This chapter is developed in three sections, namely language position in ancient period, medieval period and British period in India.

### A. LANGUAGE POSITION IN ANCIENT PERIOD

India is a multilingual country. The Census of India 1971 listed 1652 mother tongues spoken in India.[1] Out of these, 15 languages spoken by 87% of the population are listed by the Constitution of India.[2] Many of them have an enormous wealth of literature and their literary tradition can be traced back over centuries. In others the literary tradition reaches back more than a thousand years and possibly much more ancient. What is surprising is not their multiplicity but the common elements and strong affinities amongst the various Indian languages. The multiplicity and the variety of speech forms can be easily accounted for if we keep in view the vastness of the country with diverse ethnic elements and socio-cultural forces of historic and prehistoric past.[3] The common elements and strong affinities found among the various Indian languages is due to the fact that India has all along been one nation with one culture and one national language. In fact when Indian languages grow into standardised literary languages and gain currency in a wider area, they develop their literary styles very much different from the popular speech forms of the people. Languages developed with distinct phonology, vocabulary and grammatical features of their own.[4,5,6] As all Indian literary languages including the

Dravidian ones have freely drawn upon Sanskrit from the very beginning and Arabic, Persian, English etc. in later periods, they have similarity with regard to their phonological and grammatical structure, vocabulary and semantic constructs and prosodic and stylistic features. All the literary languages of India are habitually drafted to meet every new situation or requirement for expression of a new idea, of shade of meaning upon that vast, that inexhaustible treasure house of vocabulary, phrase, idiom and concept, comprised by the Sanskrit language and its literature.[8] The literary tradition in different Indian languages have, for this reason, strong identities, in their literary forms and contents.[9,10] So, in spite of being placed in different family groups in languages, semantically and functionally the modern Indian literary languages can be considered just only a few dialects of one and the same language.

**The Languages of India**

Since Indian population is a conglomeration of different racial strata, there is naturally multiplicity of languages. We have a whole collection of Non-Indo European Languages overlaid by the Indo-Aryan languages. Among them, the former include the Dravidian languages of South and those spoken by aboriginal semi-civilised tribes. Broadly speaking, the most important ones are the Dravidian and the Aryan languages. The languages belonging to four major language families of the world i.e. the Austric, Tibeto, Chinese, Dravidian and Indo-European are spoken here. Besides, there are a couple of languages which may be put down as "Unclassified."[11] Chatterji's views in this regard are important. He says, "there are fundamental differences in the structure and vocabulary among these but contact among them for 3000 years and more, particularly through masses of Austric, Dravidian and Sino-Tibetan speakers adopting Aryan has led to the imposition upon each other or to common characteristic which may be specially called Indian and which are found in language belonging to three families, Austric, Dravidian and Aryan.... overlaying their diversity. There is thus in Indian languages at the present day an Indian character which forms one of the bases of that 'certain underlying uniformity of life from the Himalayas to Cape Comorin, that general Indian personality which has been admitted even by Sir Herbert Risley, otherwise so sceptical about India's claim to be considered as one people.[12,13] It is for this typical linguistic characteristic that India is considered to be a single 'linguistic area' i.e. an area which includes languages belonging to more than one family but showing traits in common, which are found not to belong to the other members of (at least) one of the families.[14] Emeneau, therefore asserts that "certainly the end result of the borrowings is that the languages of the two families Indo-Aryan and Dravidian, seem in many respects more akin to one another than Indo-Aryan does to the other Indo-European languages.[15]

**The Indo-European family of languages**

This family includes the languages used in most of Europe, India and a large area between these two subcontinents. Max Muller and some others writers termed it as the Aryan speech. Later on, the term Arya was restricted to the oldest branch of this family the Indo-Iranian ,[16] i.e. the language of those people who called themselves as the Aryans. But the term is rejected altogether by the linguists because of its racial connotations. The Indo-Keltic was one suggested but was not accepted.[17] German scholars call it Indo-Germanic on the ground that during a certain period, Indian languages in the east and Germanic in the west, marked the bounds of this family. But since that period new branches have been recognised and Keltic, now forms the western limit.[18] The name Indo-European is accepted by practically all the scholars for it does not so much suggest that the language can be traced solely to these countries but that the Indo-European language predominated here.

**The Branches of the Indo-European Family**

The Indo-European family includes a large number of languages and is widely spread in the world. It consists of ten major and a few minor languages which are classified as under Satam and Centum - two major groups on the basis of the treatment of Indo-European palatal series. This line of division was first made clear by Ascoli in 1870, who pointed out that the present Indo-European speech possessed a set of palatal sounds.[19,*,20] Centum group is comprised of Greek, Hittite, Italic, Celtic, Germanic and Tokhrian, whereas Satam is constituted of Indo-Iranian, Balto-Slavic, Albenian and Armenian. Though these languages are placed in the two exclusive groups – Satam and Centum, in many respects they quite resemble each other.

**The Regions where the Indo-European languages Originated**

This complex relationship of the languages aroused a curiosity in the minds of the scholars as to whence the Indo-European languages originated. A number of theories have been propounded by the Western and Indian scholars who tried to assign the probable regions as the homeland of the Indo-European languages and as such the original homeland of the Indo-European people. Max Muller was the first who suggested the Pamir tableland and the adjoining regions of Central Asia as the homeland of the Indo-Europeans*. After a few years Letham of Cambridge suggested that Scandinavia was a more likely place while Giles, another scholar from the same university refers to Hungary as the original homeland of the Indo-Europeans. Later on, some German Scholars tried to prove that the North Germany was the homeland of Indo-Europeans. Some other group of scholars establish the homeland in the regions of Lithuania and the neighbouring districts of Poland. The Hittite Inscriptions containing the names of Vedic divinities have led the scholars to assume the upper reaches of the Euphrates and the Tigris as the homeland where the Indo-European languages originated.

Several Indian scholars deeply versed in Sanskrit ventured to suggest India their homeland. Amongst them, Tilak's arguments in favour of North Polar region as their ancient homeland sound very convincing. By another group of scholars, on the basis of distinction between Centum and Satem languages as the representatives of the Europeans and Asiatic languages of Aryan family, the home of the Aryan is sought to be fixed somewhere on the border land between Asia and Europe, say in South Russia. The latest opinion, however, is that of Schrader of Breslau who places the home of the Indo-Europeans in the region about the South Volga and the Northern shores of Caspian sea.

In spite of so many cogent views expressed by a number of renowned scholars, the question of the original homeland of the Aryan remains unsolved and as such, the place, where the Indo-European languages originated is yet to be decided. But, it is clear that, while moving from their homeland, the Aryans moved in two different directions - Iran and India.

**Immediate route in India**

Grierson assumes that the Aryans did not come to India in one single invasion but clan after clan, speaking related and mutually understandable dialects. They continued to arrive for a long period. It is generally accepted that they found their way from Bactria through the passes of Hindu Kush mountains into Afghanistan and thence into the regions of Punjab.[21,22,23] The Aryans then moved eastwards and settled down into the Madhyadesh - the midlands between the two great rivers Ganga and Jamuna and so this region came to be known as the Arya-Varta. It was this land where Hindu Aryan culture was finally fixed.[24]

The Aryan clans that arrived later on, soon surrounded the first settlements, which consequently expanded in all directions. In the north they reached the Himalayas, right upto Kashmir. In the south they reached the sea through Gujarat. In the west they reached almost to the Indus and in the east upto Banaras. On the evidence of the Vedic hymns Macdonnel has come to the conclusion that Aryans first settled down in the region of 'Saptsindhu' i.e. Kubha or Saraswati, Indus and its tributaries; then moved Eastwards, and occupied the Midlands, i.e. region between Ganga and Jamuna and then further moved Eastwards upto the 'Sadanira'.

Of the three later Vedas, the *Sam Veda* is clearly connected with the *Rig-Veda*. Its contents are chiefly derived from the *Rig-Veda*. The hymns reveal nothing new about the whereabouts of Aryans.

The *Yajur-Veda* introduces to us a geographical area different from that of the *Rig-Veda*. By this time the Aryans had spread further to east. All the recensions of the *Yajur-Veda* point to the territory in the middle of Northern India occupied by the neighbouring peoples of the Kurus and Panchalas. The country of the former is called Kuruksetra. It lies in the plain between the Sutleja and the track bounded by the two small rivers Drsadvati and Sarasvati and extending south-eastwards to the Jamuna. It corresponds to the modern district of Sirhind, closely connected with the eastward of this region, was situated the land of the Panchalas, which, running south-east from the Meerut district to Allahabad embraces the territory between Jumuna and Ganges called Doab ("The Waters").

The geographical data contained in the *Atharva-Veda* are but few and furnish no certain evidence as to the region in which its hymns were composed.

The inhabitants of Indian Aryans never had sufficient leisure to fuse themselves into one homogeneous nation, but kept up their separate culture, their languages*,[25] and their customs, though of course very much modified by mutual contact, as follows : "Since very ancient times, different races with their different types of culture came into India and settled down there, and according to their society and civilisation they developed their way of life and ideas of being. We have thus the primitive Negrite tribes, probably the most ancient people to make India their home : no proof has as yet been found that man of any type had evolved from some kind of anthropoidope on the soil of India. Then these were followed by Austric tribes from the West - from West Asia, and these in turn by the Dravidians also, from the West. The

Aryans next followed and from the North-east and North came Tibet Chinese Tribes. . . . After, the Aryans came to India and settled down there, they gave a form to the life of the Indian people. . . . With their superior organisation the Aryans welded all the various elements into a united whole, . . . . and the Aryans' language was one of the most important factors in the evolution of India, humanity in its history, its religion and thought in its characteristic culture, for this language became the vehicle, the symbol as well as the expression of the composite culture that grew upon the soil of India ... the Aryan language came to be indissolubly linked with the culture of India at various epochs and in various areas."[26]

**The Ancient Language of India**

The most ancient available work not only in Sanskrit, but in all the languages of the world, is *Rig-Veda.* Though there is a difference of opinion among the scholars about the age of the Vedas, yet, some attempts have been made to fix their time approximately. Max Muller assigned the *Rig-Veda* nearly to 1200 B.C. Benfoy recalls it as early as 2000 years before the Christian era. Macdonnell fixed a period, which can hardly be less remote than 1000 B.C. Winternitz agrees to 1500 B.C. and Whitney has placed the migration of the Aryans into the Indus land in the 16th century B.C. and hence he regards the period of the Vedic hymns from 2000 B.C. to 1500 B.C. Jacobi determines the period of *Rig-Veda* to be at least 4000 B.C. Haug, on the ground of a passage, in the Vedanga, fixes the period between 2400 B.C. to 2000 B.C. All these theories are based upon a consideration and comparison of language and thought. There are, certain other theories, based on, astronomical data in the *Rig-Veda*. Tilak in his *Orion*, on the basis of tradition recorded in the *Rig-Veda*, tried to fix a period not later than 4000 B.C. Diksit in his *Jyotish Shastra* has hit upon one passage in the *Satpath Brahman* which points to a period about 8000 B.C. to be of that Brahman. The *Taitriya Sanhita* is 200 years older than *Satpath Brahman* and the *Rig-Veda Sanhita* is still older than *Taitriya Sanhita*.

**The Language of the Vedas**

This has been agreed upon by all the scholars that Sanskrit is the earliest language to develop a literature and art among any of the ancient nations.[27,28] The two other Aryan languages are the Iranian and the Dardic languages and that the first record of this literature is known as the Vedas. Though so old and voluminous in extent, *Rig-Veda* has been preserved for us in a form corrected to a syllable by oral tradition.

According to Whitney, 'The exceeding age, the remarkable conservation of primitive material and forms, the unequalled transparency of structure give Sanskrit an undisputable right to the first place among the tongues of Indo-European family. It displays clearly their doubtful etymologies illustrating the law of research, which must be followed in their study and in that of all other languages.'

The object and aim of philology is to learn what man is, by what man had been. Sanskrit has been recognised as the language even older and more primitive than Greek and Latin. At least Sanskrit enables us to have a glimpse into the activities of the South-eastern branch of Aryans. And if Sanskrit is so important in its primitiveness and transparency, where with can we begin its study if not with the Vedic idiom?

Since a large number of Vedic hymns is religious in character, the scholars have termed the Vedic language as an "artificial dialect", "priestly dialect", "class language" or even the "caste-language" — i.e., the language of the Brahmanas. The language of the Vedas is *hieratic* and conventional. The various indications of language such as vocabulary, style, grammar meters and ideas clearly show that the different parts of the *Rig-Veda* represent chronologically different stages. They were not composed by one single poet but by different generation of sages extending over a long period.

The hymns of the *Atharva Veda* deal with the charms, spells and black magic. We find poems relating to happiness of peasants, cowherds, shepherds and merchants. The nature of the hymns shows that it was more related to and had greater contact with the masses, which shows that the language used must have been understood by the people in general. It seems that there was a difference between literary and colloquial language at that time. The language of the *Upanishads* though poetic, was fully understood and followed by the common man. The evidence of the *Upanishads* shows that almost all of the branches of knowledge such as science, grammar, prosody, phonetic, physiognomy, demonology, religion, philosophy, law, medicine, astronomy, etc. were treated in Sanskrit language. It was in constant use of teaching. Literary discussions were held in Sanskrit. The public religious rites and domestic rituals were recorded and carried out in Sanskrit. Education was in the hands of the Brahmanas. There are sufficient Vedic as well as Pauranic evidences to show that the instruction of the people of all classes was the duty of the Brahmanas. The medium of instruction at various stages of education must have been

Sanskrit since there is no proof of existence of any language other than Sanskrit.

Sanskrit is rich enough in literary forms as well as in contents. The intellectual and philosophical activities of the nation have been very well recorded in this language. The combination of emotional appeals and intellectual needs which is visible in this ancient language is wonderful.

It is surprising that we notice no regional dialects, in spite of the fact that the Aryan invaders were frequently moving from one place to another and the hymns were composed at different places. To quote Macdonell, "... throughout the hymns, in spite of the number of authors, essentially the same language prevails. It is quite possible to distinguish differences of thoughts, style and poetical ability, but hardly any differences of dialect."[29]

Vedic language was quite flexible in nature and was not stereotyped by grammatical rules. The spoken forms of the Vedic language had several forms of the same word, e.g. भवति was spoken as भवति, भवत् and भवात् . Both the forms देवाः and देवासः were in use (for plural of the word देव ). There were several suffixes to denote the sense of तुमुन् (तुमर्थसे सेन् नसे–असेन्–कसे–कसेन्–अध्यै–अध्यैन् कध्यै कध्यैन् शध्यैन् तवै ,तवेङ्ग तवेनः[30] Similarly there were four कृदन्त प्रत्यय i.e तवे केन केन्य and त्वेन . Such instances can be multiplied. This proves that Sanskrit cannot have been a mere literary and school language because there are early traces of its having had regional variations. Panini (5th century B.C.) has specifically distinguished between Vedic Sanskrit and Bhaṣ (i.e., the spoken language). We find certain words which are quite distinct from the priestly vocabulary. Possibly, the spoken Vedic was more modern and less complex than that of the Vedic hymns. Both Yask and Panini have recorded the peculiarities of Eastern and Northern Sanskrit. Katyayan (3rd century B.C.) refers to local divergences and Patanjali (2nd century B.C.) had specified words occurring in single districts only. The later *Sanhitas,* the *Brahmanas,* the *Aranyakas* and the *Upanishads* give indication of dialectic mixtures. Some forms are phonetically more advanced than these normal in the *Rig-Veda.* Many new words were borrowed from non-Aryans, such as, Mundas and Dravidians, with whom the Aryans came into contact.

Thus, it is clear that till 2nd century B.C. Vedic Sanskrit was actually spoken in Aryavarta, i.e. the region lying between the Himalayas and the Vindhya range. The variations in the spoken language were so numerous that the communication became difficult. Hence a need to regularise the language arose and Panini had to write an extensive grammar on the subject. In the process, the words, commonly used were retained while those in lesser use were dropped. Thus gradually, the language took a definite shape. This form of language came to be known as Laukik Sanskrit.

The earliest literary works in Laukik Sanskrit are the two epics, i.e., the *Ramayana* and the *Mahabharata*. The former narrates the story and exploits of Rama while the latter is based on the mutual rivalry and the consequent war between the Kaurvas and the Pandavas. In fact the number of subjects dealt with in the *Mahabharata* is so great that it has become virtually an encyclopaedia, not only dealing with the four-fold aim (Dharma, Artha, Kama and Moksha) of human life but also narrating many episodes, dialectic mater, duty of the kings and philosophical discourses, cosmogony and psychology, principles of ethics, legends, parables, dialogue, moral aphorism and so on. In these two epics we find a rich vocabulary extended by derivations and composition of new words according to recognised types. Numerous words can be found, which, though old seem to be new because they do not exist in the Vedic literature. Mention may also be made here of another class of works i.e., the *Puranas*. The evidence shows that both the Epics and the Puranas were recited in Temples, Assembly halls, royal courts and at sacrificial sessions. We hear that Valmiki taught *Ramayana* to Kush and Lava, who recited it at the Ashvamedh sacrifice performed by Rama. Puranas were definitely meant for that class of the society which was not entitled to Vedic education such as the ladies and the Shudras.

Sanskrit was not merely a literary and school language but was actually spoken in the whole of the Northern India between the Himalayas and the Vindhya range. Many rules given by Panini are meaningful in the context of the spoken language alone. Patanjali refers to it as used in the 'world'. He describes the legend of a headgroom disputing with a grammarian about the etymology of the Sanskrit word 'Suta'.[31] That establishes the fact that education to the common man must have been imparted in Sanskrit. The legend of the 'Bhikkus' to Buddha to adopt Sanskrit - the language of the elite, as the medium of his speeches refers to Sanskrit as a commonly used language. Hiuen-Tsiang also records that it was used by Buddhists and Jains also. The fact that Asvaghosa, who flourished in 2nd century A.D., had to compose his works in Sanskrit in order to propagate his doctrines clearly, shows, that Sanskrit had regained its temporarily lost-position and appealed to the masses even more than Prakrit. The tradition has it how a wood-cutter was pained to hear बाधति instead of बाधते from a king who sympathised with his lot. In *Naisadh Charitam* by Sri Harsa, the kings gathered there for Svayamvara, were asked to converse in Sanskrit so that they might not face the problem of understanding the different dialects.

**Pali**

The next stage of development in the language of the Aryans is known as Pali which was the sacred language of the Southern Buddhism. Nearly 2500 years before, this, language was used in regions where Hindi is spoken at present. There are different opinions regarding the derivation of the term Pali. European scholars derive it from Pali, a row or line of leaves of a book, then the book itself and lastly the canon embodied in the book and its language. Some of the Buddhist scholars think that Pali means language of the common people. Jacobi calls it a dialect at the root of the literature Pali and calls it 'Pali-Stufe'.[32] A section of scholars thinks that the language of Patliputra was called Pali, whereas others believed that it was a 'rustic language' — the language of the village i.e. Pali derived from Pal. The word Pali is also supposed to have been derived from Paliyay पालीयाय the Magadhi form of the word Pariyay परिचय and in a way it denoted the language used by Buddha for his teachings. Some others believe that in course of time, the spoken Vedic in some of the regions, was known as Pali, for the hard consonants of Sanskrit became soft in Pali. Several scholars[33] have expressed their views that Pali was originally Magadhi. Though, basically, it was not the language of Magadh, it was adopted as the official language by the Magadh kings due to its utility and importance. No doubt, it was greatly influenced by the native language of Magadh. Thus, gradually, Magadh itself developed into Pali. Mahatma Buddha used it as a medium of his preachings. The originals of *Tripitak* 'Recollections of Buddhist teachings' are in Pali. Buddha himself held the view that the instruction should be imparted in a common language, which could be understood and followed by the masses. Hence, he rejected the suggestion of his followers to preach in Sanskrit on the ground that it was the language of the elites and he contended that the preachings should be communicated in the language of the common man. In the region of Kosi, Kuruksetra and Himachal, Vindhyachal Buddha preached in Pali. Teachings were imparted orally. Thus, the language which was prevalent among the masses, in Central

India was Pali. As the disciples of Buddha included people from different regions like Magadh, Vaishali, Kashi and Koshala etc. they must have got their own dialect but due to common association and communication they used Magadhi as link language. But naturally the different dialects must have influenced common language Magadhi. Thus, Pali was developed by Buddha monks and became interregional language of Central India. Since its centre was Magadhi, obviously it influenced Pali to a large extent and hence it became famous as Magadhi. Still, it was a flexible language and had regional variations. According to Keith,[34] the language of the Buddhist literature was undoubtedly the spoken language of the educated, which was developed keeping in view the requirements of the elite. During this period, the regional dialects came to be four i.e. Northern, Western, Central, Eastern and Southern.

There is another view held by Kuhn, the German Indologist that the dialect of Ujjain, was the basis of the literary Pali. Franke, another German Indologist in his 'Pali' and 'Sanskrit' also holds that the home of literary Pali must be within the region around Ujjain.[35]

Pali has got its own background, syntax, distinct idioms, vocabulary, literary forms and style. It is full of regional words and phrases. It was a lively spoken language and not rigid like Sanskrit. But the differences between the old Sanskrit and the Pali are not as great as to conclude that they do not represent successive steps in the development of the Vedic language. The discussions in religious assemblies were held in Pali. Unfortunately, with the decline of Buddhism, the use and influence of Pali language and literature dwindled.

**Prakrit**

In the beginning, Sanskrit and the spoken language of the masses were not very much different but by the time of 5th and 6th century B.C., they had become quite distinct. To learn Sanskrit was not an easy job and required much practice and toil. It was because of this reason that Mahavir and Buddha preached in the language of the masses, which, later on was known as Prakrit. The word Prakrit has been derived from the word 'Prakriti' meaning (i) the place of origin and (ii) from the masses. If we take the first meaning then it would mean that it would have been derived from the Sanskrit language. The fact that with a slight change in the consonants in Sanskrit words we get Prakrit words lends support to this view. If we take the second meaning then it would denote the language which was not bound by the grammatical rules and which differed from region to region and from person to person. This proves that the latter literary Prakrits were derived from the natural language of the common man.

The word 'Prakrit' denoted the Prakrits used in dramas. The Prakrit referred to by grammarians, the Prakrit of poetic compositions just like Saptasati of Hal and the Prakrit of Jain religious literature. When the Kharosti inscriptions in Central Asia (in Turkistan) and manuscript of Dhammpadạ was found, their language was called Prakrit. Thus, in a wider sense the medieval stage of the development of Sanskrit language was named Prakrit and Pali was also included in it. Asoka, who was a follower of Buddhism, made Prakrit as the official language and got his inscriptions inscribed in this language. For several hundred years, Prakrit was used in inscriptions. The Prakrit of the inscriptions of King Kharvel show the maturity of the language. Even though Sanskrit gained an important position during the Gupta period (5th century A.D. onward) yet Prakrits were not abandoned.

As we have said before the use of Buddhist Pali i.e. Pali was abandoned due to the decline of Buddhism in 10th century A.D. but, it was still in use in Ceylon, Burma and Siam. The Jains retained the Prakrit. Some Brahmana scholars also used it in dramas, poetry and grammar.

There were more than one Prakrit in use. The most important among them are :—

1. *Ardh Magadhi* : A mixture of Magadhi and other Prakrits. Mahavir preached in this language and the ancient scriptures of the Jains were also composed in this language. The greatest quality of this language was that it was understood by people of all castes and regions. The Ardh Magadhi of now extant Jain Sutras, is closer to Maharashtrian than Magadhi language.
2. *Jain Maharashtrian* : It is a bit different from general Maharashtri. In a very short period it acquired a definite shape. The religious teacher of the teachers of Svetamber sect of the Jains composed several stories, *stotra*, poetical compositions and grammar.
3. *Jain Saurseni*: It was adopted by the Digamber sect of the Jains and was quite akin to 'Sursen'.
4. *Maharashtrian* : It is known to be the best Prakrit. Mahakavi Dandin in his *Kavyadarsh* (1/35) regards it as the best Prakrit. In Prakrit Grammar also, this is the first to be mentioned. It was mostly used in lyrics. In Sanskrit dramas, the ladies and

Vidusakas used Saurseni in conversation and Maharashtrian in verses. Some scholars have also concluded that Maharashtrian was a peculiar form of the Saurseni.

5. *Saurseni* : It was spoken in the regions of the Sursenas i.e. round about Mathura. Generally the Prakrit speaking characters in the dramas used this Prakrit.
6. *Magadhi* : It was the Prakrit of the eastern regions and confined to the ancient Magadha. The lowly characters in the dramas spoke in Magadhi. Some inscriptions have also been found in this Prakrit.
7. *Paisachi* : It is a famous Prakrit. Even though none of the work written in this language is available at present, it is said that Gunadhyay composed his *Brihatkatha* in Paisachi. It is also called Bhutbhasa. There is a difference of opinion regarding its place of origin. Some say that it was the language of the Central India while others assign it to North-West. In fact, that, Ghosa consonants of Sanskrit became Aghosa consonants in Paisachi, tends to assign it to the North Western regions.
8. The Avanti, Dhakki and Sahari are in fact the subdivisions of Maharashtrian and Saurseni and Magadhi.
9. The Prakrit used in inscriptions of Asoka is separately mentioned. It never became a purely literary language. It had regional variations e.g. in the inscriptions of Dhauli and Junagarh (in Central India), Magdhi is prominent. In Girnar inscriptions, conjunct (संप्रयुक्त) consonants are found.
10. *Kharosti Prakrit* - It is the language of inscriptions found in Chinese Turkistan. This resembles with the Paisachi of North West. Non-Aryan words are also found in this Prakrit.

The evidence of the Sanskrit dramas clearly proves that various Prakrits were in use along with Sanskrit. The Prakrits relating to the different regions were spoken in one and the same drama. The hero, the king, the male characters of the highest and the middle status and female ascetics spoke in Sanskrit. Vidusak, though Brahmin, used two forms of Prakrit, i.e. Saurseni in prose and Maharashtrian in verse. The female characters, children of highest society and the officials of higher rank also used Saurseni in prose and Maharashtrian in verse. The servants spoke Magadhi. The Ahiras, the dacoits, the robbers and the gamblers spoke Abhiri, Paisachi and Avanti. Apbhramsa was the language of the barbarian tribes and the inferior characters. Some dramas such as *Karpur Manjri* of Raj Sekhar are written completely in Prakrit. Grierson has observed that the multilingual character of dramas is not surprising, for even now-a-days, the domestic servants speak in their own mother tongue and they are understood by others.

**Apbhramsa**

Apbhramsa is the connected link between the Prakrits and the Modern Indian Languages. The earliest reference to Apbhramsa is found in Patanjali's *Mahabhasya*. There it has been used in a wider sense. All forms which did not conform to the Sanskrit grammar were termed as Apbhramsa. He regards all Prakrits as Apbhramsa. The sage Bharat in his *Natyasastra* used the word विभृष्ट Vibhrashta in the sense of Apbhramsa. The references made by him show that such words were used in poetry also. Bhamah[36] is the first critic on poetry who acknowledges Apbhramsa along with Sanskrit and Prakrit as the languages used in poetry. Dandin[37] has also referred to it as Kavyabhasa and connects it with Abhiras. Udbhat, Rudrat and his commentator the Jain prose writer Namisadhu[38] (1069 A.D.) mentioned some varieties of Apbhramsa. Subsequently Rajshekhar,[39] Anandavaradhan,[40] Mammat,[41] Bhoj,[42] Vagbhatta,[43] Ram Chandra Gunchandra,[44] and others have referred to Apbhransa as the language of the poetry which shows that it has established its status as a literary language.

The grammarians and the critics have referred to several forms of Apbhramsa. The grammarians have simply enumerated Nagar, Upnagar, Abhir, Gramya, Brachad, Apbhramsa without giving peculiarities of any one of them. Bhoj[45] has quoted several verses from Avanti, Lati, Abhiri, Gaurjari, Kashmiri, Paurstya and other Apbhransas. Gradually the Apbhransa was accepted as literary language and the works in it gained recognition from scholars and royal courts. For several centuries it remained the literary language of the Northern India along with Sanskrit and Prakrit - till 16th century A.D.

**Modern Indian Languages[46]**

The origin of modern Indian languages can be traced to different forms of Prakrit viz. the Maharashtri, the Saurseni, the Ardha-Magadhi, the Magadhi and the Paisau. Thus the Marathi is derived from Maharashtra Apbhramsa. The Gujarati, the Rajasthani a group of several dialects, the Punjabi and the Western Hindi, also a group of closely allied dialects are to be traced to Saursen Apbhransa; the Eastern Hindi a group of dialects to the Ardha-Magadha Apbhransa and the Oriya, Bengali, Behari and Assamese to the Magadhi Apbhransa proper. The

Sindhi from the Vracada and the Lahnda Kashmiri are probably derived from the Paisach Apbhransa. Besides these, there are the Himalayan dialects - Garwala, Kumaoni and Nepali, which are called by Grierson the Pahari languages and by Hoernle the Northern Gaudian. Bhandarkar seems to include them among the dialects of Hindi.

It would not be out of place to discuss the topography of these vernaculars and their sub-dialects.

Marathi is bounded on the South by the district of Canara, on the south-east and east by the Satpura and Vindhya ranges. The various sub-dialects are Konkani, Daccini and the one spoken in and about Kolhapur and Ratnagiri.[47] Bhandarkar adds some other dialects like the Karnari, the Goanese, the Malwari, the Savantvadi, the Chitpawni, Salsetti and Khandesi. Besides, there are the Poona or the Central dialect and the Berari.

*Gujarati* - The Gujarati is bounded on the South and East by the Marathi and Khandesi speaking districts, on the North by Marwar Central Indian states speaking Rajasthani and Western Hindi and on the West by the Kachi and the sea. There are no remarkable dialectal variations in Gujarati. The Gujarati is a composite language, having elements of Lati, the Prakrit of Dandin, the Saurseni Apbhransa and even foreign elements that it gathered from the language of heterogeneous immigrants.

*Rajasthani* - The various dialects of Rajasthani are Marawari. Jaipuri, Mewari, Malwi and one or two minor ones. These dialects are surrounded on the West by Sindhi and Lahnda, on the North by Lahnda Punjabi, on the east by Braj and Bundeli and on the south by Marathi, Khandeshi and Gujarati.

*Punjabi* - The Punjabi language is spoken in Punjab, except the Western most part along the banks of the Indus. The Punjabi has two well marked dialects, the standard language on Amritsar and the Malwi of the South Eastern Punjab.

The Western Hindi is a group of various dialects such as Hindustani, the Bangaru, the Braj Bhasa, the Kannoji and the Bundeli. Roughly speaking, part of Eastern Punjab, Western half of the Uttar Pradesh, Bundelkhand the Gwalior region is the region of these dialects.

The Eastern Hindi is a group of dialects named Avadhi or Purvi, the Bagheli and the Chattisgarhi. It is spoken over the Eastern part of the Uttar Pradesh, Madhya Pradesh excluding Nagpur and the east and west Chota Nagpur.

The Oriya is a language of the modern Orissa, South Madnapur,

Southern most corner of Bihar, a little portion of Chota Nagpur, Sambal Pur and the upper part of the Ganjam district. It has Bengali and Bihari on the North, Eastern Hindi on the West the Telugu on the South and the sea on the east.

The Bengali is the language of the lower Bengal Province, a part of Chota Nagpur and a part of the Assam Valley. It shows two clear cut dialects i.e. the Sanskrit ridden Bengali of the educated classes and the genuine vernacular of the masses. It may also be classified into (i) the Central dialect of Calcutta and the region round about it. (ii) The Eastern dialect of Rangpur Maiman Singh, Dakka, Barisal and (iii) Western dialect of Nadiya and twenty four parganas. The Bihari is the name of a group of dialects spoken in Bihar. There are three main dialects — the Maithili, Magahi or Magadhi and Bhojpuri. It has Eastern Hindi, Oriya and Bengali to its south and the Bengali to its East. On the North are the Himalyan dialects.

The Assamese language is spoken in the Northern most portion of Assam, in the valley of Brahmputra river in Assam. There are two principal dialects - one in the east, round Shiv Sagar and the other in the west.

Sindhi - Sindhi is spoken in the Sindh province along both the banks of the lower Indus. It has three main dialects, the Siraiki, the Lari and the Shareli, which are spoken in the Upper Sindh, Lower Sindh and the desert of Thar respectively.

The Lahnda, is spoken in eastern Punjab along the banks of the Upper India. The dialects of Lahnda are many — Pothwari, Chibhali, Tinaoli, Ubhachi, Thalli, Khatrani are some of them.

Kashmiri is spoken in Kashmir and is a Paisachi dialect. It has two dialects, one full of Sanskrit words and the other having Persian, Arabic words in abundance.

Then there are the Pahari languages or the Northern Gaudian, which include Gharwali, the Kumaini and the Nepali and other Himalayan languages. They are spoken in the lower Himalayan ranges from the Satluj in West to the Gogri in the East.

> "Near about 100 B.C. — At about the same date, some schools were teaching the sacred dramatics, history, aesthetics and the eighteen vernacular scripts of India."[48]

From all that has been said about the historical development of different languages from Sanskrit to modern Indian languages, one fact is clear, that at no time, India had been a unilingual nation. Even at the time when Vedic hymns were being composed in stylised Sanskrit the spoken form of Sanskrit was different from the literary language. The difference ultimately gave rise to different Prakrits, one of which, was Pali itself. In due course, these languages became impure, which, in turn gave rise to Apbhransa. From these Apbhransas, again, the modern Indian languages evolved. To quote Keith, " They remind us of the salient fact, that, at any given moment in India,there were in active use, several forms of speech varying according to the class of society." The fact remains that India has been a country of diverse social groups spread over the vast region of the sub-continent. For that matter, a common mode of communication for the vast land was neither feasible, nor linguistically relevant. Hence, is the development of the multilingual nature of the country. In the midst of the variety of tongues and their varied forms, the functional aspects of languages in different regions were not lost sight of. The three distinctly marked functions of mode of communication could be easily detected and they were (i) the language of the common man for mutual man-to-man communication and in variegated roles of social personal life; (ii) the language of the court, where the common man and the administration chose a medium for communication where the need arose and (iii) the language of the scriptures for spiritual upliftment, the language of the erudition, culture and religious pursuits. Looking at the position of languages, Indians had always been using three languages or even more than three.

## B. LANGUAGE POSITION IN MEDIEVAL PERIOD

In spite of the fact that India has always been a multilingual country, there has been only one court-language and there has been a common link language. As far as the evidence goes, this position was enjoyed by Sanskrit till and advent of the Muslims. From the middle of the 4th century A.D. India passed through great turmoil. Foreign invaders, like the Greek, the Sakas, the Huns, the Mongols and the Arabs came and tried to uproot the Hindu civilisation, culture and their language. But, Sanskrit language continued to be in use as the national medium of communication. It was the language of the religion, the ritual and the literature. During the Greek rule in Indian territory, people were bilingual. The coins found on the southern side of the Caucasus show the inscriptions inscribed on them in two languages — one was Greek and the other, barbaric in character. About the latter, some of the scholars are of the opinion that, as it is written from right to left, it shows a peculiarity of the Arab family, supposed to be the Persian. These circumstances suggest Pahlvi as the language. Many other scholars discover in the coins, certain words of Sanskrit origin which they conclude that it may be the language of Zend or some of the dialects of India.[49] It naturally leads of the conclusion that at that time, languages like Pahlvi and dialects of Sanskrit must have been in use at the official level and as such must have been taught too. In North India, the dialects used by higher classes were not far removed from Sanskrit, but, in South, the Dravidian languages were developing on different lines. During the Gupta age (324 to 4th century A.D.) known as 'the Golden Age' and 'the Classical Age', Sanskrit developed at its highest level. The replacement of Prakrit by Sanskrit as the court language gave it a position of pre-eminence. Evidences show that apart from Sanskrit and different dialects, Dravidian languages were in use. Among the different subjects learnt by the princes at the court of King Rajvahana, were all scripts and languages,[50,51] Prince Chandrapida, a royal pupil acquired proficiency in all the alphabets and all the dialects of the country.[52]

By the end of the 10th century A.D., Hinduism absorbed Buddhism. The Brahmanas regained their influence on the masses. The Sanskrit language was used as an instrument of unifying the country. As education was in the lands of the Brahmanas who used to impress and mould the masses, the medium of instruction in the field of education must have been Sanskrit.

In about 1000 A.D. Mahmud of Ghazni's invasion proved more than a militant movement only. He introduced Persian language and literature by destroying Brahmanical educational centres and killing the learned Brahmanas who performed the role of the teachers in India. This was a great set back to Hindu education. But, "the Mohammadon scholars", says Albaruni - the historian "were dependent for knowledge in different fields, on Hindu scholars, with the result that Indian Mathematics, Astronomy, Astrology, Philosophy, Medicine and Physiology etc. were studied and translated in Persian and Arabic by the Mohammadons.[53, 54] On the basis of the above facts, it may be presumed that these languages must have been taught either in the regular schools or in some sort of unconventional institutes. From 1174-1206 Mohammad Gauri established his power in Delhi. He is reported to have destroyed temples at Ajmer and built in their places, mosques and madrasahs. To mosques, were attached Maktabs i.e., the places where elementary education was given. The medium of education was Persian - a language brought through Arabs viz Persia to India. A knowledge of Arabic language was also compulsory for

Mohammadons, because, it was the language of religion and a knowledge of Quran - their religious book; was compulsory for them. Madrasahs were meant for higher learning. In today's language madrasahas can be termed as Colleges. They were generally attached to mosques, where, the subjects taught were of higher level but the medium of instruction, as usual, was Persian. The teachers called, were, from Persia, Arabia and Central Asia. Among the teachers and students seminars and discussions were held and the medium of communication used to be Persian language. Other Sultans like Kutub-Ud-Din, Bakhtiyar, Altmash, Razia Begum, Nasir-Ud-Din, Balban, Ala-Ud-Din, Ghiyas-Ud-Din Tughlaq, Mohd. Tughlaq, Feroz Shah and others all gave impetus and patronage to Persian language and literature by opening Makhtabs and madrasahs where the medium had always been Persian. Therefore, it can be concluded that a knowledge of two languages viz. Arabic and Persian was compulsory for the Mohammadons. The great Bahmani king named Firuz was a great linguist. Farishta records that in his harem there were ladies of various races, such as Arabians, Caucacians, Georgians, Turks, Europeans, Chinese, Afghans, Rajputs, Bengalies, Gujaratis, Telinganese, Marhattas and others with each of whom he could converse in the latter's own language.[55] He could read the Bible. Probably, he learned Hebrew from the Jews living on the Malabar coast for many ages.[56] Such being the case, it can be established that at least, the Kings had knowledge of several languages. To cut short, the period from 1206-1526 was a period of literary activity. The court extended patronage to Muslim scholars and to those, who wrote in Persian. There is no evidence to show that writers in Sanskrit or Indian languages were patronized.[57] At the court of Hindu kings Sanskrit flourished. In Pathshala, where the elementary education was given, this language was the medium of instruction and for higher education, they were attached to monastries. There too, the medium was Sanskrit. In Sikandar Lodi's time, the Muslim kings and chiefs opened the gates of Sanskrit learning to non-Brahmanas also. Even Muslims were allowed to learn this language. It was the first time, as the history records, that both the communities i.e. the Hindus and the Muslims began to study each other's language. The driving force behind this, was the pecuniary advantage given to the Hindus, who, particularly the Kayasthas, started learning Persian language and literature. The Muslim rulers, in turn, gave them employment in administration. Firoz Shah, for instance, gave to two Hindus very responsible posts in his administration.[58,59] They not only learnt the language, but also contributed to it by composing prose and poetry in Persian. Similar instances we find of Muslims who studied Sanskrit and had written also in it. Mohd.-Al-Beruni, the great historian (11th century A.D.) studied Sanskrit and established a close contact with Indian scholars of the age. The Arab astronomer Abu Mashar studied astronomy for 10 years in Banaras.[60] In 12th century A.D. the book *Sandesh Rasak*, in Apbhramsa — spoken dialect of Sanskrit was written by Abdula Rahman, a Mohammedan. The dialect Hindi had also developed by this time into a language of literature. The great heroic poem *Prithviraj Raso* by Chanbardai was written during this period. The inter-communication between the Mohammedans and the Hindus resulted in the evolution of a new dialect - a mixture of Persian, Arabic and Hindi words, which, in due course of time developed into a new language known as 'Urdu'. The word 'Urdu' literally means 'Camp'; but the Mughuls in India, used it with regard to the 'Imperial Camp'. Thus, the Camp language, emerged between 1206-1506, or a little earlier. Originally, it was called Zaban-i-Hindawi and subsequently Urdu; it was spoken in Delhi and in surrounding districts. Rapidly, it came into common use in North India. In fact the dialect, Zaban-e-Hindawi when written in Devanagari scripts, was called 'Hindi' and while in Persian script it was called 'Urdu'.[62] Amir Khusrau (1253-1326) used Hindi words in his writings. He had written on Indian themes also. His language is an admixture of Persian and Hindi words. In his famous Masnavi entitled *Nuh-Siphr* (Seven-Skies) he referred to the languages and dialects of the people. "Now in India, every province has a peculiar dialect of its own. There is, for instance, Sindhi, Lahauri, Kashmiri, Kanarese, Dhur-Samudri, Tilandi, Gujari, Mabari, Gauri, Bengali and Awadhi," but says he, further, that, "in Delhi and all around it, the current language is the same Hindawi, that has been in use in India from ancient times and has been used for all forms of speech. It is this Zaben-e-Hindawi in Persian script, which was made the court language by some of the Muslim rulers like Ibrahim-Adil Shah II who made the Daccni Urdu his court language in place of Persian.[63]

By the end of the 13th century the country faced an abrupt halt to the intellectual expansion due to the vast destruction of the centres of learning and the universities by the Turks and Mongols in the North India. The Indian empire was divided among the different small states. There chiefs were busy in consolidating their own positions and did not bother about the welfare of the country. But, there were still some liberal minded Muslim rulers in Kashmir and Bengal who patronized Sanskrit and Modern Indian Languages. Zain-Ul-Abedin of Kashmir (1420-1470) employed Sanskrit and Hindi scholars in his court. Nasir-Ud-Din Nusrat Shah (1518-1533) was a great patron of Bengali literature.[64] In the provinces, the Hindu converts to Islam retained the local vernaculars in their mother tongue. During the period of the Sultanate of Delhi (1206-1526), led by the saints and religious reformers, a movement known as the 'Bhakti Cult' became responsible for the evolution and enrichment of Indian vernaculars, mainly because the reformers preached their teachings to the masses in their mother tongues. This way, they enriched languages like Hindi, Bengali, Marathi, Maithili, Gujarati etc. Public accounts began to be kept in Hindi instead of Persian during the reign of Ibrahim-Adil Shah I (1534-1537).[65] By the end of the second half of the 16th century A.D. the Mughuls established a fairly stable empire in India.

Baber (1526-1530) was the first Mughal Emperor in India. He knew three languages viz., Arabic-the language of *Quran*, Persian-the language of the court and Turkish, his mother tongue. As he was a staunch supporter of Islam, he also continued with the same syllabus and medium of instruction which his predecessors followed. At some of the provincial courts, Muslim rulers brought out works in Sanskrit. In South and North, 'Urdu' became the medium of inter-communication between the Turko-Afghan rulers and the native people.

Humayun (1530-1540 ; 1555-1556) learnt Hindi, besides Turkish, Arabic and Persian. During his rule, all these languages flourished. No change was introduced in the existing educational pattern. Persian continued to be the court language, and as such the language of literature and medium of instruction in Makhtabs and Madrasahs.[66] Such being the situation, it can be concluded that the highest status in the field of education was given to Persian language. The reasons were the following :-

i) Persian was the language of the ruling class.
ii) Consequently it was made the court language and thus the language of literature and medium of instruction.
iii) Those, who knew this language were naturally given higher posts in the administration of the country.

The period between 1540-'45 evidenced the rise of Sher-Shah Suri. He issued new silver coins, on which, his name, title and the place of mint were inscribed in Arabic character. Some of his coins bore his name in Devanagari script. That shows, that, all the three scripts viz.,

Arabic, Persian and Devanagari were in use at that time. It seems that there must have been some people who knew not only the three languages but the scripts as well.

Akbar (1556-1605) was a patron of learning. He encouraged both types of education - Muslim as well as Hindu. The age saw the revival of ancient learning. His period is known for cultural renaissance. Both the communities - Hindus and Muslims used to study each other's language and literature. With the result, many Hindus were appointed as the teachers of Persian. He established a translation department, where, with the collaboration of Persian and Sanskrit scholars works in Arabic, Turkish and Sanskrit were translated into Persian. The first attempt in this direction was the compilation of Persian - Sanskrit Lexicon, known as *Parsi-Prakash*.[67] Besides, some works in Greek and Kashmiri were also translated into Persian language. Eminent scholars in Sanskrit, Arabic and Persian were employed. He was the first Mughul Emperor to extend patronage to Sanskrit. Poets and scholars in Sanskrit adorned his court.

Hindi was the medium of instruction in the schools attached to temples. A number of Muslims also learnt this language. Akbar liked Hindi poetry. He himself composed verses in Hindi.[68] Poets in Hindi language were patronized by him. Consequently the 16th and 17th centuries became "the Augustan Age of Hindustani literature." The first writer of fame after 1526 was 'Jayasi' who in 1540 wrote *Padmavat*.[69] The well known Hindi poet of his age Abdur Rahim Khankhana was well versed in Persian, Arabic, Turkish, Sanskrit, Hindi and Rajasthani.[70] Akbar's sons knew many languages like Persian, Arabic and Hindi. Since in his reign, some Portuguese missionaries came, the Emperor allowed his sons to learn Portuguese too. As the Hindi language was being patronized by the Emperor, it was developing as the language of the Central Hindustan and of the wandering saints.

In spite of encouragement and patronage given to Sanskrit and Hindi languages the Emperor Akbar, by all means emphasised Persian, which was made compulsory for all the state officials. In the realm of languages, Persian became the polite language of all India.[71] It was supposed to foster nationality among the different communities. Seeing the importance given to Persian language in the administrative work, even Todar Mal — a Hindu finance minister of Akbar, ordered the official accounts to be kept in Persian.[72] This regulation compelled many Hindus to study that language. The *Ain-e-Akbari* recorded the names of 59 most eminent Persian poets at Akbar's court.

Regarding the Arabic, it is said, that those who desired, the language was taught to them. The scholars of this period paid more attention to language. In his 'Ibadatkhana' notable scholars from different religions and sections, Parsi priests and Christian missionaries from Goa used to have academic discourses.

During his reign, the Mughul Imperial service was manned mostly by foreigners. It consisted of Turks, Mongols, Uzbegs, Persian, Arabs, Afghans, Mohammadans and Hindus. According to Blochmann, 70% of them were foreigners, who had come from Central Asia for service or had settled in this country for one or two generations.[73] Apart from these, there were some Abyssinians and Armenians. Since there was no check on immigration, many nationalities from Europe and Asia, such as, the Portuguese, the English, the Chinese, the Japanese, the Turks, the Jewish and Parsis came to this country. For the communication within a particular community, it is certain, that the languages of the different communities mentioned above, must have been taught to respective communities. But for a common and wider communication, there must have been some common means of expression and, that, possibly could be "Hindustani", which was written in two scripts - Persian and Devanagari. While in Persian, it was recognised as 'Urdu' and in 'Devanagari', it used to be called as 'Hindi'[74] It was from this time that the hybrid tongue of 'Urdu' or, the language of the camp - a mixture of Persian and Hindi attained the status of a separate language,[75] which was being used as the lingua-franca in most of the parts of the India.[76,77] "The growth of Urdu", says Majumdar, out of the mingling of Persian, Arabic and Turkish words and ideas with languages and concepts of Sanskrit origin is a proof of the linguistic synthesis of the Hindus and the Muslims.[78]

By all these instances, it will not be unjustified to say that at least by the end of 16th century a knowledge of two languages was given to Hindus and Muslims. "The *Quran* which is in Arabic is chiefly read by the Musalmans, who also study the Persian languages."[79] In some cases they knew more than two languages, "Tipu Sahib, the last sovereign of Mysore, understood several oriental languages and possessed a library enriched with all sorts of European and Eastern works."[80]

Akbar's son and successor Jahangir was crowned in 1605 and remained as the King till 1627. He also took keen interest in restoring the desolate maktabs and madrasahs and supplied them with teachers and pupils. Such schools, says Della Vella[81] existed in his time in every town and village Education in these schools was imparted through Persian. Jahangir employed Persian, Sanskrit and Hindi poets in his court and followed the policies of education laid down by his predecessors.

Shah-Jahan (1627-1658), like Akbar, encouraged Persian, Sanskrit and Hindi languages. Scholars of these, adorned his court. His son 'Dara-Shikoh' was a scholar of Arabic, Persian, Sanskrit and Hindi languages. He enriched the Persian literature by translating *Upanishads* into Persian.

Aurangzeb (1658-1707) was an orthodox Musalman. As such, he believed in the supremacy of Islam and tried to convert all the Hindus to *Muslims*. This policy very much affected the policy of education, subsequently the language policy. Historians believe that he took interest in education to spread Islam and not to advance the welfare of the people. He demolished many a temple and Hindu centres of learning. Brahmana teachers were either compelled to get converted into Islam or they were to face execution consequently. Sanskrit and Hindi languages diminished to a great extent owing to the withdrawal of court partronage. Urdu flourished in the Deccan. Persian language and literature were encouraged. Throughout the school and college education i.e. in maktabs and madrashas Persian and Arabic were taught. Aurangzeb himself was the master of three languages i.e. his mother tongue, Turkish, Persian and Arabic. He believed that a king should be familiar with the languages of surrounding nations. He made efforts also for raising Arabic language as the language of law and sciences.[82] In his reign, Persian language enjoyed the highest status in the curriculum, because, it was the medium of instruction throughout the educational ladder from the elementary to the higher. Discussions and seminars were held in this language. Persianised Urdu was the lingua-franca.

## C. LANGUAGE POSITION IN BRITISH PERIOD

India had commercial relations with the countries of the west from very ancient times. Many people of different countries from the West had come here for trade and commerce. Vasco-da-Gama, the discoverer of India, when first reached by sea-route Calicat in 1498, found that the education was at progress. Then came the Portuguese merchants. They did not confine themselves with the trade only, but, became ambitious to establish their supremacy in the Eastern seas. They settled down in Diu, Daman, Salretta, Bassein, Chaal, Bombay, San Thome near Madras and Hugli in Bengal. By the 18th century they lagged behind in the field of Indian trade with the result that they could not make advances in the cultural field. So, their language too could not spread.

In 1600 A.D. the English East India Company secured a royal charter for trade and commerce in India.[83] They were followed by the Dutch, Spanish and French traders, who established their factories in India, but, it was the English people, who could influence Indians by their commercial goods. Later on, they succeeded in establishing their rule over this land, which ultimately brought as tremendous change in the educational system of the country. Some of the historians are of the opinion, that during that early period, the East India Company was primarily a commercial concern and as such they did not bother about the education of the people of India. But N. N. Law, the great historian (in education) points out, that, even at that time, the company was engaged in proselytizing activities resulting into teaching of English language, mainly because the reading of their religious book *Bible* was essential for the Christians. It is to be remembered that, during that period, the elementary education was given to the trading and commercial classes. Sanskrit was taught as the language of religion in Sanskrit pathshalas. Arabic and Persian were taught in maktabs and madrasahs. Urdu was the spoken language amongst the Mohammedans, but, it was not rich enough to be used as the medium, of instruction. Persian continued to be the court language. There were a few schools where Bengali was also taught with Persian. In 1698 the missionaries, whose only aim was conversion of the natives and teaching the *Bible* got permission for working in India from the Parliament of England. The famous missionary clause was inserted in the charter of the company, when it came for renewal. The clause directed the English knowing missionaries to learn two more language viz. Portuguese, because, it was understood by the lower staff of the company and the native language of the country where they had to reside. In the schools, opened for the employees of the company, Portuguese was the medium of instruction. Mention may be made here, that the missionaries taught the *Bible* through the mother tongue of the natives as the convert Christians belonged to the lower strata of the Hindu society, who could not understand any other language except their own. Hence, the missionaries assiduously studied the Indian languages, compiled dictionaries, wrote books on grammar and translated the *Bible* into them. In fact, the languages of India were rich enough that the Bible could be translated in these languages easily and, therefore the missionaries did not think it proper to ignore the native languages. Sherring observed that '... New Testament has been translated and actually printed in thirty one Indian languages and dialects.... Serampur

Press (West Bengal) alone printed *Bible* into twenty languages and in addition books for schools and colleges.[84] As a result, the growth and development of Indian language, which suffered in the reign of Aurangzeb, due to the absence of royal patronage, again stepped forward. It should not be forgotten that knowledge of English language through Indian vernaculars was given only to the employees of the East India Company. Schools were found where the classical languages viz. Sanskrit, Persian and Arabic were taught. Evidences show, that, Indian vernaculars were also taught that Hindustani in Devanagari and Persian scripts were also flourishing.

An absolute change in educational system, resulting into an abrupt change in the policy of teaching English language, adopting it as the medium of instruction and language to be used for the administration of the country came only after 1765, when the company became a political power in India. Instead of learning the languages of this country, multiple in number, it was thought proper that the natives should learn the language of the ruling class, which was only one. Thus, the Directors of the Company decided to extend their educational activities to teach the Indians as a whole. But, due to the dearth of text-books in vernaculars and lack of enough funds with the Government, it was considered proper that, instead of teaching the masses, they should teach the upper classes of the society. It was decided that its only duty was to encourage classical learning in Sanskrit, Arabic and Persian on traditional lines, and that the ancient system of education, which the,Hindus and Muslims, had inherited was good enough for them for all practical purposes. The company, therefore, aimed at the encouragement of the traditional oriental learning in Sanskrit, Arabic and Persian. The centres of higher learning, for instance, Calcutta Madrasah (1781) and Banaras Sanskrit College (1792) were started. The Calcutta Madrasa was primarily meant for the higher education of Mohammedans. The syllabus included Natural Philosophy, Theology, Law, Astronomy, Geometry, Arithmetic, Logic, Rhetoric, Oratory and Grammar all according to Islamic culture. On the grounds of the evidences available during the Mughal period, it can be assumed that the medium of instruction must have been Persian. Arabic, as the language of religion was also taught. Later on, an English class was attached to this Madrasah.[85]

In Banaras Sanskrit College, the subjects taught, were Theology, Ritual, Medicine, Music, Mechanic, Arts, Grammar, Prosody, Sacred Lexicography, Mathematics, Metaphysics, Logic, Law, History,

Ethics, Philosophy and Poetry. The medium of instruction was Sanskrit. In Delhi, schools, were founded for the instruction of children of the Zamindars or peasantry, where Persian language was taught. Side by side some other schools were opened, where, English language was taught. The first three among them were established in 1785 at Tanjore. Ramnad and Shivganga[86] with the object of teaching English to Indian children. Funds were allocated for their maintenance by the court of Directors. Some liberal minded scholars from England took interest in making arrangements for the teaching of different Indian languages. For instance, in the Fort William College of Calcutta, founded by Lord Wellesley on 10th July 1800, the languages intended to be taught were, Sanskrit, Arabic, Persian, Bengali, Hindustani, Telugu, Tamil and Kannada.[87] In the same year after the Sepoy Mutiny at Velllore, in 1800 the missionaries were expelled from the country since their activities were not relished by the Hindoo and Muslim residents and the efforts of enriching the Indian languages by translating into them, not only Bible, but other English classics also, were hampered with. However, the missionaries did not sit idle. They raised their voice in England against the Directors of the East Indian Company and tried to seek permission from the Parliament in England for missionary work in India. They got support from Charles Grant, a member of the Parliament. He held the view, that, to bring about understanding between the rulers and the ruled, the oppressed class must be enlightened by education in English.[88] He also suggested the adoption of English as the language of the Government.[89] He said that Portuguese and Bengali clerks understood English as well as Hindustani.[90] Therefore, he advised the Parliament of England to educate the Indians to rid them of their ignorance and superstitions and for their education the medium of instruction was decided to be English His suggestions influenced the policies of British Government; with the result, the Parliament passed the educational clause known as 43rd section of Charter Act 1813. In this Charter of the company, the Governor-General in Council was directed to fix a certain amount of rupees in each year for the revival and improvement of literature, the encouragement of the learned natives of India and for the introduction and promotion of a knowledge of the sciences among the inhabitants of the British territories in India.[91,92,93] Following this Act, a State System of Education was begun in all the three British territories known as the Bengal, Bombay and Madras Presidencies. It is interesting to note that in spite of the fact that the work for education was begun simultaneously in the three Presidencies, the policies regarding teaching of languages were altogether different.

When the Directors of the company took over the administration of Bengal, they found the elementary education being imparted in path-shalas and maktabs. The syllabus consisted of three R's and religious myths and legends. Because the higher education was confined to the study of classical Sanskrit in tols, it is natural that the medium of instruction in elementary centres of learning must have been Sanskrit. Similarly in maktabs, the syllabus was limited to a knowledge of three R's and religious myths and legends. Persian as the medium of instruction and Arabic as the language of religion were taught. Higher education was given in Madrasahs where Arabic and Persian were the media of instruction and subjects of studies too. Grammar, classical literature, logic, philosophy, law and religious texts formed the main elements of higher study in tols and *Madrasahs*.[94,95] After manipulating the situation, it was decided, that, besides recognising the Calcutta Madrasah and Banaras Sanskrit College, some other centres for teaching classical languages should be established. But, Raja Ram Mohan Roy, an eminent Indian educationist and a scholar of several languages including Sanskrit, Arabic, Persian and English opposed it. Instead, he suggested that, institutions should be established for teaching Western sciences through English language. He believed, that what the country needed was not "What was known two thousands years ago", but a more liberal and enlightened system of education. The Government not only opened the new institutes for classical languages but also the printing and publication of Sanskrit, Arabic and Persian books were undertaken on a large scale. For translation of English books into classical languages, scholars in Oriental Sciences were employed. East India Company also sanctioned grants-in-aid to the missionaries, for teaching the natives through their mother tongues. In most cases the missionary schools taught English side by side with the vernacular languages.[96] The convert Indians educated in missionary schools were provided job opportunities which, naturally raised the demand for learning English language. Conclusively by the first half of the 19th century, English classes were attached to the colleges at Agra and Calcutta. In Delhi and Banaras, a number of English schools were opened. Provision was made for selling English books. In 1833 Raja Ram, Mohan Roy advocated for English to be the Court language and emphasised that the Indians should also be given opportunity to participate in the government's working. This naturally impelled Indians to take English oriented education. To meet this demand for leaning English language, the missionaries switched over to English medium in secondary Schools and Colleges.[97] On the other side, general Committee of Public Instructions (appointed in 1823 for the Bengal Presidency) was insisting on classical education. The members of the Committee recommended in 1823 to the Governor-General that in order to bring Western learning to their fellow countrymen the Indian teachers should be proficient in both Hindu and Mohammedan learning and English.[98] Consequently, it is presumed that in the early 1823, at least three languages were advised to be studied, if there had to be brought a synthesis among the different religions and linguistic groups of India.

In fact, the ambiguous nature of the above mentioned educational clause led to the implementation of different forms .of language policies. A number of controversies with regard to the interpretation of the clause it self, bifurcated the committee into two different groups. No doubt, it was this 43rd section of the Charter Act of 1813, which created a chaos in the field of education, particularly for teaching the number of languages, because, no special and explicit directions were given with regard to the following :-

The term 'literature' did not clarify whether it meant Sanskrit, Arabic, Persian or English literature.

Who were the learned natives of India? Did it mean scholars in Eastern or Western Sciences?

The phrase 'the introduction and promotion of a knowledge of sciences' did not at all indicate to Eastern Sciences or Western Sciences?

Moreover, no directions were given regarding the language to be used as the means of instructing the natives the above mentioned literature and sciences.

As far as the latter part of the clause i.e. the introduction and promotion of the sciences among the inhabitants of the British territories in India' was concerned, none of them differed except on the issue of the 'medium', through which a knowledge of sciences, of course western agreeable to both the parties, i.e. the Orientalist and the Anglicist should be communicated. So far as the question of the medium of instruction was concerned, one school of thought expressed the view that all the education should be imparted through the English language. The other group believed in making the classical languages of India - Sanskrit, Arabic and Persian as the media for teaching Western sciences. Yet another group believed that the vernaculars of India could be the appropriate medium for this purpose. These controversies among the eminent scholars led to the implementation of different language policies, resulting into efforts made for the development and growth of the vernaculars of India. For instance, funds were allocated for the printing and publishing of classical works available till then, mostly in manuscript forms. Stipends and scholarships were distributed among students for advanced learning in Oriental Sciences and translation work from English books into classical languages was encouraged by appointing scholars and teachers in Oriental Sciences.

For the spread of English language among the Indians, efforts were made at official level. Macaulay - President of the General Committee of Public Instructions and the Law member of the Executive Council of the Governor-General, presiding over the Anglicist Party[99] advocated for English language to be used not only as the medium of education but, also advised the Government to adopt it as the official language. In support of his views, Bentinck the then Governor General of India in 1837 got the Persian discontinued as the court language. Though vernaculars were suggested in lieu of Persian[100, 101] English began to be used at the official level. Moreover, the Government decided to use the funds sanctioned by the Directors of the Company for propagating the European sciences. His policy was again reaffirmed by the Governor-General Auckland in 1839. There years after, according to the regulation introduced by the British Government of India in 1844 for the Government jobs, preference used to be given to English knowing persons. These attempts made at official level naturally gave an impetus to the demand for learning English language. Vernaculars were not considered to be the appropriate means of instruction on the grounds of being not rich enough. In Bengal, English enjoyed the highest status in the field of education and in the society as well. Classical languages were relegated the secondary place. Vernaculars had no place at all.

Mountstuart Elphinstone, as the Governor General of India established Bombay Native Education Society for the education of the natives of Bombay between 1823-1840. In the schools run by the society, mother tongue as a medium was used to teach English and other subjects. The syllabus of the primary schools included three R's viz Reading, Writing, Arithmetic. Other subjects taught were History of India and England, Geography, Astronomy, Natural Philosophy, Algebra, Geometry and Trigonometry and all these subjects were taught through the mother tongues of the natives of Bombay.[102]

Attempts were made to give the highest education like Engineering and Medical, through the medium of vernaculars.[103, 104] The Elphinstone Institute itself had two different departments of teaching languages. English was taught in the department of English while Marathi and Gujarati were taught in the vernacular department. It had Hindustani branch also, where Hindustani was taught. In Poona Sanskrit College, Sanskrit was taught as usual. The other subjects like Dharmasastra and Vyakrana were taught in Sanskrit.[105, 106] 'Candy' the Superintendent of the College considered it to be the most fertile language and emphasised the learning of this language by every teacher. He believed that for effective teaching teachers in other Indian languages must be acquainted with Sanskrit language. To quote 'Candy', "I look on every native who possesses a good knowledge of his own mother tongue, of Sanskrit and of English, to possess the power of rendering incalculable benefit to his countrymen.[107,108,109] In other words he considered the knowledge of at least three languages essential. He had realised that the spoken languages or the mother tongues of the masses can only become the true media of their education. Further he said that the vernacular could be strengthened and enriched by Sanskrit while English could supply knowledge to the students. He recommended that without a grammatical knowledge of the native tongue, the students should not be admitted to the Zilla English school. On the other side, in 1831 a petition was submitted to the government asking that no native should be admissible after a time into a public office who could not read, write and speak the English language.[110] That resulted into the establishment of English schools in almost every district in the province. In Bombay mother tongues of the natives were given highest status while English enjoyed the second position. Classical languages of India were altogether ignored.

The Collector of Bellary in 1823, reported that Madras had arrangements for teaching English, Tamil, Persian, Mahratta, Telugu and the Carnataka languages in a large number of schools. Besides these, there were twenty three centres of instruction where, theology, astronomy, logic and law were taught through Sanskrit medium.[111] In spite of Munro's (the collector of Madras) proposals for the improvement of indigenous schools for the education of masses, no fruitful results came out. Teaching of English language was intensively emphasised and a result it enjoyed the higher status in Madras. Comparatively Indian Classics and vernaculars were neglected.

In North India, arrangements were made for teaching Hindi and Urdu, and other subjects through the medium of mother tongue.[12]

English was not a flourishing language as it was confined within the four walls of the college.[113] In Punjab, besides Hindi, Persian, Arabic and Sanskrit, Gurmukhi was also taught.[114,115] Charles Wood - the President of the Board of Control, in his Despatch of 1854 advised to use vernaculars as the medium of instruction for masses and to achieve this goal it recommended that Indian languages should be enriched by the translation of English books. In high schools, English was to be studied as one of the subjects and should not be used as the means of instruction. It was specifically mentioned that the said language was not to be taught as one of the compulsory subjects, rather, it should be taught as one of the optionals. Moreover, it was repeatedly emphasised that English was not to replace any of the Indian languages. Another condition imposed on learning of English language was, that it should be taught after the student had acquired sufficient knowledge in the language of the district.[116] That means, Wood recommended a knowledge of three languages, viz. Mother tongue because it was used as the means of instruction, local language (if it differed from mother tongue) in case he wanted to learn it and English language - if he opted for it. As English was the means of instruction at higher level of education, a student going for higher education was decidedly to bc acquainted with three languages viz. at the school level, the mother tongue, local/district language at local level and English at higher level of education. Stress was laid on the study of the vernaculars *pari-passu* with English in schools. Besides, a suggestion was made to establish the institution of university professorships for vernaculars (Modern Indian Languages), Sanskrit, Arabic and Persian for the advanced study (i.e. in Oriental Science).[117] Unfortunately, the policy of teaching languages by the government signified in the above mentioned 'Despatch' could not be implemented properly. Missionaries, usual, kept themselves busy in imparting English education through English language. Moreover, the Mutiny of 1857, was considered as the sole result of the Wood's despatch of 1854. Therefore, the recommendations given by the said despatch, though being quoted in every decision were seldom acted upon. Because of the growing dissatisfaction and restlessness among the people, administration of the country was transferred from company to the crown. It was thought over, that, one of the main causes of this volcanic revolt (Mutiny of 1857) might be the imposition of European Sciences on Western lines. Therefore, Stanley, Secretary of State for India, in 1859, suggested the vernaculars to be the medium of instruction in India. He urged upon the government to advance enough funds for translating the best English treatises into the vernacular languages of India. He also recommended some rewards for the best translations and the maintenance of the existing institutions for the study of the classical languages of India.[118] When the control of education was transferred to the Government of India in 1871, it was expected that the stress would be laid on the teaching of the languages of India and, that the mother tongue might become the medium of instruction at all the educational levels but, nothing concrete was done to achieve this end. Sitaramayya records that inspite of the apathy towards Indian languages, in 1875, there were as many as 475 newspapers mostly in provincial languages.[119] Though the Despatch of 1854 suggested 'Professorship' in the Indian languages and classics, nothing fruitful was done in practice. Arrangements were made for teaching Indian vernaculars in the affiliated colleges, but soon the efforts were made to stop it. The Indian Education Commission in 1882-1883 suggested that in all the provinces of British India, vernaculars should be used for the instruction till middle school stage only. English was to be taught as a subject, because, it was expected that the student would learn how to read, speak and write English so that in High school he could gain what was being instructed to him through English medium.

As the demand for English learning materially increased during this period, many more schools were opened for teaching English language. The India Education Commission did not make any effort to raise the status of Indian languages in secondary schools. The study of English began even before the pupil had obtained a good knowledge of his mother tongue. In fact, the primary object of secondary school education was to teach English language rather than imparting a knowledge of European sciences.[120] Although Lord Curzon, the Viceroy of India in 1901, realized that because of the dominance of English in Indian schools, the vernacular languages of the country had "shrivelled and pined", he did nothing to discourage the use of that language as a medium of instruction. Indeed his criticism of the low standard of English in secondary schools indirectly led to more attention to it.[121] This exaggerated importance given to English hindered the use of modern Indian languages as media of instruction at the secondary stage. Moreover, Curzon did not accept the principle of compulsory education demanded by the Indian leaders like Gopal Krishna Gokhale and others. He rather ridiculed them saying that the 'Indian intelligentsia deliberately or habitually deviated from the truth.[122] and, as such, it is he

(Curzon) only who knew and could decide what was to be taught to the Indians. He therefore, discarding the expansion of education of the natives, spoke in favour of qualitative reform only. That enraged the people of India as they had realized that the excuse of paucity of funds for the development of Indian languages was indirectly raised in favour of the growth of English language only, because the expansion in education was achieved by Indian enterprise.[123]

In the Report of the Indian Universities Commission, appointed by Curzon in 1902, it was recommended that at the entrance examination one of the four compulsory subjects should be 'Second Language' which was defined as (a) an Oriental or European Classical language or (b) an Indian or Continental European Vernacular language. In Allahabad and Punjab Universities no option of a vernacular language was given. In Punjab, a candidate could take a fifth optional subject which might be a vernacular language, elementary science or a second classical language. At the intermediate Examination, a second language defined as "An Eastern or Western Classical or Modern European Language" was compulsory. Madras University alone added the option of a Modern Indian Language. This makes it clear that except in Madras, the study of Modern Indian Language was neglected in the ordinary course of the university which is important enough to be the sole cause in the slow development of Indian languages.[124] It can be mentioned here that in the Grants College in Bombay, medical books were written in modern Indian languages, especially in Marathi. Instruction was given through Marathi, later on in Gujarati. Scholarships and stipends, by some of the leading Indians were given to those students who studied through these languages. But owing to the general neglect of Modern Indian Languages, the attempts of giving medical education through Marathi or Gujarati and teaching through the mother tongue was discontinued by about 1880.[125] With all these happenings around, the educated class of the country opposed Curzon. The masses of the country developed a spirit of nationalism under the Swadeshi movement led by the Indian National Congress founded in 1885, under the Presidentship of Mrs. Annie Besant. People raised their voice in favour of 'Domination of English to go.' They demanded that it should not be used as the medium of instruction and that a proper place should be given to the modern Indian languages. Subsequently, in Lahore, Hardwar, Shantiniketan and Benaras, even higher education was given through the peoples' own mother tongues.

Mahatma Gandhi suggested that instead of English to be used at the official level in India, Hindustani should be the national language of the country and that English should not be used as the medium of instruction at any stage of education.[126] According to the Resolution of Indian Education Policy of 1904, Calcutta Madrasaha made the vernacular language a compulsory subject of study for the Intermediate examination. "No scholar in a secondary school should, even then, be allowed to abandon the study of his vernaculars, which should be kept up until the end of the school course."[127, 128] The Indian University Commission suggested a serious study of the Indian vernaculars at all stages of education. But the study of Modern Indian languages was not sufficiently emphasised in Indian Universities in 1921-22 owing to an emphasis on English and classical languages.[129] In 1921-1937, when Indian first obtained the control of Educational Department, it was expected that the Modern Indian Languages as media of instruction at the secondary stage would be used but English continued to be the medium in several schools because of its use as the medium of instruction at the University level and because of the medium of examination in 'Government Competitive Examination'. In multilingual areas English was adopted as the medium of instruction. In Hindi-Urdu areas, a departmental order was issued that the Indian languages used for the instruction must be easily understood by Hindi and Urdu speaking pupils. The difficulty of different scripts, viz. Devanagari, Persian and Roman gave rise to a feeling that a 'mixed-language' might develop, which of course will be better than Sanskritised Hindi or Persianised Urdu.[130] English continued to be the medium at University stage.

In 1937, when Provincial autonomy was introduced in eleven provinces of British India, it was suggested that the vernacular languages should so far as possible be the media of instruction throughout the High or Higher secondary schools, but, English should be a compulsory language for all pupils in these schools.[131] The same year, Mahatma Gandhi evolved a scheme of education known as the Wardha Scheme or Basic National Education which envisaged compulsory free education for seven years and for that, the mother tongue was to become the means of instruction. He recommended for wiping off the teaching of English, not only in basic schools but in all schools throughout India, at least till the students have acquired a regular education for seven years through their mother tongue. He also advised to evolve a 'common language' for India.[132] The policy of using the mother tongue as the medium of education in all High schools was reaffirmed in 1944. It was decided that English should be a secondary language in academic as well as technical schools. The mother tongue, English and Modern Languages were decided to be taught as the common subjects.[133] To conclude one may say that the language policy implemented by the Mughal Emperors like Akbar and Aurangzeb in India was changed altogether under the British rule. Even Persian, as the court language was replaced by English. It is unfortunate to note that in spite of the suggestion given in 1837 by Bentinck, the then Governor General of India in favour of vernaculars to be used as the court languages no step was taken in that direction.[134]

History reveals the fact that the Indian vernaculars were always neglected by the British Government. It was in the British regime that Sanskrit, once the spoken language of India was for ever listed as the 'ancient language' of India, mainly because of the deep-rooted desire among the Britishers to crush the Indian languages, civilization and culture. With the result, from time to time, the British Government had to appoint different commissions to suggest the various means and policies, which could be fruitful in bringing peace and harmony between the rulers and the ruled and not for the prosperity or advancement of the native language or literature. But it should not be forgotten that when the printing press was established, it printed books in Indian vernaculars also.

Sharp in his education records [135] observes, that, there existed two different systems of education, according to which two different language policies were in practice. First, as the indigenous system of education in which, classical languages of India and the vernaculars of India were being used as the medium of instruction and as the subjects of study. A number of mission schools taught Indian languages. According to the other system of education in numerous schools, run by the missionaries, English was used as the means of instruction and as one of the subjects of the curriculum. While in some other missionary schools, Western education was given through 'Modern Indian Languages'. These two systems went on peacefully side by side.[136]

The position of different languages, classical, vernaculars and English differed from time to time due to the different policies by different authorities in India. A section of liberal minded English men like Munro, Thompson, Elphinstone, Macdonell, Winternitz, Colebrooke and others were great admirers of oriental literature. They recommended the study of the oriental literature for the other Europeans. One fact must be kept in mind, that, in spite of the pecuniary gains advanced by the Britishers to the English knowing peoples, the Muslims refused to learn it. Majority of the Muslims stressed on the learning of their own languages. Though the British policy regarding teaching of English language was always emphatically implemented, 'Curzon' - the Viceroy of India was not averse to the learning of Indian vernaculars. Mahatma Gandhi the foremost amongst the Indian leaders, laid emphasis on Hindustani, to be used as the means of instruction in High Schools, and recommended to develop a 'common language' - acceptable to all. But, English continued to be used as the medium of instructions in quite a number of schools English occupied a permanent position in the curriculum. Modern Indian languages enjoyed a secondary position and Sanskrit, Arabic and Persian languages were relegated to the position of classical languages.

## D. LANGUAGE SITUATION IN PRE-INDEPENDENCE ERA

It was in 1623 that the East India Company commenced its operation in Indian soil. In the early years of the British rule, the authorities were more concerned with the revival of Indian learning than with imparting of what was known as 'English Education' and what mainly implied the English language as well as the scientific knowledge of the West. The founding of the Calcutta Madrasa in 1781, by Warren Hastings and the Banaras Sanskrit College in 1792 was an attempt to encourage the promotion of Indian learning. The first recognition during the British regime of governmental responsibility for organising general system of education in the country came in 1813 with the provision of Rs. 1 lakh being allotted to education. This grant was intended principally for the advancement of learning in the classical languages such as Sanskrit, Persian and Arabic. During these years it was supposed that the Hindus had as good a system of faith and morals as most people and it would be madness to give them any kind of learning other than what they possessed.[137]

Following the renewal of the Company's Charter in 1813 there took place one of the first great debates relating to the education policy in India. In short, the Orientalist school, wanted to encourage the cultivation of the classical language and literatures of India, whereas the Anglicist or modern school wanted to inculcate knowledge of modern sciences through English language. It was a historic event when Raja Ram Mohan Roy along with others advocated the latter school. Following famous minute recorded by Macaulay in this connection, a resolution was passed in 1835 by William Bentinck, the then Governor-General, laying down that all funds would henceforth be spent in imparting to Indians a knowledge of English literature and science. Notwithstanding this resolution, Wood's Despatch of 1854 (described as the Magna Carta of English Education in India), embodied a clear recognition of the importance of the indigenous language of the country in the educational system. The Despatch while enunciated the aim of education as the diffusion of the improved arts, science, philosophy and literature of Europe laid down that the study of the spoken languages of India was to be encouraged and that both English language and the spoken language of India were to be regarded as the media for the diffusion of European knowledge. It was noted that in the absence of a high order of education in addition to the problem of overcoming the difficulties of a foreign language, the improved European knowledge should be conveyed to them through one or the other vernacular languages. The knowledge thus having been obtained first by the classes undergoing higher education through the medium of English was meant to be percolated to the masses.

There was more promise in the Despatch than was carried out. The literature of Indian languages recorded an impressive development till the thirties of the present century. The period of the 19th century represented a great renaissance in the indigenous literatures but the expression confined itself to poetic compositions of a traditional and semi-religious character. The indigenous languages were not studied as a rule beyond then elementary stage and the higher formalized education of the country was largely through Sanskrit, Persian and Arabic in tols and madrasas. It follows then that certain developmental difficulties in the indigenous languages started growing - a situation which could have been avoided. One finds a parallel situation in Japan after the incursion into Japanese waters in 1857 by Commodore Perry. The zeal behind the advancement of scientific knowledge of the West did not sweep the Japanese people to any limit as to cause a madness in them to overemphasize the real need of the knowledge relevant to West in at the cost of national interest. They retained the Japanese language for that purpose. Systematic steps were taken in Japan to sends out bands of young men for taking education in fields of scientific advance. Gandhiji's reference to this parallel situation (*Harijan*, 1942)[138] was an eye opener for all. In spite of the fact that Japanese script was difficult the Roman script was not adopted by them to have an access to western knowledge. At the same time those who learnt the English language and acquired the knowledge, enriched the Japanese thought with knowledge which the West alone could give.

Of course the situation in Japan and in India was different because

India was by then a British colony and Japan not. The developmental deficiencies that were found inherent in Indian indigenous languages and literature resulted from the practice that was followed in the system of education in the country in subsequent years. The percolation theory, unlike in Japan, did not work here. Education meant to instruct people in Western science which could be imparted at the higher level and through the medium of English language. The greater part of the educational system continued to be the English language, through English medium. The Indian languages, not being used either for purposes of an educational medium or in the higher spheres of administration, judiciary legislation, and Indian public life failed to develop the expressions required for all aspects of life. Thus, the part of Wood's policy regarding use of Indian languages as a medium of instruction for the sciences was not so diligently followed as the one relating to the encouragement of western science.

Consequent upon the demand from politically conscious Indian population for more opportunities for higher education in English, a knowledge of the English language- as distinct from the thought to which it opened an access - was itself looked upon as the key to political advance to begin with and for much better gain for later years in various aspects of life.

One cannot deny the side effect of introduction of English education. With the advent of knowledge of English and of English literature, the Indian languages blazed into a large number of new lines of literary composition, social plays, the short story, the novel, the essay etc. The advent of the printing press resulted in bringing about an unprecedented development of literature in the regional languages. Thus English language gained importance in the Indian soil. While regional languages were being studied in different regions, the position of English as a subject of study was made compulsory., English as a medium of instruction, in addition to the subject of study gained in popularity and use. Sanskrit an Arabic were retained as classical languages of study but occasionally as an option to some other subjects such as science, mathematics and the like.

## E. LANGUAGE SITUATION AFTER INDEPENDENCE

India got independence on 15th August, 1947. The partition of the country which resulted into the displacement of millions and millions of people affected not only the political and economic environment but also the cultural sphere. Likewise it had its impact on education as well.

The so-called 'refugees' belonged to different linguistic groups. Naturally, when they settled here permanently, they looked forward for the protection of their interests not only in education but in services also. Even after partition, the Muslims, whose number far exceeded the number of those who migrated to Pakistan, remained in India. They naturally wished that Urdu-their Mother tongue- should get its due place. On the other side the Indian Intelligentsia felt that the language-policy and the system of education in India should undergo certain changes. Therefore, it was thought necessary that the education policies as well as the language policy of the country should be moulded in a way that could suit, the growing needs and requirements of the country in a sovereign state. English was made the official language of the country, it was also compulsory language of study in the entire educational system or the country.

In fact it was "horizontal bilingualism,[139,140] which prevailed in the administration. English was in use in the Secretariat of the Central Government, provinces and district headquarters, but at sub-district and Tehsil levels, both English and regional languages were in use. At the lowest level only the regional languages were used. The people employed in subordinate services knew their mother tongue and regional language, while the officers who belonged to All India Services were required to know not only English but desirably the mother tongues of the inhabitants of the provinces where they were posted. Instruction in Indian language of the province where they were posted, was an essential part of their training.[141,142,143,144] The knowledge of English was a 'must' since the medium of examination was English. Hindi or Hindustani had a distinguished position, because for certain All India Services, the knowledge,of Hindi/Hindustani used to be compulsory" Particularly the learning of Hindi or Hindustani was obligatory for the defence services us well as for higher services such as the Indian Customs Services (Formerly known as Imperial Customs Services) even during the British rule.[145] Judiciary used both English and regional languages. Above the district level, English was the language of the court, though the permission was granted to give the oral evidence in regional languages if need be. In the district courts, although English and regional languages were used, judgements, decrees and orders were invariably given in English. In lower courts, the regional language was used. Though English occupied an important position because of its continuous use in administration and judiciary yet the regional languages were used simultaneously. In the princely states of the country, Indian languages were used as official and court languages.[146] Since the knowledge of English language was considered essential for higher jobs, naturally it occupied an important place in the field of education. Those, who aspired to join the All India Services tried to join English medium schools. At the same time the national leaders were aware of the view that they must have a common national language. A discussion that was held on the topic and views expressed by some of the members of the parliaments concluded, that, the language which contained more Sanskrit words could become the lingua-franca of the country because Sanskrit was the source of most of the Indian languages. While deciding the language policy of the All India Radio, Hindustani was considered to be the most proper language, since it was understood by the common people and could be written in both Persian and Devnagari characters.[147]

Keeping all these factors in mind, the Government of India then asked the Central Ministry of Education to put forward some of the schemes which could bring certain innovations in the educational system of the country. The Central Ministry of Education, in turn, appointed different committees like an Indology Committee, University Educational Commission, Secondary Education commission, the Committee on Medium of Instruction and so on.[148] On the suggestion of the Indology Committee, the Government of India, decided to preserve the rare manuscripts in Sanskrit, Prakrit, Arabic and Persian, for which, the grant-in-aid was given to the voluntary organisations.[149]

It goes without saying that the position of three language formula is deeply concerned with the educational system of the country. It is incumbent in the Union government and the state governments so far as their legislative and executive powers extend respectively to consider and implement suggestions relating to the educational system with a view to its orientation towards helping to accomplish a solution of the country's language problem. The obligation of the government's administrations machinery is also envisaged in the Article 45 of the Directive Principles of the State Policy in the Indian Constitution, "The State shall endeavour to provide within a period of ten years from the commencement of this Constitution, for free and compulsory education for all children until they complete the age of fourteen years." The education system of the country is the most important formal agency to give effect to the fulfilment of this directive but the educational system cannot function without the proper language to give expression to the State's commitment to educate its citizens.

The Official Language Commission made an apt statement; "In pursuance of this objective the above provision envisages that the entire Indian electorate should undergo a course of education which would equip it for the purpose of taking an interest in the governance of the country." (p.73) The Commission members were unanimous in stating that the task of regional languages in matters of rousing the enthusiasm of the different regions undoubtedly was significant. But in terms of the need for pan-Indian communication, only an Indian language should be adopted. This certainly could not be done by the English language. Henceforth come a strong recommendation suggestive of the constitutional provision already envisaged in the Constitution, that is, the literacy should be given in Hindi so as to enable the common man to take part in the country's affairs. The educational system must therefore be oriented to achieve the imparting of a sufficient literacy in the Hindi language by the age limit of fourteen years, so that every citizen, if so inclined, may be in a position to comprehend and keep in touch with the public affairs.

The decision to use Hindi as the official language of the union was already embodied in the Constitution which was came into force on 26th January, 1950. A little prior to the inauguration of the Constitution but appropriately after the independence of India, the University Education Commission made recommendations, touching the matter of languages. It is surprising to note that although the precise solution embodied in the constitutional provisions bearing upon languages was not before the Commission, as it reported, the Union Education commission suggested that the education of the country would need three languages in its system. Closely following the constitutional directives on language formula which numbered minimally three, came the recommendation of the Secondary Education Commission (1952-53) of the languages to be studied in schools. Soon after these two Commissions, the Official Language Commission was formed by the Government of India to go into the details of the language package that should be implemented in the education system of the schools and colleges. Each of these Commission's recommendations must be carefully examined to arrive at the proper understanding of the language issue.

The recommendations of the University Education Commission touched the matter of languages and showed a full comprehension of the nature of the Indian language problem and the likely directions in which its solutions could be attempted. The recommendations in regard to the medium of education were-

that (i) for the medium of instruction for higher education English be replaced as early as practicable by an Indian language which cannot be Sanskrit on account of vital difficulties;

that (ii) pupils at the higher secondary and University stages be made conversant with three languages- the regional language, the Federal language and English (the last one in order to acquire the ability to read books in English).

that (iii) higher education be imparted through the instrumentality of the regional language with the option to use the federal language as the medium of instruction either for some subjects or for all subjects;

that (iv) English be studied in High schools and in the Universities in order that we may keep in touch with the living stream of ever-growing knowledge.

The recommendations of the Secondary Education Commission should also be examined. The Secondary Education Commission said, "During the Middle school stage a child should be taught at least two languages. English and Hindi should be introduced at the end of the Junior Basic stage, subject to the principle that no two languages should be introduced in the same year." It also observed as regard the study of Hindi - that "In view of its becoming the official language of the centre and of some states, every pupil at the secondary stage should be give an opportunity of acquiring a basic knowledge of the language and it be left to him to develop it according to his needs. From this point of view it is stated that Hindi should be taught during the Middle school or the Senior Basic stage." Furthermore, with reference to the position of language studies, it observes "We however, feel that under the present circumstances it should be possible for a child to learn three languages. It is no doubt true the scripts being different the strain will be a little heavy, but we believe that it is easier for the child to learn these languages at an early than at a later stage." The perspectives of these two Education Commissions and those of the Official Language Commission, though different, the ultimate analysis point out great consistency than inconsistencies amongst these recommendations.

On the basis of these findings, the Central Advisory Board of Education and the Secondary Committee recommended that:—

a) The medium of instruction in the educational institutions should be changed over from English to regional languages although it might cost an extra expenditure on printing of question papers.

b) The teaching of English should start at the end of the Junior Basic stage, i.e. after 5th class and should be compulsory throughout the secondary stage i.e. from VI to X class.

The Committee appointed by the Ministry of Education on the Medium of Instruction reported that in some of the provinces in a number of schools, vernaculars and regional languages substituted English as the medium of instruction. For instance,. in West Bengal, Bengali was introduced in various examinations as the medium of most of the subjects. In erstwhile Coorg though all the English medium sections in Government Secondary schools were converted into Indian language medium sections yet, it was still taught as a compulsory subject in English Middle and High schools. Thus, in a large number of schools although English as medium was discarded as primary and secondary levels, it continued to be taught as one of the compulsory subjects throughout the High school stage in all the provinces.[150]

At the University level English continued to be the medium of instruction due to two main reasons :-

i) The knowledge of English was considered essential for the better prospects of life, for, it was noticed that English knowing intelligentsia had better chances in the All India Services. Therefore, the study of English be continued.

ii) The text books containing advanced knowledge in regional languages were not available. [151]

The question to abolish this foreign language was discussed in the meeting of Central Advisory Board of Education (now onwards it would be known as CABE) and in the All India Educational Conference. It was decided that the replacement of English by some Indian languages should be gradual, for which, a minimum period of five years was considered necessary. It is interesting to note that in the 1st meeting of the CABE and in the All India Educational Conference, held in free India, it was suggested that international scientific terminology in English prevalent at the international level, should be retained and incorporated in Indian languages with the necessary prefixes and suffixes where words with a specific and unambiguous meaning do not exist in the indian languages concerned.[152] In the changed circumstances some reforms in the Marathi, Gujarati and Kannada scripts were thought to be necessary. But, no decision could be taken about any change. Education being a state subject local government[153] could change the language policy according to their requirements. The Board had also postponed to consider the memorandum given by the Madras Government on the use of Roman scripts for learning Hindustani as a lingua-franca for India. The plea taken was, that, it was too early to make a definite recommendation on the matter.[154]

Under such circumstances, the Government of India decided to forgo the study of English by adopting the Basic education at the national level. Since there was no place for English in the syllabus of basic education, it was presumed that the English language taught in other non-basic schools, could easily be replaced by some Indian language. The CABE had already agreed that no provision for teaching English should be made in the junior basic schools i.e. upto class V.[155] For the medium of education, mother tongue was to be used. At the same time, a demand was raised in the country for the formation of province on the linguistic basis. But it was not accepted on the ground that country would become weaker if it was divided into small component elements.

The Secondary Education Committee set up for giving suggestions on the study of different languages, at school level, in 1948, recommended the study of three languages, namely the mother tongue, national or federal language-Hindi and English. It was decided that mother tongue should be taught compulsorily for the first five years i.e. at the Junior Basic stage., Federal language (Hindi) was supposed to be learnt for the next3 years, i.e. in VI, VII and VIII classes and English was to be introduced after VIII class and was to continue for a 4 years i. e. throughout the secondary stage, as long as, it remains the medium of instruction in the University.[156,157] It was also suggested that the study of three languages was desirable at the school level. Out of these three languages, mother tongue should be the first language; federal language should be the second and English should be taught as the third language with the condition that the federal language Hindi, different from the mother tongue should not be introduced earlier than class III. The appropriate period for the inclusion of federal language in the school syllabus was considered to be from III to V Class. Since English was given 3rd position, it ceased to be taught at primary level in most of the schools. In Uttar Pradesh, English started to be taught from VI class instead of Class III. Orissa introduced the teaching of Hindi in middle schools. In Bihar also the study of a language other than the mother tongue was declared compulsory for the minorities.[158] In Delhi, Punjabi was introduced in the vernacular middle schools.[159,160] In Madras also, a decision was taken in favour of the study of vernaculars *pari-passu* with English in schools. Besides English, students, were required to learn Regional language and one of the four languages viz. Hindi, Sanskrit, Arabic and Persian.[161, 162] As a result the students were supposed to learn three languages simultaneously.[163] But, all these three languages were not assigned the same status in the schools curriculum. Throughout the secondary stage, regional language as the 1st language, Hindi as a second language and English as the 3rd language were prescribed in the school syllabus.[164]

At many places it was noticed, that, though the instructions were given to make provisions to teach mother tongue if it was different from the regional language in practice, it was not followed. The students were compelled to study the regional languages or those mother tongues only which were available to opt for. For example Urdu, the mother tongue of some non-Bengali Muslim of West Bengal was by order replaced by state language - Bengali, in Sakhawat Memorial Girls High school. An institution was established for the Muslim students whose mother tongue was Urdu.[165]

The pursuance of this language policy could be dangerous for the peace of the country, as much as. it denied the legitimate claims for the mother tongue,. The Government therefore issued the orders in Bengal to open two sections in each class one for Bengali medium and the other for Urdu medium with Bengali as a compulsory subject.[166] The CABE was also against the retention of English medium in the educational institutions and as such it recommended the use of mother tongue as the common medium at middle and high school stages of education.[167] In the meeting of the Provincial Ministers Conference held in Delhi in August 1949, it was decided that for the medium of instruction especially at the school level mother tongue should be used. The regional language was however to be a compulsory subject throughout the secondary stage.[168]

These changes made in the school curriculum, did not affect the curriculum at higher level of education. In January 1948, the Government of India appointed a committee to consider the medium of instruction at higher level. In this committee, headed by Dr. Tara Chand, the then Education Adviser to the Government of India, the decision was taken in favour of Indian languages to replace English as the medium of instruction. Certain difficulties in this sort of replacement were also envisaged, for instance, the lack of suitable textbooks and technical terms in Indian languages and in international communication. The lack of unanimity regarding the use of Indian languages also helped in the constitution of English medium. In spite of that, the Calcutta University allowed the students for the Intermediate, B.A.(Pass), B.Sc. and B.A. Commerce; to answer their papers in one of the two media viz. Bengali and English. The Banaras Hindu University adopted Hindi as the additional medium of instruction in all the subjects except in English and Modern Indian Languages. Nagpur University decided to have Hindi or Marathi as the medium of instruction from 1950 for both Intermediate Arts and Science courses, while Sagar University decided in favour of Hindi medium to be introduced from 1950 onwards.[169, 170]

It was also suggested by the committee that within five years from 1950 English medium should be replaced by Modern Indian Languages, but no heed was paid to that. The Committee further suggested a compulsory test in Hindi during the 1st degree course of the University but passing the examination was not considered necessary. The Committee recommended the use of Devanagari script for English language. In case of regional language, the use of Devanagari script, besides their own scripts was suggested. But, the use was discretionary on the part of the State Governments. Subsequently no common scripts could be developed.

From among the different dialects of Hindi, such as Avadhi, Maithili and Bhojpuri etc. western Hindi was considered to be the largest group because the maximum number of variations/ dialects of Hindi language, like Brij Bhasha, High Hindi, Maithili, Magadhi, Bhojpuri and Urdu were/are considered to be closely allied to western Hindi. Even Urdu, having a totally different script is considered to be closely related to this Hindi. The provincial governments therefore were advised to take steps to prescribe the teaching of federal language-Hindi, not only in all the classes of higher secondary schools but in degree colleges and universities as well.[171]

The Radha Krishnan Commissions (now onwards it would be referred as R.K. Commission) further expressed the view that, since India is a multi-lingual country, due importance and recognition should be given to all the languages rich in vocabulary and literature.[172] That would enable every region and province to take its proper share in the administrative activities of the Government which, ultimately will promote inter-provincial understanding and solidarity.[173] To achieve this aim, the R.K. Commission recommended that the students were required to learn one of the regional languages besides Hindi- the federal language. In case, the mother tongue and the regional language were the same, a provision was made to teach either the classical language or one of the Modern Indian Languages different from Hindi. Since Sanskrit the classical language is the ancient language it was advised to be taught in place of Modern Indian Language.[174] After a great discussion it was added as the 14th language in the Constitution of India. For maintaining contacts with other countries and to keep in touch with the advanced knowledge, the R.K. Commission further advocated the study of one more language which could be used at the international level. Those days, English was the only foreign language used as the official language. Naturally, the suggestion for the study of one of the international languages had gone in favour of English. Though the R.K. Commission agreed with the views expressed by the Secondary Education Committee in 1948, that the predominent position of English during the British period had been the main cause for the illiteracy of the masses and for the poor development of Indian languages, yet its study was declared essential for the students at both the school and college levels. Moreover, the motto of our country was to create a classless society[175] in a Sovereign Democratic Republic[176] where the Government of India had already committed to give equal opportunities to all the citizens.[177] the learning of English was made compulsory for all. Pandit Nehru, the then Prime Minister said, "But the fact remains that from the point of view of both convenience and utility, English is obviously the most important languages for us.[178]

Keeping into consideration the position enjoyed by English language, even after independence discussions were held in the Constituent Assemblies and CABE, to give it a permanent recognition in the Constitution of India,[179] but that could not be materialised because of its being a foreign language.[180] Pandit Nehru, also observed, "But it will have to be inevitably a secondary language meant for a relatively restricted number of people."[181] In spite of the fact that the Commission advised to retain the study of English permanently in the universities because of its being an international language,* the facility was given to the students for learning a European language – French/German in lieu of English if they desired so in the secondary schools.[182] The Commission not only agreed with the suggestion of the Secondary Education Committee set up in 1948, regarding the obligatory study of three languages viz. mother tongue/regional language, Hindi and English compulsorily at the school level but advised to make the study obligatory at the college level too.[183] It was also decided that all these three languages should neither be introduced simultaneously into the same class, nor should be continued in XI and XII as they are considered to be the outgoing classes.[184]

Regarding the medium of instruction, the RK Commission recommended the use of mother tongue as the medium of education in the schools. The Secondary Education Committee had already given its opinion in favour of mother tongue as the medium of education. "If India is to be a Sovereign Democratic Republic[185] in true sense; then every citizen should be given a right to get his/her education through the medium of his/her mother tongue.[186] In case of linguistic minorities, the Commission suggested that the school authorities should make special arrangements for teaching through mother tongue if the number of the students opting for a particular language comes to 40. Even a separate school could be established for this purpose if the number of such students in the school was sufficient and the medium of instruction in such school was to be the language of the pupils.[187,188] Subsequently the CABE advised the Provincial Governments to make necessary arrangements for imparting education through mother tongue, especially in the metropolitan cities where the mobility of the people speaking different languages was higher. They were also asked to recognise such schools where education was imparted through the mother tongue of the students.[189] After 5th class, Sampurnananda, the well-known educationist and the Chairman of the CABE suggested that "It is right, proper, necessary and urgent that the language of the province should be the common medium of instruction for the people."[190] Consequently the school authorities were advised, that, for switching over from English to the medium of regional language an option should be given to the students to answer either in mother tongue or regional language for the first two years after the junior or basic school.[191]

For the higher level of education, it was decided that English should be retained as the medium of instruction. "This Conference resolves that in the University stage of Education, English be retained as the medium of instruction till the regional languages are developed to take its place;[192] although the aim was to be the replacement of English by an Indian language as the medium of instruction. The R.K. Commission further advised not to sacrifice standard of teaching and learning for this change over.[193] It was also recommended that the scientific terminology in English or in some international language should be retained so that a contact between the scientific developments in other countries may be maintained.[194, 195]

The Government of India examined the report of RK Commission and accepted its recommendations. The Universities and the Provincial

Governments were therefore asked to take early steps for their implementation.[196] Even though there was a desire to do away with English - the official language, still they were not prejudiced against the teaching of some of the 'Foreign Languages including English. On 1st February, 1949, a 'School of foreign languages' was started where instruction were given in French, Persian, Chinese, Arabic, Russian and German. Though the school was meant for the armed forces yet, it was kept open [197,198] for the admission of the officers from other Ministries too.

In pursuance of the recommendations given by the Radha Krishnan Commission in 1948-49, the Government of West Bengal made arrangements in the schools for teaching Hindi, Urdu, Gujarati, Assamese, Oriya and Tamil upto Matriculation stage. Facilities were provided for teaching through these languages. It was also advised to start separate classes for them in case the number of the students speaking a particular language fulfilled the requirement regarding the number.[199] In Bombay, facilities were provided for teaching in Marathi, Gujarati, Canarese (Kannada) and Urdu.[200] The Uttar Pradesh Government recognised Bengali, Gujarati and Marathi as media of instruction at Secondary stage in addition to Hindi, which was the recognised medium of instruction at that stage. Sampurnananda, the then Education Minister of U.P. conveyed at the meeting that the use of Urdu as medium of education would not be in the interest of the students, for, Hindi was to become the medium of instruction at all the levels of education in the coming 5 years. He, further explained, that, Urdu was not the language of any province and as such no minority could claim it as its language.[201] Even then the Government of Punjab made arrangements for introducing Urdu medium.[202] In spite of Tamil being the regional language, Madras Government provided the facilities for teaching upto matriculation, through Kannada, Malayalam and Telugu also. In all other states only the regional language was the recognised medium of instruction.[203] It might be interesting to note that Hindi was taught as one of the subjects in Madras even before independence. "It is gratifying to learn that Hindi is increasingly spreading in Tamil Nadu", so said Pandit Nehru.[204] Later, the Madras Government sent a proposal for teaching Hindustani in the Roman or Regional script in the regions where Hindustani was not the regional language. Although the proposal was accepted by the Board, it was resolved that the script of the language must be taught to the students either in the schools or at the college level.[205]

Since most of the provinces remained indifferent towards the suggestions given by the RK Commission, it was felt necessary, that, unless some steps were taken in this direction at the Central level, the result might not be satisfactory. The Government of India, therefore, reviewed all the recommendations and wanted to implement certain policies of education regarding the teaching of languages as suggested by the Radha Krishnan Commission, for which the requisite provisions were made in the Constitution of India. The Preamble of the Constitution states that the people of India resolved to constitute the country into a Sovereign Democratic Republic giving her citizens their fundamental rights to conserve distinct language and script.[206] Not only an assurance was given to the minorities to protect their interests[207] but 'Education' was placed in the 'State List' in the Constitution of India.[208] Obviously 'Education' was declared as a 'State-subject' giving freedom to the states to mould the curricula of their educational institutions according to their requirements. The minorities were given not only the right to establish their educational institutions for the progress of their own languages, culture and religion but, the State Governments were also asked not to discriminate at the time of giving grant to such educational institutions.[209] The Constitution further provides the safeguard to the interests of minorities by declaring that the President may direct the State to give official recognition to a language if he was satisfied that it was spoken by a substantial proportion of population in that particular state.[210] One more Article 350-A was included in the interest of minorities according to which facilities were to be provided for the instruction in mother tongue at the primary stage of education to children belonging to linguistic minority groups.[211,212]

Keeping in view the multilingual character and different racial elements in the country, the Government recognised 14 major languages to which Sindhi was later added by an amendment in the constitution.[213] Thus, it was clear that these 15 languages [214] were given equal status. Since all these 15 major languages of the country could not be used at the official level due to practical difficulties Hindi in Devanagari script was recognised as the official language,[215] although from the commencement of the Constitution, for a period of 15 years English numerals and English language were to be continued at the official level. Though, Hindi was not considered rich enough to be used immediately as the official language yet, it was to replace English language because "the vocabulary, diction, alphabetical system or script of Hindi is much more akin to the other Indian languages than

English."[216] In case, Hindi was developed to the extent that it could occupy the place of the official language, then the President could direct the use of Hindi language and Devanagari forms of numerals in addition to English with the international forms of Indian numerals for any or all the official purposes of the Union.[217] The Parliament could pass a law for retaining the use of English or for using the Devanagari numerals for the purposes mentioned in the law after the said period of 15 years. [218] The English language was to be continuously used not only at the official level of the country but in the Supreme Court and the High Courts also.[219] Besides, the Bills introduced in both the Houses of the Parliament and in the Houses of the legislature of a state would be in English. Acts passed at both the central and state levels would be in English.[220] Although the English had been given the highest status by its continuous use at the official level, in the courts and in the proceedings of the Parliament, a special clause was inserted in the Constitution of India to bring the other languages at par with the English language. It is articulated in one of the clauses that with the previous consent of the President, the Governor of a particular state may authorise the use of Hindi or any other official language of the state in the proceedings of the High Court. But the judiciary, while giving decrees, orders and judgements would use English only.[221] Under similar directives the bills introduced in and the acts passed could also be in a language other than the English language, with the condition that a translation of the same in the English language will be published in the official Gazette of that State. [222] Though the Constitution has recognised the use of English language for 15 years for the administration of the country and as the language of the 'Highest Court' in India yet, the provision was made to give freedom to the person to use any language used at the Centre or in the State for getting redressed his grievances.[223] Obviously besides the use of English and Hindi the Constitution emphasised and gave the privilege of using the mother tongue also.[224]

For communication purposes, at inter-state level and between a State and the Union, the Constitution provided the use of English with the provision that the States were free to use Hindi or any other language, if their legislatures passed such a law.[225]

Thus, English by its continuous use, retained its eminent position by superseding Hindi. With the result the demand of English schools became more pertinent. Even in the schools, where vernaculars were taught, students wished that they knew English. Naturally, it occupied the primary position in the syllabi of educational institutions, because the aspiring students had high hopes to get Government jobs if they had enough knowledge of this language. It was envisaged that after 1965, Hindi was to be used at the Centre for all official purposes within or after 15 years, from the commencement of the Constitution. It was also considered an essential subject for the study and because the instruction till primary level was supposed to be given in the mother tongue of the child,[226] the knowledge of that too became inevitable for the students. Obviously the study of three languages viz. Hindi, English and Modern Indian Language has been declared in the Constitution of India.

By protecting the fundamental rights of her citizens the Government had an obligation to develop all the Indian languages, especially Hindi — the official language.[227] It was calculated that 3,50,000 new terms had to be evolved to keep pace with the advanced knowledge in English. The Ministry of Education, therefore, in 1950 constituted a Board of Scientific Terminology which helped in developing the vocabulary in Hindi as well as in other regional languages.[228] By 1961, 2,90,000 words had been evolved.[229] For the propagation of Hindi, the Government of India adopted a number of measures. For instance a basic grammar of Modern Hindi was prepared, the keyboards for Hindi typewriters and teleprinters were designed and the suitable short hand notations for Hindi and other modern Indian languages were undertaken for designing. Besides, Hindi was introduced in the school curricula in almost all the States and Union Territories. That resulted in an increased demand of Hindi teachers. Various steps were taken to promote Hindi in states like Assam, e.g. Hindi which was taught as a compulsory subject upto class VIII, was declared as a compulsory subject upto class X, but optional in class XI.[230] In the Telangana area, Hindi used to be taught as a compulsory subject from class IV and from class VI in some parts of Andhra Pradesh. In some of the schools of Andhra Pradesh, it was taught as an optional subject in Class IV and V. As the form and structure of written language differs from syntactic form of spoken language, the University Education Commission advised to draw a distinction between the written and spoken forms of Hindi. It was decided by the University Education Commission in 1948-49,[231] that the written form of Hindi should draw more from the parent language — Sanskrit so as to bring it closer to the languages of non-Hindi speaking areas,such as Bengal, Assam and Maharashtra etc., while the spoken form of Hindi should be made easier so that it should be commonly understood.[232] Consequently, the

Government of India introduced an Article in the Constitution whereby emphasis was laid on the efforts to be made for the enrichment of Hindi language by drawing primarily on Sanskrit and secondarily on other languages.[233] Since a decision had already been taken by the Government of India that the associate official language English would be replaced by Hindi within fifteen years from the commencement of the Constitution in case, Hindi was enriched to the extent that it would be used for the official purposes of the Union,[234] it was decided by the CABE, that special efforts and extensive preparations had to be made for this change over throughout the country, particularly in those areas, where the regional language was not Hindi. For instance, a special officer in the State of Trivandrum was appointed who was advised to take active measures for teaching Hindi in the Schools. It was also recommended that the number of the periods for teaching Hindi should be increased in the schools of non-Hindi areas.[235] The Board further advised that the efforts for popularising Hindi should be made not only for those who were to be recruited in Government jobs in future but among those also who were already in Government services. For such Government employees, who were not conversant with Hindi and for those whose mother tongue was different from Hindi; it was thought essential that a course in Hindi for a period of 6 months to a year may be instituted, because, all the Government employees were required to pass a test in Hindi. In 1952, Hindi classes for non-Hindi knowing Central Government employees were started at three centres in New Delhi and in 1953 some more classes were opened.[236,237] Prizes were also recommended for those who attained proficiency in regional languages of the areas where they were posted,[238] and for those, who aspired for Government jobs, the following suggestions were given:-

i) At the time of recruitment in Central Services it was suggested that a compulsory paper in Hindi for all the examinations should be introduced and passing in it should be made obligatory;
ii) Prizes should be awarded to those, whose mother tongue was not Hindi, but, who acquired proficiency in Hindi;
iii) At the level of Higher Education in non-Hindi areas, a Hindi-Department should be opened in the Universities so that the students, who wish to study the language, may have the necessary facilities to opt for it. Subsequently it swelled the demand for text-books of graduate and post-graduate levels. For meeting this challenging demand, the universities, wishing to take the

publication work of Hindi books required at the graduate and post-graduate levels should be granted monetary help by the Government of India and a prize should be instituted for the author of the best Hindi publications for the year.

iv) The Government should encourage and support the agencies who make voluntary efforts in this direction.[239]

Subsequently, efforts for propagation of Hindi were made on official and non-official levels. For instance, a new Hindi section was both opened on the official level, in the Ministry of Education, and a central organisation called the Hindi Shiksha Samiti was set-up on the non-official level to advise the Ministry for the development and promotion of Hindi language, especially in non-Hindi areas.[240] Efforts were also made to develop Modern Indian Languages for protecting the interests of linguistic minorities and to preserve Sanskrit and other classical languages like Persian and Arabic etc. Naturally, it gave rise to such questions as to how many languages out of those recognised by the Constitution of India, should be taught at different levels of education and what languages should be used as the media of instruction in schools and colleges. The more pertinent question was to decide the place of two official languages viz. English and Hindi, in the School curriculum. The CABE therefore advised the Government of India to appoint a Commission on Secondary Education to give its consistent views on these issues.

The Commission, appointed in 1952-53 observed that, besides Hindi, English and one of the Modern Indian Languages, the Study of Sanskrit a language preserving the Indian culture and religion was also necessary. With the result, the number of languages to be learnt compulsorily in the schools varied from three to five in different states. Firstly, in the regions, where Hindi was/is the mother tongue, regional as well as the language of the Centre, the number of the languages to be learnt will be three only, namely, Hindi as the mother tongue, regional language and the language of the Union; English as one of the international language and Sanskrit the classical language. Secondly, in the regions, where Hindi is the regional language but not the mother tongue of the people, the students would be required to learn one more language, besides the three mentioned above, for, the mother tongue was different from Hindi which continued to be the regional and official language. Thirdly, in the non-Hindi speaking states, where the mother tongue, regional language and the federal language were not the same but three different languages, the students would have to learn five languages. Naturally, there was no uniformity in the syllabus of the school curriculum as far as the teaching of languages was concerned. Since the Commission observed that a definite policy of teaching languages should be laid down,[241] which could be implemented throughout the country, it was thought proper that the importance of the languages decided to be taught in the schools, should be reconsidered.

For obvious reasons, the highest importance among all the languages was given to mother tongue. Regarding the importance of learning 'regional language' the Commission suggested that the students should acquire the knowledge of this language too, for, it was generally used by the majority of the people in that region. The study of Sanskrit was also thought to be necessary, because, it was the source of most of the Indian languages and had appealed from the cultural and religious points of views. It was also recommended that the facilities should be provided for teaching other classical languages such as Persian, Arabic, and Latin.

While discussing the importance of teaching English on compulsory basis, the members of the Commission were divided. One group advocating for the study of English argued that for keeping the country in touch with the advanced knowledge of science in other countries, the knowledge of English should become indispensable.

The other group opposed it on the ground that the greater importance given to English in the past had not only hindered the growth of modern Indian languages but had been a great cause for the subsequent neglect of different subjects in the school curricula. "It is unnatural and inconsistent to have a foreign language as a compulsory subject at any level education."[242] But keeping in view the advantages of learning English, it was decided that it should continue to occupy an important place in the curricula of secondary schools, [243,244] where it could be taught as a compulsory subject for a period of 5-6 years after the basic stage of education i.e., after the first 7 or 8 years of a child's education.[245] Referring to the other countries, like the U.S.S.R., Japan and France, where facilities are provided for learning more than one foreign language, the Commission suggested that the provisions should be made for teaching other foreign languages in India too.

As English played the role of a 'link-language' in the country, under the British rule, it was decided unanimously, that, if English was to be replaced, the country would again be in need of some 'link' or 'common' language with a common script.[246] Since Hindi is the Official language of the Centre and as such is expected to become the lingua-franca of the country, [247,248] the Commission advised to take steps for making Hindi compulsory, as a part of the school curriculum, [249,250] because it would promote national unity and solidarity.[251] Consequently, almost all the States and Union-Territories introduced Hindi as a subject of study in the curricula of their schools. Due to the autonomy given to States in the field of 'education'[252] (Education being the State subject) disparity with regard to study was natural. For instance, in some of the States Union Territories, it remained a compulsory subject but not necessarily as medium of instruction. While in others, the result of the examination in Hindi language was not considered for promotion to the next class. There were other states also, where instructions were given to the schools to provide the facilities for compulsory teaching of Hindi language to the students but it was left on the choice of the students, whether to opt for it or not. Besides, Hindi was not considered a subject for examination in these schools.

For the development of Hindi and its popularisation in non-Hindi speaking areas as well as among the Members of Parliament financial grants were given by the Central Government to different agencies promoting the cause of Hindi and to the needy Hindi writers in non-Hindi areas. In regional languages also, the Government of India gave awards to the authors of books written in Indian languages.[253,254] An assurance was also given to extend help to promising writers and publishers in all the Indian languages (recognised by the Constitution of India)[255] The Commission regretted to say that the language teachers were not only paid poorly but, hardly knew the pedagogy of languages. With the result, students seldom took initiative and interest in learning Hindi in non-Hindi areas.

On the educational side in particular the Commission had a discussion on the issues of language to be used as the medium of instruction in the schools. In 1949, the CABE had already passed a resolution that the mother tongue was is the best medium of education. The Commission, therefore, recommended that it should be followed at least upto the primary level of education.

On the advice of CABE and following the suggestion of the Secondary Education Commission in 1952, in most of the Secondary Schools under Government management in some states the medium of education was changed from English to Hindi 'regional languages. It was expected that the use of the Indian languages as the medium of instruction would be helpful in raising the standard, of education. Unfortunately the standard of both teaching and learning deteriorated.

Immediately, an Advisory Council for Secondary Education was set-up to find out the cause responsible for the fall of academic standard in the schools and to advise the Central and State Governments to take corrective measures. It was suggested that one of the reasons for the fall of standard was the removal of English from the list of the compulsory subjects in the schools.[256] The Council therefore recommended that the provision should be made for compulsory teaching of three languages at the secondary stage. Two different formulas were suggested for the said purpose. In one of the two variations of the three language formula, a choice was given to the State Government to opt for one language either of the four combinations namely, mother tongue/regional language, a composite course of mother tongue and regional language; a composite course of mother tongue and classical language or a composite course of regional language and classical language. Hindi or English was to be taught as the 2nd language and for the 3rd language a choice was given to opt for one of the Modern Indian languages or Modern European languages on the condition that it should be different from the 1st and 2nd languages. The result was that neither the knowledge of English, nor the learning of any other Modern European language was compulsory for the students at any level of education. While in the other variation of the three language formula, not only the learning of English/Modern European language was thought to be compulsory, but the knowledge of Hindi was also considered indispensable for non-Hindi speaking students and the knowledge of one of the Modern Indian languages besides the language taken as 1st and 2nd language, was declared compulsory for Hindi speaking students. As for the medium of instruction the Council advised to retain mother tongue/regional languages at the secondary level of education.

On this suggestion for compulsory teaching of three languages, the State Governments were asked to give their consent and adopt either of the three language formulas given by the Council. Being the language of the Union, though Hindi occupied the primary place yet it was still considered poor in vocabulary. It was observed that Hindi was not rich enough to replace English as the official language of the country even after the expiry of 5 years from the commencement of the Constitution though the President of India in 1955, circulated an order with regard to the use of Hindi language and Devanagari form of numerals in addition to the English language and the international form of numerals for the official purposes. The order provided for the use of Hindi while corresponding with the other countries and international organisation and the formal documents to be issued to the diplomatic officers were also supposed to be in Hindi.[257] The Government of India, therefore, in pursuance of Article 344 of the Constitution of India in 1956 appointed a Commission known as the Official Language Commission so that definite views and recommendations could be given with regard to the development of Hindi – the Union language and teaching of languages in the educational institutions. The Commission observed, that, for maintaining the high academic standard the knowledge of English should be made essential for the students. In other countries too, the Commission said, that for keeping abreast of scientific advances in the world, an advanced foreign language was taught as a 2nd language in their educational system and English as the 2nd language was the choice of many countries.

As there were significant purposes, of teaching a foreign language, the Commission advised to mark distinction between the two different purpose of teaching English as a foreign language. For instance, while teaching it for using the language for special purposes, English should be taught as a subject and principally as a language of comprehension. But if the purpose was to use English as the principal or general medium of education and administration as well as of public life, and the day to day business of the country, then it should be taught as a 2nd but in literary form. Whatever might be the purpose the study of English should not be made compulsory but should be taught as an optional subject and that too, to the students who were willing to pursue higher studies, English would have to be cultivated by appropriate categories of persons.[258] The duration of the period for learning/teaching was limited to 5 years at the secondary stage i.e. before the school leaving certificate examination. Since English was not taught in the Basic schools, the students passing out of Senior Basic schools could not seek admission to High Schools. The CABE recommended to introduce English into Senior Basic Schools in the corresponding classes of High Schools.[259] Perceiving the importance of teaching English the Commission gave its consent in favour of the legitimate demand for including English language into the VIII Schedule of the Constitution of India.[260] The Commission also advised the Government to make a provision to empower the presiding authority for permitting the Members of the Parliament to address the House in English if they were unable to express in Hindi/mother tongue even after 15 years of the commencement of the Constitution.[261] Thus, the importance given to English language, on one side raised the status of the language and on the other side, the number of the students opting this language increased more and more.

About the teaching of Union language and other Modern Indian Languages, the Commission referred to the Article 45 in the Constitution according to which free and compulsory education was to be given to the children till the age of 14 years. During this period of eight years of compulsory schooling, the students were supposed to learn two languages, viz., mother tongue in the first 4-5 years, and Hindi in the next 3-4 years. It was also decided that the students should acquire sufficient literacy in Hindi so that they might be in a position to comprehend and keep in touch with the activities of not only the Union Government but with the trends and movements of public life at an India level. Therefore, the Commission recommended that the study of Hindi language should be declared indispensable for all the citizens of the free country,[262] but, the level at which it had to be made compulsory, should be left to the discretion of the State Governments.

The Commission further suggested that the students, who took their education after the 8 years of compulsory schooling, should continue learning of Hindi language with English till they finished their S.L.C. examination. Obviously in their case, the period of learning Hindi, would automatically be increased by one or two years more than the period of learning English language. Furthermore, the Commission pointed out that the suggestion given by the people in Hindi speaking States that they must learn one of the South Indian languages as the 3rd language in the schools was rejected by the southern representatives.[263]

Replying to the argument that the South Indian candidates would ultimately have to learn Hindi – a language of a different family which, the candidates from Hindi speaking states would not have to do, the commission said that the former would have constant occasion to use Hindi in the discharge of their duties. On the contrary, Hindi speaking students might not necessarily have the opportunity to use a language belonging to Dravidian family. The Commission also rejected the suggestion of adopting two Union languages one from the Aryan family and the other from the Dravidian family.[264]

In spite of these arguments the Commission suggested that the learning of one of the South Indian languages should remain in the list of optional subjects for Hindi speaking students but attempts should be made on voluntary basis all over the country for the learning of South Indian languages and acquiring the knowledge of South Indian civilization and culture. Regarding the ancient languages like Sanskrit, Pali, Prakrit, and Apabhramsa etc., the Commission felt concerned over their strong influence on current Indian languages and as such, it was decided that Sanskrit and other ancient languages should be studied systematically by the students. Since the issue was separately under the consideration of Government, the Commission did not express any views on this matter. The efforts were to be made to develop Hindi the Union language in a way that it could be used as a coherent force in the different ministries and departments.[265]

Though, the Official Language Commission suggested that the statutes of the Government should necessarily be written in Hindi, yet it did not recommend the restrictions to be imposed on the use of English for any of the purposes of the Union Government. Further, it recommended that all the Government statutes in English should be translated not only in Hindi but in other Regional languages too.[266] Regarding the use of the forms of numerals, the Commission left the choice on the State Governments to use either the international form or their own forms of numerals for the internal purposes of State administration. At the Central level the international forms of numerals were supposed to be used.[267] The Roman as well as the numerals in regional languages could be used.

For developing new terminology in Indian languages, the Commission advised to explore the indigenous terms current in the past and the terms which were currently used at present in day- to-day life. The international terminology should be retained only, when such terms were not available provided they should be simple and precise.

Although the Commission realised, that, ultimately the entire proceedings including the judgments and decrees of the Supreme Court would be in Hindi, their authoritative translations should be available in the language of the concerned party whose mother tongue was not Hindi. In the High Court also, the language used would be Hindi and if necessary a translation of the same should be provided in regional languages while in the Lower Courts, the proceedings should continue in the languages best understood by the people as was the practice in the past also. For instance, in some of the Indian princely states like Baroda, Gwalior, Hyderabad, Jammu and Kashmir and Patiala not only the Lower Courts but the High Courts also had been working in in their regional languages even at the time of the integration of the states into the Indian Union by 1950. Although the use of Hindi the Union language and regional language was suggested for the proceedings of the Courts, the commission concluded that for maintaining the judicial unity, the entire Statute book of the country should be available in Hindi language facilitating inter-state communication.

Regarding the language to be used as the medium of instruction, the Commission observed that only 1% of the total population had linguistic ability in English language. It therefore could not be used as the general medium of education at national level. Although Sanskrit happened to be the parent language of most of the Indian languages yet for practical problems it also could not be used as medium throughout India.

The obvious linguistic medium for all India purposes is Hindi language, because, it is not only the language to be used between the Union and the state or at inter-state communication level but has been recognised as the language of the Union also. Besides, the number of the people who can understand and speak the language is higher than those of other regional languages. Since the other Indian languages have been given appropriate and similar place as to Hindi language in the Constitution of India, their claim of being used as the medium of education cannot be ignored. It is possible that the regional languages may be adopted as the media of instruction at the lower level of education and a common medium of Hindi or English may be followed at the higher level of education.[268] It was suggested that some courses in Humanities might be taught in the regional languages and for subjects of common interest Hindi might be the suitable medium. In other faculties, particularly in higher courses of science and research, English might be the appropriate language to be continued as the medium. For legal education, the Commission advised, that the facilities should be provided for teaching through both Hindi and regional languages. Although the Commission advocated the autonomy of the Universities, it was suggested that the decisions taken by the Universities, with regard to the medium, should be according to the National Language Policy. Though the Commission suggested that for removing the alienation between the educated class from the rest of the community English medium at higher level of education should be replaced by some Indian language · languages. In the educational institutions of science and technology two languages viz., Hindi and regional languages should be followed as the media of education. The common medium of Hindi language should be adopted for the students coming from different linguistic regions and for the students coming from one and the same linguistic regions, their regional language should be used as the medium of their education. In fact, for achieving the linguistic equilibrium, the linguistic pattern and the linguistic media must be allowed freedom to develop not only in response to the needs and requirement of the situation, but also on the opportunities available for the learners.[269] The Commission further pointed out that in the personal and social dealings in national life at pan-India levels a single linguistic medium was of the highest significance.

In the field of the Public Service Examinations, the Commission realised that the media of these examinations should be the same as that of the educational system of the country. After the independence, since most of the States in the country shifted from English medium to the media of regional languages, the media of Public Service Examinations, should also be the regional languages. It was pointed out that it might result into the decentralisation of the entrance examination and later on it might create a necessity of introducing a 'quota system' for the purposes of recruitment to All India Services. It was further explained that under the 'quota system' the allotment of vacancies would be by languages offered as the medium for the examinations and not by domicile in the linguistic state.

It was further clarified by the Commission that a non-Hindi speaking candidate offering Hindi medium and Hindi speaking candidate opting other than the Hindi medium would have the right to compete under the said system. The Commission also considered the case of Hindi speaking candidates, who were/are benefited for not appearing in the compulsory paper in Hindi, which would be indispensable for the non-Hindi speaking candidates. It was suggested that to counterbalance the advantage gained by the Hindi speaking students by not appearing in the compulsory paper in Hindi, they might be required to offer a paper from the following group of subjects – Anthropology, South Indian History, South Indian Literature or such other cultural subjects on South India or an Indian language from the VIII Schedule other than Hindi and the medium of writing this paper would be the same as the linguistic medium of general examination. The Commission further suggested that a provision should be made for testing the candidates in English language even after the medium was changed from English to regional languages. The result was that English continued to be the medium of education in non-Hindi speaking states while it was replaced by Hindi in Hindi speaking states.[270] Subsequently, the students had to learn not only three languages but their distinct scripts as well. To minimise the burden of learning three scripts, the Commission discussed the possibility of adopting a common script for all the languages. Even the eminent national leaders and thinkers like Tilak, Gandhi, Nehru and others reflected on this issue and advocated for the adoption of a common script adopted for writing all the Indian languages, for, it would further the cause of unity and integration of the people belonging to different linguistic groups. Besides, it would facilitate the learning of three languages in all the regions. A 'Parishad' known as 'Eklipi Vistar Parishad' was also started under the patronage of some of the judges, like Justice Mitra, Iyear and others.[271] Out of the two scripts – Devanagari and Roman, the former was preferred as the best known script, because, almost all the Indian scripts including Devanagari had not only been derived from the Brahmi script but had almost the same alphabet as that of Brahmi. Among the scripts of the Indian languages, except in Tamil, Devanagari was the script which accounted for the largest number of such alphabets and as such, it had the strongest claim for adoption as the common script. The Commission, therefore recommended that the other Indian languages should also be written in Devanagari script in addition to their own scripts.[272] On the other hand, the Roman was discarded because there were no practical advantages to be gained.[273] For the development of the Union language and other regional languages the Commission recommended that an autonomous body in the form of a National Academy of Indian Languages as a single agency should be set up. The members of this agency should be the representatives from the Union and State Governments, Universities and literary associations in different regional languages. Besides, a Central Library of literature of all Indian languages and a National Institute for training of language teachers should also be established.[274] The Commission concluded by suggesting that for the citizens of a polyglot country, study in different languages should be encouraged.

Although in the context of our modern needs the CABE advised the State Governments to introduce the compulsory teaching of three languages in the Secondary Schools, they were asked to exempt the students from the compulsory from the teaching of regional language in the Anglo Indian Schools provided the students learnt the Union language Hindi. It was argued that the parents of those students being the Government employees were supposed to be transferred from one state to another. Besides the students seeking admission to higher than

VII class, were also asked to be exempted from the compulsory learning of regional language in case they came from such schools, where the regional language was not taught.[275] Obviously disparities in the implementation of the language policy were bound to occur not only from one State to another but within the State itself. Although in some of the Schools only two instead of three languages were taught, it did not affect the status assigned to these languages. Hindi was considered secondary in comparison to the mother tongue regional languages and English was given the status below in the school curricula.[276] Surprisingly while evolving a language formula, English, a foreign language, was placed as the 3rd language to be learnt but in practice, English continued to be the first or the second language. The CABE observed that the majority of the States were in favour of the second formula where English or a modern European language was put as the second language. In those cases, where neither Hindi nor any other Modern Indian Language, was the mother tongue, Hindi or any Indian Language was to be learnt as the third language. Though English still continued to be the official language of the country yet, being a foreign language, it was considered to be more difficult than any other Modern Indian Language so the time allotted to the teaching of English was more than to the teaching of any other subject. All the more, due to a higher number of job opportunities in and outside the country, more emphasis was laid on its learning. Visualising this phase of learning three languages viz. mother tongue regional language or a composite course of compulsory language with mother tongue regional language, English Modern European Language and Hindi Modern Indian Language, the CABE advised the Government to accept the 'Three Language Formula' as an all India policy for teaching languages.[277]

Though Sanskrit is the source of most of the Indian languages, yet, it was not given any satisfactory place in the three language formula, which was accepted by a number of States in the country. The Union Government felt concerned over it because the knowledge of this language would enable the students to know the cultural heritage of the country and thereby help in the maintenance of the national solidarity. For evolving an all India policy of education in which Sanskrit could be given proper place, the Union Government in 1956, appointed a Commission for suggesting the ways and means for promoting the study of Sanskrit. The Commission pointed out that the Calcutta University had already made one of the classical languages compulsory for the students, who wanted to appear in the entrance examination for joining higher courses in the colleges. Although the University provided facilities for teaching classical languages like, Sanskrit, Arabic, Persian, Latin and Greek, the majority of the students offered Sanskrit. The University of Calcutta in those days had a very wide jurisdiction including not only Bengal, Assam, Bihar, Orissa, the United Provinces (now known as U.P.), Punjab and Ajmer, but Burma and Ceylon also.[278] Throughout this wide area, Sanskrit studies necessarily found a place in the schools and the students began to study Sanskrit as a compulsory subject. For the Muslim students the facilities were provided for teaching Arabic and Persian while for Anglo Indian students, Latin and Greek were made available. Bombay and West Bengal offered an option between Pali, Ardh Madaghi, Prakrit and Sanskrit at the secondary level of education. In Madras, Sanskrit was placed in the list of optional languages, viz., Telugu, Kannada, Tamil and Malayalam. Although Sanskrit occupied an important place in the school curricula in almost all the States, it could not be declared compulsory throughout the country because of its being a difficult language. Though the Commission did not approve the suggestion for teaching Sanskrit as a non-examination subject after the school hours, yet, it put forward the four language formula in which the study of Sanskrit was to be compulsory. The CABE rejected it simply on the ground that it would entail an extra burden on the students. There was another possibility that people would prefer Sanskrit to Hindi and ultimately it would be Hindi that would suffer. Since the provision had already been made for teaching of Sanskrit as an optional subject or a composite course of Sanskrit with mother language or regional language, the CABE advised not to alter or modify the three language formula.[279] The recommendation was accepted by the Government of India.[280]

Thus, the three language formula received increasing acceptance throughout India. Even the Madras Government in 1957, at an All Party Convention, accepted, the three language formula under which the study of Hindi was to be made compulsory in addition to the study of English and mother tongue/regional language in non-Hindi speaking areas and the study of another Indian language different from mother tongue/regional language and Hindi alongwith the study of English and Hindi was supposed to be compulsory in the Hindi speaking states.[281, 282]

The clauses 4 & 5 of the Article 344 of the Constitution of India lay down that a Committee should be constituted to examine the recommendations of the Commission on Official Language and to report to the President their opinion thereon. Accordingly, the Government in 1958 appointed a Committee known as the Committee of Parliament on Official Language.

The Committee reported, that while deciding the language policy of the country, due regard was given to the people of all interests. Even the linguistic capacity of the existing government employees were considered. The Committee further observed that although an early change over from English to Hindi at the official level was desirable, it should be so developed that it might not only be effective but, also should not cause any dislocation and inconvenience to the linguistic minorities in Hindi and non-Hindi speaking areas. Similarly a thought should also be given to the growth of Hindi language in non-Hindi areas. The Constitutional provisions had already been made where the directives were given to introduce Hindi as the official language gradually. At the first stage, Hindi was to be in use in addition to English obviously, English being the principal official language occupied the foremost position in administration, education and courts of the country while Hindi being the subsidiary official language continued to be secondary in position during the first 15 years from the commencement of the Constitution. In the next stage, restrictions might be imposed on use of English and Hindi should be used progressively for the official purposes of the Union in principle. Though Hindi was to be used progressively at official level yet, it did not enjoy the highest status in practice, because of the continuous use of English at the official level.

With regard to the suggestion that the Government officials of 45 and above, most learn Hindi, the Committee visualised that no condition should be imposed on them for learning it. The Committee considered the question of the use of Hindi language in the courts. It was recommended that the judgments, decrees and orders should be passed in English only, although Hindi might be used in the proceeding of the High Courts and even in the Supreme Court. In case, an earlier sanction was sought from the President for the use of Hindi, while giving judgments etc., it should be accompanied with an authorised English translation. Over the question of equating Hindi with non-Hindi speaking candidates in competitive examinations for all India . and higher Central Services, the Committee suggested that there should be three compulsory papers of equal standard in Hindi, English and Modern Indian Language and for the medium of Examination the option should be given for using either English or Hindi. The University Grants Commission (now onwards it would be referred as U.G.C.) also considered several times between 1954-56 and again in 1959, the question of the language to be used as the medium of instruction in the Universities and reached the conclusion that for maintaining the academic standard in education, English should be retained as the medium for some time more, although an Indian language should take over its place.[283]

Soon after in November 1960, in a Conference of Education Ministers, it was observed, that, certain disruptive tendencies threatening the unity of the country were on the rise in India. They realised, that since language was closely bound up with deepest emotions, there was always a need for balancing regional sentiments with national interest in an atmosphere of tolerance and understanding.[284] Therefore, in May 1961, under the Chairmanship of Sampoornananda, a Committee on Emotional Integration was appointed to study such problems and to suggest the positive measures for promoting integration. The Committee expressed the opinion that language policy was one of the most potent forces which if planned with far-sightedness might bring unity, otherwise, disruption in the country.[285] The Committee visualised that if the Official Language was different from the link language, it was the former, which, would occupy an important place in the school curricula, for the education of the child was related to the prospects of his career. As a result the school children would be burdened with learning of more than one script in the schools, for instance, the students would have to learn the scripts of English – the official language, Hindi – the common link language, the mother tongue and the regional language if it was different from the aforesaid three languages. The Committee, therefore, concluded that the language crises were due to the multiplicity of scripts and as such the suggestion for evolving a common script was preferred by all.

An example was cited of such countries as Turkey, Malaya, Phillipines, Indonesia and Vietnam for accepting the Roman as a common script for all their languages. Even China and USSR were quoted for using Roman script in the past before developing their Cyrillic script. The Committee recommended that the people in Hindi speaking areas should agree to the use of Roman script for an interim period. In non-Hindi speaking areas, although an option should be given to learn Hindi in either of the three scripts, viz. Devanagari, Roman and regional at the High School stage the Devanagari script[286] must be taught to them. The CABE reported that the efforts were being made by the Ministry of Education to publish selected books from all the regional languages in Devanagari script. It further recommended the publication of original text[287] on the page in Devanagari script and on the opposite page an easy translation in Hindi of the original text.

The Committee also discussed the stages at which the study of three different languages should be considered desirable. The members of the Committee expressed an opinion that the objectives of teaching languages at all the stages of education should be defined so that a decision could be taken for introducing compulsory study of three languages at a particular stage/stages. At the primary stage, the Committee opined that the objective of teaching a language should be to develop the speech of the child so that, he could express, read, and write correctly. Naturally, the mother tongue would be the appropriate language to teach at this level of education. At the Junior level, i.e., from VI to VIII class, emphasis should be laid on promoting integration. The teaching of a regional language different from mother tongue, would therefore be a right step in this direction. English as a language used in science and technology should also be introduced at this stage, so that the students pursuing higher education might not face any difficulty in grasping the subjects because of its continuance as the medium of higher education and might also consult standard reference books.[288] It was expected that the students, after learning Hindi and English for three subsequent years after the primary level of Education would be able to converse and write to the people outside their state and thereby help in the progress of national integration. It was also suggested that in lieu of the regional or modern Indian Language, the willing students could offer one classical language, such as Sanskrit, Arabic or Persian. It was further suggested that at High School level the languages taught should be those, which were used in vocational and higher courses of education.

The Committee also discussed the languages to be studied at the college level. The decision was taken in favour of the continuance of three language formula where the study of regional language in addition to Hindi and English was recommended. The students taking up vocational courses were not supposed to burden themselves with the study of three languages. The Committee concluded that as a large number of students might leave the school by the end of VIII class, they were supposed to know three languages, mother tongue/regional language, Hindi and English.

Referring to the views of Dr. Penfield, one of the recognised neurologists of the world the CABE not only justified the teaching of English – a foreign language latest by the end of Junior Basic Stage (i.e. after V class) ; but also advised to introduce it at an earlier stage[289] on the ground that the child could pick up a foreign language most quickly at the early (teen) age.[290] For creating an understanding and bringing unity among the different language groups of India, the CABE reported that the Committee appointed by the Ministry of Education for making a survey of the terms common to Hindi and other languages, finished the work and the dictionaries had been published. Similarly, the Board advised that the preparation of the glossaries should also be completed sooner, so that the same word carrying different meanings in different languages, might not confuse the learners.[291] Meanwhile the Rajasthan Government put a proposal of introducing two types of public examination for Higher Secondary candidates with compulsory English and without English. In spite of the fact that the largest number of the students failed due to English and that a large number of students who did not go for higher education had no use of English, the learning of this language was considered absolutely essential on the ground that the students were generally unable to decide at an earlier age whether they would proceed for higher education.[292] The Government of India thus passed an order that 'English should be the principal official language and Hindi the subsidiary official language till 1965.[293] The Committee further suggested that the Universities must institute diplomas in Modern Indian Languages, for instance, the Universities in non-Hindi and Hindi speaking areas might start giving diplomas in north Indian and South Indian languages respectively. Although the University students must be encouraged to take up one such language which did not belong to the family of their mother tongue; the Committee recommended not to make its study compulsory.[294,295]

The three language formula recommended in 1956, by the CABE in consultation with the State Governments was discussed again in the Chief Ministers' Conference held in August 1961. Although the Conference accepted the teaching of three compulsory languages at the Secondary level of education, some alteration/modification was thought to be necessary in the context of national integration.[296,297,298] The Conference resolved that instead of regional language/mother tongue both these languages should be taught in case the mother tongue of the child was different from the regional language. Under the 2nd group of languages provision should be made for teaching Hindi in non-Hindi speaking areas and any Indian language different from the mother tongue and regional language in Hindi speaking areas. No change was suggested for English/Modern European language to be taught as the third language.[299,300,301] Although Sanskrit was excluded from the first group of languages in which it was to be taught in a composite course either with the mother tongue or regional language, it could be placed in the second group of languages if the term 'Indian Language' was interpreted as it was. As it is obvious, the term Indian Language was taken to be as 'Modern Indian Language', and not the Indian language. With the result the Central Sanskrit Board set up by the Government of India to advise her on the teaching of Sanskrit was shocked at this new scheme of teaching languages in the schools, because, it had no place for Sanskrit, which was considered to be essential for proper understanding of Modern Indian Languages[302,303,304] as well as of Indian culture and civilisation. They, therefore, passed a resolution against this new policy of teaching three languages. "Resolved that the Central Sanskrit Board views with concern the simplified three language formula, recommended for adoption, at the secondary school stage, by the Chief Ministers' conference as the formula does not provide scope for teaching of Sanskrit as a composite course with regional language or mother tongue in the Secondary/ Higher Secondary Schools.[305,306] Moreover, under the simplified formula of languages the students would have to learn four instead of three languages as mother tongue, and regional language as they were two different languages. Hindi in non-Hindi speaking areas while any modern Indian language different from the former ones in Hindi speaking areas and English/Modern European Languages as the 4th language.[307] The National Integration Conference held in Sept./Oct. of the same year i.e. in 1961 urged, that, while teaching a Modern Indian Language under the second group of languages preference should be given in the Hindi speaking area to the teaching of a language out of the languages of South Indian group.[308,309,310,311] As has already been mentioned no Commission appointed by the Government of India approved it. Even the Supreme Advisory Body (CABE) to the Government of India had ruled out this suggestion. It was, therefore, decided that the "three language formula" evolved earlier, where, on the choice of the students, Sanskrit was to be taught in a composite course either with the mother tongue or the regional language; Hindi/Modern Indian Language respectively in non-Hindi and Hindi speaking areas and

English or Modern European Language was to be taught as the third language, should be continued for teaching languages at the Secondary level of education. [312, 313, 314]

The question of the languages, spoken by the minority group, was also discussed in one of the meetings (29th) of the CABE held in 1962. The Board was informed by the Ministry of Education that the provision had already been made in some of the States to teach the children of minority groups in their mother tongue. It was expected that the other States would soon follow the same policy. The Board (CABE) decided that the laws, rules and regulations available in the official language of the State, should also be translated in the minority language if that linguistic group constitutes 15% to 20% of the population regarding the status given to such language as that of another official language of the state, it was notified that this language might not only be spoken by the 60% of the total population but should also be one of those major languages specified in the VIII Schedule of the Constitution, while in the Hill Districts of Assam, Darjeeling and West Bengal, even those languages could be recognised which were not mentioned in the Indian Constitution. In the internal administration between the State and District headquarters, the CABE recommended that the use of the Union language – Hindi or English in addition to the use of the official language of that State should also be permitted. The candidates appearing for the entrance examination being held for the State Services, should be given an option to use any of the three languages viz. official language of the State, Hindi/English as the medium of their examination. Since the knowledge of the State language should be an essential qualification for such services, a proficiency test in the official language of the State should be given to the selected candidates during the period of their probation.

Regarding the medium of instruction at the Primary level of education, the Chief Ministers' Conference, the National Integration Conference and the Ministry of Education expressed the opinion that vigorous efforts should be made to impart education in/and through the mother tongue, of the child. At the Secondary level of education, it was noticed that the mother tongue was not being used as the medium of instruction in all the States and Union Territories. As the students, after the secondary stage of education, either go for vacationing, or step in colleges for higher education, English as well as Modern Indian Languages should be continued as the medium. [315, 316] It was further advised that in the Adivasi areas and Hill Districts of Assam, Darjeeling and in West Bengal, special arrangements for teaching through the mother tongue may be made.[317] The National Integration Committee upholding this view intimated that even the regional language in addition to Modern Indian Language[318] and English could also be used as the medium at the secondary level of education.

At the higher level of education, though Hindi because of its being the National as well as the link language of the country, was considered to be the suitable medium of instruction in all Indian Universities,[319] yet, English was retained as the medium till Hindi was adequately developed for the purpose of advanced education in all the branches of knowledge. Besides this "change over" is made acceptable to the academic world.[320,321] It was also informed that instruction through regional languages in addition to English was started in Andhra, Baroda and Gujrat Universities.[322] In the Universities of Allahabad, Bihar and Gorakhpur and in others, where English was not used as the medium of instruction for any of the University-courses, necessary provisions should be made to teach English as a second language.[323,324] The CABE, also realised the importance of having a common language in the Universities, otherwise the absence of such a language could lead to isolation of certain universities. For instance, the students, who got their education through Hindi medium, naturally would not be able to communicate with those having other Indian Languages as their media of education. Similarly, those students, who would have English medium would be segregated from others. Hence, the imperative need of such a common language was emphasised and, that may be Hindi or English. "Ultimately it will have to be Hindi"* in spite of repeating this 'slogan' the Board realised that in the present circumstances, English might continue till the time Hindi should enrich itself enough to replace English as the 'link language'. Besides, from the point of view of international communication, for the growth of modern knowledge in science, industry and technology in India, the importance of the knowledge of English the widely known 'Internatioanl Language' was realised. Taking into consideration all the facts and the Constitutional directives, the Board advised the different linguistic groups to retain the scientific and technical terminology for use at the International level. Subsequently, the Central Government declared that 'English' would continue as the "Associate Official Language" even after Hindi was installed as the Official language of the country. Notwithstanding the expiration of the period of 15 years from the commencement of the Constitution, the English language may, as from the appointed day (26th January 1965) continue to be used, in addition to Hindi –

a) for all the purposes of the Union for which it was being used immediately before that day and

b) for the transaction of business in the Parliament.[325]

This order further clarified that a translation in English/Hindi would be accompanied if necessary in communication at the State level or between State and the Union.[326] Although the use of both Hindi and English was permitted at the official level of the country, the rules ensured the services of the Central Government Employees, though they might not have, the proficiency in both the languages.[327] The CABE also suggested that when English at higher level of education was to be replaced by some regional language or Hindi, the change should be brought initially in the first 3 years of Degree courses in the Colleges. For all other courses, including those of Science in the first 3 years too, English medium should be continued.[328] The suggestion was also welcomed in the Conference of Vice-Chancellors held in October 1961.[329] In spite of the fact that the three language formula was suggested for the school teaching, it was 'bilingualism' which with the consent of the Government of India,[330] prevailed in the field of education. At the primary level mother tongue/Modern Indian Languages and at the secondary level Modern Indian Languages were continued as the medium of instruction, though English medium had also been in use in some of the Secondary Schools. Obviously the students who joined Higher Education were found with varying attainments in their knowledge of English language which was continuously followed as the medium in majority of the Universities. To get the students acclimatised to the new medium of English at the higher level of education a 'Two year Intermediate Course' after the school education was considered beneficial,[331] for their adjustment in the colleges. In fact, efforts were made to give equal status to all the three languages to be taught in the the schools. The mother tongue/regional language grouped under the heading of 'Modern Indian Languages' and the other language English were the two languages being taught as the subjects and also to be used as the medium of education. Though the time allotted for teaching them used to be of varied duration, yet, the attempts were made in the direction of equalising their status in the school syllabus, for instance, in the school, where modern Indian languages as well as English were used as the media for arts and science subjects respectively, the status of these two languages was brought at par while it differed in respect to each other when English and Hindi were followed as two different media in separate different schools.

Three Language Formula Implementation Committee of the Education Ministry was also appointed in April 1963 by the Chief Ministers' Conference, to review the programme of teaching languages in the schools.[332] The Committee informed that, though the Madras Government made Hindi a subject of examination, yet, the marks obtained in it were not counted for promotion to the next class as well as for the eligibility of the University Courses of Studies. It welcomed the decision of the U.P. Government to introduce English as a compulsory subject and the teaching of other modern Indian languages in addition to Sanskrit in the schools.[333,334,335] The Committee pointed out that the provision of teaching a Classical Language[336] need not be in lieu of Modern Indian Language, but might be as a part of a composite course of mother tongue/regional language or as an elective subject. Obviously a study of 4 languages was considered essential for the Hindi speaking states, where mother tongue/regional language with Sanskrit, one of the Modern Indian languages different from the mother tongue/regional language and English were supposed to be learnt compulsorily at the school stage. As the students after finishing the school education are expected to have an adequate knowledge of the languages the teaching of language should be provided at least for a period of three years in the continuous course. The Committee further recommended a 100% grant for the teaching of Modern Indian languages in the Hindi speaking areas as was being given to non-Hindi speaking States for teaching of Hindi.[337]

Though the Committee (The Three Language Formula Implementation Committee) expressed the satisfaction on the progress to be made in implementing the three language formula, yet, it expressed the wish that the formula should be implemented in a way, that, it could secure a large uniformity in all the States and Union Territories, for instance, in regard to the place of languages in the school curriculum, the selection of languages other than the mother tongue or regional language and the standard of proficiency to be aimed at. The Board (CABE) advised the Ministry of Education to review periodically the progress made in this regard and the results were to be reported to CABE.

It reaffirmed its recommendation that the mother tongue should be used as the medium of instruction at all the stages of education. But, at the University stage, the common link language either English or Hindi must necessarily be used as the medium of instruction in order to facilitate the movement of teachers and students from one state to another.[338] M.C.Chagla, as the President of CABE, emphasised the fact that in India, there is a necessity of one language as a great unifying force in the world of scholarship and judiciary.[339]

At the time of Chinese aggression in 1962, a necessity was felt of reassessment of values and re-phasing of the educational programmes for, only education can develop knowledge, discipline and loyalty in times of emergency. The Government of India, therefore, appointed an Education Commission under the Chairmanship of Dr. D.S. Kothari in July 1964 to advise the Government on "The national pattern of education and on the general principles and policies for the development of education at all stages and in all aspects.[340,341] As language is the only means of communication, without which no knowledge can be transmitted and it is the first item which a child learns, the Commission also considered the issue of languages to be taught to the students. Though the Commission gave its consent in favour of teaching three languages to the school students, yet, it decided to review the language policy keeping in view the fact that English, has been recognised as an 'Associate Official Language', of the Indian Union for an indefinite period. Under this modified or graduated three language formula the first language to be learnt was either the mother tongue or the regional language, the second was, either Hindi the official language or English the associate official language so long as it exists and the third was, either a modern Indian language, or a foreign language not covered yet, (i.e. Under Ist and 2nd languages) and other than that used as the medium of instruction. It follows, then, that neither Hindi was compulsory though it is the official language of the country, nor English was essential, although it is an important international language to learn. Besides, a foreign language other than English could be opted in place of an Indian language.[342] Thus, the most important objective of integrating the different States and the Union Territories, of the three language formula could have remained unachieved.

As this formula of teaching three languages differed from the formula, that, had acquired some acceptance in the country earlier, the Government waited to renew consultations with the State Governments subsequent to the 1967 elections.[343] In the same year i.e. in 1967 Triguna Sen the then Union Education Minister set up a twenty eight member committee of the Members of Parliament to review the recommendations of the Education Commission of 1964-66 and to propose a national policy on education.[344, 345] This Committee unanimously recommended a 'two language formula'. A student was required to learn only two languages: the mother tongue from class I to class X and one other language, which could be any language [346,347] and was to be continued from class V to X.[348] Provision was to be made for teaching the 3rd language also, but, on optional basis in classes VIII to X and the facility was given to the student to offer a 3rd language of his choice. This formula gained some weight as the language load on the students was reduced from 'three' to 'two' only. It may be interesting to note that one newspaper reported that 'the Education Minister – Triguna Sen himself became a party to the decision to replace the three language formula by a two language formula. [349,350] Since there was no compulsion to learn the Official language Hindi in non-Hindi speaking areas according to this two language formula, the Committee modified its proposal by making compulsory the study of Hindi or English as a 3rd language for a period of three years from Class VIII to class X. [351, 352, 353, 354] Soon, a Conference of State Education Ministers was held in which a uanimous decision was taken in favour of teaching three languages viz. Mother tongue, Hindi and English compulsorily to all the school students. [355, 356] Enlightening on the study of the classical languages the Commission expressed the opinion that either it should be taught in a combined course of the mother tongue or on an optional basis after VIII class.[357]

Teaching of these three compulsory languages was advised by the Commission, at lower secondary level i.e. between Class VIII to Class X, for the language learning would become a heavy load for the students of upper primary level i.e. from VI to VIII class. The Commission argued that some of the students would have left the school after finishing their free and compulsory education till 14 years of age. The remaining students, therefore, would be less ,who can have better teacher personnel and larger facilities to learn the languages. Hence, the appropriate stage for teaching the three compulsory languages would be the lower secondary stage i.e. between VIII to X class. But, S. Panandikar, the neurologist - educationist member of this Commission, following the lines of Penfild suggested the compulsory learning of three languages at the upper primary level i.e. from VI to VIII classes.

as it is the ideal age for learning languages.[358] The Commission also viewed the suggestion for teaching three languages for more than a period of three years and for their continuation at the University stage. It did not accept to continue with it, even at the higher secondary stage (i.e. after X class in other words between X to XI or XII class), for, the students would have less time to devote in gaining the advanced knowledge of subjects, like science and mathematics, due to the heavy load of curriculum. It was pointed out, that, for intensive study of languages of course, more than a period of three years is required, but, a short period with favourable conditions yielded better results e.g., well qualified, but, trained teachers and the use of the scientific methodology of teaching languages.[359,360,361] The stage at which the students start learning languages and to the extent they are motivated to learn them, are equally important pre-requisites for learning the languages.

Regarding the languages to be used as the media of education the Commission confirmed the claim of mother tongue to be used as the medium of instruction. The CABE also reaffirmed its recommendation that the Indian languages should be adopted as the media of education at all stages of school education. As the different mother tongues were being used as the media, the CABE pointed out to the growing necessity of production of literature in all the 14 languages recognised (till then) by the Constitution. It was suggested that, such books should be supplied to the different libraries and educational institutions, but, should equally be made available for the learners. Regarding the Indian languages to be used as the media at higher level of education, the Ministry of Education suggested that urgent steps should now be taken to adopt them as media of education, at the University stage.[362,363] The CABE regretted to say, that since adequate literature was not available, a policy of 'festinalenti', or proceed slowly should be followed.[364] Since "The Government of India accepted in principle that the Indian languages should now be adopted as media of education at all stages",[365] it (the Government) from 1968-69 offered upto Rs. 1 crore to each State Government, having Universities in their jurisdiction, for producing Text Books, translation work and other useful literature in Indian languages to be used as the higher level of education. It is significant to note that a provision of Rs. 50 crores was proposed for this scheme in the 5th Five Year Plan.[366]

It may not be out of place to mention here, that, two journals *Secondary Education* and *Youth* bilinguals in Hindi and English were published by the Publication Unit, that constitutes, the agency of the Union Ministry of Education.[367]

The Commission was also aware of the problem of learning different scripts with different languages, as every language has a script of its own. Very often, the students are required to learn not only three languages but three scripts as well, which ultimately increases the load of learning languages. It was, therefore, recommended to adopt a common script, either Roman or Devanagari for all the languages with a condition, that in case Roman was preferred for learning Hindi in non-Hindi speaking areas, Devanagari script should be taught later on.

As the main focus of the Commission was on the difficulties faced while implementing the three language formula, it highlighted the general opposition to heavy language load in the school curriculum, the resistance held by the people to the study of Hindi in some non-Hindi speaking areas and the lack of motivation for the study of an additional modern Indian language in the Hindi speaking areas, besides creating the un-real situation in which the 3rd language was taught.

The CABE in its 35th meeting decided to revert to the decision[368] made by the National Integration Conference held in September - October 1961. It urged that a modern Indian language, preferably of the South Indian Group should be taught as the 3rd language in Hindi speaking areas.[369,370] A resolution was also adopted in the Parliament in 1968, where inter-alia, it was resolved that :

> "Whereas it is necessary for promoting the sense of unity and facilitating communication between people in different parts of the country that effective steps should be taken for implementing fully in all states the three language formula evolved by the Government of India, in consultation with the State Government;
>
> This House resolves that arrangements should be made in accordance with that formula for the study of a modern Indian language preferably one of the Southern language apart from Hindi and English in Hindi speaking areas and of Hindi alongwith the regional language and English in the non-Hindi speaking areas.[371]

As the trained teachers for teaching modern Indian languages were not available in Hindi speaking areas, the Government of India decided to establish four 'Language Teaching Centres' to be located at Bhubaneshwar, Mysore, Poona, and Patiala in a phased manner. It may be significant to note that only the Mysore Centre made provision of teaching South Indian languages.[372] These Centres were also given the responsibility of publishing literature on language teaching.[373] Besides, the financial grants were to be given to those Institutions also, which made arrangements on voluntary basis for teaching languages to adults. The Government of India assisted them upto 75% of their approved expenditure for teaching Hindi and modern Indian languages respectively in non-Hindi and Hindi speaking areas.[374] The Board (CABE) further suggested that cent per cent central assistance should be released in time for the Centrally sponsored schemes for Sanskrit education.[375] It also retained the suggestion given in its 15th Meeting in 1949 that, provision should be made for teaching to the linguistic minorities not only their mother tongues but regional languages also. That should continue till the secondary stage of the school education so that they can have larger and better job opportunities and can become part and parcel of that state.[376]

The standing Committee of CABE in 1973 agreed with the view that efforts should also be made to impart instruction in tribal languages and to achieve success in this direction, the Board (CABE) suggested, that, special allowance and other facilities should be given to teachers working in tribal areas.[377] Regarding the teaching of 'Foreign Languages', the Board expressed the opinion, that teaching of foreign languages other than English should be encouraged in the Universities and a reasonable proficiency in any of the international languages should be aimed at.[378]

As the Government of India continues to be committed to implement the three language formula evolved in 1961 and resolved in the Parliament in 1968, the State Governments in June 1982, were requested to take full advantage of the schemes and facilities being provided by the Government for its implementation.[379] Some of the States raising opposition against its implementation are Tamil Nadu, Karnataka, West Bengal and Maharashtra.[380] Even in the Union Territory of Delhi the seat of the Central Government, the three language formula is not implemented in the form, it is envisaged by the Government itself.[381]

## Notes and References

1. Report of the Census of India 1971; Language Handbook on mother tongues in Census. New Delhi : Ministry of Home Affairs. 1972. p.. xvi.
2. Report of the Official Language Commission. 1956. p. 19.
3. *Ibid.*

4. Coldwell, R., J.L. Wyatt and T. Krishnamehari Pillai. (Eds). *Comparative Grammar of Dravidian or South Indian Family of Languages, U.S.A.* : Telegraph Books. 1980 p. 81.
5. Munshi, K.M. *Gujarat and its Literature*. Bombay : Bhartiya Vidya Bhawan. 1954. Introduction.
6. Keay, F.E. *Indian Education in Ancient and Later Times*. 2nd Edition Geoffrey Cumberlege: Oxford University Press. 1938.
7. Chaturvedi and B.V. Mohale. *op. cit.*, p. 10.
8. Report of the Official Language Commission 1956. p. 249.
9. (Edited by) Nagendra. *Indian Literature*. Agra: Laxmi Narain & Sons. 1959 p. xxvi.
10. Munshi, K.M. *Gujarat and its Literature from Early Times*. Bhartiya Vidya Bhawan. 1967 p. xxiii.
11. Taraporewala. *op. cit.* p. 208
12. Chatterji, S.K. *Language and Linguistic Problem*. 3rd Edition. Madras : Oxford University Press. 1945
13. Sarkar, A. *Handbook of Languages and Dialects of India*. Calcutta. 1964 p. xii.
14. Murray, B. Emeneau; Dell Hyness and A. Harpper. Eds. *India as a Linguistic Area in Language, in Culture and Society* International Edition. 1966 p. 650.
15. *Ibid.*
* The term is now old fashioned and has been degraded by unpopular uses.
16. Virginia, P. Clark; Pault, A. Eschholz and Alfred F. Rose, eds. *Language*. New York : St. Martin's Press 1977 p. 43.
17. Taraporewala. *op. cit.*
18. *Chamber's Encyclopaedia of Education*. London : George Newnes Ltd. 1950. pp. 353-54.
19. Taraporewala. *op. cit.*, p. 268.
* All the varied languages of the vast family resemble each other in structure; they also share some of their vocabulary; individual words, are recognizable as stemming from the same language matrix.
20. Harney and others. *Area Handbook for Afghanistan*. Washington: U.S. Govt. Printing Press 1973. p. 85.
* The name Indo-European has no radial or ethrological counotation. It simply means to designate the people (of whatever race or country) who spoke or speak Indo European Langues.
21. Dutt, N.K. *Aryanization of India*. Calcutta: Mukhopadhyaya & Sons. 1970.
22. Raja, C. Kanhan. *Survey of Sanskrit Literature*. Bombay: Bhartiya Vidya Bhawan 1962. p. 3
23. Macdonell. *A History of Sanskrit Literature*. Delhi : Motilal Banarsi Das 1962. p. 118.
24. Taraporewala. *op. cit.*, p. 228.
* Grierson in *Lingustic Survey of India* has enumerated 129 different Languages and 544 different dialects of India.
25. Ahmad, Z.A. *System of Education*. Calcutta: Longman Green and Company Ltd. 1929. p. 215.
26. Chatterji, S.K. *Indo-Aryan and Hindi*. Eight Lectures delivered in 1940 before the Gujarat Vernacular Society, Ahmedabad. Published in Calcutta: Mukh-ópadhyaya & Sons 1969. p. 2.
27. Mishra, S.S. *A Comparative Grammar of Sanskrit*, Greek and Hittite. Calcutta: The World Press Pvt. Ltd. 1968
28. *Chamber's Encyclopaedia of Education. op. cit.*
29. Macdonell. *op. cit.*, p. 37.

30. Panini. *Ashtadhyayie*. Varanasi: Chaukhamba Surbharti Prakashan. 1976
31. Patanjali. *Mahabhasya*. Poona: Bhandarkar Oriental Research Institute. 1972 p56.
32. Referred to by Gune, P.D. *An Introduction to Comparative Philology*. Poona: Poona Oriental Book House. 1950
33. Windisch. 'Uber den sprachlichen charakter der Pali esp. p. 23. cf also Grierson. *Home of Literary Pali.* p.117 *of the* Bhandarkar Commemoration volume.
34. Keith, A.B. *History of Sanskrit Literature*. London: Oxford University Press. 1920
35. Franke, R. Otto. *Pali and Sanskrit.* Germany. pp. 1902 131-32.
36. Bhamah. *Kavyalankar*. Patna: Bihar Rashtrabhasa Parisad. 1962 I : 16 & 28.
37. Dandin. *Kavyadarsha.* Delhi: Meharchand Lachmandasa. 1973 I. 32, 36 and 37.
38. Bhamah. *Kavyalankar.* Bombay: Nirnay Sagar. 1928 II. 12.
39. Rajshekhar. *Kavyamimamsa*. Varanasi: Chaukhamba Vidyabhawan. 1982. pp. 6, 19, 33, 48, 50 54, 55.
40. Anandavaradhan. *Dhuanyalaka*. Banarasa: Chaukhamba Sanskrit Series. 1953 III. 7.
41. Mammat. *Kavyprakasha*. Part I. Banaras: Chaukhamba Vidyabhawan 1955 pp. 42, 59, 67, 88 90, 91, 345.
42. Bhoja. *Saraswatikan thavaran*. Varanasi: Chaukhamba Orientalia. 1976 2, 10, 13, 17.
43. Vagbhatta. *Vagbhattalankar*. Varanasi: Chaukhamba Publications. 1977
44. Gunchandra, R.C. *Natyadarpana*. Part I. Baroda: M.S. University. 1929 p. 209.
45. Bhoja. *Shringarprakasha.* Mysore: Coronation Press. 1955 pp. 102-3.
46. Gune, P.D. *op. cit.*, pp. 255-64.
47. Hoernle. *Gaudian Languages*. p. 3 cited by Gune, P.D. *op. cit.*
48. Venkateshwara, S.V. *Indian Culture through the Ages*. New York: Longmans, Green 1928. p. 112.
49. Elphinstone. *Ancient India*. Calcutta: Chitranjan Avenue 1953. pp. 37-38.
50. Dandin. *Dashkumar Charitam*. Vol. III. Bombay: Sanskrit and Prakrit Series. 1919 p. 22.
51. Majumdar, R.C. (ed). *The History and Culture of the Indian People*. Vol. III "The Classical Age." Bombay: Bhartiya Vidya Bhawan. 1954 pp. 23-24.
52. Bana Bhatta. *Kadambari.* Kashi: Pandit Pustakalaya. 1959 125f.
53. Vide 'Preface' *Alberauni's India* 1914. Translated by Sachau. London : Kegan Paul, Trench, Trubner & Co. Ltd. 1910, 1914.
54. Cited by Law, N.N. *Promotion of Learning* in India during Mohammedan Rule. Delhi : Idarah-1 Abadiyat -1 1973 p. 13.
55. Farishta Vol. II. pp. 369-70. Cited by Law, N.N. *op. cit.*, Ch. 8.
56. Scots' *Deccan* Vol. I p. 74. Cited by Law, N.N. *op. cit.*
57. Shriwastava, A.L. *Medieval Indian Culture*. Agra: Shiv Lal Agarwala and Co. 1964 p. 100.
58. Law, N.N. *op. cit.*, p. 112.
59. Keay, F.E. *Indian Education in Ancient and Later Times.* Oxford: Geoffrey Cumberledge Univ. Press. p. 1938 112.
60. Majumdar, R.C. *An Advanced History of India*. London: Macmillan & Co. Ltd. 1948 p. 275.
61. Shriwastava, A.L. *op. cit.* , p. 113.
62. *Ibid* p. 113.
63. *Ibid*. p. 118.
64. Shriwastava, A.L. *Mughal Empire* (1526-1803 A.D.). Agra: Shivlal Agarwal & Co. 1953 p. 6

65. Law, N.N. *op. cit.*, Ch. VIII.
66. Jaffar, S.M. *Education in Muslim India.* Delhi : Idarah; Adaliyat. 1936
67. Shriwastava, A.L. *Mediaeval Indian Culture. op. cit.*, p. 107.
68. *Ain-e-Akbari* Vol. I (English Translation) p. 520 Cited by Shriwastava, A.L. *Mediaeval Indian Culture. op. cit.*, p. 111.
69. *Ibid.* p. 110
70. Majumdar, R.C. *An Advanced History of India. op. cit.*, p. 581.
71. Spear, P. India-*A Mediaeval History.* Ann Arbor: The University of Michigan Press. 1961. p. 136.
72. Mukherji, L. *History of India*. Calcutta: Mandal Brothers and Cop. Ltd. p. 363.
73. Shriwastav, A.L. *The Mughal Empire. op. cit.*, p. 221.
74. 'It is this form of Hindi often spoken of as Hindustani'. Percival, S. *India - A Medieval History.* Ann Arbor: The University of Michigan Press. 1961. p. 136.
75. *Ibid.*
76. Grierson. *Ethnology, Religion, Language* and Literature of India. Delhi: Indian Documentation Service. 1975 p. 35
77. Keay, F.E. *op. cit.*, p. 116.
78. Majumdar, R.C. *An Advanced History of India. op. cit.*
79. Shoberl's *Hindustan in Miniature*. Vol. iv. pp. 215-16. Cited by Law, N.N. *Promotion of Learning in India during Mohammedan Rule. op. cit.*, p. 96.
80. *Ibid.*
81. Cited by Shriwastava, A.L. *Mughal Empire* (1526-1803). *op. cit.*, p. 527.
82. Keay, F.E. *op. cit.*, p. 128.
83. Majumdar, R.C. *An Advanced History of India. op. cit.*, p, 633.
84. Sherring, M.A. "A History of Protestant Missions in India". p. 75. Quoted by Narullah and Naik. *A Students' History of Education in India.* Bombay: Macmillan & Co. Ltd. 1956. p. 36.
85. Sharp, H. *Educational Records 1781-1839 Part-I.* New Delhi: Bureau of Education India. 1920 p. 26.
86. *Ibid.* pp. 29-34.
87. Chatterjee, K. *English Education in India–Issues and Options*. Delhi: The Macmillan Co. of India Ltd. 1976 p. 121.
88. Majumdar, R.C. *op. cit.*, p. 816.
89. Chatterjee, K. *op. cit.*, p. 121.
90. *Ibid.* p. 84.
91. Sharp. H. *Educational Records of India*. Part-I. *op. cit.*, p. 22.
92. Vakil and Natrajan. *Education in India*. Bombay: Allied Publishers. 1948
93. Nurullah and Naik. *A Students' History of Education in India.* (1800-1947). *op. cit.*
94. Keay, F.E. *op. cit*. p. 15.
95. Majumdar, R.C. *op. cit.*, p. 816.
96. Shriwastava, B.D. *The Development of Modern Indian Education.* Bombay: Orient Longman Ltd. 1953 p. 164.
97. Narullah and Naik. *op. cit.*, p. 97.
98. Chatterji, K. *op. cit.*, p. 11.
99. *Chamber's Encyclopaedia of Education.* Vol. VIII. London: George Newnes Ltd. 1950. pp. 754-55.
100. Vakil and Natrajan. *Education in India op.cit.*
101. Tarachand. *Impact of Western Culture* Vol. II. Allahabad: The Indian Press (publication) Ltd. 1967. Ch. IV. p. 198.
102. Nurullah and Naik. *op. cit.*, p. 68.
103. *Ibid.* p. 52.

104. Vakil and Natrajan, *op. cit.*, p. 71.
105. *Ibid.* pp. 74-78.
106. Report of the Board of Education for 1840-41. pp. 24-28.
107. *Ibid.* p. 35
108. Vakil and Natarajan. *op.cit.*, p. 76.
109. Nurullah and Naik. *op.cit.*, p. 69.
110. Vakil and Natrajan. *op.cit.* p. 73.
111. Sharpp. *op.cit.*, p. 65.
112. Tarachand. *op.cit.*, p. 199
113. *Ibid.*
114. Nurullah and Naik. *op. cit.*, p. 78.
115. Tarachand. *op. cit.*
116. Vakil and Natrajan. *op. cit.*, p. 138.
117. *Ibid* pp. 139-43.
118. *Ibid.* p. 145.
119. Sitaramayya, Pattabhi. *The History of the Indian National Congress.* Vol. I (1885-1935) Bombay: Padma Publications Ltd. 1935. p. 10.
120. Nurullah and Naik. *op. cit.*, p. 161-71.
121. Shriwastava, B.D. *op.cit.*, p. 220
122. Nurallah and Naik. *op. cit.*, p. 212.
123. *Ibid.* pp. 210-11.
124. *Ibid.* p. 162.
125. *Ibid.* p. 163.
126. Vakil and Natarajan. *op. cit.*, p. 263
127. *Ibid.* p. 262.
128. Government of India Resolution. Para 24.
129. Nurullah and Naik. *op. cit.* p. 258.
130. *Ibid.* p. 296.
131. Vakil and Natarajan *op. cit.*, p. 173.
132. Patel. The *Educational Philosophy of Mahatma Gandhi.* Allahabad : Navjivan Publishing House. 1953 p. 113-43.
133. Nurullah and Naik. *op. cit.*, p.347.
134. Howell. *Education in British India.* p. 40. Cited by Vakil and Natarajan. *op. cit.*, p.130.
135. Sharp, H. *op. cit.*, p. 79.
136. *Ibid.*
137. Report of the Official Language Commission 1956. p. 24.
138. *Ibid.*
139. Rao, P. Kodanda. *Rational Language Policy for India.* Bangalore: Committee for English. 1965 p. 9
140. Nayar, Baldev Raj. *National Communication Language Policy in India.* New Delhi. Fredrich a Praeger. 1969 p. 97.
141. Ram Gopal. *Linguistic Affairs of India.* Bombay: Asia Publishing House 1966. p. 197
142. Nurullah and Naik. *op. cit.*, pp. 31 40.
143. Shriwastava, G.P. *The Indian Civil Service : A Study in Administrative Personnel.* Delhi : S.Chand. pp. 1965 110-13.
144. Nayar, Baldev Raj. *op.cit.*, pp. 98-99.
145. Report of the Committee of Parliament on Official Language. India: Ministry of Home Affairs. 1958. pp. 16-17. (Here in after referred to RCPOL),
146. Nayar, Baldev Raj. *op.cit.*, pp. 98-100.

147. Legislative Assembly Debates. 11th March, 1947. Vol. III. New Delhi: Superintendent, Assembly Branch, Parliament House Library. 1947.
148. A Review of Education in India (1947-61) First Year book on Education. New Delhi: N.C.E.R.T. 1961
149. *Ibid.*
150. Education in India. 1947-48. Calcutta: Government of India Press. 1951.
151. Keay. *A History of Education in India and Pakistan since 1947-48*. Oxford University Press. 1949.
152. CABE (1935-60) Silver Jubilee Souvenir, 14th Meeting January 1948. Item No XIII. MInistry of Education, Government of India 1960.
153. *Ibid.* Item No, XIV.
154. CABE January 1947. New Delhi: Ministry of Education, Government of India. 1960.
155. *Ibid.*
156. Report of the Committee under the Chairmanship of Dr. Tarachand in 1948.
157. Education in India, 1948-49. Pamphlet No. 128, New Delhi: Government of India, Ministry of Education. 1952.
158. Rai Chaudhri, H.N. *Our Language Problems.* Calcutta: Uppal press. 1958 p. 3.
159. *Education in India 1948-49*: New Delhi: Government of India, Ministry of Education 1952.
160. Report of the Committee under the Chairmanship of Dr. Tarachand in 1948.
161. *Education in India 1947-48. New Delhi*: Government of India, 1951.
162. Bureau of Education, Ministry of Education, Government of India. Pamphlet No. 51.
163. Education in India 1947-48. *op. cit.* Ch. 1.
164. Education in India 1948-49. *op. cit.*
165. Rai Chaudhri, H.N. *op. cit.*, p. 3.
166. *Ibid.* pp. 3-4.
167. Report of the CABE. Jan. 1948. Government of India, Ministry of Education. 1960.
168. Rai Chaudhri, H.N. *op. cit.*, p. 3.
169. *Education in India 1948-49. op. cit.*
170. Report of the Committee under the Chairmanship of Dr. Tara Chand. April 1948. Publication No. 124.
171. Report of the Radha Krishnan Education Commission 1948-49. p. 321.
172. The chief languages of India according to the Census of India 1931 were 13 namely, Assamese, Bengali, Hindi, Gujarati, Kashmiri, Marathi, Oriya, Panjabi, Urdu, Malayalam, Kannada, Tamil, and Telugu. The Report of the Constituent Assembly 1947. New Delhi.
173. Report of the Radha Krishnan Education Commission 1948-49. p. 321.
174. *Constituent Assembly Debates*. Vol. IX, p. 1401. 30th July to 18th Sept. (Only a suggestion given by different people).
175. *Ibid.* p. 1331.
176. *The Constitution of India*. New Delhi : Government of India Press. 1950.
177. *Ibid.*
178. *Constituent Assembly Debates*. Vol. IX, p. 1414. 30th July to 18th Sept. 1949. Government of India.
179. *Ibid.*
180. *Ibid.*
181. *Ibid* p. 1414.

* "English is an international language and of the catastrophic events do not after the present picture of the world force it will soon be the world language." Report of the University Education Commission. (1948-49. p. 316.

182. *Ibid.*
183. *Ibid.* p. 326.
184. *Ibid.*
185. Indicated in the 'Preamble' to our Draft Constitution 1950.
186. Report of Radha Krishnan Commission 1948-49. p. 35.
187. Report of CABE,, 15th Meeting 1949. Government of India, Ministry of Education. 1960.
188. Report of Radha Krishnan Commission 1948-49. Government of India. 1950. p. 324.
189. Report of CABE, 15th Meeting 1949. Government of India, Ministry of Education. 1960.
190. *Ibid.*
191. *Ibid.*
192. Report of Radha Krishnan Education Commission 1948-49. Part II. pp. 665-814.
193. Report of CABE, 15th Meeting 1949. Govt. of India, Ministry of Education 1960.
194. Report of CABE 1944. Govt. of India, Ministry of Education. 1960.
195. Report of Radha Krishnan Commission 1948-49. pp. 312-14.
196. Education in India 1948-49. New Delhi: Govt. of India 1950.
197. Statement of the Activities of the Ministries during 1948-49 Section VI. New Delhi: Ministry of Defence. p. 11.
198. *Constituent Assembly. Debates* 1949.
199. Report of the CABE, 15th Meeting 1949. Govt. of India. 1960.
200. *Ibid.*
201. *Ibid.* pp. 222-23.
202. *Ibid.*
203. *Ibid.*
204. Letter from Nehru, dated 16th May, 1931.
    *Constituent Assembly Debates* Vol. IX, 30th July to 18th Sept., 1949. Govt. of India. 1949.
205. Report of CABE, 15th Meeting 1949. New Delhi: Govt. of India. 1960.
206. *The Constitution of India.* Article 29 (1).
207. *Ibid.* Article 29 (2).
208. *Ibid* VII Schedule.
209. *Ibid.* Articles 30 (1), 30 (2) and 337.
210. *Ibid.* Article 345 and 347.
211. *Ibid.*
212. Report of the Committee of Parliament on Official Language 1958.
213. *The Consiitution of India.* VIII Schedule. p. 311.
    (21st Amendment Act 1967).
214. *Ibid.* VIII Schedule. p. 452. Assamese, Bengali, Gujarati, Hindi Kannada, Kashmiri, Malayalam, Marathi, Oriya, Punjabi, Sanskrit, Sindhi, Tamil, Telugu and Urdu.
215. *Ibid.* Article 343 (1). XVII Part. Ch. I. p. 220.
216. Report of the Committee of Parliament on Official Language 1958. Ch. II.
217. *The Constitution of India.* Article 343 (2).
218. *Ibid.* Article 343(3).
219. *Ibid.* Article 348(1).
220. *Ibid.* Article 348(1) and (3).
221. *Ibid.* Article 348 (2).
222. *Ibid.* Article 348 (3).
223. *Ibid.* Article 350.
224. *Ibid.* Article 348 (2) and 350-A.

225. *Ibid.* Article 346.
226. *Ibid.* Article 350-A.
227. *Ibid.* Article 344.
228. A Review of Education in India 1947-61. First Yearbook of Education. New Delhi: Ministry of Education. 1961. p. 53.
229. *Ibid.*
230. *Ibid.*
231. The University Education Commission 1948-49. Ch. IX. Medium of Instruction.
232. Report of the CABE 17th Meeting 1950. Govt. of India. 1960.
233. The *Constitution of India*. Article 351.
234. *Ibid.* Article 343(2) and 344.
235. Report of CABE 18th Meeting 1951. Govt. of India. 1960.
236. Report of CABE 1953-54. Govt. of India. 1960.
237. Report of the Secondary Education Commission. 1952-53. p. 250.
238. Report of CABE, 17th Meeting 1950. Govt. of India. 1960.
239. *Ibid.*
240. Report of CABE, 19th Meeting 1952. Govt. of India. 1960.
241. Report of the Mudaliar Commission 1952-53. Ch. "Study of Language"
242. *Ibid.*
243. *Ibid.*
244. Report of the Conference of English Professors called by the Central Government. 1953.
245. *Ibid.*
246. Report of the CABE 1938. Govt. of India. 1960.
247. Report of the University Education Commission 1948-49.
248. Report of the Secondary Education Commission 1952-53. Ch. "Study of Languages".
249. *Ibid.*
250. Report of the Conference of Hindi Professors called by the Central Government in January 1953.
251. *Ibid.*
252. *The Constitution of India*. List II, State List. p. 310.
253. Report of CABE 21st Meeting 1953-54. Govt. of India. 1960.
254. Report of Secondary Education Commission 1952-53. p. 250.
255. *Ibid.*
256. Report of the CABE, 23rd Meeting, January 1956. Govt. of India 1960.
257. Copy of the Ministry of Law, Notification No. S.R.O. 938-A (S.No. 2). The Constitutional Hindi Language for Official purposes order 1955. New Delhi : Government of India, Department of Official Language, Ministry of Home Affairs.
258. Report of the Official Language Commission 1956. Ch. IV
259. Report of CABE 24th Meeting 1957, p. 343 Item 3-g.
260. *Ibid.* No. 24, para 19.
261. *Ibid.* Ch. IX, No. 78, para 2
262. *Ibid.* Ch. VI, No. 40, para 12
263. *Ibid.* Ch. VI, No. 41, para 13.
264. *Ibid.* Ch. IV, No. 15, para 7.
265. *Ibid.*
266. *Ibid.* Ch. VII.
267. *The Constitution of India*. Article 343.
268. Report of the Official Language Commission 1956. Ch. VI.

269. *Ibid.* para 15.
270. *Ibid.* para 69.
271. *Ibid.* p. 220.
272. *Ibid.* Ch. XIII.
273. *Ibid.*
274. *Ibid.* pp. 39-40.
275. Proceedings of the Meeting of CABE held in 1957. New Delhi: Government of India. 1960.
276. *Ibid.*
277. The Proceedings of CABE Silver Jubilee Souveanir, New Delhi: Ministry of Education, Government of India. 1960. p. 345.
278. Report of the Sanskrit Commission. New Delhi: Government of India Press. 1958. Ch. V.
279. Report of the CABE. 26th Meeting, Silver Jubilee Souvenir, New Delhi: Ministry of Education, Government of India Press. 1960. No. 9.
280. Report of the CABE. 28th Meeting, Silver Jubilee Souvenir, New Delhi: Ministry of Education, Government of India Press. 1961.
281. Quoted by Mohan Kumaramangalam, S. *India's Language Crisis.* Madras: New Century Book House. 1965. p. 39.
282. Nayar, B.R. *op. cit.*, Ch. V.
283. Report of the CABE 28th Meeting. New Delhi : Silver Jubilee Souvenir 1961. Ministry of Education, Government of India. 1960.
284. Report of the States Reorganisation Committee. New Delhi : Ministry of Home Affairs. 1956.
285. Report of the Committee on Emotional Integration. New Delhi: Ministry of Education, Government of India. 1962.
286. *Ibid.*
287. Proceedings of the CABE, 25th Meeting 1958. Silver Jubilee Souvenir. New Delhi : Ministry of Education, Government of India. 1960. No. 13.
288. The Report of the Kunzroo Committee referred in the Meeting of CABE 1958. New Delhi : Government of India. 1960.
289. The Report of the Proceedings of CABE 29th Meeting. New Delhi : Government of India. 1960.
290. Penfield, cited in the 27th Meeting held by CABE 1958. New Delhi : Silver Jubilee Souvenir, Government of India Press. 1960.
291. *Ibid.* Item No. 13.
292. Report of the Proceedings of CABE, 27th Meeting. New Delhi: Ministry of Education, Govt. of India. 1960.
293. Copy of Ministry of Home Affairs Notification No. 2/8/60-OL dated 27th April, 1960, Compilation of Orders regarding the use of Hindi.
294. Report of the Proceedings of CABE 28th Meeting 1961. New Delhi : Government of India. 1962.
295. The Report of the Committee on Emotional Integration. New Delhi : Ministry of Education, Govt. of India. 1962.
296. Report of the Chief Ministers' Conference. New Delhi : Government of India. 1962.
297. Report of the CABE, 29th Meeting, New Delhi : Government of India. 1963.
298. Shrivastava, G.N. 1970. *The Language Controversy and the Minorities*. Delhi : Atma Ram & Sons. Ch.VI.
299. *Ibid.*

300. Report of the Commission for Linguistic Minorities ; Fourth Report. Delhi Manager of Publications. 1962. pp. 92-93.
301. Nayar, Baldev Raj. *op. cit.*
302. Report of the Conference of Chief Ministers. New Delhi : Government of India. 1962.
303. Report of the Proceedings of CABE. 29th Meeting. New Delhi: Government of India. 1963.
304. Shrivastava, G.N. *op. cit.*, pp. 37-41.
305. Supplementary paper under Item No. 3(i) of the Agenda in the Resolution passed by the Central Sanskrit Board in the 8th Meeting held at New Delhi on the 7th Dec. 1961.
306. The Report of the Procedings of CABE 29th Meeting. New Delhi : Government of India. 1963.
307. *Ibid.*
308. Report of the Conference on National Integration. New Delhi: Government of India. 1962.
309. Report of the Proceedings of CABE 29th Meeting. New Delhi: Government of India. 1963.
310. Report of the Kothari Commission. New Delhi: Govt. of India Press. 1966.
311. Shrivastava, G.N. *op. cit.*, Ch. VI.
312. Report of the Proceedings of CABE 29th Meeting. Govt. of India. 1963.
313. *Ibid.* 30th Meeting. Govt. of India. 1964.
314. Shrivastava, G.N. *op. cit.*, Ch. VI
315. The Report of the Conference of Chief Ministers. New Delhi: Government of India. 1962.
316. The Report of the Proceddings of CABE. 29th Meeting. New Delhi : Government of India. 1963.
317. *Ibid.*
318. Modern Indian Languages mentioned in the VIII Schedule of the Constitution of India.
319. The Madras Government stated that if and when English ceased to be the medium of instruction in respect of any of University courses of study in this state, it should be replaced by Tamil and not by Hindi (Cited by the Report of the 29th Meeting of CABE. p. 46. para 9.)
320. The Report of the National Integration Conference. NEw Delhi : Govt. of India. 1962. para 15.
321. The Report of the Proceedings of CABE 29th Meeting.
322. The Report of the Proceedings of CABE 28th Meeting. Agenda - Medium of Instructions in the Universities. New Delhi : Government of India. 1962.
323. The Report of the Kunzroo Committee. New Delhi : Government of India. 1962.
324. The Report of the Proceedings of CABE 29th Meeting. New Delhi : Government of India. 1963.

* Reaffirmed in almost all the Meetings of CABE.

325. The Official Languages Act. 1963 (Act No. 19 of 1963) Resolution and Rules. Government of India. Simla : Ministry of Home Affairs, Department of Official Languages. 1980. p. 4.
Compilation of orders regarding the use of Hindi issued by the Ministry of Home Affairs for special purposes of the Union; serial No. 7. New Delhi : Department of Official Languages, Government of India. Ch. III.
326. *Ibid.*

327. The Official Languages Act. 1963 (Act No. 19 of 1963) Resolutions and Rules. Simla : Home Ministry, Government of India. 1980. p. 6.
328. The Report of the Proceedings of the 29th Meeting of CABE. New Delhi : Government of India. p. 46.
329. *Ibid.*
330. *Ibid.* para 10. Suggested formula of All India Policy.
331. The Report of the Proceedings of CABE 29th Meeting. New Delhi : Government of India. 1963. p. 48.
332. The Report of the Proceedings of CABE 30th Meeting. New Delhi : Government of India, Ministry of Education. 1964. p. 296.
333. *Ibid.* pp. 355-56.
334. Report of the Proceedings of the 7th State Education Ministers' Conference. New Delhi : Ministry of Education, Government of India Press. 1965. p. 111.
335. Nayar, B.R. *op. cit.*, Ch. V.
336. The Classical Languages - Sanskrit, Persian, Arabic and Latin.
337. The Report of the Proceedings of CABE 30th Meeting. New Delhi : Ministry of Education, Government of India. 1964 pp. 355-56.
338. Report of the CABE. 30th Meeting held in 1963. New Delhi : Ministry of Education, Govt. of India. 1964. p. 307
339. Report of the CABE. 31st Meeting held in 1964. Published in 1965. p. 17.
340. Report of the Education Commission 1964-66. p. ix.
341. National Policy on Education. New Delhi : Government of India Press. 1974. p. 1.
342. Report of the Education Commission 1964-66. p. 334.
343. Nayar, Baldev Raj. *op. cit.*, p. 158.
344. *The Overseas Hindustan Times* (New Delhi), April 13, 1967
345. Nayar, Baldev Raj. *op. cit.*, p. 159.
346. The *Statesman Weekly* (Calcutta), April 29, 1967.
347. Nayar, Baldev Raj, *op. cit.*, p. 159.
348. *Ibid.*
349. *Ibid.* p. 160.
350. *The Overseas Hindustan Times,* May 11, 1967.
351. Report of the Education Commission 1964-66. pp. 335-36.
352. Report of the Committee of Members of Parliament on Education 1967. .Faridabad : Government of India Press. 1967. pp. 3-4.
353. Report of the *Hindu Weekly Review,* May 1, 1967.
354. Nayar, Baldev Raj. *op. cit.*, p. 159.
355. *Ibid.* p. 160.
356. The *Hindu Weekly Review*, May 1, 1967.
357. Report of the Education Commission 1964-66. p. 343.
358. Report of the Education Commission 1964-66. pp. 337-38.
359. *Ibid.* p. 334.
360. John, V.V. *Education and Language Policy*, Bombay : Nachiketa Publications. 1969. p. 48.
361. *The Hindustan Times,* April 18, 1968.
362. Report of the Education Commission 1964-66. p. 8.
363. National Policy on Education 1968. *op. cit.*, p. 3.
364. Report of the CABE 33rd Meeting held in 1967. Published in 1968. p. 128
365. *Ibid.* p. 133
366. Report of the CABE 36th Meeting held in 1972. Published in 1973. p. 110.

367. Report of the CABE 32nd Meeting held in Oct. 1965. Published in 1966.
368. Report of the CABE 35th Meeting held in 1970. Published in 1971. p. 93.
369. *Ibid.*
370. Shrivastava, G.N. *op. cit.*, p. 40.
371. Report of the CABE 39th Session. 1983. p. 71
372. Report of the CABE 35th Meeting held in 1970. Published in 1971. p. 94.
373. *Ibid.* 39th Session. p. 72
374. *Ibid.* 35th Meeing held in 1970. pp. 94-95
375. *Ibid.* p. 114
376. *Ibid.* p. 95.
377. *Ibid.* 38th Meeting held in 1975. Report Published in 1976. p. 25.
378. *Ibid.* p. 50.
379. *Ibid.* 39th session. Report published in 1983. p. 72.
380. *Ibid.* pp. 72-73
381. *Lok Sabha Debates* - 7th Series. New Delhi : Lok Sabha Secretariat starred question, dated 3.12.1981.

# 5 Field Work- School Survey

The historical perspective presented in several previous chapters revealed the complex phenomenon that existed in determining the status of language learning in the Indian Education system. The Government of India in the post-independence era, attempted in numerous ways by setting up Commissions and Committees to arrive at a sensible practical language formula which could preserve the integrity and unity of the land through a national language on one hand and could promote the excellence and standard of the various regional languages and literature worthy of attention.

The investigator was intrigued to find out the present position of three languages learning in vogue in some schools in the Union Territory of Delhi with a view to establishing the genuineness with which the educationalists in the land had implemented the language policy. Delhi should be known as a seat of the Union Territory and also the capital of India. State owned schools are by and large Hindi medium schools where a strong bias is maintained for teaching of Hindi both as a subject and a medium of instruction. There are also a number of minority schools with regional languages as media of instruction at the early primary level and English as a medium at the secondary and senior secondary levels. There are the third category of schools in Delhi which are run on progressive school pattern and which follow English medium right from Class I onwards. In fact schools in Delhi are classified very much on the medium of instruction that the schools follow. The rest of the school curriculum remains the same. At this point of the present study it would be worthwhile to examine the language situation in some mother tongue medium schools in Delhi and unravel the problems and difficulties if any associated with it.

## Analysis and interpretation

After the data collected, the scheme of analysis was decided upon. It was though desirable to present the data collected from students, language teachers and men in public in three separate sections, wherein each section should fall under three sub-sections again for complete analysis, such as :

a) Presentation of tables.
b) Description/interpretation of the data.
c) The discussion.

It would seem feasible that under each classification regarding the sources of data, viz., students, teachers and public, the relevant interpretation and discussion need be placed to facilitate the proper understanding of the meaning of the data. The scheme of analysis followed was :

| | |
|---|---|
| 1. Students questionnaire (Sample = 300 students) | Tables<br>Observations<br>Discussion |
| 2. Written opinionnaire from teachers (Sample = 67) | Table<br>Observation<br>Discussion |
| 3. Structured interview Schedule (Sample = 100) | Table<br>Observation<br>Discussion |

**a) Treatment of data from student's questionnaire (L.S.)[1] :**

There were ten major tables with one sub-table emanating from the major issues contained in the languages questionnaire administered to 300 students of Class X of senior secondary schools.

The tables intend to present the data on a total sample of 300 drawn from six schools. Hence the observation would be based on the total sample. The reactions of the total sample group are tabulated, described and discussed in this chapter. The case of each school in the form of case reports would be presented separately.

The language study questionnaire (LSQ) was administered to six groups each of fifty students from class X in six different schools, where different languages were not only taught as the subjects but were also used as the media of instruction. The Sample group took thirty to forty five minutes to fill in the LSQ and they did attempt to answer the questions to the best of their ability and satisfaction. The schools taken for the study were as follows :

| |  |  |
|---|---|---|
| 1. | Nutan Marathi Senior Secondary School, Deshbandhu Gupta Road, New Delhi. | Hindi Medium School |
| 2. | Delhi Public School, Mathura Road, New Delhi | English Medium School |
| 3. | Fatehpuri Muslim Senior Secondary School, Fatehpuri, Delhi | Urdu Medium School |
| 4. | Shree Guru Tegh Bahadur Senior SecondarySchool Sisganj Gurdwara, Chandni Chowk, Delhi | Punjabi Medium School |
| 5. | Raisina Bengali Senior Secondary School Reading Road (Mandir Marg), New Delhi | Bengali Medium School |
| 6. | Sindhi Education Society Baba Nebhraj Senior Secondary School, Lodhi Estate, New Delhi | Sindhi Medium School |

At the outset, information regarding the linguistic background of the students was sought, following which, data regarding the family background were collected and treated. The questionnaire responses collected from the students highlighted five broad sections, namely -

1. Information regarding family background, which included the languages spoken by their parents, the parents' education and their financial position.
2. Language environment at the learning centre.
3. Language environment of the children i.e. the use of various languages while communicating to different categories of people in their surroundings.
4. Use of language/languages in varied situations.
5. Students' opinion about the learning of three languages.

Since language is acquired best in the early childhood, in the company of parents and members of the family, it became necessary to enquire about the parents' education, their occupation, their language repertoire and their approximate income as these were likely to affect the growth of language/(s) pattern in young children. It is often commented that the education and profession of parents have an impact on the linguistic development of the child, even when the mother tongues of the parents are different. In some cases, professions of parents who have had to do with various languages during their course of life may enhance the possibilities in children of knowing languages other than those, offered in the school. The general atmosphere of the home is an index of the youngsters' language background. The following few paras deal with the information regarding the family background of these sample groups in respect of the education, occupation, languages and income of the families of the sample groups of the schools under study. Students of this sample group mentioned seven different mother tongues. The data in Table-1 indicates all the above facts of information.

Information regarding the mother tongue of students, the region they belonged to, and the languages generally used by their parents were sought through the LSQ. Languages used by the parents of this sample group were not only those, which were mentioned by the informants as their mother tongues, viz., Hindi, Urdu, Punjabi, Bengali, Sindhi, Marathi, and Konkani, but, Gujarati, Nepali, and English were also found in vogue. The Hindi mother tongue group comprised 106 students. Out of them one hundred and one (101) belonged to Hindi speaking areas and the remaining five (5) hailed from non-Hindi speaking states. The languages used by the mothers of these Hindi mother tongue students were not only Hindi, but Urdu, Punjabi, Gujarati, Nepali, and English as well. It is rather surprising to note that although these students had Hindi mother tongue the mothers of two students used only English and the mothers of eighty seven students used only Hindi while talking to others. The mothers of sixteen students had been using two languages out of whom, nine used English in addition to Hindi, four used Punjabi and Hindi, two used Gujarati and Hindi both and the mother of one student used Nepali in addition to Hindi. A single mother was found to be using three languages Hindi, English and Urdu.

The fathers of eighty students in the Hindi mother tongue group comprising 106 students, used only Hindi. Out of English speaking fathers of twenty students, eight fathers used only English, whereas the other twelve used both Hindi and English. The fathers of two students used Punjabi with Hindi and of another two students used Gujarati with Hindi and the father of one student communicated in Nepali and Hindi while talking to others; one of the hundred and six students, mentioned that he had no father.

The following conclusions could thus be drawn from the data ;

i) Hindi was the most widely used language among the parents, although it was used more frequently by mothers.

ii) English was the second language in use but the fathers used it more frequently than the mothers.

iii) Punjabi was the third language in vogue, whereas the use of Gujarati and Nepali was almost nil in comparison to Hindi and English languages.

**TABLE 1**

**The Mother tongue of the students, the regions they belonged to and the languages generally used by their parents**

| Mother tongue of the students | Hindi only | Pun. only | Urdu only | Ben. only | Sin. only | Mar. only | Eng. only | H P | H U | H B | H S | H G | H N | H E | E K | E P | E U | E B | H E P | H E P | H E B | H E, O | P Urdu | Total | Region: Hindi speaking area | Region: Non-Hindi speaking area |
|---|---|---|---|---|---|---|---|---|---|---|---|---|---|---|---|---|---|---|---|---|---|---|---|---|---|---|
| Hindi 106 (35.33) | M87 (82.1) | | | | | | 2 (1.38) | 4 (3.77) | | | 2 (1.88) | | | | 9 (8.57) | | | | 1 (0.9) | | | | | 106 (100) | 101 (95.23) | 5 (4.72) |
| | F 80 (76.19) | | | | | | 8 (7.52) | 2 (1.9) | | | | 2 (1.9) | | 1 | | 12 (11.43) | | | | | | | 105 (100) | | | |
| Urdu 52 (17.33) | M | | 49 (96%) | | | | | 2 (3.92) | | | | | | | | | | | | | | | | 51* (100) | 52 (100) | – |
| | F | | 39 (76.17%) | | | | | 3 (5.88) | | | | | | | | | 8 (15.69) | | | 1 (1.96) | | | | 51 (100) | | |
| Punjabi 51 (17) | M 4 (7.48) | 31 (60.78) | | | | | 2 (3.92) | 5 (9.80) | | | | | | | | 5 (9.80) | | | | | 4 (7.84) | | | 51 (100) | 37 (72.55) | 14 (22.45) |
| F | 5 (10) | 20 (58) | | | | | 4 (7.8) | 2 (4) | | | | | | 2 (4) | | | 3 (6) | | 4 (8) | | | | 1 (2) | 50 (100) | | |

| Mother tongue of the students | | Hindi only | Pun. only | Urdu only | Ben. only | Sin. only | Mar. only | Eng. only | H P | H U | H B | H S | H G | H N | H E | E K | E P | E U | E B | H E P | H E P | H E B | H E, O | P Urdu | Total | Region: Hindi speaking area | Region: Non-Hindi speaking area |
|---|---|---|---|---|---|---|---|---|---|---|---|---|---|---|---|---|---|---|---|---|---|---|---|---|---|---|---|
| Bengali 50 (16.67) | M | | | | 38 (77.55) | 1 | | 3 (6.12) | | | | 1 | | | | | | | 2 (4.03) | | | | | 4 (8.17) | 49* (100) | 28 (56) | 22 (44) |
| | F | | | | 32 (64) | 5 (10) | | | 1 (2) | | | 6 (12) | | | | 6 (12) | | | | 50 (100) | | | | | | | |
| Sindhi 38 (12.67) | M | 3 (7.89) | | | | 35 (92.11) | | | | | | | | | | | | | | | | | | | 38 (100) | 36 (94.71) | 2 (5.26) |
| | F | | 2 (5.56) | | | 28 (77.78) | | 2 (5.56) | | | | 4 (11.1) | | | | | | | | | | | | | 36 (100) | | |
| Marathi 2 (0.67) | M | | | | | 2 (100) | | | | | | | | | | | | | | | | | | | 2 (100) | | 2 (100) |
| | F | | | | | | | 2 (100) | | | | | | | | | | | | | | | | | 2 (100) | | |
| Konkani 1 (0.33) | M | | | | | | | | | | | 1 (100) | | | | | | | | | | | | | 1 (100) | | 1 (100) |
| | F | | | | | | | 1 (100) | | | | | | | | | | | | | | | | | 1 (100) | | |

| Mother tongue of the students | Hindi only | Pun. only | | Urdu only | | Ben. only | Sin. only | Mar. only | Eng. only | H P | H U | H B | H S | H G | H N | H E | E K | E P | E U | H E B P / H E P B / H E O / P Urdu | Region: Total Hindi speaking area / Non-Hindi speaking area |
|---|---|---|---|---|---|---|---|---|---|---|---|---|---|---|---|---|---|---|---|---|---|
| M | 94 (31.54) | 31 (10.4) | 49 (16.44) | 38 (12.75) | 35 (11.74) | 2 (.67) | 5 (1.68) | 9 (3.02) | 2 (0.67) | 3 (1.01) | 2 | 1 (.31) | 10 (3.4) | 1 (.67) | 5 (1.68) | 2 (.34) | 4 (1.34) | 1 | 4 (1.34) | | |
| F | 87 (29.5) | 29 (9.83) | 39 (13.22) | 32 (10.85) | 28 (19.49) | | 22 (7.46) | 4 (1.36) | 3 (1.02) | 4 (1.36) | 2 (.68) | 1 (.34) | 15 (5.08) | 3 (1.02) | 8 (2.71) | 6 (2.03) | | 4 (1.36) | 1 | 6 (2.03) | 1 |

N.B. (1) The fathers of 5 students and the mothers of 2 students were not alive.
(2) Figures against M stand for Mother and agaist F stand for Father.
(3) Figures within parentheses indicate the percentage.

iv) The multilingual environment was more obvious in case of mothers. The fathers had a surrounding constituting of Hindi, Punjabi, Gujarati, Nepali and English languages, whereas, in case of mothers Urdu was also an additional language in use with the aforesaid languages.

*Urdu mother tongue group* : The other largest group of fifty two students constituted of Urdu mother tongue students belonging to the Union Territory of Delhi. Significantly, very little variation was found in the languages used, by the parents. The mothers of forty nine students conversed in Urdu only, while two mothers used Hindi also in addition to Urdu, the mother of one student was not alive.

The language variation was found almost nil in the case of mothers when compared to that of fathers, although the majority of fathers (39) had been using generally Urdu language only. The fathers of eight students talked in English and Hindi, whereas the fathers of other three students used Hindi in addition to Urdu. The father of a single student had been using three languages, viz., Urdu, Hindi and English. One of fifty two students in this group, mentioned that he had no father. Thus it was clear that:

i) Urdu was being used most frequently by the Urdu mother tongue group of parents, the mothers used almost Urdu alone, whereas, ten fathers used Hindi and English apart from Urdu.
ii) English was not at all used by mothers.
iii) Urdu, English and Hindi were the languages respectively in use by both the parents.

*Punjabi mother tongue group* : In a group of fifty one Punjabi mother tongue students, 37 belonged to Hindi speaking region, while the rest 14 of them belonged to non Hindi speaking states. A large majority of Punjabi mothers used only Punjabi language.

The mothers of ten students used to speak in two languages, half of whom used Hindi, whereas another half used English alongwith Punjabi. The mothers of four students used three languages namely Hindi, English and Punjabi while conversing with others. It was surprising that six Punjabi mothers did not use Punjabi at all during conversation.

The fathers of twenty nine Punjabi mother tongue students communicated in Punjabi only, five fathers used Hindi only, four used English only. Fathers of two students used both Hindi and English another two used Hindi and Punjabi, three used English alongwith Punjabi, four used three languages i.e. Punjabi, Hindi and English while talking; father of one student used as many as four languages which were known as Punjabi, Hindi, Urdu and English. These findings could be summarised as :

i) Punjabi was the more commonly used language with this group.
ii) A small number of fathers used Punjabi only as compared to mothers. However, it was not at all by eleven fathers.
iii) Hindi was the second language in use among both the parents; and
iv) English was another language used by both of them but its use was found least as compared to Punjabi and Hindi.

*Bengali mother tongue group* : In another group of fifty students mentioning Bengali as their mother tongue 28 belonged to Hindi speaking states and the remaining 22 came from non-Hindi speaking regions in this group. The majority of the mothers (38) conversed in Bengali only. The mothers of four students used both Hindi and English together with Bengali. The mothers of three students used Hindi along with Bengali whereas the mothers of two students used English in addition to Bengali while talking to others. The two mothers did not use Bengali at all but English, though one of them communicated in Hindi too.

In case of fathers, only thirty two used Bengali exclusively while talking to others. The remaining eighteen were English speaking fathers. Out of whom six used English in addition to Bengali and the other six used three languages, namely, Bengali, Hindi and English while conversing. The fathers of six students did not use Bengali at all as five of them used only English, whereas one used Hindi and English both. It would be concluded that :

i) Although Bengali was the most commonly used language among the Bengali mother tongue parents, its use was more common in case of mothers.
ii) Hindi was equally used by both fathers and mothers.
iii) The frequency in use of English and Hindi was about equal in case of mothers.
iv) English was more frequently used by fathers and as such, English was the second common language used among the parents of Bengali mother tongue students.
v) Hindi was the third language used by them.
vi) The language variation was limited to three languages viz., Bengali, Hindi and English which were being taught in the school.

*Sindhi mother tongue group* : In case of thirty eight Sindhi mother tongue students, the largest majority of 36 students belonged to Hindi speaking areas and the rest two to non-Hindi speaking areas. The mothers of thirty five students used Sindhi while the mothers of the remaining three students used Hindi also in addition to Sindhi.

The fathers of thirty two Sindhi students generally used Sindhi language, although four of them used Hindi also in addition to Sindhi, whereas four fathers did not use Sindhi at all. Of these, two used only Hindi and two communicated only in English.

It might be concluded that :

i) As usual, the use of Sindhi mother tongue was more common in case of mothers, although considerable number of fathers had also been using Sindhi language.

ii) No Sindhi mother, like those of Urdu speaking mothers, talked in English.

iii) The fathers had been conversing in English, but, it was less frequently used than Sindhi and Hindi languages.

iv) The language variation was almost nil in case of mothers, whereas, it was more visible in case of fathers, who communicated in three languages viz. Sindhi, Hindi and English.

*Marathi and Konkari mother tongue groups* : Marathi was the mother tongue of only two and Konkani was the mother tongue of only one student. All these three informants hailed from non-Hindi speaking areas. The Marathi mothers used no other language but Marathi while the mother of the only Konkani student held communication not only in Konkani but in English also.

The fathers of two Marathi and one Konkani students used only English while talking to others.

As usual, the mothers of these groups too, had been using mother tongues, Marathi and Konkani, which were not used by the fathers in these two groups. Fathers had been using only English language in communication.

By summing up it could be said that :

i) Hindi was the only language which was being used in varying frequencies by the mothers of all the linguistic groups.

ii) In all the mother tongue groups, the maximum use of mother tongue was visible in case of mothers although the fathers of the students also had been using it in their circle.

iii) Although English was in use more in case of fathers, its use was insignificant when compared to the use of mother tongue and Hindi.

iv) The use of English was almost nil in case of mothers.

v) Hence, the language most commonly used by the parents was the mother tongue. The other language commonly used by them was Hindi. Only some of the parents used English which occupied the 3rd position whereas mother tongue and Hindi occupied first and second positions respectively.

vi) In case of two Marathi students, none of the fathers seemed to use Marathi.

vii) Altogether the group of parents comprised speakers of six distinct independent languages, namely Hindi, Urdu, Punjabi, Bengali, Sindhi, and English besides fifteen combinations of more than one language; still the unilingual parents constituted the vast majority.

Among the fathers and mothers, who were using other languages, in conversation, the percentage of fathers using other languages was quite high as compared to that of mothers. The reason was due to the fact, that there were more fathers, who were graduates and post-graduates as compared to mothers. This could be seen from Table 2.

**TABLE 2**

**Parents' Education and Occupation**

| *Education/ Occupation* | | *Illiterate* | *Upto Lower Secondary (till VIII class)* | *Upto Senior Secondary (Upto XII class)* | *Upto Graduate* | *Upto Post-Graduate* | *Total* |
|---|---|---|---|---|---|---|---|
| Business | M | 1 = 0.34% | --- | --- | 1 = 0.34% | -- | 2 = 0.67% |
| | F | 5 = 1.69% | 33 = 11..19% | 24 = 8.14% | 43 = 14.58% | 9 = 3.05% | 114 = 38.64% |
| Service | M | --- | 3 = 1.01% | 4 = 1.34% | 14 = 4.70% | 9 = 3.02% | 30 = 10.07% |
| | F | 4 = 1.36% | 8 = 2.71% | 51 = 17.29% | 59 = 20% | 49 = 16.6% | 171 = 57.97% |
| Not in Service | M | 47 = 15.77% | 77 = 25.84% | 86 = 28.86% | 45 = 15.10% | 11 = 3.69% | 266 = 89.26% |
| | F | -- | -- | 4 = 1.36% | 6 = 2.03% | -- | 10 = 3.39% |
| Total | M | 48 = 16.11% | 80 = 26.85% | 90 = 30.20% | 60 = 20.13% | 20 = 6.71% | 298 = 99.33% |
| | F | 9 = 3.05% | 41 = 13.90% | 79 = 26.78% | 108 = 36.61% | 58 = 19.66% | 295 = 98.33% |

.M Stands for mothers and F stands for fathers.

As indicated in the Table above, the fathers appeared more educated than mothers; also unlettered mothers were more in number (16.11%) than unlettered fathers (3.05%). The wide range of educational standard was recorded more in case of fathers from lower secondary to post-graduate level and absence of such higher educational level was significantly noted in the case of mothers.

On the occupational level, only 10.67% mothers were shown to be having some kind of earning by service and business. The rest were all housewives. Fathers, as heads of the family, were all earning members except in case of 3.39%. Maximum number of them were in service (57.97%); quite a good number (38.64%) were in business.

By summing up the educational and occupational background of the parents of the students, it could be concluded:

i) that a very small number of parents were found unlettered;
ii) that 16% mothers and only 3% fathers were illiterates ;
iii) that the number of educated and earning fathers was higher than those of mothers; the majority of them were not only educated but also employed ;
iv) that although fathers being the heads of the families were all in some sort of job, the language variation in their case was confined primarily to regional language, English and Hindi. It was however seen that the language used at home by parents was mainly the regional language/mother tongue although fathers were found to be using more than one language at home at times. In some cases fathers were found to be using English in preference to the mother tongue/regional language.

Information regarding the financial background of the families of the students was presented in Table 3. Looking into the family structure, more than 1/3 (39%) belonged to the higher income group. Out of the remaining (61%) of the total number 30% each belonged to the middle and lower income groups.

Thus, the information regarding financial background of the students, whose language status was being investigated would be summarised as :

i) a very small number of mothers was found as earning women;
ii) father's education was evenly distributed from lower secondary to post-graduation ;
iii) father's income was also relatively assured.

**TABLE 3**

**Financial Background : Families of Students**

| *Name of the School* | *Below Rs. 500/- Per month.* | *Between Rs. 500/- and 1500/- per month* | *Above R.s 1500/- per month* | *Total* |
|---|---|---|---|---|
| Nutan Marathi Sr. Secondary School | 20 = 40% | 14 = 28% | 16 = 32% | 50 |
| Delhi Public School | — | 3 = 6% | 47 = 94% | 50 |
| G.T.B.* Khalsa Sr. Secondary School | 25 = 50% | 12 = 24% | 13 = 26% | 50 |
| Fateh Puri Sr. Secondary School | 20 = 40% | 21 = 42% | 9 = 18% | 50 |
| Raisina Bengali Sr. Secondary School | 9 = 18% | 23 = 46% | 18 = 36% | 50 |
| S.E.S.B.* Nebhraj Sr. Secondary School | 17 = 34% | 19 = 38% | 14 = 28% | 50 |
| Total | 91 = 30.33% | 92 = 30.66% | 117 = 39% | 300 |

* Guru Teg Bahadur
* Sindih Education Society Baba

Information regarding language(s) learnt at different levels and language(s) used as media by school students were furnished in the Table 4. With a view to finding out whether the students in the schools learnt their mother tongue and the languages which were generally being used by their parents, a question was asked about the languages learnt and the languages used as media of instruction at different levels of school education.

*Hindi mother tongue group* : Out of one hundred and six students who belonged to the Hindi mother tongue group nearly 71% students at the primary level learnt two languages in addition to Hindi i.e. 63.2% learnt English and 8% (7.55%) learnt Punjabi in addition to their mother tongue Hindi. The remaining 29% learnt one language i.e. Hindi only. It is interesting to note that although the mother tongue of this sample group of 106 students was Hindi, 33% of them had their education through English medium.

At the lower secondary level of education, i.e. from VI to VIII class, three languages were essentially taught in the schools. Out of these three languages, Hindi and English were compulsory, option was given for the 3rd language only. Hence, in this group of 106 Hindi mother tongue students, the majority of them i.e. 70% learnt Sanskrit, 21% learnt Punjabi, 7.5% learnt French and 1% each learnt Russian and German as their 3rd languages. Regarding the languages used as the media of instruction it was found that the largest number of the students (68.9%) had their education through Hindi medium. The next largest number of the students (24%) had English medium in English medium school and the minimum number of the students had their education through Punjabi in Punjabi medium school.

Since only two languages were compulsory at the Secondary level of education, the maximum variation of languages learnt was found at this level. Out of one hundred and six Hindi mother tongue students, the highest percentage (74%) of the students was found to be opting for Hindi with English. Although eighteen students had opted for Sanskrit, twelve (11%) had offered English and 5.66% had opted for Hindi, with Sanskrit common to each. Ten students opting for Punjabi were also divided in two different combinations viz. Punjabi + Hindi and Punjabi + English which were respectively nine (8%) and one (0.94%) in number. The languages used as the media of instruction at this level emerged as Hindi, English and Punjabi for sixty five (61%) thirty nine (37%) and two students (2%) respectively. It is significant to note that the students opting for Hindi/English as one of the two languages was almost at par

**TABLE 4**

**'es learnt and the languages used as media of insturction at different levels of schools of school education.**

| | Pu | Si | H Ur | H Pu | H Si | H E | H E Ur | H E B | H E Si | | Class VI to VIII: H E Skt | H E Pu | H E Ur | H E Si | H E Fr | H E Rus | H E Ger | HE B Skt | HE Ur Ar | HE Ur Per | H | E | P | Ur | B Si |
|---|---|---|---|---|---|---|---|---|---|---|---|---|---|---|---|---|---|---|---|---|---|---|---|---|---|
| | | | | 8 7.55% | | 67 (63.21%) | | | | | 74 69.81% | 22 20.75% | | | 8 7.55% | 1 | 1 | | | | | | | | |
| | | | | | | | | | | | | | | | | | | | | | (73) (23.6%) | (25) (68.9%) | (8) (7.5%) | | |
| % | | | | 34 65.38% | | | 1 1.92% | | | 6 11.54% | 1 1.92% | | 23 44.23% | | | | | | 10 19.23% | 18 34.62% | | | | | |
| ;%) | | | | | | | | | | | | | | | | | | | | | (1) | (1) | (50) (96.15%) | | |
| | | 10 | | 30 1.96% | | | | 58.82% | | | 18 35.29% | 23 45.1% | | | 10 19.61% | | | | | | | | | | |
| %) | | (9) (17.64%) | | 19.6% | | | | | | | | | | | | | | | | | | (19) (37.25%) | (23) (45.09%) | (17.64%) | (9) |
| | | | | | | | | 50 100% | | | | | | | | | | | 50 100% | | | | 50 100% | | |

| Pu | Si | H<br>Ur | H<br>Pu | H<br>Si | H<br>E | H<br>E<br>Ur | H<br>E<br>B | H<br>E<br>Si | | Class VI to VIII<br>H<br>E<br>Skt | H<br>E<br>Pu | H<br>E<br>Ur | H<br>E<br>Si | H<br>E<br>Fr | H<br>E<br>Rus | H<br>E<br>Ger | HE<br>B<br>Skt | HE<br>Ur<br>Ar | HE<br>Ur<br>Per | H | E | P | Ur | B Si |
|---|---|---|---|---|---|---|---|---|---|---|---|---|---|---|---|---|---|---|---|---|---|---|---|---|
| | | | | 1 | | 11<br>28.95% | | | 36.84% | 14<br>15.79% | | 6<br>7.89% | | | 3<br>76.32% | 29 | | | | | | | | |
| | (26)<br>(68%) | | | | 10<br>26.32% | | | | | | | | | | | | | | | (12)<br>(32%) | | | | (26)<br>(68%) |
| | | | | 1<br>50% | | | | | | 2<br>100% | | | | | | | | | | (2)<br>(100%) | | | | |
| | | | | | 1 | | | | | | | | | 1<br>100% | | | | | | | (1)<br>(100%) | | | |

| Class IX and X | | | | | | | | | | | | | |
|---|---|---|---|---|---|---|---|---|---|---|---|---|---|
| H Pu | E Skt | E P | E B | E Si | H E Skt | H E Si | E Ur Ar | E Ur Per | H | E | Pu | H Ur | Si |
| 9 8.49% | 12 11.32% | 1 | | | | | | | (65) (61.32%) | (39) (36.79%) | (2) (1.89%) | | |
| | 1 | | | | | | 20 38.46% | 30 57.69% | (1) | (1) | | (50) (96.15%) | |
| 6 11.76% | 4 7.84% | 9 17.65% | | | | | | | (19) (37.25%) | (28) (55) | (4) (7.8%) | | |
| | | | 35 70% | | | | | | | (50) (100%) | | | |
| | | 1 | | 1 | 1 | 25 65.79% | | | (9) (24%) | (3) (8%) | | | (26) (68.4%) |
| | 1 50% | | | | | | | | (1) (50%) | (1) (50%) | | | |
| | | | | | | | | | | (1) (100%) | | | |

theses show the languages used as media of instruction at different levels of school education and the figures outside show the ifferent levels of school education.

*Urdu mother tongue group* : Urdu had been recorded as the mother tongue of fifty two students at the primary level of education. The majority of these students (79%) learnt Hindi also in addition to Urdu while the remaining 21% learnt Urdu only. Out of the former group of 79% of the students, 12% had learnt English also alongwith Urdu and Hindi. A single student could not get an opportunity to learn his mother tongue Urdu, though he learnt two languages Hindi and English.

When asked about the languages being used as the medium of education all of them, but one, had stated Urdu as the medium. The only one student had his education through English medium.

At the lower secondary level of education, twenty-eight students (54%) had an opportunity of learning classical languages too, besides the three compulsory languages – Urdu, Hindi and English, eighteen (35%) out of these, opted for Persian, whereas ten (19%) had offered Arabic as the fourth language. The remaining twenty four students (46%) learnt only three languages of whom, twenty three (44%) learnt Urdu, Hindi and English whereas one student (2%) learnt Hindi, English and Sanskrit, since no other option was given.

Regarding the medium of education, it was perceived from the Table 4, that fifty students (96%) had their education through Urdu medium of the remaining two, one student (2%) had Hindi medium and another (2%) had English medium at this level of education.

At the Secondary level of education although two languages were supposed to be taken, thirty (58%) had opted for Persian with Urdu and English whereas 20 (38%) had offered Arabic with the same combination of two languages i.e. Urdu and English. The number of the students offering these two classical languages had been enhanced from the number of the students opting for them at the lower secondary level of education. Out of the remaining two students (4%) opting for English 2% had offered Hindi and another 2% had opted for Sanskrit as the 2nd languages.

The largest number of the students (96%) had gone for Urdu and English media simultaneously whereas 2% each had gone for Hindi and English media separately.

*Punjabi mother tongue group* : Though Punjabi was the mother tongue of fifty-one students, yet, all of them did not learn it at the Primary level of education. Although 59% had learnt two languages, none of them had offered Punjabi; instead they learnt Hindi and English. Out of the remaining 41% students, 19.60% learnt Hindi only and another 19.60% learnt Hindi and Punjabi as the two languages. The remaining single student (2%) had learnt English only at this level of education.

All these languages viz. Punjabi, Hindi and English were also mentioned as the languages used as media of instruction. English was offered by 51%, Hindi by 31% and Punjabi was offered by 18% students, as the medium of instruction at the primary level of education.

At the lower secondary level of education, two languages Hindi and English remained common, but, compulsory languages for all. Since three languages are compulsory at this level of education, the students had to go for the 3rd language also. The Table 4 – shows that the number of the students opting for Punjabi was enhanced from 20% (at the primary level) to 45% at this level, 35% of the students had opted for Sanskrit, whereas 20% had offered French.

Punjabi, Hindi and English, all the three languages were mentioned being used as the media of instruction for this group. Significantly the maximum number of the Punjabi mother tongue students had their education through English medium and the least had Punjabi medium. To be more accurate 45% of the students had their education through English medium and 37% had opted Hindi medium; only 18% of the students had offered Punjabi as the medium of their education.

At the secondary level of education the largest number of the students, i.e. nearly 63% had opted for Hindi with English. About 18% of them had offered Punjabi and English whereas 12% and 8% respectively had offered Hindi with Punjabi and English along with Sanskrit.

Regarding the languages used as media of instruction, the Table 4 - shows that the Punjabi mother tongue students had opted for three different media i.e. English, Hindi and Punjabi. The majority of the students (55%) had offered for English medium. Of the remaining 45% Hindi medium was opted by 37.3% students, whereas the minimum percentage of the students (7.8%) had gone for Punjabi medium, although 31% of Punjabi mother tongue students had been recorded as hailing from Punjabi medium school.

*Bengali mother tongue group* : As there was no other school in the total sample of the study in which Bengali student was found, the sample for Bengali students consisted of fifty students only from the school, in which Bengali language had been followed as the medium of instruction. At the primary level of education the informants learnt three languages. In addition to their mother tongue Bengali, they learnt two more languages which were mentioned as Hindi and English, Bengali was the medium for 50% and English for another 50% of this group.

At the lower secondary level of education, students in this school, instead of three learnt four languages. Apart from Bengali, English and Hindi, Sanskrit was taught as the fourth compulsory language in this school.

All the students (100%) in this group of fifty students had opted Bengali medium.

At the secondary level of education, option was given between Bengali and Hindi, 70% of these students had offered Bengali whereas 30% had offered Hindi with English remaining the compulsory language for all. Though the provision was made for Bengali medium also yet, the students of this group opted English medium.

*Sindhi mother tongue group* : There were thirty eight students who mentioned Sindhi as their mother tongue. 37% of the students learnt three languages viz. Sindhi, Hindi and English at the primary level of education; 29% had learnt Hindi and English whereas 26% learnt Sindhi with Hindi, 5% of the remaining students learnt Hindi only and 3% learnt Punjabi along with Hindi.

Sindhi and Hindi were the two languages which were adopted as the media of education at the primary level of education, 68% of the Sindhi students opted for Sindhi medium, where as 32% of the informants had offered Hindi medium.

At the lower secondary level of education, the highest percentage (76%) of the students had opted for Sindhi with Hindi and English, 16% of them had offered Sanskrit and 8% had gone for Punjabi with Hindi and English, remaining common but compulsory languages with both the combinations (of languages).

Sixty eight per cent of Sindhi speaking students had their education through Sindhi medium while 32% had Hindi medium.

At the secondary level of education, all the Sindhi mother tongue students learnt English with different combinations of languages at this level of education. Twenty six students (68%) of them learnt three languages and the remaining 12 students (32%) learnt two languages. The larger group opting for three languages was found to be having two combinations of three languages, 25 students opted for Sindhi with Hindi and English and the remaining student (1) (2.63%) opted for Hindi, English and Sanskrit. Among the students opting for two languages the largest number of the students consisting of 10 (26.3%) learnt Hindi and English whereas one each of the remaining two students learnt Punjabi with English and Sindhi with English.

*Marathi and Konkani students* : Only two informants out of a sample of three hundred students had mentioned Marathi as their mother tongue and another single student mentioned Konkani as his mother tongue. One of the Marathi students learnt only Hindi whereas the other Marathi and the only Konkani student learnt two languages viz. Hindi and English. One of the Marathi students had opted for Hindi medium whereas the others including the Konkani student had their education through English medium.

At the lower secondary level i.e. from VI to VIII class, all the three students learnt three languages. The two Marathi students opted for Hindi, English and Sanskrit with Hindi medium whereas the only Konkani student learnt Hindi, English and French with English medium.

At the secondary level of education, one of the two Marathi students opted for Hindi and English while the other had opted for Sanskrit and English combination. The Konkani student had a combination of Hindi and English. Regarding the medium of education, the facts revealed that both Hindi and English languages were used as the media of education. One of the Marathi students had his education through Hindi medium. The other Marathi and the only Konkani student had their education through English medium.

The conclusion drawn from the above data were :

1. At the primary level of education –
   - (a) The data collected revealed the fact that not only one but two to three languages were also being taught. Though English was not the mother tongue of any informant in this sample group of 300 yet it was found to be in use as the medium of education in certain cases.
   - (b) Though English was one of the languages to be learnt at this level of education yet, it was not the first choice at this level.
   - (c) Though Hindi was discovered as the mother tongue of 106 students in this sample of 300 yet in certain cases it came out to be the first choice of non-Hindi mother tongue groups also e.g. Punjabi mother tongue group.
   - (d) Out of a sample of 300 students, 58% learnt 2 languages; 23% learnt 3 languages and the remaining 19% learnt only one language. It is significant to note that 100% of Bengali; 37% of Sindhi and 12% of Urdu mother tongue students learnt three

languages whereas 80% of Punjabi; 71% of Hindi and 63% of Urdu mother tongue students learnt 2 languages. The remaining students learnt only one language.

(e) Languages being used as the media of education differed from one mother tongue group to another. For instance, Urdu mother tongue group was restricted to Urdu medium whereas the largest number of Punjabi students (26) had their education through English medium. Sixteen and nine Punjabi students had their education respectively in Hindi and Punjabi medium. Bengalees were divided equally between Bengali and English media. The remaining students had Hindi and their respective mother tongues as the media of education.

2. At the lower Secondary level of education –

(a) Students in this sample group learnt not only English but the other foreign languages like French, Russian and German. They also learnt classical languages – Sanskrit, Arabic and Persian.

(b) Hindi and English were compulsory for all the mother tongue groups.

(c) All the Bengali mother tongue students and 54% of Urdu mother tongue students learnt four languages at this level of education.

(d) All the Bengali students, 96% Urdu speaking and 68% Sindhi mother tongue students had their education through their respective mother tongues whereas the Hindi and Punjabi students had opted three media languages. Some of them had gone for Hindi, others for English, and yet some others had gone for Punjabi medium.

3. At the secondary level of education – Although Hindi and English both were found to be the choice of the students their relative place differed from one mother tongue group to another mother tongue group. English was the main choice in most of the cases. Next to English preference was for Hindi followed by their respective mother tongues.

4. Regarding the medium of education, it was found that both Hindi and English languages were equally used as media of education at the secondary level.

After perceiving the various languages learnt by the students, a questionnaire was constructed to find out whether they had developed all the four linguistic skills viz. understanding, speaking, reading and writing in those languages (Table 5). Besides whether they could understand and speak those languages which were not learnt but acquired from environment.

**TABLE 5**
**Language attainment and four language skills**

**TABLE 5 (a) Understand only**

| Language/ Mother tongue | Punjabi | Bengali | Assamese |
|---|---|---|---|
| Hindi<br>106 | 14<br>13.20% | 4<br>3.77% | --<br>-- |
| Urdu<br>52 | 2<br>3.84% | -- | -- |
| Punjabi<br>51 | -- | 1<br>1.96% | -- |
| Bengali<br>50 | 12<br>24% | -- | 20<br>40% |
| Sindhi<br>38 | 6<br>15.78% | -- | -- |
| Marathi<br>2 | -- | -- | -- |
| Konkani<br>1 | 1<br>100% | -- | -- |

**TABLE 5(b) Understand & Speak only**

| Language/ Mother tongue | Punjabi | Sindhi | Konkani |
|---|---|---|---|
| Hindi<br>106 | 16<br>15.09% | -- | -- |
| Urdu<br>52 | -- | -- | -- |
| Punjabi<br>51 | 28<br>54.9% | -- | -- |
| Bengali<br>50 | -- | -- | -- |
| Sindhi<br>38 | 2<br>5.26% | 9<br>23.68% | -- |
| Marathi<br>2 | -- | -- | -- |
| Konkani<br>1 | -- | -- | 1<br>100% |

**TABLE 5 (c) Read only**

| Language/ Mother tongue | Arabic |
|---|---|
| Hindi<br>106 | -- |
| Urdu<br>52 | 1<br>1.92% |
| Punjabi<br>51 | -- |
| Bengali<br>50 | -- |
| Sindhi<br>38 | -- |
| Marathi<br>2 | -- |
| Konkani<br>1 | -- |

**TABLE 5 (d) Write only**

| Language/ Mother tongue | Eng. | Skt. |
|---|---|---|
| Hindi 106 | 1 ·0.94% | 11 10.37% |
| Urdu 52 | -- | -- |
| Punjabi 51 | 3 5.88% | 3 5.88% |
| Bengali 50 | -- | -- |
| Sindhi 38 | 4 10.52% | -- |
| Marathi 2 | -- | -- |
| Konkani 1 | -- | -- |

**TABLE 5 (e) Understand Speak and Read only**

| Language/ Mother tongue | French |
|---|---|
| Hindi 106 | -- |
| Urdu 52 | -- |
| Punjabi 51 | 1 |
| Bengali 50 | -- |
| Sindhi 38 | -- |
| Marathi 2 | -- |
| Konkani 1 | -- |

**TABLE 5 (f) Read only write only**

| Language Mother tongue | Eng. | Skt. | Arabic | French |
|---|---|---|---|---|
| Hindi 106 | 12 11.32% | 28 26.41% | -- | -- |
| Urdu 52 | 30 57.69% | 1 | 20 38.46% | -- |
| Punjabi 51 | 8 15.68% | 4 7.84% | -- | 1 |
| Bengali 50 | -- | -- | -- | -- |
| Sindhi 38 | 12 31.57% | 5 13.15% | -- | -- |
| Marathi 2 | -- | 1 | -- | -- |
| Konkani 1 | -- | -- | -- | -- |

**TABLE 5 (g) Understand, Read and Write**

| *Language* Mother tongue | English | Sanskrit | Punjabi | Persian | French | Russian |
|---|---|---|---|---|---|---|
| Hindi 106 | 31 = 29.24% | 32 = 30.18% | 3 = 2.83% | | 4 = 3.77% | 1 |
| Urdu 52 | 20 = 38.46% | – | – | 30 = 57.69% | – | |
| Punjabi 51 | 8 = 15 68% | 10 = 19.60% | – | – | 3 = 5.88% | |
| Bengali 50 | – | 40 = 80% | – | – | – | – |
| Sindhi 38 | 20 = 52.63% | 1 = 2.06% | – | – | – | – |
| Marathi 2 | 1 = 50% | 1 = 50% | – | – | – | – |
| Konkani 1 | – | – | | – | – | – |

**TABLE 5 (h)**

**Understand, Speak, Read and Write**

| Language/ Mother tongue | Hindi | English | Punjabi | Urdu | Bengali | Sindhi | Marathi | Sanskrit | French |
|---|---|---|---|---|---|---|---|---|---|
| Hindi 106 | 106 100% | 62 58.49% | 19 17.92% | | | | | 3 2.83% | 4/8 50% |
| Urdu 52 | 43 82.69% | 2 3.85% | | 52 100% | | | | | |
| Punjabi 51 | 51 100% | 32 62.74% | 23 45.09% | | | | | 1 1.96% | 5/10 50% |
| Bengali 50 | 50 100% | 50 100% | | | 50 100% | | | 10 20% | |
| Sindhi 38 | 38 100% | 2 5.26% | | | | 29 76.31% | | | |
| Marathi 2 | 2 100% | 1 50% | | | | | 2 100% | | |
| Konkani 1 | 1 100% | 1 100% | | | | | | | 1/1 100% |
| Total 300 | 291 97% | 150 50% | 42 14% | 52 17.33% | 50 16.67% | 29 9.66% | 2 0.67% | 14 4.66% | 10 3.33% |

*Understand only* : Punjabi, Bengali and Assamese were the three languages which the informants had mentioned that they could only understand though these were not their mother tongues.

Punjabi language was understood by 12% of the students drawn from all the non-Punjabi mother tongue groups. As shown in the Table 5(a) the number of the Hindi students was the highest followed by Bengali, Sindhi and Urdu mother tongue students who understood Punjabi. There were four Hindi and one Punjabi speaking student who had claimed to understand Bengali. Assamese was mentioned to be understood by the 40% Bengali sample group.

*Understand and speak only* : The informants had mentioned three modern Indian languages – Punjabi, Sindhi and Konkani which they could not read and write but could understand and speak. Though there were 51 students, who had mentioned Punjabi as their mother tongue yet, more than 54.90% of them could neither read it nor write it. Fifteen per cent (15.09%) of the Hindi mother tongue and 5.26% of the Sindhi mother tongue students could understand and speak Punjabi language. Twenty four per cent (23.68%) of the Sindhi mother tongue students could only understand and communicate in their mother tongue. They could neither read it nor write it.

*Read only* : Only one Urdu mother tongue student had mentioned such languages as Arabic which he could only read but was unable to write it, though the script of Arabic was known to him.

*Write only* : Similar was the condition with the skill of writing, although the scripts of both English and Sanskrit were known to the students. Though English was the compulsory language for all the mother tongue students 10.52% of Sindhi, 5.88% of Punjabi and 0.94% of the Hindi mother tongue students could develop only the skill of writing down the script of English. In Sanskrit language 10% of the Hindi and 6% of Punjabi mother tongue students (opting for Sanskrit) mentioned that they developed only one skill and that was the skill of writing the script.

*Read and write only* : The students of all the mother tongue groups had mentioned such four languages as they could read and write but they could neither understand them nor they could communicate in those languages. Out of these four two were classical languages, viz. Sanskrit and Arabic. The remaining two were the foreign languages namely English and French. All the 100% of students offering Arabic as one of the classical languages in the school could develop none other skill but reading and writing in it; 26% out of 151 students stated that they could only read and write the language 21% of the total sample of 300 informants (for English was a compulsory language for all) could develop only the skill of reading and writing in English whereas 6% of French offering students could read and write French language.

*Understand, speak and read only* : A single Punjabi mother tongue student had mentioned that he could not write French, although he could read, understand and communicate in that language.

*Understand, read and write only* : In all 6 languages were recorded in which the students could not communicate but they could understand them. Besides, they could read and write them. Sanskrit, Persian, English, French, Russian and Punjabi were such languages in which the informants could not develop the skills of speaking. All the students (100%) opting for Persian, 56% of Sanskrit and 39% of the French offering students could not develop the skill of speaking in the said languages. Similarly 26.33% of English knowing students 1% in case of Punjabi offering students and a single student opting for Russian were found in the same boat.

*Understand, speak, read and write* : All the students in all the mother tongue groups except in Sindhi and Punjabi mother tongue groups could develop these four linguistic skills in their respective mother tongues. It is surprising to note that only 76% of Sindhi and 45% of Punjabi mother tongue students could develop the four skills in their respective mother tongues.

In English, 100% of Bengali, 63% of Punjabi and 58% of Hindi mother tongue students could develop the skills of understanding, speaking, reading and writing. A meagre percentage of Sindhi and Urdu students (5% and 4% respectively) could do so in English.

Hindi was the only modern Indian languages in which maximum number of the students of this sample groups of 300 could develop all the 4 linguistic skills. It was in case of Urdu speaking group where 83% of them could develop all the four linguistic skills.

In respect of other languages, it was perceived, that, 86% of those students who opt for Punjabi in the Hindi mother tongue group could develop these four linguistic skills in Punjabi. French was offered by 19 students. Out of them 53% of the students and 9% of 151 Sanskrit students could understand, speak, read and write French and Sanskrit respectively.

By summing up it can be concluded that :

1. Bengali mother tongue students were found more keen towards learning languages since, 100% of them understood, spoke, read and wrote not only in the language mentioned by them as their mother tongue, but in Hindi and English also. Even 50% of them claimed to develop all these four skills in Sanskrit.
2. Ninety seven per cent of the students of all the mother tongue groups knew Hindi to the extent that all the four linguistic skills were developed in their case.
3. Fifty three per cent of the students opting for French, had developed these 4 skills in French whereas only 50% of the sample group could develop these skills in English.
4. Out of three classical languages – Sanskrit, Arabic and Persian taught in the schools, it was only Sanskrit in which the students developed the four linguistic skills, although the percentage of such students was pretty low.

After determining the level of the skill development in the languages learnt, it seemed necessary to find out whether the languages learnt in the schools were difficult for them to learn. Table 6 (a) brought out a list of 6 languages that the students mentioned to have perceived as difficult to learn which were formally taught to them in the schools. The classical languages, foreign languages, regional language/mother tongue and Hindi were recorded by them in descending order as the difficult languages. Out of the 201 students, who had opted for classical languages such as Sanskrit, Arabic and Persian, 31% of them perceived difficulty in learning them.

Among the group of foreign languages, English was learnt as a compulsory language by all the 300 students of this sample group. Twenty six per cent of these students found it difficult to learn. The other foreign languages – French, Russian and German were considered to be more difficult to learn than English.

Among the group of modern Indian languages being learnt as the first language/mother tongue languages returned were found to be 7 in number viz., Hindi, Urdu, Punjabi, Bengali, Sindhi, Marathi and Konkani. Since Marathi was not taught in any of the schools, taken for the study, all the two students found it difficult to learn. Only two Bengali, one Punjabi and one Sindhi student mentioned that their respective mother tongues were difficult to learn.

TABLE 6 (a)

**Languages difficult to learn**

| *Mother tongue of the student* | *Hindi* | *Urdu* | *Punjabi* | *Bengali* | *Sindhi* | *Marathi* | *Sanskrit* | *Arabic* | *Persian* | *French* | *German* | *Russian* | *English* |
|---|---|---|---|---|---|---|---|---|---|---|---|---|---|
| Hindi<br>106 | 106<br>-- | | 22 = 20.75%<br>(12) = (54.55%) | | | | 74 = 69.8%<br>(16) = (21.62%) | | | 8 = 7.55%<br>(1) | 1 | 1<br>(1) = (100%) | 106<br>(21) = (19.81:) |
| Urdu<br>52 | 52<br>(4) = (7.69%) | 52<br>-- | | | | | 1<br>(1) | ·20 = 38.46.%<br>(4) = (20%) | 30 = 57.59%<br>(20) = (66.67%) | | | | 52<br>(22) = (42.31%) |
| Punjabi<br>51 | 51<br>(3) = (5.38%) | | 23 = 45%<br>(1) = (4.34%) | | | | 18 = 35.29%<br>(5) = (27.98%) | | 10 = 19.61%<br>(3) = (30%) | | | | 51<br>(15) = (29.41%) |
| Bengali<br>50 | 50<br>-- | | | 50<br>(2) = (4%) | | | 50<br>(14) = (28%) | | | | | | 50<br>(4) = (8%) |
| Sindhi<br>38 | 38<br>(4) = (16%) | | 3 = 7.39% | | 29 = 76.32%<br>(1) = ( ) | | 6 = 15.79%<br>(2) = (33.33%) | | | | | | 38<br>(14) = (36.34%) |

| *Mother tongue of the student* | *Hindi* | *Urdu* | *Punjabi* | *Bengali* | *Sindhi* | *Marathi* | *Sanskrit* | *Arabic* | *Persian* | *French* | *German* | *Russian* | *English* |
|---|---|---|---|---|---|---|---|---|---|---|---|---|---|
| Marathi<br>2 | 2<br>(2) = (100%) | | | | 2 | | 2<br>(1) = (50%) | | | | | | 2<br>(2) = (100%) |
| Konkani<br>1 | 1<br>(1) = (100%) | | | | | | | | | 1 | | | 1 |
| Total<br>300 | 300<br>52<br>(14)<br>(4.67%) | -- | 48 = 16%<br>(13)<br>(4.33%) | 50 = 16.67%<br>(2)<br>(0.66%) | 29 = 9.67%<br>(1) | 2 = 0.67%<br>-- | 20 = 6.67%<br>151 = 50.33%<br>(39)<br>(13%) | 30 = 10%<br>(4)<br>(1.33%) | (2)<br>(0.66%) | 19 = 6.33%<br>1<br>(4)<br>(1.33%) | 1<br>-- | (1) | 300<br>(73)<br>(26%) |

N.B. Figures within parentheses show the language difficult to learn. Figures outside the parentheses show the languages learnt.

2) In classical language the percentage is calculated out of the students who had opted for it.

Regarding the other modern Indian languages or regional languages it was discovered that both Punjabi and Hindi were the difficult languages. It may be recalled that Bengali, Sindhi and Marathi as the 3rd language were not provided for teaching.

As can be seen in Table 6 the Hindi mother tongue group perceived the classical languages – Sanskrit and the foreign languages – English, French, German, Russian and the modern Indian language – Punjabi difficult languages to learn. Fifty five per cent of the Punjabi opting students (12 students out of 22 opting Punjabi), 22% of those who opted for Sanskrit; 20% in English faced difficulties in learning the said languages. Only one out of 8 students opting for French found it difficult to learn.

All the Urdu mother tongue group found the classical languages – Arabic and Persian difficult to learn. Eight per cent of Urdu mother tongue students (i.e. 4/52) found Hindi also difficult to learn.

In Punjabi mother tongue group also the classical languages, foreign languages and Hindi languages were discovered as the difficult languages to learn. Thirty per cent of those opting for French, 29.41% found English, 28% of Sanskrit students and 6% of the Punjabi mother tongue group found Hindi to be a difficult language.

In Bengali mother tongue group, 28% and 8% of the students found respectively classical language – Sanskrit and English languages difficult to learn.

In Sindhi mother tongue group, 33.33% found Sanskrit a difficult language to learn. Besides, 37% and 16% respectively found English and Hindi languages difficult to learn.

In the Marathi mother tongue group, all the two students found English and Hindi difficult languages. One of them faced difficulty in learning the classical languages – Sanskrit also.

The only Konkani student found only Hindi a difficult language.

**Conclusion :**

1. Among all the mother tongue groups, the maximum variety of languages (7) were opted by the Hindi mother tongue group and as such the number of languages found to be difficult to learn was maximum in this group only.
2. The students found not only the classical language and foreign languages difficult but the modern Indian languages also difficult to learn. In a few cases, even the language learnt as mother tongue was discovered difficult for them.

3. Urdu was the 2nd mother tongue group opting for five languages – besides their mother tongue. They found the classical languages - Arabic, Persian and Sanskrit difficult languages. Besides, English and Hindi were also difficult for them.
4. Punjabi was the 3rd mother tongue group opting for four languages in addition to their mother tongue they faced difficulty not only in learning their mother tongue but in learning the Classical language – Sanskrit, English, French, Hindi and Punjabi in that order.
5. The Sindhi mother tongue group also opted for 5 languages. They found Sanskrit, English and Hindi difficult languages. One of the Sindhi students found his mother tongue also a difficult language.
6. Bengali mother tongue group opted for 4 languages. They found the classical language – Sanskrit, English and their mother tongue Bengali difficult languages to learn. Hindi in their case was not found to be a difficult language.
7. All the two Marathi students found Sanskrit, English and Hindi as the difficult languages.

Summing up, it can be concluded that –

1. All the 3 classical languages – Sanskrit, Arabic and Persian were considered to be the most difficult languages followed by English, modern Indian languages, Hindi and the respective mother tongues.
2. English was recorded as a very difficult language to learn for the Urdu mother tongue group.
3. Hindi was considered the least difficult language. None of the Bengali and Hindi mother tongue students perceived it as a difficult language to learn.

Although the students had mentioned various languages which were perceived by them, not easy to learn, it was not clear as to what was the level up to which they had learnt those languages viz. classical languages, foreign languages, mother tongue/regional language and Hindi. Hence, another question was put to them in order to find out their difficulties in terms of linguistic skills and tabulated in Table 6(b).

TABLE 6 (b)

**Languages difficult to learn in terms of skills**

| *Mother tongue of the students* | *Mother tongue* | | | | *Classical Language* | | | | *English* | | | | *Hindi* | | | |
|---|---|---|---|---|---|---|---|---|---|---|---|---|---|---|---|---|
| | *U* | *S* | *R* | *W* | *U* | *S* | *R* | *W* | *U* | *S* | *R* | *W* | *U* | *S* | *R* | *W* |
| Hindi 106 | 18 | 15 | 14 | 19 | 27 | 42 | 21 | 18 | 29 | 37 | 25 | 22 | Nil | Nil | Nil | Nil |
| Urdu 52 | 11 | 4 | 13 | 7 | 34 | 50 | 34 | 9 | 24 | 50 | 34 | 13 | 12 | 2 | 9 | 3 |
| Punjabi 51 | 9 | 7 | 10 | 11 | 14 | 17 | 11 | 14 | 16 | 21 | 15 | 17 | 8 | 8 | 8 | 8 |
| Bengali 50 | 9 | 5 | 4 | 8 | 24 | 27 | 24 | 27 | 3 | 3 | 3 | 4 | 5 | 3 | 3 | 4 |
| Sindhi 38 | 7 | 10 | 12 | 12 | 6 | 4 | 6 | 2 | 11 | 16 | 17 | 14 | 9 | 9 | 10 | 12 |
| Marathi 2 | — | — | — | — | 2 | 2 | 1 | 1 | 1 | 1 | — | — | — | — | — | — |
| Konkani 1 | — | — | — | — | — | — | — | — | — | — | — | — | — | — | — | — |

On probing deeper the specific problems for different mother tongue groups, it was seen that not only the skills of speaking and understanding classical and foreign languages were difficult but reading and writing too created problems. In fact the classical languages – Sanskrit, Arabic, Persian and the foreign languages were equally difficult for all the mother tongue students except in case of Bengali speaking students, who considered the classical language – Sanskrit the most difficult one. At least 54% of the Bengali students were found to be weak in all the four linguistic skills viz., understanding, speaking, reading and writing in Sanskrit. In English they had the least number of the students who faced difficulties in terms of linguistic skills. As for Hindi, which was the mother tongue/regional language for the larger group of students, four non-Hindi mother tongue groups i.e., Urdu, Punjabi, Bengali and Sindhi spoke about difficulties of various types ranging from understanding, speaking, reading and writing. But, in case of regional language the difficulties were many more than those expressed for Hindi language.

**Conclusion :**

1. The informants of this sample group could not develop all the four linguistic skills in classical languages.
2. The skill development was not satisfactory even in English language in all the mother tongue groups barring the Bengali mother tongue group. In their case it was found that English was even less difficult than their mother tongue.
3. The students were found weak even in regional languages. The Table 6(a) shows that in case of regional languages which in certain cases were recorded as the mother tongues also, the difficulties were many more than those expressed for Hindi language.
4. Hindi was the only language in which the largest number of the non-Hindi mother tongue students had developed all the four linguistic skills. None of the Hindi speaking students mentioned any such difficulty.

Out of the three languages learnt in the school, Sanskrit was not the spoken language, and hence its use in environment was out of question. The languages which could be expected to be used were not only the respective mother tongues of the different mother tongue groups mentioned in the schedules, but Hindi and English also.

TABLE 7 (a)

Languages Students spoke to various persons

| Mother Tongue | Languages | Father | Mother | Brothers & Sisters | Grand Parents | Servant | Neighbours | Teachers | Friends |
|---|---|---|---|---|---|---|---|---|---|
| *1* | *2* | *3* | *4* | *5* | *6* | *7* | *8* | *9* | *10* |
| Hindi | H | 67 = 63. 20% | 77 = 72.64% | 45 = 42.45% | 46 = 43.39% | 96 = 90.57% | 72 = 67.92% | 51 = 48.11% | 39 = 36.79% |
| 106 | E | 9 = 8.49% | 1 | 4 | – | – | 3 | 11 = 10.38% | 3 |
| | Pu | 1 | 1 | – | 4 | 1 | 1 | – | – |
| | H+Pu | 1 | 6 = 5.66% | 4 | 2 | 6 = 5.66% | 10 = 9.43% | 10 = 9.43% | 15 = 14.15% |
| | H+E | 25 = 23.58% | 19 = 17.92% | 15 = 14.15% | 4 | 3 | 16 = 15.09% | 32 = 30.18% | 37 = 30.90% |
| | H+Pu+E | 2 | 2 | 4 | 2 | – | 4 | – | 12 = 11.32% |
| | H+Si+E | – | – | – | – | – | – | 2 | – |
| Urdu | U | 40 = 76.92% | 46 = 88.46% | 21 = 40.38% | 27 = 51.92% | 34 = 65.38% | 33 = 63.46% | 26 = 50% | 22 = 42.30% |
| 52 | H | – | – | 3 | – | 11 = 21.15% | 5 = 9.61% | – | 1 |
| | E | – | – | – | – | – | – | 1 | – |
| | U+H | 7 = 13.46% | 4 | 5 = 9.61% | 2 | 7 = 13.46% | 12 = 23.07% | 20 = 38.46% | 24 = 46.15% |
| | H+E | – | – | – | – | – | 1 | 2 | 2 |
| | U+E | 2 | 1 | 10 = 19.23% | – | – | – | 3 | 3 |
| | U+H+E | 2 | – | 2 | – | – | – | – | – |
| | U+H+Pu | – | – | – | – | – | 1 | – | – |

contd...

| *1* | *2* | *3* | *4* | *5* | *6* | *7* | *8* | *9* | *10* |
|---|---|---|---|---|---|---|---|---|---|
| Punjabi | Pu | 15 = 29.41% | 22 = 43.13% | 13 = 25.49% | 16 = 31.37% | 4 | 9 = 17.64% | 2 | -- |
| 51 | H | 5 | 8 = 15.68% | 3 | 6 = 11.76% | 31 = 60.78% | 21 = 41.17% | 10 = 19.6% | 6 = 11.76% |
| | E | 4 | 1 | 5 | 1 | -- | 1 | 10 = 19.6% | 5 |
| | H+Pu | 7 = 13.72% | 7 = 13.72% | 5 | 4 | 12 = 23.52% | 9 = 17.64% | 8 = 15.68% | 12 = 23.52% |
| | H+E | 11 = 21.56% | 8 = 15.68% | 8 = 15.68% | 2 | 3 | 9 = 17.64% | 16 = 31.37% | 21 = 41.17% |
| | Pu+E | 2 | 2 | 1 | 1 | -- | -- | 1 | -- |
| | E+Fr | -- | -- | 1 | -- | -- | -- | -- | -- |
| | H+E+Pu | 4 | 3 | 4 | 3 | 1 | 2 | 4 | 7 = 13.72% |
| Bengali | B | 23 = 46% | 36 = 72% | 14 = 28% | 20 = 10% | 7 = 14% | 1 | 9 = 18% | 2 |
| 50 | H | -- | -- | -- | -- | 40 = 80% | 3 | -- | -- |
| | E | 5= 10% | -- | 3 | -- | -- | 2 | 11= 22% | 1 |
| | B+H | -- | 1 | -- | -- | 1 | 15 = 30% | -- | 2 |
| | H+E | -- | -- | -- | -- | -- | 12 = 24% | -- | 1 |
| | H+Pu | -- | -- | -- | -- | 2 | -- | -- | -- |
| | B+E | 18 = 36% | 10 = 20% | 13 = 26% | 5 = 10% | -- | -- | 21 = 42% | 11 = 22% |
| | B+H+E | 4 | 3 | 4 | 1 | -- | 12 = 24% | 9 = 18% | 32 = 64% |
| | B+H+Pu | -- | -- | -- | -- | -- | 2 | -- | -- |
| | H+E+Pu | -- | -- | -- | -- | -- | 2 | -- | -- |
| | B+H+E+Pu | -- | -- | 1 | -- | -- | 1 | -- | 1 |

*contd...*

| 1 | 2 | 3 | 4 | 5 | 6 | 7 | 8 | 9 | 10 |
|---|---|---|---|---|---|---|---|---|---|
| Sindhi | Si | 19 = 50% | 21 = 55.26% | 7 = 18.42% | 12 = 31.57% | -- | 1 | -- | -- |
| 38 | H | 3 | 5 = 13.15% | 16=42.10% | 3 | 29 = 76.31% | 26 = 68.42% | 11 = 28.94% | 17 = 44.73% |
| | E | 1 | -- | -- | -- | -- | -- | -- | -- |
| | Si+H | 10 = 26.31% | 12 = 31.57% | 6 = 15.78% | 2 | 9 = 23.68% | 4 | 12 = 31.57% | 9 = 23.68% |
| | Si+E | 1 | -- | -- | -- | -- | -- | 2 | -- |
| | H+E | 2 | -- | 3 | -- | -- | 7 = 18.42% | 9 = 23.68% | 7 = 18.42% |
| | H+Pu | -- | -- | -- | -- | -- | -- | 1 | 1 |
| | Si+H+E | -- | -- | -- | -- | -- | -- | 3 | 4 |
| Marathi | Mar | 1 | 2 | -- | 2 | 1 | -- | -- | -- |
| 2 | H | -- | -- | -- | -- | -- | 2 | -- | -- |
| | Mar+H | -- | -- | -- | -- | 1 | -- | 1 | 1 |
| | Mar+E | 1 | -- | -- | -- | -- | -- | -- | -- |
| | H+E | -- | -- | -- | -- | -- | -- | 1 | 1 |
| Konkani | E | -- | -- | 1 | -- | -- | -- | 1 | -- |
| 1 | H | -- | -- | -- | -- | 1 | -- | -- | -- |
| | E+K | 1 | 1 | -- | 1 | -- | -- | -- | -- |
| | H+E | -- | -- | -- | -- | -- | 1 | -- | 1 |

**TABLE 7 (b)**

**Number of the languages spoken by the students of different mother tongue groups with different persons**

| *Mother tongue/ Languages* | *Father* | | *Mother* | | *Brothers & Sisters* | | *Grand Parents* | | *Servants* | | *Neighbours* | | *Teachers* | | *Friends* | |
|---|---|---|---|---|---|---|---|---|---|---|---|---|---|---|---|---|
| | *2Lg.* | *3Lg.* | *2Lg.* | *3Lg.* | *2Lg.* | *3Lg.* | *2Lg.* | *3Lg.* | *2Lg.* | *3Lg.* | *2Lg.* | *3Lg.* | *2Lg.* | *3Lg.* | *2Lg.* | *3Lg.* |
| Hindi 106 | 26 | 2 | 25 | 2 | 19 | 4 | 6 | 2 | 9 | – | 26 | 4 | 42 | 2 | 52 | 12 |
| Urdu 52 | 9 | 2 | 5 | – | 15 | – | 2 | – | 7 | – | 13 | 1 | 25 | – | 29 | – |
| Punjabi 51 | 20 | 4 | 17 | 3 | 15 | 4 | 7 | 3 | 15 | 1 | 18 | 2 | 25 | 4 | 21 | 7 |
| Bengali 50 | 18 | 4 | 11 | 3 | 13 | 4 | 5 | 1 | 3 | – | 27 | 16 | 21 | 9 | 14 | 32 |
| Sindhi 38 | 13 | – | 12 | – | 9 | – | 2 | – | 9 | – | 11 | – | 24 | 3 | 17 | 4 |
| Marathi 2 | 1 | – | – | – | – | – | – | – | 1 | – | – | – | 1 | – | 1 | 0 |
| Konkani 1 | 1 | – | 1 | – | – | – | 1 | – | – | – | 1 | – | – | – | 1 | – |

Besides, the other Indian languages were also being used, although these were not recorded as their mother tongues. This information had been tabulated in two Tables 7(a) and 7(b). Table 7(a) dealt with the languages that the students used to speak to the persons including parents and others as they themselves recorded on paper. Table 7(b) indicated the six language groups speaking in two and three languages with different persons.

In the Hindi mother tongue group, apart from mother tongue, the languages used with parents were found to be Punjabi and English whereas, with brothers and sisters were Hindi and English only. Both the grandparents and servants, the informants spoke only in Hindi while with neighbours, teachers and friends they communicated not only in Hindi and English but to some extent in Punjabi also. English was used more frequently with teachers and friends.

In Urdu mother tongue group, three languages viz. Urdu, Hindi and English were used for communication purposes in descending order. The use of Hindi was found more common with neighbour and in the circle of teachers and friends. In fact, very few Urdu speaking students communicated in English that too with brothers/sisters, teachers and friends.

In the Punjabi mother tongue group apart from their mother tongue, Hindi and English were frequently used with parents, brothers, sisters and grandparents. The Punjabi speaking students used their mother tongue (Punjabi) less frequently while communicating with servants, neighbours, teachers and friends. In their case more common language was found to be Hindi. The data collected revealed that the Punjabi mother tongue group used Hindi followed by their mother tongue for communication purposes.

In the Bengali mother tongue group, the languages found to be in common use were recorded as their mother tongue – Bengali, English and Hindi. This group of Bengali students communicated more often in Bengali and English except while speaking with servants. Sixty four per cent of the Bengali students talked with their friends in Hindi and English in addition to their mother tongue (Bengali). Bengali, English and Hindi were the 3 languages used frequently in descending order by this group.

In the Sindhi mother tongue group, Sindhi was used for conversation purposes with both parents and grand-parents only. It was found that in this mother tongue group also, like that in Punjabi mother tongue group Hindi followed by their respective mother tongues was the most frequently used language. English was used very little by this group.

**Conclusion :**

1. The students belonging to Hindi, Urdu and Bengali mother tongue groups mostly communicated in their respective mother tongues with the people around them whereas the students of Punjabi and Sindhi mother tongue groups used Hindi frequently while speaking to various people around them.
2. The use of two languages was also perceived, which were recorded as the respective mother tongues and Hindi/English. The Urdu and Sindhi mother tongue groups communicated in their respective mother tongues and Hindi mostly whereas the remaining mother tongue groups used mostly their respective mother tongues and English.
3. Though the use of three languages was also perceived, yet it was found to be very little. Besides, only Punjabi and Bengali mother tongue groups used 3 languages such as their respective mother tongue and Hindi in addition to English. The other mother tongues groups used 3 languages rarely.
4. Regarding the use of other 2 languages like Punjabi, Sindhi, Marathi and Konkani, their use was perceived as the respective mother tongues, but their use as the other common languages was almost insignificant.
5. Among all the mother tongue groups, the most prominently used languages were found to be their respective mother tongues, Hindi and English in that order.

For finding out the frequency of the use of languages, eight situations were chosen under this section of Table 8. The analysis of the data attached had shown that the use of different languages by all the mother tongue groups in all the situations varied. The data collected were tabulated in two tables namely 8(a) and 8(b). Table 8(a) dealt with on the one hand, the six mother tongue groups and language and combination of languages each group showed using in 8 varied situations posed by the investigator. Table 8(b) highlighted the number of the students using languages found in the six mother tongue groups in those very eight situations specified.

**TABLE 8 (a)**

**The Language used in various situations**

| *Mother tongue* | *Languages* | *Play ground* | *Conversation with* different linguistic groups | *Shopping* | *Reading books* other than textbooks | *Reading* newspapers | *Watching* films | *Listening* to radio | *Saying* prayer to God |
|---|---|---|---|---|---|---|---|---|---|
| 1 | 2 | 3 | 4 | 5 | 6 | 7 | 8 | 9 | 10 |
| Hindi 106 | Hindi | 59 55.7% | 49 46% | 61 57.1% | 43 40.56% | 36 33.96% | 44 41.5% | 54 50.94% | 68 64.15% |
| | English | 2 1.88% | 28 26.41% | 16 15.09% | 17 16.03% | 23 21.69% | 1 0.94% | 3 2.83% | -- |
| | Punjabi | -- | -- | -- | -- | 1 0.94% | -- | -- | 2 1.88% |
| | Marathi | -- | -- | -- | -- | -- | -- | -- | 2 1.88% |
| | Sanskrit | -- | -- | -- | -- | -- | -- | -- | 1 0.94% |
| | H + Sindhi | -- | -- | -- | -- | 2 1.88% | 3 2.83% | 4 3.77% | 1 0.94% |

*contd....*

| 1 | 2 | 3 | 4 | 5 | 6 | 7 | 8 | 9 | 10 |
|---|---|---|---|---|---|---|---|---|---|
| | H+Punjabi | 12<br>11.32% | 10<br>9.43% | 7<br>6.6% | 11<br>10.37% | 11<br>10.37% | 13<br>12.26% | 9<br>8.49% | 7<br>6.6% |
| | H + Marathi | -- | -- | -- | -- | -- | -- | -- | 8<br>7.54% |
| | H + Sanskrit | -- | -- | -- | -- | -- | -- | 1<br>0.94% | 4<br>3.77% |
| | H + English | 31<br>29.24% | 18<br>16.98% | 21<br>19.81% | 27<br>25.47% | 30<br>28.3% | 44<br>41.5% | 31<br>29.24% | 13<br>12.26% |
| | H + Pu + E | 2<br>1.88% | 1<br>0.94% | 1<br>0.94% | 4<br>3.77% | 2<br>1.88% | 1<br>0.94% | 4<br>3.77% | -- |
| Urdu<br>52 | Urdu | 23<br>44.23% | 10<br>19.23% | 24<br>45% | 11<br>21.15% | 2<br>3.84% | 1<br>1.92% | 5<br>9.61% | 16<br>13.76% |
| | Hindi | 2<br>3.84% | 6<br>11.53% | 13<br>25% | 3<br>5.76% | 2<br>3.84% | 16<br>30.77% | 17<br>32.69% | -- |
| | English | 1<br>1.92% | 3<br>5.76% | 1<br>1.92% | 2<br>3.84% | 7<br>13.46% | 2<br>3.84% | 1<br>1.92% | -- |
| | Marathi | -- | -- | -- | -- | -- | -- | -- | 1<br>1.92% |
| | Ur + Hindi | 7<br>13.46% | 11<br>21.15% | 9<br>17.30% | 8<br>15.38% | 9<br>17.3% | 12<br>23.07% | 10<br>19.23% | -- |
| | Ur + English | 10<br>19.23% | 8<br>15.38% | 2<br>3.84% | 4<br>7.69% | 9<br>17.3% | 4<br>7.69% | 2<br>3.84% | -- |

*contd....*

| 1 | 2 | 3 | 4 | 5 | 6 | 7 | 8 | 9 | 10 |
|---|---|---|---|---|---|---|---|---|---|
| | H + English | 8<br>15.38% | 11<br>21.15% | 2<br>3.84% | 2<br>3.84% | 6<br>11.53% | 11<br>21.15% | 13<br>25% | -- |
| | Ur + Arabic | -- | -- | -- | -- | -- | -- | -- | 35<br>67.3% |
| | Ur + H + E | 1<br>1.92% | 3<br>5.76% | 1<br>1.92% | 15<br>28.84% | 17<br>33% | 6<br>11.53% | 4<br>7.69% | -- |
| Punjabi<br>51 | Punjabi | 1<br>1.96% | -- | 25<br>49.01% | -- | -- | -- | -- | 13<br>25.49% |
| | Hindi | 21<br>41.17% | 19<br>37.25% | -- | 10<br>19.6% | 10<br>19.6% | 13<br>25.49% | 15<br>29.41% | 18<br>35.29% |
| | Sanskrit | -- | -- | -- | -- | -- | -- | -- | 2<br>3% |
| | English | 5<br>9.80% | 22<br>43.13% | 8<br>15.68% | 18<br>35.29% | 21<br>41.17% | 5<br>9.8% | 4<br>7.84% | 3<br>5.88% |
| | French | -- | 1<br>1.96% | -- | -- | -- | -- | -- | -- |
| | H + Punjabi | 8<br>15.68% | 1<br>1.96% | 2<br>3.92% | 7<br>13.72% | 6<br>11.76% | 6<br>11.76% | 8<br>15.68% | 10<br>19.6% |
| | H + Marathi | -- | -- | -- | -- | -- | -- | -- | 1<br>1.96% |
| | H + English | 14<br>27.45% | 6<br>11.76% | 15<br>29.41% | 11<br>21.56% | 13<br>25.49% | 24<br>47.05% | 16<br>31.37% | 4<br>7.84% |

contd.....

| 1 | 2 | 3 | 4 | 5 | 6 | 7 | 8 | 9 | 10 |
|---|---|---|---|---|---|---|---|---|---|
| | Pu+ English | 2<br>3.92% | -- | -- | -- | -- | -- | -- | -- |
| | E + Marathi | -- | -- | -- | -- | -- | 1<br>1.96% | -- | -- |
| | H+E+ Pu | -- | 2<br>3.92% | 1<br>1.96% | 3<br>5.88% | 1<br>1.96% | 2<br>3.92% | 7<br>13.72% | -- |
| Bengali<br>50 | Bengali | 13<br>26% | -- | -- | 6<br>12% | -- | 2<br>4% | 2<br>4% | 41<br>82% |
| | Hindi | 3<br>6% | 10<br>20% | 21<br>42% | -- | -- | 2<br>4% | 6<br>12% | -- |
| | English | -- | 19<br>38% | 3<br>6% | 9<br>18% | 32<br>64% | 2<br>4% | 1<br>2% | -- |
| | Sanskrit | -- | -- | -- | -- | -- | -- | -- | 5<br>10% |
| | B + Hindi | 11<br>22% | 2<br>4% | 2<br>4% | 1<br>2% | -- | 1<br>2% | 2<br>4% | -- |
| | B + Sanskrit | -- | -- | -- | -- | -- | -- | -- | 4<br>8% |
| | B + English | 4<br>8% | -- | -- | 17<br>34% | 8<br>16% | 2<br>4% | 1<br>2% | -- |
| | H + English | 4<br>8% | 14<br>28% | 22<br>44% | 6<br>12% | 2<br>4% | 12<br>24% | 27<br>54% | -- |

*contd....*

| 1 | 2 | 3 | 4 | 5 | 6 | 7 | 8 | 9 | 10 |
|---|---|---|---|---|---|---|---|---|---|
| | E + Punjabi | -- | -- | 1<br>2% | -- | -- | -- | -- | -- |
| | B+H+E. | 15<br>30% | 5<br>10% | 1<br>2% | 10<br>20% | 8<br>16% | 29<br>58% | 11<br>22% | -- |
| Sindhi<br>38. | Sindhi | -- | -- | 1<br>2.63% | -- | -- | -- | -- | 5<br>13.15% |
| | Hindi | 22<br>57.89% | 18<br>47.36% | 23<br>60.52% | 20<br>52.63% | 13<br>34.21% | 17<br>44.73% | 23<br>60.52% | 20<br>52.63% |
| | English | -- | 1<br>2.63% | -- | -- | 2<br>5.26% | -- | -- | -- |
| | Punjabi | -- | -- | -- | 1<br>2.63% | -- | -- | -- | -- |
| | Sindhi+Hindi | 3<br>7.89% | 5<br>13.15% | 3<br>7.89% | 1<br>2.63% | -- | 2<br>5.26% | 1<br>2.63% | 13<br>34.21% |
| | Sindhi + Eng. | 1<br>2.63% | 1<br>2.63% | -- | -- | -- | -- | -- | -- |
| | H + Punjabi | -- | -- | -- | -- | 2<br>5.26% | 3<br>7.89% | 2<br>5.26% | -- |
| | Hindi + Eng. | 12<br>31.57% | 12<br>31.57% | 11<br>28.94% | 15<br>39.47% | 21<br>55.26% | 14<br>36.84% | 10<br>26.31% | -- |
| | S + H + E | -- | 1<br>2.63% | -- | 1<br>2.63% | -- | -- | 2<br>5.26% | -- |

contd......

| 1 | 2 | 3 | 4 | 5 | 6 | 7 | 8 | 9 | 10 |
|---|---|---|---|---|---|---|---|---|---|
| | H + E + Pu | -- | -- | -- | -- | -- | 2<br>5.26% | -- | -- |
| Marathi<br>2 | Hindi | -- | -- | 1<br>50% | -- | -- | 1<br>50% | -- | -- |
| | English | -- | 2<br>100% | -- | 1<br>50% | 1<br>50% | -- | -- | -- |
| | Sanskrit | -- | -- | -- | -- | -- | -- | -- | 1<br>50% |
| | Hindi + Marathi | -- | -- | -- | -- | -- | -- | 1<br>50% | 1<br>50% |
| | H + English | 2<br>100% | -- | 1<br>50% | -- | -- | -- | -- | -- |
| | H+E+Marathi | -- | -- | -- | 1<br>50% | 1<br>50% | 1<br>50% | 1<br>50% | -- |
| Konkani<br>1 | English | -- | 1<br>100% | -- | 1<br>100% | 1<br>100% | -- | 1<br>100% | -- |
| | H + English | 1<br>100% | -- | 1<br>100% | -- | -- | 1<br>100% | -- | -- |

The Hindi mother tongue group was seen as depicted in the Table 8(a), using their mother tongue by and large in playground 55%; in conversation with different linguistic groups 46%, in shopping 57%, in reading books other than textbooks and newspapers 40% and 34% respectively, in watching films 41%; listening to radio programmes 51% and in offering prayers 64%. Some of the students of same group were using English by and large in playground 2%, in conversation with different linguistic people 44%, for reading books and newspapers 24%, in watching films and listening to radio 4%. While Hindi in one combination with Punjabi and in another with English were seen in quite a high per cent being used for these different situations mentioned above. To be brief, 41% of this population used 2 languages in the playground etc. The number of the students using 3 languages was found small. The use of Sanskrit was limited to the offering of prayers only. As far as using languages as a media tc receive information, there was relatively greater use of all languages for the Hindi mother tongue group. In comparison to languages as media, reception was greater than language used as expression.

*Urdu mother tongue group* : Urdu for expression was very common in comparison to Urdu being used for reading and listening. The Urdu mother tongue group in Table 8(a) was found using their mother tongue. Urdu by and large in playground 44%, in conversation with different linguistic persons 19%, while shopping 45%, reading books other than textbooks and newspapers 21% and 4% respectively, watching films 2%, listening to radio 10% and in saying prayers 14%. The same group was seen using Hindi by and large in playground 4%, in a company of different linguistic people 12%, in shopping 25%, in reading books other than textbooks and newspapers 6% and 4% respectively. Maximum use of Hindi was made by them in listening to radio and watching films respectively 33 and 31% each. Fifty per cent (25 students) of the Urdu mother tongue students used two languages in the playground. The students using a combination of Urdu with English (10) exceeded the group speaking Urdu with Hindi (7). The remaining 8 students using 2 languages did not at all communicate in Urdu but in Hindi and English while playing in the playground. Sixty seven per cent of the Urdu mother tongue students offered their prayers in Urdu and Arabic whereas the remaining 14% said their prayers in Urdu only. As many as 17 students were using Urdu, Hindi and English in reading newspapers, 15 in reading books other than textbooks, 6 watching films, 4 listening to radio. These were all having to do with the skills of reading and listening but 4 to 5 Urdu speakers recorded that they were using the three languages Urdu + Hindi + English in conversation as well in the playground, in talking to people and in shopping.

Like the Hindi mother tongue group, the Urdu mother tongue group also used three language – Urdu, Hindi and English in various situations as can be seen in Table 8(a). They did not use Punjabi at all. The frequency of the use of (Urdu) mother tongue was the highest. Hindi and English were found to be the 2nd and 3rd languages respectively in use.

*Punjabi mother tongue group* : The Punjabi mother tongue group was found to be using only their mother tongue Punjabi very little except while shopping where 49% of the sample of 50 Punjabi mother tongue students used it. The Punjabi speaking group was seen using Hindi by and large between 19% to 41% in all the 8 varied situations. The same group was using English rather than Hindi or Punjabi on more occasions like reading books, newspapers, listening to radio, watching films and in conversation with others. The group recorded to be using Hindi and English together also in many situations. There was a very minimum percentage of students amongst these 51 who used the three languages Hindi, English and Punjabi on rare occasions. In their case too, the languages spoken were found to be three viz., Hindi, English and Punjabi. It is significant to note, that the frequency of the use of mother tongue was found to be minimum. Hindi occupied the first place whereas English was placed as the second most frequently used language.

*Bengali mother tongue group* : The Bengali mother tongue group was found to be using [Table 8(a)] Bengali by and large in playground 26%, in reading books other than texts 12%, in watching films and listening to radio 2% each and in saying prayers 82%. Next language in preference seen in use by this group was English and then Hindi. Then comes Bengali + Hindi very much used in the playground whereas Bengali and English in use for reading books and newspapers. Hindi and English were seen being used by the group in conversation, shopping, listening to radio and on some occasions like reading books other than textbooks. The maximum use of 3 languages in the mother tongue group was found while watching films. It is significant to note that the skills both of speaking and expressing were much more developed in this mother tongue group. Another significant point with this Bengali mother tongue sample group was that English as well as Bengali were seen prominently being used. Next combination of languages was Hindi and English. The prominent feature of this mother tongue group was that they were using the 3 languages in large number in comparison to other mother tongue groups. More languages were seen in use in respect of reception of information than in respect of expression through language.

*Sindhi mother tongue group* : The Sindhi mother tongue group consisted of 38 students. Table 8(a) shows that this group did not use their mother tongue but used Hindi and English. The use of Hindi by and large was discovered in playground 58%, in company 47%, in shopping 61%, in reading books and newspapers 53% and 34% respectively, in watching films 45%, in listening to radio 61% and in saying prayers 53%. English was used by a very few students. The number of the students using 2 languages was observed in this mother tongue group also. Three such combinations were found in vogue. It was discovered that the largest group consisted of those Sindhi students who used Hindi with English. The second larger group used Hindi with Punjabi followed by the group using Sindhi with English.

Table 8(b) showed that the number of the students using 2-3 languages was minimum in this sample group. Like the two, previously analysed Punjabi and Bengali mother tongue groups, the Sindhi mother tongue group also used their mother tongue Sindhi minimum in all the domains. Hindi and English were the two languages found in frequent use in descending order.

Marathi mother tongue group though consisted of two students only yet they did not use their mother tongue to the maximum extent. English, HIndi and Marathi were placed in order in their case. The only Konkani student used English maximum.

Keeping these facts in mind, the following conclusion can be drawn –

### TABLE 8 (b)

**Number of the languages used in various situations by the students of different mother tongue groups**

| *Mother tongue/ Language* | *Play-ground* | | *Conver-sation with different linguistic groups* | | *Shopping* | | *Reading books other than text-books* | | *Reading news-papers* | | *Watching films* | | *Listening to radio* | | *Saying prayer to God* | |
|---|---|---|---|---|---|---|---|---|---|---|---|---|---|---|---|---|
| | 2Lg. | 3Lg. | 2Lg. | 3Lg. | 2Lg. | 3Lg. | 2Lg. | 3Lg. | 2Lg. | 3Lg. | 2Lg. | 3Lg. | 2Lg. | 3Lg. | 2Lg. | 3Lg. |
| Hindi 106 | 43 | 2 | 28 | 1 | 28 | 1 | 38 | 4 | 41 | 2 | 57 | 1 | 41 | 4 | 33 | -- |
| Urdu 52 | 25 | 1 | 30 | 3 | 30 | 1 | 14 | 15 | 24 | 17 | 27 | 6 | 25 | 4 | 35 | -- |
| Punjabi 51 | 24 | -- | 7 | 2 | 17 | 1 | 18 | 3 | 19 | 1 | 31 | 2 | 24 | 7 | 15 | -- |
| Bengali 50 | 19 | 15 | 16 | 5 | 28 | 1 | 24 | 10 | 10 | 8 | 15 | 29 | 30 | 11 | 4 | -- |
| Sindhi 38 | 16 | -- | 18 | 1 | 14 | -- | 16 | 1 | 23 | -- | 19 | 2 | 15 | 2 | 13 | -- |
| Marathi 2 | 2 | -- | -- | -- | 1 | -- | -- | 1 | -- | 1 | -- | 1 | 1 | 1 | 1 | -- |
| Konkani | 1 | -- | -- | -- | 1 | -- | -- | -- | -- | -- | 1 | -- | -- | -- | -- | -- |

1. All the mother tongue groups used more than one language in the domains mentioned in this Table.
2. The data revealed that the linguistic skill of speaking was not as developed as the other skills of understanding and reading.
3. Though in every mother tongue group, three languages were found to be in vogue yet, the Bengali mother tongue group recorded the largest number of the students using 3 languages. Next in order was Urdu mother tongue group while Sindhi mother tongue group showed a very negligible number of students using 3 languages, Punjabi group used three languages in much less number whereas Hindi group showed very meagre use of three languages.
4. It was natural that all the 6 mother tongue groups showed greater use of language/languages in the respective domain in comparison to using languages for expression. As students, it appeared to be a very heartening trend because this is the period when receiving knowledge is greatly emphasised than expression.

For finding out the frequency of the use of various languages in different situations it was discovered that –

1. *In playground* – Hindi was used by 55% of the Hindi speaking students; 44% of the Urdu speaking and 26% of Bengali speaking students used their respective mother tongues by and large while playing. Only 2% of Punjabi speaking students used their mother tongue in this situation. None of Sindhi students communicated in their mother tongue during the same situation.

Regarding the maximum use of a language while playing it was noticed that 98% of Hindi, 97% of Sindhi and 84% of Punjabi speaking students used the Hindi language, whereas, only 62% of Bengali and 35% of Urdu students conversed in Hindi. On the contrary students rarely talked in English, although the Bengali mother tongue group was the foremost in talking in English in this situation. The next groups in order were found to be Punjabi, Urdu and Sindhi.

i) Three languages were being used in a situation like playground.
ii) Hindi followed by the respective mother tongue was the language most commonly used.
iii) English was also used in the playground.
iv) Punjabi was used by Punjabi and Hindi students only. None of the other mother tongue groups communicated in Punjabi in the playground.

2. *In a gathering of different linguistic people –*

i) The maximum use of Hindi language was perceived in case of 95% of Sindhi students, 74% of Hindi speaking students, 62% of Bengali, 60% of Urdu and 55% of Punjabi mother tongue students, though all of them used other languages also with Hindi. In comparison to it, English was used by 76% of Bengali mother tongue group; 59% of Punjabi mother tongue group; 48% of Urdu mother tongue group; and 44% of Hindi mother tongue students in a gathering of different speech communities. Nine per cent of Hindi mother tongue and 5% of the Punjabi mother tongue group occasionally used Punjabi also.

ii) On analysing the whole sample, it was found that both Hindi and English were being used by all the mother tongue students but English was more common amongst Bengali and Punjabi students. However, the use of English was found to be more prevalent amongst the Bengali students as compared to the group of Punjabi students.

The students belonging to Hindi and Urdu mother tongue groups used their mother tongues most frequently as compared to other mother tongue groups, as Punjabi, Bengali and Sindhi students used their mother tongues only rarely while talking in a gathering of different linguistic groups. Thus it became very clear that Hindi was the language, which acted not only as the best means of communication but the most preferred language in a gathering of different language speaking people.

3. *In shopping* – The use of mother tongue while shopping was quite common in case of Hindi speaking, Urdu speaking and Punjabi speaking students. Out of whom 85%, 69% and 55% were using their mother tongues respectively. Sindhi and Bengali students used their mother tongues very rarely while shopping. It was Hindi language which was more commonly used in this situation. Almost 97% of Sindhi and 92% of Bengali and 85% of Hindi mother tongue students communicated in Hindi while shopping. In comparison to it only 50% to 10% of the students belonging to different linguistic groups in this sample, conversed in English language.

Thus, it is obvious that Hindi was being used as the most common language followed by their respective mother tongues and English while shopping.

4. *Reading books other than textbooks* – On analysing the data, it was revealed that 80% of Hindi speaking students, 73% of Urdu speaking students, 68% of Bengali and 20% of Punjabi speaking students read books in their respective mother tongues. A negligible 5% of Sindhi students read books in their mother tongue. For reading purposes the different mother tongue groups read the books, other than the textbooks in Hindi and English languages besides, reading them in their respective mother tongues. It is significant to note that Sindhi students read books in Hindi only whereas most of the Urdu mother tongue students read the books in Urdu only. English books were most frequently read by Bengali, Hindi and Punjabi students.

The percentage of reading books in Hindi was undoubtedly higher. 100% of Sindhi, 80% of Hindi, 61% of Punjabi, 54% of Urdu and 34% of Bengali mother tongue students read books in Hindi language, English books were read by 84% of Bengali students, 63% of Punjabi mother tongue students and 45% of Hindi mother tongue students, 44% of Urdu and 42% of Sindhi mother tongues students read books other than text books in English.

It is concluded that the majority of the students preferred to read books (other than their textbooks) in Hindi, English and in their respective mother tongues in descending order.

5. *Reading newspapers* – On the whole quite a good number of students read newspapers in their mother tongues. The majority of the students reading newspapers in mother tongue was found in Hindi mother tongue group as 76% of the students read newspapers in Hindi which was their mother tongue. Of the remaining mother tongue groups 71% of Urdu; 32% of Bengali; and 14% of Punjabi speaking students read newspapers in their respective mother tongues. None of the Sindhi students read newspapers published in their respective mother tongues.

Majority of the students belonging to different linguistic groups in a sample of three hundred students read Hindi as well as English newspapers. Hindi was once again given preference as 98% of Sindhi, 76% of Hindi, 54% of Urdu, 39% of Punjabi and 20% of Bengali mother tongue students read Hindi newspapers. English was given only a slightly more preference if compared to Hindi as 100% of the Bengali students, 59% of Punjabi students, 75% of Urdu speaking students, 52% of Hindi speaking students and 60% of Sindhi speaking students read English newspapers. In this domain Hindi lost its frequency as the number of those reading newspapers in English was higher.

6. *Watching films* – Hindi movies were found to be most popular among the students of almost all the linguistic groups in this sample as 100% of not only Hindi mother tongue students but Sindhi mother tongue students also watched Hindi movies. Punjabi and Bengali students percentage was counted at par i.e. 88% whereas 86% of Urdu mother tongue group watched films in Hindi. 100% of Hindi, 68% of Bengali, 44% of Urdu, 16% of Punjabi and 10% of Sindhi mother tongue groups watched movies in their respective mother tongues. In comparison to this 90% Bengali mother tongue, 61% Punjabi mother tongue group, 44% Urdu mother tongue group, 43% Hindi and 42% Sindhi mother tongue groups watched English movies.

Considering the sample on the whole it was revealed that Hindi movies were found to be most popular amongst all the different linguistic groups of this sample. English movies followed by movies in regional languages became popular in that order. One thing should be remembered that as situated in the Hindi belt, the maximum use of Hindi in films could be obtained. The regional media programmes were few and far between. Hence, the preference for Hindi movies.

7. *Listening to Radio* – The radio programme relayed in the regional languages some of which were recorded as the mother tongues of 5 major groups in this sample, were found not less popular but English programmes were preferred more as 97% of Hindi mother tongue group; 40% of Urdu mother tongue group, 32% of Bengali mother tongue group; 29% of Punjabi speaking students; 8% of Sindhi mother tongue group listened to programmes relayed in their respective mother tongues whereas 82% of Bengali mother tongue group, 53% of Punjabi mother tongue group, 38% of Urdu mother tongue students, 36% of Hindi mother tongue group and 32% of Sindhi mother tongue groups listened to English programmes. Since more time is given for the broadcast of Hindi programmes, it was found that the largest number of the students used to listen to Hindi programmes e.g. 100% of Sindhi population, 97% of Hindi mother tongue students, 92% of Bengali, 90% of Punjabi, and 85% of Urdu mother tongue students stated that they listened to Hindi programmes. The non-availability of the mother tongue medium programmes could be a major condition influencing the preference recorded here.

8. *Saying prayer to God* – The data collected revealed that in all the mother tongue groups except that of Sindhi, offered their prayers in their respective mother tongues. Some of them were found saying their prayers either in classical languages or Hindi.

Information regarding language(s) for writing for different purposes was gathered in Table 9. The frequency of use of a particular language is the highest if it is used in writing also. Whether the sample group had developed the skill of writing to that extent that they could express their original ideas and thoughts in writing on certain topics, a question was put to them regarding the use of languages for writing down diary, literary articles, letters to friends and letters to relatives. The facts revealed that 40%, 42%, 41% and 50% of the Hindi mother tongue students respectively wrote down diaries, literary articles, letters to friends and relatives in their mother tongue Hindi. It is significant to note that 32%, 12%, 25% and 20% of the 106 Hindi mother tongue students tried to express themselves respectively in the form of diary, literary articles, letters to friends and relatives in English also. The combinations of two different languages (Hindi + English and Hindi + Punjabi) for writing purposes was also perceived with the Hindi mother tongue students. Sixteen per cent of them maintained their diaries in Hindi and English both. A slightly higher per cent i.e. 24% of the Hindi mother tongue students had been writing down literary articles in both Hindi and English languages. An equal per cent of 22% each corresponded with their friends and relatives in Hindi as well as in English. Though the Hindi speaking students expressed themselves in Hindi and Punjabi also, but the percentage of such students was found to be low. The remaining percentage of students did not respond. That showed that they were not used to writing diaries, literary articles, letters to friends or relatives.

Out of a sample of 52 Urdu students, 56%, 42%, 37% and 48% respectively wrote down diary, literary pieces, letters to friends and relatives in their mother tongue, Urdu. Though they used two languages also for these purposes yet the number of such students was not high. Two such combinations viz. Urdu + Hindi and Urdu + English were recorded by them. Thirty seven per cent of the Urdu students used to write down literary articles in both Urdu and Hindi languages. Twelve per cent and 17% corresponded respectively with friends and relatives in Urdu and Hindi, whereas 25% and 17% corresponded with friends and relatives in Urdu and English. The remaining percentage observed silence. That showed that they were not used to writing down diary, literary articles, letters to friends and letters to relatives.

**Table 9**

**Languages used for writing for different purposes**

| *Mother Tongue* | *For writing/ Languages* | *Diary* | *Literary articles* | *Letters to friends* | *Letters to relatives* |
|---|---|---|---|---|---|
| Hindi | Hindi | 42 = 39.62% | 45 = 42.45% | 44 = 41.50% | 53 = 50% |
| 106 | English | 34 = 32.07% | 13 = 12.26% | 27 = 25.47% | 21 = 19.81% |
| | HE | 17 = 16.03% | 25 = 23.58% | 23 = 21.69% | 23 = 21.69% |
| | HPu | 2 = 1.88% | 3 = 2.83% | 5 = 4.71% | -- |
| | HEP | -- | 2 = 1.88% | -- | 2 = 1.88% |
| | | 95 = 89.62% (11) (10. 37%) | 88 = 83.0% (18) (16. 98%) | 99 = 98.39% (7) (6.60%) | 99 = 93.39% (7) (6.60%) |
| Urdu | Urdu | 29 = 55.76% | 22 = 42.30% | 19 = 36.53% | 25 = 48.07% |
| 52 | Hindi | -- | 1 = 1.25% | 2 = 3.34% | 3 = 5.76% |
| | English | 1 = 1.92% | -- | 1 = 1.92% | -- |
| | UH | -- | 19 = 36.53% | 6 = 11.53% | 9 = 17.30% |
| | EU | -- | -- | 13 = 25% | 9 = 17.30% |
| | HE | 1 = 1.92% | -- | 7 = 13.46% | 3 = 5.76% |
| | UHE | -- | 2 = 3.84% | 2 = 3.84% | 1 = 1.92% |
| | | 31 = 59.61% (21) (40.38%) | 44 = 31.61% (8) (15.38%) | 50 = 96.15% (2) (3.84%) | 50 = 96.15% (2) (3.84%) |

contd.....

| Mother Tongue | For writing/ Languages | Diary | | Literary articles | | Letters to friends | | Letters to relatives | |
|---|---|---|---|---|---|---|---|---|---|
| Punjabi | H | 13 = 35.40% | | 11 = 21.56% | | 7 = 13.72% | | 6 = 11.76% | |
| 51 | E | 15 = 29.41% | | 6 = 11.76% | | 22 = 43.13% | | 19 = 37.25% | |
| | HE | 5 = 9.80% | | 12 = 23.52% | | 7 = 13.72% | | 9 = 17.64% | |
| | HPu | 4 = 7.81% | | 7 = 13.72% | | 6 = 11.76% | | 8 = 15.68% | |
| | HEPu | 1 = 1.96% | | 1 = 1.96% | | 4 = 7.84% | | 5 = 9.80% | |
| | | 38 = 74.50% | (13) (25.49%) | 37 = 72.54% | (14) (27.45%) | 46 = 90.19% | (5) (9.80%) | 47 = 92.15% | (4) (7.84%) |
| Bengali | Bengali | 18 = 36% | | 7 = 14% | | 4 = 8% | | 23 = 46% | |
| 50 | English | 14 = 28% | | 12 = 24% | | 24 = 48% | | 5 = 10% | |
| | BE | 12 = 24% | | 13 = 26% | | 15 = 30% | | 19 = 38% | |
| | HE | 1 = 2% | | -- | | 2 = 4% | | 1 = 2% | |
| | BHE | 5 = 10% | | 12 = 24% | | 5 = 10% | | 2 = 4% | |
| | | 50 = 100% | | 44 = 88% | (6) (12%) | 50 = 100% | | 50 = 100% | |
| Sindhi | Sindhi | -- | | -- | | -- | | 1 = 2.63% | |
| 38 | Hindi | 22 = 57.39% | | 24 = 55.26% | | 18 = 47.36% | | 16 = 42.10% | |
| | Sindhi+H | 2 = 5.26% | | 2 = 5.26% | | -- | | 4 = 10.52% | |

contd...

| Mother Tongue | For writing Language | Diaiy | | Literary articles | | Letters to friends | | Letters to relatives | |
|---|---|---|---|---|---|---|---|---|---|
| | HE | 11 = 23.94% | | 9 = 23.62% | | 18 = 47.36% | | 15 = 39.47% | |
| | SE | -- | | -- | | -- | | 1 = 2.63% | |
| | SHE | -- | | 1 = 2.63% | | 1 = 2.63% | | -- | |
| | | 35 = 92.10% | (3) (7.89%) | 33 = 36.34% | (5) (13.15%) | 37 = 96.36% | (1) (2.63%) | 37 = 97.36% | (1) (2.63%) |
| Marathi 2 | Marathi | -- | | -- | | -- | | 1 = 50% | |
| | English. | 2 = 100% | | -- | | 1 = 50% | | -- | |
| | MH | -- | | -- | | -- | | 1 = 50% | |
| | HE | -- | | -- | | 1 = 50% | | -- | |
| | MHE | -- | | 2 = 100% | | -- | | -- | |
| | | 2 = 100% | | 2 = 100% | | 2 = 100% | | 2 = 100% | |
| Konkani 1 | English | 1 = 100% | | 1 = 100% | | 1 = 100% | | 1 = 100% | |

N.B. : Figures in parentheses mention those students who did not write diary, literary articles, letters to friends and letters to relatives, and as such they were not included in the sample while calculating the percentage.

Punjabi mother tongue students (51) were found less prone to the habit of using their mother tongue for writing purposes. Though they were found to be using HIndi and in certain cases English too yet, the use of English was perceived more common with them, as 29%, 12%, 43% and 19% of the Punjabi mother tongue students respectively wrote down diary, literary articles, letters to friends and letters to relatives in English, whereas 25%, 22%, 14% and 12% expressed themselves in Hindi in that order. Although two combination of Hindi + English and Hindi + Punjabi languages were also recorded, the percentage of the informants using Hindi and English was higher than the percentage of the informants using Hindi and Punjabi. The data showed that 10%, 24%, 14% and 18% of them respectively wrote down diary, literary articles; letters to friends and letters to relatives in Hindi as well as in English. The percentage of the Punjabi mother tongue students using Hindi and Punjabi was lower as has been recorded in the Table 9. 8%, 14%, 12% and 16% respectively wrote down diary, literary articles, letters to friends and letters to relatives in Hindi as well as in Punjabi. In this group also, quite a good number of the students mentioned that they were not in the habit of maintaining diary or write down literary articles and letters to friends or relatives.

The sample of Bengali mother tongue students consisted of 50 students. In their case, the use of English was found to be more common except in writing down the diaries, which they maintained in their mother tongue Bengali. The facts revealed that 36%, 14%, 8%, and 46% respectively wrote down diary, literary articles, letters to friends and letters to relatives in Bengali, whereas 28%, 24%, 28% and 10% of the informants expressed themselves in English in that order. The number of the students using 2 languages viz. Bengali + English was also noticeable as 24%, 26%, 30% and 38% respectively wrote down diary, literary articles, letters to friends and letters to relatives in Bengali and English. There are two important features with this group—

i) they used three languages - Bengali, HIndi and English for writing purposes and (ii) only 12% of the students were not found in the habit of writing down literary articles. All the others recorded that they were used to writing down diaries, literary articles, letters to friends and relatives as well.

The Sindhi speaking populations in this sample group of 38 students was found the least in making use of their mother tongue

Sindhi. Hardly 3% of the students corresponded with their relatives in Sindhi. The use of Hindi was more prominent with this group as 58%, 55%, 47% and 42% of them wrote down diary, literary articles, letters to friends and letters to relatives in Hindi. They also used two different combinations of two languages viz., Sindhi + Hindi and Hindi + English. It is significant to note that the percentage of the Sindhi students using Hindi + English was higher than those using a combination of Sindhi + Hindi language. Twenty nine per cent, 24%, 47% and 39% of them expressed themselves in the form of diary, literary articles, letters to friends and letters to relatives in Hindi and English both, whereas 5% each expressed themselves in the form of diary and literary articles in Sindhi + Hindi. Only 11% of them used two languages Sindhi + Hindi while corresponding with relatives.

Two Marathi mother tongue students in the sample group of 300 students, had been using English more than the exclusive use of their mother tongue Marathi. They used HIndi also while writing down literary articles and letters to friends. A single Konkani student had been writing in English only.

To conclude thus,

1. Hindi was the language used more frequently by all the mother tongue groups except the Bengali mother tongue group for writing purposes. It was used by Sindhi mother tongue students, more frequently than even the Hindi mother tongue students.
2. Urdu and Bengali mother tongue students had been found using Hindi more while writing down literary articles rather than in other areas of writing mentioned in the schedule.
3. Sindhi as the mother tongue found no place in the field of writing.
4. The frequency of the use of Hindi was again perceived to be the highest followed by the respective mother tongue and English for the purpose of writing.
5. The number of the Bengali mother tongue students was the least who were not used to writing diary, literary articles, and letters to friend/relatives.

After finding out the languages used in different domains and situations, it was thought necessary to seek their opinion regarding the language studies (Table 10) in their schools. Though the students had been using their respective mother tongues and Hindi mostly yet, more than 50% of the students gave their consent in favour of the study of three compulsory languages, which they said, had helped them in

TABLE 10

**Students' Opinion regarding effect of learning three languages on other subjects**

| Opinion of Students | *Helped in studies* | *Adversely affected* | *No effect* | *No response* | *Total* |
|---|---|---|---|---|---|
| Hindi 106 | 75 = 70.75% | 5 = 4.71% | 2 = 1.88% | 24 = 22.64% | 106 |
| Urdu 52 | 24 = 46.15% | 8 = 15.38% | 6 = 11.53% | 14 = 26.92% | 52 |
| Punjabi 51 | 27 = 52.94% | 13 = 25.49% | 3 = 5.88% | 8 = 15.68% | 51 |
| Bengali 50 | 23 = 46% | 9 = 18% | 7 = 14% | 11 = 22% | 50 |
| Sindhi 38 | 22 = 57.89% | 4 = 10.52% | 6 = 15.78% | 6 = 15.78% | 38 |
| Marathi 2 | 1 = 50% | 1 = 50% | -- | -- | 2 |
| Konkani 1 | -- | -- | -- | 1 = 100% | 1 |
| Total out of 300 | 172 = 57.33% | 40 = 13.33% | 24 = 8% | 64 = 21.33% | 300 |

their studies. Twenty one per cent of them kept silent on this issue whereas 13% of the sample population informed that the study of compulsory three languages had adversely affected their studies. The picture of the use of three languages for various purposes by the students in some schools in Delhi should be considered a specific one under the circumstances obtaining in the Hindi belt of the Union Territory. The conclusions therefore had limited applications only.

**Discussion**

"The process of interpretation is essentially one of stating what the results (findings) show in the light of the previous analysis concerning the gathering of data."[1] Such an interpretation will ultimately help in implementing the language policy more vigorously and may also help in planning the language policy of the country from a different angle, in case, there are certain widespread trends in learning particular languages and using different languages in practical life. As the study was limited to the Union Territory of Delhi, the facts were explained keeping in view the cosmopolitan character of the city. As had been observed earlier, two major languages i.e. Hindi and English were used as media and taught as subjects also. In the present sample group it was found that Urdu as a subject was taught in two schools and used as a medium in one only. Both Bengali and Sindhi were taught as subjects in two different schools. The same schools provided these languages as media also. Punjabi was used as the medium in one school, but was taught as a subject in two schools. A single Delhi Public School offered foreign languages. Only with the exception of the Urdu medium school, Sanskrit was taught in all the schools under survey. Arabic and Persian were offered by the Urdu medium school only.

**Table 1**

From the point of view of mother tongues, five prominent groups emerged. The largest group, 35% of the total, had Hindi as their mother tongue. The percentage of the students was 17 in use of each of Urdu, Punjabi and Bengali. Compared to it, a very meagre percentage i.e. 1% had Marathi and Konkani each as their mother tongue. The students having other regional languages as their mother tongues were conspicuous by their absence. It meant that the regional language schools offered various regional media only up to primary stage and did not continue such media in the upper stages of education. It was observed that out of a sample of 300 students, 254 belonged to Hindi speaking region but only 106 had Hindi as their mother tongue. Five out of them did not belong to Hindi speaking region. This showed that even those students, who did not belong to Hindi speaking region had Hindi as their mother tongue. It was another thing that their number was very small. It was not unnatural if it was kept in mind that a considerable number of people, hailing from different states were now settled in Delhi. Under the three language formula, Hindi and English being compulsory, the option remained only in case of the choice of the third language. Even there the choice was nullified, for the facilities of teaching each or many of the scheduled mother tongues did not exist in schools, because, certain restrictions and limitations regarding the number of the students were required before a particular language was introduced in a school.

The survey revealed that no provision existed for teaching Punjabi, Marathi and Urdu languages in Nutan Marathi Senior Secondary School, in spite of the fact that these were the languages mentioned by the students studying in that school as their mother tongues. The same was true with Shri Guru Tegh Bahadur Khalsa Senior Secondary School, where Sindhi, being the mother tongue of certain students was not provided for in the school. In 'Public Schools', where the Government control was minimum, the importance of the teaching of regional/Indian language was ignored. For example in the Delhi Public School, a large number of languages say 8 were taught. Preference was given for teaching foreign languages such as, English, French, Russian and German. Only two regional languages – Punjabi and Urdu were being taught. Even these two were not provided at the primary level, though the students belonging to these mother tongues were there. Under the required conditions they could have facilities provided for their primary education through mother tongues. But this was not insisted upon and therefore not provided for, subject to the usual condition approved by the Education Ministers' Conference (1949) that the minimum number of such children should be 10 in a class or 40 in a school.[2,3] Besides, these languages were not continued for teaching at the college level. Even at the senior secondary level in this particular school, no provision was made for continuing the teaching of these Foreign languages except English. The teaching of one more foreign language along with English, was not in accordance with the Government policy of teaching languages, because, as per three language formula, only English was permitted.

It would not be out of place, to recall here, that even in ancient times, as far back as in Buddhist period, the importance of teaching vernaculars/mother tongues, was accepted. During the British rule also, in 1882, the Indian Education Commission had not only recognised the importance of the study/teaching of the Major Indian languages, but, laid equal stress on the need of the study of Tribal languages.[4]

After independence, in August 1949, the Commission for Linguistic Minorities adopted a resolution at the Provincial Education Ministers Conference and the same was approved by the CABE also.[5,6] The resolution stated, "It shall be endeavour of every state and of every local authority with the state to provide adequate facilities for instruction in the mother tongue at the primary stage of education, to children belonging to linguistic minorities groups and the President may issue such directions to any state as he considers necessary or proper for securing the provision of such facilities."[7] The Article relating to this policy of the Government had been interpreted differently, because it said nothing about the use of these languages as the media of instruction. "In the study of the status of link languages in the educational system, one may conveniently ignore the primary school stage, where the accepted policy is, that, the medium of instruction and the language for instruction should be the mother tongue."[8]

Out of a sample of 300 students, the largest group that of 106 students belonging to four schools, had Hindi as their mother tongue. In the other two schools, the students had either Urdu or Bengali as their mother tongues, as in these schools, admission was given only to those children who had a linguistic background of these languages. Moreover, the education and profession of their parents had an indirect impact on the linguistic background of the children. Thus it is seen that however desirable it had appeared to arrange for education in the child's mother tongue it was not possible to get the child's education in his mother tongue always. To what extent this situation affected the proper implementation of the three language policy would be seen at a later stage.

**Table 2**

The enquiry into parents' education and occupation in a bid to finding out its relationship with the language status of children studying in school stood justified on the ground that – (i) the standard and quality of language that a home generated could be seen in the number of languages that the parents used, (ii) the level of education that the parents had, (iii) the language most commonly used at home for communication with children and the implicit encouragement that might help towards building a positive language learning attitude in the children. According to the finding of this table, of the two parents, fathers seemed more educated, normally knowing more than one language and exposed to wider professional world or so. Both education and profession wise the sample population of the 300 children appeared to be more in the atmosphere favouring multilingual exposure than otherwise.

**Table 3**

The socio-economic level of the population of this sample group was divided into three categories – viz. low, middle and high income groups. The largest number of the parents having business formed the higher income group, the next being 'middle income group'. Similarly four levels of education of the parents were identified viz. upto lower secondary level (till VIII class); senior secondary level (till XII class); graduation and post-graduation.

An interesting feature got revealed in the income distribution and the distribution of sample population in the 6 schools under study. Among the highest income group (above Rs. 1500 p.m.) 94% of the Delhi Public School population belonged. The next group belonging to this category was Raiseena Bengali group (38%). The groups in descending order were Nutan Marathi Senior Secondary School 32%, Sindhi Education Society Senior Secondary School 28%; Khalsa Senior Secondary School 26% and Fatehpuri Urdu Medium School 18%. Contrary to this Delhi Public School group below Rs. 500 had no parent from the sample population. S.G.T.B. Khalsa School had 50% in this group and the rest in the descending order were Nutan Marathi Senior Secondary School 40%; Fatehpuri Urdu Medium School 40%; Sindhi Senior Secondary School 34% and Raiseena Bengali Senior Secondary School 18%. From this presentation of the income distribution, one conclusion became prominent, that more of emphasis on English medium might have resulted from better economic conditions and vice-versa. Similarly, more of reliance on Modern Indian/regional languages used were found in the middle and lower income groups. One could infer, although not conclusively proved, that better socio-economic conditions of the parents might be more conducive to the exposure to multiple language context. This, by no means, suggested that use of mother tongue/regional language was less popular among the majority of the school population. This could be examined by going through the percentage of population belonging to the lower and middle income groups.

In conclusion after going through the analysis of the data presented in the 3 tables, it became apparent that (a) wherever there had been ascendance in terms of level of education there had been greater chances of multilingual exposure. (b) The more the languages the parents however used, the more was the opportunity for wider language learning. (c) With better economic conditions encouragement to the learning of more languages, especially English increased. (d) Whatever be the desire to pick up, more than one language the basic language of the sample groups had remained their mother tongues.

**Table 4**

The interpretation took interesting turn on the data of Table 4. Information sought through this question were :

1. On languages learnt at the three school levels – primary, lower secondary and secondary.
2. On the languages offered as media of instruction by the sample group at different school levels i.e. primary, lower secondary and secondary. The analysis revealed two classes of findings and these two classes of findings would be discussed one by one. It had been found useful to talk about the findings in two forms:
   (i) when six of the mother tongue groups spread out in the sample of 300 took to learning the language/languages at different school levels, and
   (ii) the findings were also seen in terms of languages being used as media of education in the three school levels.

**Hindi mother tongue students**

It was significant to note that even at the primary level of education the Hindi mother tongue students (106) had a trend of learning two languages. In addition to Hindi mother tongue the two other languages that were learnt were English in larger number 75% and Punjabi as a second large 63%.

Though Hindi was the main medium of education of these students (at the primary level) yet 33% of them had English as the medium of their education.

The mother tongue i.e. Hindi learning continued as a main language at lower secondary level. Two other languages i.e. in all, three languages started at the lower secondary level. Besides Hindi, the other two languages were English as a second language and Sanskrit as the close third language. In few cases, combination of the three languages were Hindi, English and Punjabi and 1% of the Hindi mother tongue students had opted for in addition to Hindi and English one of the foreign languages such as French/Russain/German as the third languages.

Likewise, at the primary level, Hindi and English continued to be the media of education, but at the lower secondary level Punjabi was also used as the medium, although for a few (8) students only.

The maximum variation of languages learnt was found at the secondary level of the school education. Hindi and English were offered by the majority of the Hindi mother tongue group. The other combinations found were English and Sanskrit; Hindi and Punjabi and Hindi and Sanskrit in order of preference.

At this level too, Hindi, English and Punjabi continued to be the media of Hindi mother tongue students but the number of these mother tongue students opting for Punjabi medium was brought to minimum (1.8%) at the secondary level of education.

In conclusion, it would not be out of place to mention that the students belonging to a particular mother tongue group were seen learning more languages in addition to the mother tongue at the primary level. They were seen learning in the lower secondary level three languages and at the secondary level the greater preference was for English while two languages were learnt. Regarding media languages also it was observed that Hindi and English continued to be used at all the three levels of school education, though Punjabi was also used as medium by a few Hindi mother tongue students at the lower secondary level.

The Urdu mother tongue group comprised fifty two students, at the primary level. Urdu as mother tongue was compulsorily learnt. Two other languages were also seen being learnt by the group i.e. Hindi (79%) and English (12%). In this mother tongue group, the interesting phenomenon as compared with the Hindi mother tongue group was that with the Urdu group mostly children learnt two languages (Urdu and Hindi) but unlike the Hindi group, there were 12% of the students who learnt Urdu, Hindi and English. The language pattern was seen expanding to three languages even at the primary level.

Urdu was the medium of education for the Urdu mother tongue students at the primary level.

At the lower secondary level, the Urdu mother tongue continued to be a compulsory language. Hindi and English also enjoyed the same position as three languages were compulsory to be learnt at this level. It was creditable, that a certain percentage (54%) of the Urdu mother tongue students learnt even four languages, such as Urdu, Hindi, English and Arabic/Persian.

Leaving aside 2 students who went for Hindi and English medium (one each), all of them had their education through Urdu medium.

At the secondary level of education learning of Urdu and English continued and the two other classical languages (Arabic 20 students, Persian 30 students) were also offered by almost all of them.

The media languages found in use were two – Hindi and Urdu. The former was used for teaching science subjects and the latter for other than science subjects.

In conclusion the Urdu mother tongue group continued learning Urdu right from the primary till secondary, learning of English started in a minimal manner (6 total) at the primary level. With this group one could find that the three languages were not an unreality even at the primary level. In the lower secondary, English and Hindi were compulsory stand by and the fourth language was the classical language – either Arabic or Persian. At the secondary level Urdu, English and Arabic/Persian were followed, which meant that this group continued three languages whereas the minimum requirements was only of 2 languages. Urdu remained the main medium language in all the three levels of school education, though Hindi was also used as medium language for teaching science subjects at the secondary level of school education.

*Punjabi mother tongue students* – The Punjabi mother tongue group consisted of 51 students in the total sample of 300 students.

There were 59% of this group who started with Hindi and English but not Punjabi. Next 20% learnt only Hindi. One student learnt only English. The remaining 20% only learnt Punjabi and Hindi. Although it was a Punjabi mother tongue group, Punjabi as a language, it appeared was less favoured by the group as a language to learn.

There were three media languages used at this level of school education. English, Hindi and Punjabi were the three media languages found to be in use in order of priority.

At the lower secondary level for this group Hindi and English remained compulsory languages to learn. However, Punjabi as a third language was offered by 45% of the students; another 35% offered Sanskrit and the rest 20% offered French as the third language. Here was a clear case of Punjabi as a less strong mother tongue and preferring to learn more of foreign languages.

Similar was the case with the media languages. Although English, Hindi and Punjabi languages stood as the media of instruction at the lower secondary level of school education, Punjabi was favoured least as the medium of education.

At the secondary level the combination of Hindi and English continued to be the main choice of the Punjabi mother tongue students.

At this level of education English maintained its position being the main medium of education. Hindi also retained its position as the medium language whereas Punjabi was brought down as the medium language offered by only 4 students out of a sample of 51 Punjabi mother tongue students.

*Bengali mother tongue students* – The total number of students in this Bengali mother tongue group was 50. All of them were found to be learning three languages at the primary level – Bengali, English and Hindi.

The medium of instruction at this level was English for 50% and Bengali for another 50%.

At the lower secondary level, all of them in the same group were learning 4 languages such as Bengali, English, Hindi and Sanskrit.

However, the medium of instruction they adopted was Bengali.

At the secondary level of education, English remained compulsory. The second popular language was Bengali 70% and Hindi 30%.

As for the medium, option was given by the school for both Bengali and English to be used as the media of instruction. In spite of this provision being made available, English was preferred by all to be the medium of instruction.

*Sindhi mother tongue students* -- There was only 38 Sindhi mother tongue students in the sample group of 300 students. Altogether 63% or 2/3rds of this mother tongue group learnt Sindhi as their mother tongue at the primary level. There was a trend of 3 languages being learnt by 1/3rd of the group Except 8% of the students in Sindhi mother tongue group the rest learnt English. This showed a preference for English even at the primary level of education.

As the medium of instruction, Sindhi was offered by nearly 70% of the students. The remaining students had offered Hindi medium.

At the lower secondary level English and Hindi were studied compulsorily. A large number to the extent of 3/4ths of the group learnt Sindhi along with Hindi and English. A small number studied Sanskrit along with Hindi and English. A very few learnt Punjabi as a third language.

At the lower secondary level the same trend of having 2/3rds of this population offering Sindhi medium and the rest of the population offering Hindi as medium continued.

At the secondary level of school education the Sindhi mother tongue group numbering about 66% continued with three languages such as Sindhi, Hindi and English.

At this level of education three media languages were found to be in use. Sindhi was the medium language for the highest number of the students. English medium was also used by a few students, though it was never found to be in use as medium at the primary as well as at the lower secondary level of school education. Obviously, Hindi was the second large medium language for the Sindhi mother tongue students at the secondary level of school education.

*Marathi mother tongue students* -- Out of a sample of 300 students only two students mentioned Marathi as their mother tongue. None of them learnt their mother tongue in the schools. One of the Marathi mother tongue students learnt Hindi only whereas the other learnt two languages Hindi and English at the primary school level. Similarly one had his education through Hindi and the other had his education through English medium.

The only two Marathi mother tongue students learnt Hindi, English and Sanskrit at lower secondary level. Hindi was the only language used as medium for them.

At the secondary level of their school education, one out of the two Marathi mother tongue students, learnt Hindi and English languages. The remaining other student had learnt English with Sanskrit. Hindi and

English both continued to be the media languages. One of the two had opted for Hindi medium and the other one had his education through English medium.

*Konkani mother tongue students* – Like the two Marathi mother tongue students the only one Konkani mother tongue student never had an opportunity to learn his mother tongue. He learnt English only at the primary level. Hindi in addition to English were the media language in his school education. At the secondary level, he learnt Hindi and English languages. The only medium language at this level was English for him.

The conclusions drawn from the above data were :

1. The largest number of the students learnt two languages at the primary level of education. Out of a sample of 300 students the percentage of such students was found to be 58%. The students learning three languages were placed next to it (23.37). The lowest percentage of the students (18.6) learnt only one language. That showed that even at the primary level of education the majority of the students learnt two languages, whereas the minimum requirement at this level was only one language to be learnt. Out of these two languages the first language to be learnt was the mother tongue and the second was English. Medium language remained the mother tongue for this sample group at the primary level of school education although the exception to this finding was Delhi Public School where English was the medium of instruction at the primary level.

2. At the lower secondary level of school education though the students were required to learn three languages yet some of them had learnt even 4 languages. Mention may be made of Urdu and Bengali media schools. They learnt English, Hindi and classical languages in addition to their respective mother tongues. At this level of education, the three media languages were found to be in use. The students had offered either their respective mother tongues or English/Hindi as the medium of their education.

3. At the secondary level of education, some of the Urdu and Sindhi mother tongue students learnt three languages even at this level of their education. In case of Urdu speaking students the combination consisted of Urdu-English and classical languages whereas in case of Sindhi mother tongue students it was mainly Sindhi, English and Hindi. Though Hindi did not remain a sub language for Urdu mother tongues students it was used as the medium language for teaching science subjects. In case of others, mother tongue followed by English remained main medium.

**Table 5**

After finding out the languages learnt by the students at the different levels of school education and use of different media of instruction it was thought desirable to find out whether the students had developed all the four linguistic skills (understanding, speaking, reading and writing) uniformly. It was further enquired to what extent members of this sample group could understand and speak languages which they might not have learnt but acquired from the environment. Hence, a question with regard to acquisition referring to four linguistic skills was constructed and put to them.

It was found that besides mother tongue English was the second language in which 50% of the students of this sample group of 300 could develop all the four linguistic skills. The Punjabi was the other regional language in which the students could develop their skills. Though quite a good number of the students had opted for classical languages yet they could not develop the skill of speaking in them. The classical languages Arabic and Persian were found to be more difficult than the classical language Sanskrit. Assamese was the other regional language which was acquired by the Bengali sample group who did not learn the language but could understand it. Similarly, Hindi and Punjabi mother tongue students could understand Bengali although they did not learn it.

**Table 6(a)**

After determining the levels of skill development in languages it was thought necessary to find out whether the students found any language(s) difficult to learn. The data revealed that the classical languages were very difficult for them to learn. Next to the classical language was found English to be a difficult language. It is significant to note that some of the students belonging to Punjabi mother tongue group, Bengali mother tongue group, and Sindhi mother tongue group mentioned their respective mother tongues difficult to them.

**Table 6(b)**

After finding out the languages difficult to learn it was probed that upto what level they had learnt those languages. The data collected revealed that speaking in classical languages was a Herculean task for them. English was the next difficult language for communication purposes whereas Hindi was the language in which all the non-Hindi mother tongue students in the sample group could develop all the four linguistic skills.

**Table 7**

In a multilingual country like India, linguistic attainment was difficult to ascertain. The language, pupils were familiar with, could be several. Some of the languages were learnt after efforts were made to learn. Some others were acquired incidentally and their number might be unlimited; also the levels of attainment in such languages could spread from simple smattering of few words or sentences to reading, writing and speaking. In Delhi, the environment is always found charged with possibilities of picking up languages even from streets and playground.

Our different language groups except Hindi comprised fifty each. So the data analysis was limited to only the group of fifty. Hindi mother tongue group was the largest i.e. comprising 106.

**Table 7(a) revealed many significant features :**

1. The Urdu mother tongue group was found to be the strongest group for the use of Urdu mother tongue while communicating with parents, brothers, sisters, grand parents and so on. Next to them for using the respective mother tongues, in the sample group were found to be the Hindi, Bengali and Punjabi mother tongue students. Sindhi mother tongue group also used Sindhi mother tongue but while speaking to servants and neighbours, its use was found to be the least.
2. The number of the students using two languages was found to be higher in Hindi, Punjabi, Bengali, Urdu and Marathi mother tongue groups in descending order.
3. The students or Bengali mother tongue group was the highest in number who communicated in three languages. Punjabi and Hindi mother tongue groups were placed (next to Bengali mother tongue students) in this category in descending order. The least number of the multilingual speakers belonged to Urdu mother tongue group.

**Table 7(b)**

clearly indicated the different languages used by the students while speaking to various persons. It was discovered, that, besides the respective mother tongues, Hindi, English and Punjabi were the languages used by the students while communicating with different persons around them. Though Marathi had been reported as the mother tongue of two students yet it was not found in use by them. Another important feature of this table was that one of the Punjabi mother tongue students also used French while communicating though its use was limited to brothers and sisters only.

The data revealed some more interesting features. Hindi was shown to be the most frequently used language by the children of this sample group. Hindi was not only learnt, but also was acquired. Hence, the highest frequency was credited to Hindi. For the convenience of analysis, a break up of a number showing the use of Hindi with neighbour by this sample group of 300, could be examined. It was shown that with neighbours 249 of the pupils spoke in Hindi. The break-up showed that 102 Hindi mother tongue group; 19 Urdu mother tongue; 41 Punjabi mother tongue; 47 Bengali mother tongue ; 37 Sindhi mother tongue ; 2 Marathi mother tongue and 1 Konkani mother tongue used Hindi while talking to their neighbours. It was not natural that this study where the sample group was drawn from primarily Hindi belt would show such high frequency in the case of Hindi for any group by the pupils as shown in the analysis above.

English was shown to be the language for next high frequency. English had been referred to as a non-mother tongue language, a compulsory second language in school curriculum and also a language of immense prospects and possibilities. Having this special functional role, that English was expected to fulfil, it was but natural that efforts were made by these students, to learn English and use it at any level of attainment. One would say that the frequency of the use of English in this metropolis might have added to their strength of frequency.

A very strong mother tongue group i.e. 52 had been seen to be sticking to the use of Urdu for communication with practically all group of people. This occupied the 3rd position in the frequency of the use of the languages. One would conclude that strength of the mother tongue had surpassed in this case all other considerations to occupy this position. The next two language groups which were very close to each another were Hindi and Bengali followed by Punjabi.

**Table 8**

After perceiving the use of the languages with different people around the students, it was pertinent to enquire whether the students used the same languages in different situations such as in a playground, company, while shopping, reading books other than textbooks and newspapers. Three other domains such as watching the films, listening to radio and for saying prayers were also taken into consideration for finding out the use of the particular language. This table was also tabulated into 2 sub-tables 8(a) and 8(b). The Table **8(a) highlighted the following important features –**

1. It was very significant to note that the use of Sindhi was found nil by the Sindhi mother tongue students in almost all the domain mentioned in this table. The use of mother tongue was also neglected by the Punjabi and Bengali students but not to the extent to which Sindhi speaking students neglected their mother tongue. Similarly, Marathi and Konkani students used mostly Hindi and English languages in different situations. It was perceived that in a mixed linguistic group Hindi and English were the two main languages found to be in use though English was less frequent than Hindi. It was natural for them as they said that prayers were offered in their respective mother tongues. The Punjabi and Sindhi students mostly said their prayers in Hindi and many other mother tongue students offered their prayers in classical languages.
2. The number of the students using two languages was found to be the highest in Urdu mother tongue group which used Urdu and Hindi mostly. Bengali and Punjabi mother tongue groups were found to be at par. The two languages used by them were discovered as Hindi and English by both the mother tongue groups.
3. The largest number of the students who used three languages in all the various situations belonged to Bengali mother tongue group followed by Urdu mother tongue group. Hindi and Punjabi mother tongue groups were found to be at par.

This shows that notwithstanding the mother tongue base, the different language groups were acquiring the basic language skills of speaking, listening and reading in 2 to 3 more languages besides their mother tongues.

**Table 8(b)** pointed out the various languages used by the different mother tongue groups under this section. It was found out that the students used by and large Hindi, English, Urdu, Punjabi and Sindhi. Punjabi was used by Urdu and Bengali mother tongue students. Even Sindhi mother tongue group did not use it much. It was not surprising to note that all the mother tongue groups consisting of 50 or more informants had been using three languages in different situations.

**Table 8(b) revealed a few more interesting features :**

By and large Hindi was shown to be the most frequently used language in all the different situations by the informants in this sample group. It was but natural as the present study was conducted in the Union Territory of Delhi which is known as the Hindi speaking area.

The second most frequently used language came out to be English though English was not found to be the mother tongue of any of the students in this sample of 300.

Urdu was discovered as the third language being used frequently by this group of student informants. It is significant to note that Sindhi was the languages which was used least even by the Sindhi mother tongue students.

**Table 9**

For determining the frequency of use of a language it was thought appropriate to enquire about the extent of use of the languages in written form. It was Hindi in which not only Hindi mother tongue students but Punjabi and Sindhi students also had been writing. Urdu and Bengali mother tongue students also had been writing in Hindi but they had been writing in their respective mother tongues more frequently. Obviously mother tongue followed by Hindi and English were the main languages used in writing to the friends or for any other purposes.

**Table 10**

After finding out the details with regard to languages learnt used as media and their use in different domains, it was thought necessary to take their views regarding the three language preference. On this question, out of 300, 64 (21.33%) did not respond at all. The largest number 172 (57.33%) recorded that the learning of three languages had helped them in their studies. Quite opposed to that view was the second group of 40 (13.33%) that recorded that it adversely affected their studies. Lastly, some 24 (8%) said that it did not have any effect on their studies.

**Summary of findings –**

While summing up the responses in students questionnaires the following conclusions were drawn –

1. In the Union Territory of Delhi, out of a total of 51 linguistic minority schools, six mother tongue medium schools which offered mother tongue medium till the secondary stage were taken for the study.
2. Though a sample of 50 students was drawn from each of six schools, the largest number of students (106) were found to be of Hindi mother tongue.
3. In all mother tongue groups, six languages were found to be in vogue in the senior secondary schools under the study.
4. It was found that the 300 students belonged to Hindi as well as non-Hindi speaking regions.
5. Though the Union Territory of Delhi is inhabited by multilingual people, the languages generally spoken by the parents of this sample group were the respective mother tongues. Besides, the use of English was found to be negligible in case of mothers. More of educated parents showed a preference for English at the higher level of school education and even as a medium of instruction in some cases. With the occupational trend of parents racing from ordinary to professional, both Hindi and English were seen used in that order. In some cases parents' preference for English surpassed that for either the mother tongue or Hindi. Socio-economic standard had an influence in the designing of the language preference so much so that with the higher income groups, English was the favourite language and mother tongue got into disuse whereas, use of Hindi showed a reasonable proportion.
6. A few mother tongue groups such as Urdu and Bengali continued learning their respective mother tongues till the secondary stage although the former changed to Hindi and the latter to English as the medium at the secondary level. In contrast Punjabi mother tongue group left at midway the learning of mother tongue. By and large Hindi was the most commonly learnt language at all three school levels and

preferred as the most useful medium also. The 2nd preference for a language medium was English and a very small minority continued the mother tongue medium at the secondary level in this Union Territory. The place of classical languages such as Sanskrit, Arabic and Persian was not less significant by any chance. Considering the different mother tongue groups the preference for the 3rd language had often fallen on the classical languages though their use was limited to offering prayers or attending rituals.

In the words of the student respondents, classical languages were considered difficult to learn followed by English. In rare cases some difficulties were expressed in a minimal measure in learning even the mother tongue. The competence in communication was very poor as expressed by the students in classical languages and in English in that order.

The data revealed that even at the primary level of education the students learnt two languages. In certain cases they learnt even three languages. Similarly, at the lower secondary level they learnt four and at the secondary level of their school education they learnt three languages instead of three and two respectively.

The use of three media languages was also observed from school to school. The science subjects were generally taught through English and Hindi languages.

The data collected also revealed the fact that the use of more than one language was a general phenomenon of this sample group of 300 students. In certain cases even three languages were discovered being in use, for instance the Bengali mother tongue group. It was also noticed, that, in a company of mixed language groups, the use of Hindi followed by English was more prominent.

Hindi followed by English was the most frequently used language in almost all the situations.

The most significant feature of this data was, that, the majority of the students stated that learning of three languages did not have any adverse effect on the learning of other subjects.

**(b) Questionnaire administered to Language Teachers-
Analysis and interpretation of data :**

As has been said earlier in the chapter on 'Procedure', a representative sample of language teachers were consulted through a questionnarie. A 5 point form of a questionnaire was constructed and administered to the language teachers, the principals of the senior secondary schools and to those who were educated and had settled down in life. Though, the policy directly affected the school students, yet, the teachers were supposed to be more responsible for its fruitful implementation and raising its status in the school curriculum.

The questionnaire in 5 point format ranging from 5 to 1 score included 11 questions.[9] It was sent to more than 100 persons, but the respondents returned were found to be 67 only. The analysis and treatment of data would be dealt into three forms –

i) Tables
ii) Observation and
iii) Discussion.

The data collected were analysed question-wise.

*Question - I* : According to the written opinionnaire the majority of the persons i.e. 54% felt that the formula would definitely raise the overall academic standard of the people, whereas 18% of the sample group totally disagreed with the notion that the three language formula would raise the academic standard of the people. Three candidates (4%) also supported (though slightly) the view that it would not raise the academic standard. A small number of 9 persons i.e. 13.43% however, felt that the formula might raise the academic standard. In other words, they were not very sure of the ultimate outcome. Ten per cent of the sample population neither agreed nor disagreed with it.

*Question-II* : When asked whether the formula would help in increasing mobility of the people, 55 persons (82%) gave a reply in the positive while 9(13%) felt that it might help in promoting the mobility.

*Question-III* : An almost equal number of people 51 (76%) also felt that the study of three languages would help in the development of communication also. The number of person who agreed slightly with it was 9(13%) whereas 4(6%) observed silence in this respect.

*Question-IV* : Forty eight persons (72%) believed that the learning of three languages would promote national integration. Their view was supported by 10 persons (i.e.15%).

*Question-V* : Regarding the availability of occupational opportunities, the sample group of 41 (61.19%) agreed that the study of three languages would surely enchance the occupational opportunities and thirteen people (19%) supported this view, although, they agreed slightly with it.

*Question-VI.* : Since there were three languages to be studied under the three language formula in which one of the regional languages was also to be learnt compulsorily by the students, 49 persons (73%) gave a firm reply in its favour i.e. they agreed that the formula would help in the enrichment of Indian languages. A small population of 9 persons (13%) supported this view as they said that it might help in enriching the Indian languages. Nearly 10% (6% disagreed + 4% slightly disagreed) of the sample population disagreed with it and 3% remained neutral in this respect.

*Question-VII* : An equal number (49) of the people (73.13%) expressed the opinion that the study of three languages would help in broadening the outlook of the society. Their view was supported by another 9% of the population, though they did not support it confidently. Three per cent of the population disagreed with it whereas 7% of the population surveyed, supported them. The remaining 7% remained neutral in this respect.

*Question-VIII* : Although English knowing persons are very few in number (2.7%) a large number i.e. 56 persons (83.58%) out of a sample of 67 were found to be of the view that its study would help in creating international understanding, with which, another group of 7 persons (10%) also agreed, but slightly. It may be significant to note here that none of them disagreed with it.

*Question-IX* : Since all the students had to learn three languages compulsorily, a certain number of people might not be in favour of learning all of them. Hence a question was set and included in the questionnaire. The opinion on this question was divided as almost an equal number of 23 (34.33%) people supported but another 5 i.e. 8% expressed the view that there was a need of modifying the three language formula and another group of 22 persons (33%) supported by 7 i.e. 10% expressed the view that there was no need of modification. Almost the same number and percentage of people to whom another 7 persons (10%) also agreed i.e. they said, that there was no such need. Ten persons (15%) kept themselves totally neutral in this regard.

*Question-X*: Similarly the opinion was divided on the question that the study of three languages did not constitute a burden on the students. Twenty three persons (34.33%) disagreed with the question. They were also supported by 11 persons (16%). Consequently, the number of those people who were firm in saying that the learning of three languages was really a burden on the students increased to 34 (50.50%) while 31 (27 + 4) persons (46%) agreed with the question that a compulsory study of three languages did not at all constitute a burden for the students. Three per cent (2 persons only) observed silence and remained neutral on this issue.

*Question-XI* : As a similarity to some extent is found existing in almost all the modern Indian languages because of their parent language – Sanskrit being one and the same for all, it was deemed proper that their opinion should be sought as to whether the learning of three different languages simultaneously would interfere in developing their linguistic skills. It was discovered that 36 persons (54%) out of a sample of 67 with another group of 4(6%) agreed that learning of three languages simultaneously would not interfere in the acquisition of skills of the languages being learnt, whereas, 14 i.e., 21% supported by 8 i.e. 12% of the sample population expressed their opinion that learning of three languages simultaneously would certainly clash with the acquisition of linguistic skills. Five persons i.e. 7% remained neutral in this respect.

**TABLE 11**

**Opinionnaire -- Language Teachers**

| *Answer/ Question No.* | *Disagree* | *Slightly disagree* | *Neutral* | *Slightly agree* | *Agree* |
|---|---|---|---|---|---|
| I | 12 = 18% | 3 = 4% | 7 = 10% | 9 = 13% | 36 = 54% |
| II | 2 = 3% | 1 = 1.5% | 0 | 9 = 13% | 55 = 82% |
| III | 2 = 3% | 1 = 1.5% | 4 = 6% | 9 = 13% | 51 = 76% |
| IV | 4 = 6% | 2 = 3% | 3 = 4% | 10 = 15% | 48 = 72% |
| V | 3 = 4% | 7 = 10% | 3 = 4% | 13 = 19% | 41 = 61.19% |
| VI | 4 = 6% | 3 = 4% | 2 = 3% | 9 = 13% | 49 = 73.13% |
| VII | 2 = 3% | 5 = 7% | 5 = 7% | 6 = 9% | 49 = 73.13% |
| VIII | 0 | 3 = 4% | 1 = 1.5% | 7 = 10% | 56 = 83.58% |
| IX | 22 = 33% | 7 = 10% | 10 = 15% | 5 = 8% | 23 = 34.33% |
| X | 23 = 34.33% | 11 = 16.41% | 2 = 3% | 4 = 6% | 27 = 40.29% |
| XI | 14 = 21% | 8 = 12% | 5 = 7% | 4 = 6% | 36 = 54% |

**Discussion :**

In an attempt to ascertain through opinions of teachers and administrators, the benefits or lack of it in the three language policy in vogue in the education system, the opening question was directed towards finding out the merit of the language scheme. More than half expressed agreement to the value of the three languages in the school education. Reassuringly only 18% disagreed with this view. A very small number did not pass any judgment. Some 17% were in two minds about the value of the three languages. The balance of opinion swung definitely towards the benefit side. In a progressive country limiting the avenues of information getting and also use of more than one medium for expression seemed to be an accepted phenomenon. The findings as narrated above only corroborate this particular trend in the civilized society. One would feel tempted to quote Bernstein, "The students who are good in language are good in all other subjects and those who fall in language, fall in every other subject."[10,11] In fact all education begins with languages.

For furnishing the truth that the knowledge of three languages would facilitate the movement of the people within and outside the state, a question was asked whether the knowledge of three languages would increase the mobility among them. The findings revealed that almost 100% (to be exact 95%) expressed their opinion that it would certainly increase it. None of the sample group remained neutral as in case of transfers of the parents, their wards would be admitted in any school as the three languages, mother tongue, English and regional language were being introduced in the school teaching. Besides, in search of livelihood people would not fear in migrating from one state to another due to language barrier.

When asked whether the knowledge of three languages would help in facilitating the possibilities of communication in wider areas, majority of the people expressed their opinion that it would certainly create more opportunities for communication as, almost everyone in the country might have learnt 3 languages. In practice Hindi was largely in use as a link language for the country.[12,13] English was also a compulsory language in every state and as such people would not have to learn the regional language of that state immediately. They could use Hindi as well as English at times.

As the basic objective of introducing the three language formula was to promote national integration, an endeavour was made to seek the views on the issue whether the knowledge of three languages would prove a cementing force or a destructive force. The facts revealed that 72% of the sample population believed that the different nationals of the country would come close to each other if the language barrier was removed. Another 15% of the population also supported it though with less confidence.

Knowledge of different languages would remove prejudices and misconceptions of the culture and tradition of those whose mother tongues were being learnt as regional language because each of state in India represented a micro-structure the same diversity what India as a whole may be said to represent a macro-design,"[14] and as such the cultural unity and 'national integration in a country as diverse as India is only possible through mutual respect for each other's language and the points of view,[15] because "repeatedly in the history of the world, the language-bond has proved stronger than bonds of race and blood relationship."[16] Moreover, the smoothest entry into another's heart, it is said, is through the other's language.[17] There were other people constituting 15% of the sample population, who did not agree with this view fully that the national integration would be promoted by the study of three languages, because, if the language could be a cementing force, it would be a destructive and disintegrating force as well. "Language is in itself a tension reducing instrument, by virtue of its potentialities for inter-communications. It can become both a unifying and identifying instrument in Inter-groups contexts."[18] Language therefore, was no more, the sole instrument, which helped in unifying the people. A few of the sample population disagreed with it, as it was not the language which united or divided the people, but, it was mutual understanding, cooperation and love for each other which were the responsible factors for the integration of the people of different states. Four per cent of the population was neutral. This attitude of theirs was to show the indifferentness, apathy and total opposition to the very idea. The 3% of the population who slightly disagreed with them, may be bracketed with those who disagreed on this issue.

The people knowing three languages would certainly be in a more advantageous position than those having knowledge of less than three languages as the number of channels receiving the new ideas would be narrowed. In our country both English and Hindi were used at the official level and the regional languages were found to be in use at the state level for internal administration. The knowledge of the regional language only gained by the people would narrow down their prospects as they would find themselves unable to cross the boundaries of their states due to language problem. But their job opportunities would be enhanced in case they knew Hindi and English or the official as well as the associate official language respectively. English knowing persons were put in more advantageous positions as they could take up jobs even at the international level. Some 19% of the population laid more emphasis on the development of linguistic skills rather than possessing merely the knowledge in three languages. They opined that the working knowledge of a language could be gained if not sooner, in a few months.

For the enrichment of the linguistic heritage of the country, majority of the population ensured that the various languages should be put in use. The history reveals that in India, due to the English base policy of teaching languages during the British regime, the growth of Indian languages suffered to the extent that some of them remained no more spoken. The population of this sample group assured that the inadequacies of vocabulary could be removed by developing technical words, forms and expressions of some abstruse ideas. Six per cent with another 4% of the sample population disagreed with the notion, that the knowledge of regional languages under the three language formula would help in enriching the linguistic heritage of the country, because, it was the use of a language in different domains of life, which assisted in the enrichment of languages.

As to the question, whether the learning of three languages would help in broadening the outlook and enriching the knowledge an almost equal percentage (73.13%) with another 9% of the population agreed with it as, by learning other languages, than the mother tongue, the culture and tradition of different speech-communities could be known, because, language represented culture. As the religious faiths, customs and traditions were reflected in language, reading of literature in languages, where they depicted the religious faiths of other communities, cultivated respect for other's religion and languages. Ten per cent (3% totally and 7% slightly) of the people surveyed disagreed with it, because, a period of three years was not sufficient for the extensive knowledge of a language. Seven per cent observed silence (neutral) for it was not the knowledge of a language only, which made the vision wide, but it was the knowledge of science which usually broadened the outlook.

A query was also raised whether the knowledge of English language will help in establishing international understanding and relations. An overwhelming majority of 84% answered in affirmative because, English as one of the international languages was being used by most of the countries. English is the foremost means of communication in the world today.[19] Mahatma Gandhi, the father of nation had pointed out that English language would ever retain its natural place as the international speech of commerce and diplomacy.

Obviously its knowledge would facilitate the mutual communication for trade purposes as well as for cultural exchanges.

As the three languages were to be learnt compulsorily at the lower secondary level, it was curious to ask whether the status-quo should be maintained or some alteration/modification was needed. The opinion was divided between the two i.e. 23 persons (34.33%) agreed and 22 (33%) disagreed. The people who were of the opinion that there was a need of change in the policy of teaching languages had an edge over those, who said that there was no such need though by a single role only. It appeared by the data that the persons who kept themselves neutral (15%) in this regard were indifferent to the changes visualised in the educational policies.

Similar results were observed when asked whether the learning of three languages could constitute a burden on the students as there were many other subjects to be learnt in the schools. Almost half of the population in this sample group confirmed the fact that learning of 3 languages was certainly a burden for the students, whereas less than 50% of the population opined that it did not constitute any burden. A meagre percentage of 3% of the population remained neutral, for learning had never been considered a burden for an average student.

As the three languages on compulsory basis were taught between VI to VIII classes, it was thought, that simultaneous learning of the three languages might create clashes with the acquisition of different linguistic skills. For instance, the pronunciation and accent of Punjabi words was not much different from some of the Hindi words. The students got confused in writing and also in reading some of the words, e.g. कापीयाँ in Punjabi is correct, but, it is wrong in Hindi. A student whose mother tongue was Punjabi, might go on uttering and writing कापीयाँ in Hindi also, which was not correct. Similarly, a Hindi mother tongue student might go on using कॉपियाँ while learning Punjabi as the regional language. Another example might be from Bengali language, where विनय Hindi is pronounced as विनौय Obviously 33% of the sample group expressed their opinion that simultaneous learning of three languages clashed with each other resulting into the weaker development of the linguistic skills. On the contrary, 60% of the sample population did not give their consent in its favour as the skill development in terms of linguistic skills depended on the practice of speaking and reading in the classrooms as well as outside the classrooms and not on the simultaneous learning of languages. It was the colloquial use of a language which helped in developing the linguistic skills of a person. The remaining 7% of the population neither agreed nor disagreed with this question, as the development of the linguistic skills depended on the emphasis laid on the different aspects of the language teaching e.g. on pronunciation and accent etc.

## Conclusion

In the opinion of the intellectuals, the three language formula would raise academic standard, promote mobility, develop communication and promote national integration. In addition, it would also enhance educational opportunities, enrich the linguistic heritage and broaden the outlook of the people. Almost all of them expressed in favour of retaining English because it would help in international understanding. Majority of them however felt, that, the study of three languages would constitute a burden on children, even though, it might not interfere with the acquisition of skills in different languages. A sufficient number of them approved of the present three language formula, whereas an equal number felt that it needed some modification. Thus, the intellectuals had rated highly the three language formula. Most of them expressed the opinion that the formula was not considered from the educational point of view and its implementation programme vis-a-vis the study of other subjects was not very well planned and as such, it had resulted in increasing the burden of/on the students. The question regarding the modification/alteration/addition was significantly not answered. Only 2% were bold enough to express their views regarding this aspect. The majority of them showed their apathy.

## (c) Interview Schedule for Public men

The technique of interviewing is a major tool for gathering evidence in the field. It was applied in this study for collecting data from primary sources, i.e. directly through dialogue. Social scientists view the public as a form of social organization and as a body of verbalized attitudes in a social group regarding some controversial or undetermined issue. Such issues most frequently arise in secondary group organization which characterize dynamic community life. The social scientist in studying public opinion would concern himself with a number of interrelated factors, such as (1) the nature of the various social groups who voice their opinion, (2) the social framework within which the various groups operate, (3) the nature of the social pressures which are brought to bear upon the functional groups, (4) the patterns of diverse views and positions on the issues in question and the balancing of the pros and cons which aim to resolve uncertainty and (5) the social processes which crystallized opinion on the subject. In short the whole process helps in obtaining a composite opinion formed out of the thought of several opinions.

Especially, to seek such opinions of the public the direct dialogue had its unique merit. Dalen and Mayer called the technique of interviewing the "auditory and usual clues that help the researcher get the tempo and tone of the private conversation so as to elicit personnal and confidential information and to gain knowledge about motivations, feelings, attitudes and beliefs."[20] Since the planning of languages for learning is a universal issue, the knowledge of the mental and social aspects of the people must be considered.

An effort therefore was made to gather public opinion on the language policy of the country. Being a collective product, public opinion was supposed to represent the views of the entire public. Rousseau in his first discussions of the Volonte-generale came to the conclusion that 'the most general will is also the most just and that the voice of people is the voice of God'. In fact, the policy of democratic Government is generally framed keeping in view the benefits that the masses are going to gain by it. Its efficacy should be judged by the actual benefits that the masses are drawing or not. The public opinion could be sought in two ways –

(i) either by administering the questionnaire, or
(ii) by interviewing the people from different categories.

Interview had an edge over questionnaire. In some cases the people wanted to remain anonymous due to certain reasons. Subjects sometimes refrained from expressing their views freely and honestly in a group, therefore, individual interviews were conducted. Though the thoughts were freely expressed while conducting unstructured interviews, due to the physical limitations and for having varied viewpoints on the same questions, the structured interview-schedule was drawn as this introduced the controls that were required to permit the formulation of scientific generalisation.

**Analysis and interpretation of Interview Schedule**

There were altogether four questions in the interview schedules.[21] On the question No. 1, whether Hindi should be made compulsory or optional in the non-Hindi speaking states, the opinion was almost divided.

Out of the one hundred persons interviewed fifty three were of the opinion that Hindi should be made compulsory even in the non-Hindi speaking states. Out of these, eleven were academicians, eight doctors, five businessmen, five from judiciary, four journalists, four sports persons, three government officers, two librarians, two chartered accountants, two administrators, two politicians and one I.A.S. officer also one each of the category of cartoonist, defence, police department, religious head and engineer. The remaining 47/100 expressed the view that Hindi should remain as the optional subject. Out of those, who supported this view eight were academicians, eight journalists, four librarians, four religious heads, three from the police department, three doctors, two businessmen and two from defence, two from the government department, two cartoonists, two chartered accountants, two engineers and two administrators.

In reply, to the second question i.e. whether the schools should be allowed to switch over to English medium after class V, the majority of persons was in favour of retaining the mother tongue/regional language as the medium of instruction. Out of sixty eight persons, supporting this view, fourteen were academicians, six doctors, six journalists, five businessmen, five librarians, five government officers, five from judiciary, four religious heads, four politicians, four sportsmen, three chartered accountants, two engineers, two administrators and one each from amongst the cartoonists, defence and police departments. The remaining thirty two favoured the switching over to English medium from Hindi/mother tongue medium after Class V. Of these, six were journalists, five academicians, five doctors, three from defence, two businessmen, two from police department, two cartoonists, two administrators i.e. I.A.S. officers and one each from the category of librarians, religious heads, political leaders, chartered accountants and engineers.

Regarding the continuance of English medium (Question-3) at the higher level of education 90/100 opined that the status-quo should be maintained i.e. English should be continued as the medium of education. Those who supported this view included sixteen academicians, twelve journalists, nine doctors, seven businessmen, six librarians, five from judiciary, four police officers, four sportsmen, four chartered accountants, three cartoonists, three from defence, three engineers, two administrators and two political leaders. Those who favoured the switch over to Hindi medium from English medium at the higher level of education were only ten persons out of the sample of one hundred.

On the question (No. 4) how many and which language should be learnt by the students for the development of his personality and prospects, for the interest of a society and in the largest interest of the nation, an overwhelming majority nearing almost 100% were of the opinion that learning of mother tongues was the best for the individuals (98/100); learning of Hindi was a must in the interest of society (92/100); and study of English was essential in the interest of the nation (93/100).

A religious head however, said that the knowledge of Hindi was a must for the welfare of the individual while another person, a doctor, felt that the knowledge of English was essential for the welfare of the individual. Regarding the interest of society, four persons including a doctor, a journalist, a religious head and an administrator felt that the knowledge of HIndi would be in the interest of society. Whereas another group of four persons including one businessman, two journalists and a cartoonist said that the knowledge of English was essential for the welfare of the society. Seven persons of whom two were businessmen and the remaining an engineer, a doctor, a journalist, a political leader and a librarian felt that the knowledge of Hindi rather than the knowledge of English would be more advantageous in the interest of the nation.

**TABLE 12**

**Opinion of Public men Interviewed regarding Three Language Formula**

| | | | | | | | | *Total* |
|---|---|---|---|---|---|---|---|---|
| Q-1 | | | | | | | | |
| Teaching of Hindi in non-Hindi speaking areas (States) | Compulsory | A | 11 | Jd. | 5 | P | 1 | 53 |
| | | Do | 8 | L | 2 | Pl | 2 | |
| | | B | 5 | S | 4 | R | 1 | |
| | | J | 4 | C | 1 | CA | 2 | |
| | | O | 3 | D | 1 | E | 1 | |
| | | | | | | Adm | 2 | |

*Table 12 contd.....*

| | | | | | | | | | |
|---|---|---|---|---|---|---|---|---|---|
| | Optional | | A | 8 | Do | 3 | C | 2 | |
| | | | J | 8 | B | 2 | CA | 2 | |
| | | | L | 4 | D | 2 | E | 2 | |
| | | | R | 4 | 0 | 2 | Adm | 2 | 47 |
| | | | P | 3 | P1 | 3 | | | = 100 |
| | Advantageous | | J | 6 | P | 2 | CA | 1 | |
| | | | A | 5 | C | 2 | E | 1 | |
| Q 2. | | | Do | 5 | L | 1 | Adm | 2 | 32 |
| Switch over | | | D | 3 | R | 1 | | | |
| to English | | | B | 2 | P1 | 1 | | | |
| medium by | | | | | | | | | |
| Schools | Dis- | | A | 14 | R | 4 | D | 1 | |
| after | Advantageous | | Do | 6 | Adm | 2 | P | 1 | |
| Class V | | | J | 6 | Jd | 5 | CA | 3 | |
| | | | B | 5 | P1 | 4 | E | 2 | 68 |
| | | | L | 5 | S | 4 | | | = 100 |
| | | | 0 | 5 | C | 1 | | | |
| | Status-quo | | A | 16 | O | 5 | P1 | 2 | |
| | to be | | J | 12 | R | 5 | CA | 4 | |
| Q 3. | maintained | | Do | 9 | Jd | 5 | E | 3 | |
| | | | B | 7 | C | 3 | Adm | 2 | 90 |
| continuance | | | L | 6 | P | 4 | | | |
| of English | | | D | 3 | S | 4 | | | |
| as medium of | | | | | | | | | |
| instruction | Switch over | H | A | 3 | | | Adm | 2 | |
| at higher | to | I | Do | 2 | | | | | |
| level | | N | P1 | 3 | | | | | |
| | | D | | | 3 | | | | |
| | | I | | | 2 | | | | 10 |
| | | | | | 3 | | | | |
| | | R L | | | NIL | | | | NIL |
| | | | | | | | | | = 100 |
| Q. 4 | Individual | MT | A | 19 | D | 3 | S | 4 | |
| Language | | | J | 12 | O | 5 | P1 | 5 | |
| to be | | | Do | 10 | R | 4 | CA | 4 | |
| taught | | | B | 7 | Jd | 5 | E | 3 | |
| in the | | | L | 6 | C | 3 | Adm | 4 | |
| interest | | | | | P | 4 | | | 98 |
| of | | | | | | | | | |
| | | H | R | 1 | | | | | 1 |
| | | E | Do | 1 | | | | | 1 |
| | | | | | | | | | = 100 |

*Table 12 contd...*

| | | | | | | | | |
|---|---|---|---|---|---|---|---|---|
| Society | M.T. | | | | | | | |
| | | D | 1 | J | 1 | R | 1 | Adm 1 |
| | | | | | | | | = 4 |
| | H | A | 19 | R | 4 | S | 4 | |
| | | Do | 11 | P | 4 | CA | 4 | |
| | | J | 9 | Jd | 5 | E | 3 | |
| | | B | 6 | P1 | 5 | Adm | 3 | |
| | | L | 6 | D | 2 | | | |
| | | O | 5 | C | 2 | | | 92 |
| | E | B | 1 | J | 2 | C | 1 | 4 |
| | | | | | | | | = 100 |
| | M.T. | NIL | | | | | | NIL |
| Nation | H | B | 2 | Do | 1 | P1 | 1 | |
| | | E | 1 | J | 1 | L | 1 | 7 |
| | E | A | 19 | O | 5 | P | 4 | |
| | | J | 11 | R | 5 | S | 4 | |
| | | Do | 10 | P | 4 | C | 3 | |
| | | B | 5 | D | 3 | CA | 4 | 93 |
| | | L | 5 | Jd | 5 | E | 2 | |
| | | | | | | Adm | 4 | = 100 |

| | |
|---|---|
| A | Academicians |
| B | Businessmen |
| C | Cartoonists |
| Do | Doctors |
| D | Defence (Army, Navy, AirForce) |
| J | Journalists |
| Jd | Judiciary |
| L | Librarians |
| G | Government officers |
| P | Police, Vigilance, CBI |
| R | Religious Heads |
| P1 | Politicians |
| S | Sportsmen |
| CA | Chartered Accountants |
| E | Engineers |
| Adm | Administrators (IAS officers) |

**Discussion**

Certain types of information can be secured only by direct contacts with people e.g. intimate facts of personal history, of personal habits and characteristics of family life, opinions and beliefts.[22] Since many people are willing more to give information verbally than in writing, particularly on an emotionally laden question it was thought necessary to hold an interview with the cross-section of the society, because, when qualified individuals with common or divergent backgrounds were brought together to expose a problem or to evaluate the merits of a proposition, they could present a wide range of information and varied view-points. Hence, in addition to a written questionnaire for the language teachers a separate schedule was constructed to conduct the interview with the cross-section of society because sometimes the subjects might refrain from expressing some points before a group, which they might reveal in a private interview, and which the investigator might read "between the lines" when much had not been said in words. On a written questionnaire, the scope of the response of the informants was very limited. In such a situation the doubts could neither be raised nor could be clarified. While in a personal interview all the aspects of a particular problem were fully covered as, conclusions were arrived at after discussing each and every aspect of the problem. Therefore, to make the survey more meaningful, about one hundred people including doctors, engineers, journalists, advocates and some of the politicians, administrators, academicians, members of the judiciary and so on were personally interviewed. Their considered opinions were sought on such problems as whether Hindi should be made compulsory or not; at what stage the English medium should be introduced; upto what stage it should be retained, the role of English in higher education and the usefulness of the study of mother tongue, Hindi and English, keeping in mind the interest of individual, society and nation.

The first question put to them was regarding the official language Hindi to be taught as one of the core languages under the three language formula. It was significant to note that more than 50% of the sample population suggested that Hindi should be a compulsory language for all, so that a uniformity could be maintained at the educational level. Compulsory education in Hindi would help the people from non-Hindi areas to easily join the national mainstream which predominently consisted of Hindi speaking people. This had been expressed by the

Official Language Commission 1956 also. The compulsory teaching of Hindi would thus go a long way in promoting national integration and unity in the face of huge and diverse population in the country. For instance as some of the doctors said that there was hardly any hospital in the country which did not have people of nursing profession hailing from the South India. Obviously, this had been possible because the people from the southern States were readily coming forward to learn the language which is the language of masses in our country. By making Hindi compulsory, the idea was not to impose it on non-Hindi speaking people as they were already trying to learn it voluntarily. The language if made compulsory, according to some, would hasten the learning process and make the use of language broad based to achieve the goal of national integration sooner than later. The idea behind the learning of compulsory Hindi was to have working knowledge in it to be gained in three years, which in no case should constitute that much of burden as it was claimed to be. Similarly, Hindi speaking people should not oppose the learning of one of the regional languages as a compulsory subject. The Hindi speaking people may learn one of the neighbouring non-Hindi State languages according to convenience and preference. Moreover, they were required to have a working knowledge only, of the regional language according to the Government policy of teaching languages.

Less than half the people interviewed were however of the opinion that, Hindi should not be made compulsory and students should have an option to learn it if they so desired. In that case, the students, particularly of non-Hindi speaking states would not have the feeling that the language was being imposed on them and thereby a feeling of hostility towards Hindi would not be roused. There was an inherent suggestion that non-Hindi speakers out of their own eagerness of national spirit, sense of participation and under collaboration with people in the four corners of the country, would pick up the working knowledge of Hindi in and out of their job places and places of stay within the country.

Regarding question No. 2, the majority of the sample was against the introduction of the English medium after V standard. Such a viewpoint received support from the UNESCO Resolution which stated, "It is educationally sound to extend the use of the mother tongue as late a stage as possible."[23,24] It was also observed, that, the desire to shift to English medium after the V standard was not a very common phenomenon in the state owned schools. However, the position and existence of a sizeable number of denominational schools and public schools could not be ignored wherein English medium education could continue to prevail right from class I to the whole of school education.

Turning to question No. 3 opinions were expressed by a majority of the public men, that, learning English was for the benefit of the students and a good knowledge of English would help them in their higher studies as well. English still continued to enjoy the most important position in the country's education system. The reasons put forward were several in favour of continuance of English medium instructions at the higher level. The shift over from English medium teaching to regional medium teaching should be gradual, for the reason that the stupendous expansion of knowledge if available through English must not by any chance be lost. Further, literature in ever new corners under science, technology, commerce, business management, medical and engineering branches and such other related study matters were less easily available except in English. The education should by no means suffer a setback because of language medium.

The sample population favoured the continuance of English as the medium at the higher educational level. They argued, that as the reference books in most of the subjects, periodicals, magazines etc., especially in science subjects were available in English, students could not understand them without having thorough knowledge in the language. Besides, for establishing a link among the intellectuals of the advanced countries, English medium should be continued at higher level. They further reconciled by saying that at least the terminology in science should be retained in the language, which was used and understood at the international level so that they might not face any difficulty in exchanging their views. None of them was in favour of shifting to the medium of regional languages at the higher level of education. Firstly, because the languages were not yet cultivated to the extent that, they could be used as means of transmitting knowledge and secondly because having so many regional languages as the media of higher education it would narrow down the opportunities of mutual communication in the absence of a common link language as it would be detrimental to the interests of those, who would like to opt for all India services and even for Indian Foreign Services. That would certainly hamper the unity of the country. Hindi medium was preferred to be used at the higher level of education, but by a very small number of respondents (10%). However, this group though small included academicians, administrators, doctors, and politicians. The academicians wanted Hindi at higher level of education, because, unless the language was used at the higher level of education the vocabulary of the language could not be enriched. This had been referred to also in the Report of the Official Language Commission, that if Hindi was not in use for the purpose of higher education, such as for higher atomic research, Scientific terms would not develop in that language which had been a result of the past policies according to which native languages were not studied beyond the elementary stage.[25] In its support, one would quote Govind Menon, the Chief Minister of Kerala, suggesting in *The Hindustan Times* (18th January, 1958) 'No language can develop in a vacuum. Pundits sitting in a room cannot develop a language as the history of languages has taught us. Hindi will develop only when it is put to use.' The administrators in the sample group wanted the introduction of Hindi medium at the higher level of education for two reasons. Firstly, if the language was not developed fully, its use for administrative purposes would remain limited. Secondly, if the language was introduced at the higher level of education, the coming generation of people in the administrative services would not have to undertake courses in Hindi language to learn it and if they had learnt the language earlier, they would be better equipped for administrative purposes. The doctors who were in favour of Hindi medium at the higher level of education were of the opinion that the same should help in minimising the difficulties, faced by the candidates admitted against the reserved seats in various professional courses, for at present the performance of such candidates in such course (professional courses) was very very poor and the main reason was their less understanding of the English language which not only created impediments in the understanding of the subjects, but also in the expression of their thoughts. In the opinion of the politicians, introduction of Hindi medium at higher level would encourage more people to learn Hindi voluntarily, because, learning of this language would then brighten their career prospects and they would not have this feeling that the language was being imposed on them. As a result, the resistance of the non-Hindi speaking people to the use of Hindi would slowly but surely decrease. To quote Kothari Commission, "The establishment in non-Hindi states, of colleges and other institutions of higher education which use Hindi as the medium of education, should be encouraged so that, it may serve, as provided for in Article 351 of the Constitution, as a medium of expression for all the elements of the composite culture of India."[26] Another reason given by them was, that, unless Hindi was used at the higher levels it would not be used at the international level, particularly in the United Nations Organization. Moreover, if Hindi was not encouraged, it would not get its due position and English would continue to remain at the top position.

It is heartening to learn that an overwhelming majority of more than 90% of the sample strongly favoured the 3 language formula as it was evident from the Table 12 which showed that 98% of the people thought that learning of mother tongue would be in the interest of individuals because, unless the person developed all the linguistic skills in his mother tongue, he would not be able to identify himself at the same level as others of his community and the region, 93% believed that learning of Hindi would be in the interest of society, because this would help in creating a feeling in any individual that he not only belonged to his community or region but that he was one of the mainstream of the nation and the person would be able to have a feeling of a true Indian. Whereas in the opinion of 94% learning of English was essential in the larger interest of nation, because, in the fast changing world of today, the interest of the country were not confined to the geographical boundaries but they extended to the whole of the world and therefore the knowledge of such a language was essential which was understood by a large number of people of different countries. The present opinion was naturally based upon the existing situation in which Hindi had not achieved its due place in the country, what to say at international level.

In conclusion, the analysis of the interview data was more satisfying to the investigator than what was expected. In the trend of discussion with these public men, there was not any attempt to direct or to coerce any man to show conformity with the national thinking of the three language formula. The very genuine expression of these intellectuals was an eye-opener to the extent that the position of a language which could be a mother tongue or a national language or a foreign language emerged with whole lot of sense and sensibility. An individual as a student about whose education there was concern, was predominant in the whole discussion. The individual's position as a learner where one or more than one language would be necessary to learn was made clear. It was brought to a perfect understanding that the mother tongue identifies an individual to the land where he is born, the national language identifies him with the political and social entity of a nation and an international language takes him out of the narrow boundaries and helps him to communicate with others in the broadest arena of existence. Pleasantly the three language effortlessly emerged from a discussion with these 100 celebrities, that the investigator had the fortune to contact and to talk to.

**(d) Case Study : Schools**

**1. Nutan Marathi Senior Secondary School (Co-education), Paharganj, Delhi.**

The majority of the students belonged to Hindi speaking areas, very few of them hailed from non-Hindi speaking areas. The school under the three language formula appeared to give the combination of only three languages, viz. Hindi, English and Sanskrit and the medium of instruction was Hindi. Even Punjabi and Muslim students had practically no chances to learn their mother tongues. They had to offer Hindi as the first language. The largest number of the students were from lower income group and their parents were mostly matriculates.

Though Hindi was taught as the first language/mother tongue and English as the second language even then, the students faced difficulties in learning these languages. The plight of students learning Sanskrit was worse. The capacity to converse in Sanskrit and English was very little. They understand and wrote Hindi and English well, but in case of Sanskrit, it was a 'Herculean task' for them. From the analysis of the data, regarding the use of different languages in different fields, it was noticed that the majority of the students used Hindi and Punjabi, which was quite natural, keeping in view that the Union Territory of Delhi was a Hindi speaking area and after partition, a large number of persons migrating from Punjab, had settled down in Delhi and the adjoining areas. English was used by a limited number of students. Most of the students offered their prayers in their respective mother tongues and Hindi, followed by Sanskrit. Though the students faced difficulties in learning Sanskrit yet, they had opted for it even at the secondary level of education. Even the Urdu mother tongue student had to opt combination of Hindi, English and Sanskrit. He had no chance of learning his mother tongue Urdu. Most of the students used to write diaries, articles and letters etc. in Hindi and English both. More than 60% of the students, had reported that the three language formula had no adverse effects on their learning of other subjects.

**Findings :**

1. No other language but Hindi, English and Sanskrit were taught compulsorily as the first, second and third languages respectively from VI to VIII class.
2. The frequency of the use of Hindi was the highest in almost all the domains, Punjabi was the second language in use while speaking.
3. As the students moved up for higher education, they felt more and more for English medium as in some of the sections at secondary level the school had introduced English medium. But, medium of Hindi was the choice of the largest number of the students.
4. The students could understand and speak the languages such as which were not taught to them in the schools. In certain cases, they could even read and write them.
5. Hindi occupied the primary position followed by Punjabi and English.
6. Except Hindi, no other mother tongue was taught in this school.

**2. Fatehpuri Muslim Boys Senior Secondary School, Fatehpuri, Delhi**

Though all the 50 students of the sample population in this school hailed from Hindi speaking region yet, none of them had reported Hindi as their mother tongue. Like the Bengali Senior Secondary School, in this school too, only those children were admitted who had a Urdu background and as such all the 50 students had reported Urdu as their mother tongue. The socio-economic background of these students was found lower in comparison to the students of other schools taken for survey. The educational level of their parents was also lower and as such the use of English was perceived least in their families. The students were also found weak in learning the languages, although some of them learnt Hindi and English in addition to their mother tongue even at the primary level of education. The provision was made for teaching Persian and Arabic also from VI onwards with Urdu, Hindi and English as compulsory languages. But while counting the marks only two elective languages were considered for promotion, in which the student's performance was found to be better. Similarly at the secondary level also, the students were benefited by this policy. It is surprising to note that the difficulties faced by the students were least in Hindi, although, they had difficulties in English, classical languages and even in their mother tongue Urdu. Arabic and Persian were found to be very difficult languages as the data revealed that they could only read and write them. Similar was the position of English. In different situations and domains of life Urdu was the most frequently used language followed by Hindi and English. Similarly they used to write down their diaries etc. in Urdu. When asked about the impact of learning 3 languages on the study of other subjects only 46% of them mentioned that it helped in their studies.

**Findings :**

1. Urdu was the first language which was used as the medium of instruction also from I to XII but for non-science subjects only.
2. Hindi was the second compulsory language from I to VIII and continued to be the medium of instruction for teaching science and mathematics at the secondary level i.e. in IX and X classes.
3. English was the third compulsory language. From IX onwards (upto XII) it was being taught as an elective subject. English language had the least status when compared to Urdu and Hindi but it was raised to the status of second language as it was being used as the medium for teaching science and mathematics at Senior Secondary level i.e. from XI to XII classes where Hindi had no place.
4. In this school too, provision was made for teaching three and four compulsory languages respectively at the primary and lower secondary levels of school education.
5. The school made a provision of teaching through 3 different language media viz. Urdu, Hindi and English.

**3. S.G.T.B. Khalsa Girls Senior Secondary School, Sis Ganj, Chandni Chowk, Delhi**

In a sample of 50 students, three had mentioned Sindhi as their mother tongue who had no chance to learn it in this school which had made a provision of teaching Punjabi, Hindi, English and Sanskrit only. The largest number of the students (44) belonged to Hindi speaking areas. They had mentioned Punjabi and Sindhi as their mother tongues. The students came from average income group although the educational level of their parents was lower in comparison to Urdu and Sindhi schools and as such English was not at all used in their homes. Punjabi was the main medium of education from first onwards but Hindi was also used as medium of education. English medium was introduced in one of the sections from 9th onwards. In terms of linguistic skills the students were found weak in almost all the languages but the number of such students was highest in English. As the school was situated in the upper storey of the Gurudwara in the busiest market (Chandni Chowk) of the Union Territory of Delhi, the teacher and the taught both could not concentrate fully on the studies. With the result, level of the development of the linguistic skills of the students remained low and unsatisfactory. As the Sindhi students in this sample group had no chance to learn their mother tongue they generally used Hindi in all the domains and situations. Even Punjabi mother tongue students used Hindi most frequently except while talking to their parents and grand parents. In situations like playground, shopping or in a gathering of different speech communities, Hindi was the most frequent language to be used. Similarly they wrote down their diaries, literary articles and even letters in Hindi. In spite of all the difficulties of understanding, speaking, reading and writing in different languages 70% of them realised that the study of three languages helped in their studies.

**Findings :**

1. Except Punjabi no minority languages were taught in this school although the students were found belonging to different speech communities.
2. The informants in this sample group used Hindi mostly in almost all the domains except while talking to their parents and grand-parents. In their case Punjabi was most frequently used.
3. In different domains and situations Hindi was the main language in use. Even in situation like shopping and in a gathering of different speech communities, Hindi was the primary colloquial language followed by Punjabi.
4. The socio-economic status of the parents of the students of this sample group was average. The students were found weaker in all the languages in terms of linguistic skills.

**4. Raiseena Bengali Senior Secondary School (Co-education), Reading Road, New Delhi.**

Although more than 50% of the sample population in this school belonged to Hindi speaking areas, none of them had mentioned Hindi as the mother tongue. The remaining population hailed from non-Hindi speaking states. As is obvious by the name of the school, the children of Bengali speaking families were admitted in the school and as such the mother tongue in all the 50 students was reported to be Bengali. The majority of the students came from middle income group and a very few of them came from low income group. Most of their parents were graduates who used Bengali generally at home, though Hindi and English were also used by them.

The school provided a combination of 3 languages viz., Bengali, English and Hindi at the primary level, whereas, at the lower secondary level Sanskrit was also taught as a compulsory additional language in addition to the aforesaid 3 languages. But at the time of promotion only three out of 4 languages were considered on the basis of higher marks. Bengali was the main medium of education although there was a provision for adopting English as medium. Bengali was the main medium of education, from IX onwards the school shifted to English medium. Surprisingly enough, some of the students could understand Punjabi so, although it was neither their mother tongue nor it was taught in this school. Though Assamese is more akin to Bengali yet, only 40% of them had mentioned that they could understand it. Though Sanskrit is not a spoken language 20% of this sample population claimed that they could speak in that language. Surprisingly enough, two of the students found their mother tongue Bengali difficult to learn even though the study of this language was compulsory from I to VIII. Besides, it was the main medium of education, till lower secondary level. Some of the students were found bilinguals and yet others were found trilinguals also. Bengali as the mother tongue was the most frequently used language in all the different domains and situations of life, except while shopping and talking in a company. In such situations Hindi was used maximum. They maintained their diaries, wrote letters and literary articles in Bengali, English and HIndi respectively. Significantly less than 50% of these students found that the study of 3 languages did not affect their studies adversely.

**Findings :**

1. At the primary level of education three languages viz. Bengali, English and Hindi were complusorily taught.
2. At the lower secondary level of education, one more language Sanskrit was added to these three languages.
3. The language variation in use was perceived minimum as the students were exposed to only three languages viz. Bengali, English and Hindi.

4. Hindi was the most frequently used language in a situation like shopping and in a gathering of different speech communities.
5. The students in this school had to learn one more language at the primary as well as at the lower secondary level of school education. At the primary level they learnt three and at the lower secondary level they learnt four languages.

**5. Delhi Public School, Mathura Road, New Delhi**

Students from four different communities viz. Hindi, Punjabi, Urdu and Konkani were found in the sample group of 50 students who belonged to the families of the highest income group. The educational background of these students was also the highest among all the 6 schools taken for survey, as none of the parents was found to be illiterate. The language variation was also found more in their families. Besides their respective mother tongues, the use of other Indian languages and English could be perceived in their homes. Unlike the other schools, this school had made a provision for teaching 6 elective languages with English and Hindi as the core languages. Since the students came from all the states and even from the foreign countries, the school had made a provision for teaching French, Russian and German besides Sanskrit, Punjabi and Urdu as the elective languages. But no such provision was made at the primary level of education though the students from different speech communities were found in this school. None of the students had mentioned any difficulty in English and Hindi. Significantly the school was running a 'Language-Laboratory' for improving the linguistic skills of the students where emphasis was laid on the improvement of the pronunciation and accent of foreign language. Indian languages had no place in this language laboratory.

As the educational background of the students was very high, they were found using English more in their circle, but with their parents and grand-parents they talked in their respective mother tongues mostly. In different domains of life English was most frequently used language, although Hindi was also used but less frequently than English. It is surprising to note that the Punjabi students had been offering their prayers in Hindi, though in other fields of life English was the main language used by them. In situations like shopping and conversing with servants, Hindi was used. The students maintained their diaries, wrote down literary articles and even letters in English. It is interesting to note, that although the linguistic skills of the population of this sample group were satisfactorily developed, only 62% of them found the study of 3 languages useful for their study. Twenty six percent of the students observed silence of this issue.

**Findings :**

1. English language was given the primary status in the school because, it was not only a compulsory language from pre primary to senior secondary level, but was used as the medium of instruction also at all the levels of schools education.
2. Hindi language was given the secondary status in the school curriculum. Though it was not used as the medium of instruction at any level of school education yet, it was taught as a language from pre-primary to senior secondary level of education.
3. Other languages viz. Sanskrit, Punjabi, Urdu, French, German and Russian occupied third position in the school curriculum of languages.
4. In day-to-day use, English was the main language used. Hindi was next, followed by different but respective mother tongues.
5. In certain cases, the study of regional languages as the third language was ignored, as in lieu of them (regional languages) foreign languages such as French, German and Russian were taught as the third language. English remained the first compulsory language.
6. The school had made no provision of teaching through mother tongue even at the pre-primary/primary level of school education.

**6. S.E.S. Baba Nabhraj Senior Secondary (Co-education) School, Lajpat Nagar, New Delhi.**

Though the largest number of the students (92%) out of 50 students hailed from Hindi speaking region yet they mentioned Sindhi and Punjabi as their mother tongues. The latter had no opportunity to learn their mother tongue Punjabi. Only 4 students hailed from non-Hindi speaking states. The educational background of the families of these students was average but the economic background was found above average. Although maximum number of the students had mentioned Sindhi as their mother tongue its use was found the least in their circle. The school had made a provision of teaching Sanskrit, Hindi and English at the primary level and from VI onwards one more option of Sanskrit language was given for the students. In this school too at the time of promotion higher marks secured in one of the elective languages were considered. The school had made an arrangement to impart education through the media of 3 languages. Sindhi and Hindi were adopted as media from primary to senior secondary levels. In addition to these two, English medium was also followed but, at senior secondary level. Though Punjabi was not taught in this school yet two of the Punjabi mother tongue students had mentioned that they had learnt it at the lower secondary level. They had also found it difficult to learn. English was found to be the most difficult language for these students, although the difficulty in other languages too were not less. Some of them had discovered difficulties even in learning their mother tongue Sindhi. The linguistic achievement was perceived very low in case of Sanskrit, but in English it was lowest. Significantly all these Sindhi mother tongue students had been using Hindi most frequently in all the domains except while talking to their parents and grand-parents. In situations like playground, in a gathering of different speech communities and in shopping Hindi was the most frequently used language with all the speech communities in this school. Even while offering their prayers to God, Hindi was used more frequently than Sindhi.

**Findings :**

1. Though it was a Sindhi medium school yet, Hindi and English were also used as the media of education.
2. Though Sindhi was the mother tongue of 70% of the students in this sample of 50 yet it was used least by them in their day-to-day life. Even in a situation like saying prayers to God, Hindi was the most frequently used language. In other domains of life also, the most frequently used language was Hindi.
3. The use of Sindhi was limited upto the parents and grand-parents only. In other domains and situations Sindhi had no use. It can therefore be concluded that Hindi occupied the first position followed by English and Sindhi languages.
4. Even at the primary level of school education, the students learnt three languages and at the lower secondary level, they learnt four instead of three compulsory languages.
5. This school had made a provision of using three media languages – Sindhi, Hindi and English.
6. No provision was made for teaching Punjabi as the mother tongue/regional language.

## Notes and References


* Language Study Questionnaire.
1. Good, Barr and Scates. *op. cit.*, p. 617.
2. Report of the CABE. 1947. Silver Jubilee Souvenir. 1960.
3. Report of the Education Commission 1964-66. p. 335.
4. Quoted by Thirtha, N.V. *op. cit.*, p.43.
5. Report of the Commission of Linguistic Minorities. Fifth Report. Delhi : Ministry of Home Affairs. 1963. p.125.
6. Quoted by Nayar, Baldev Raj. *op. cit.*, p. 144.
7. Article 350A. *The Constitution of India*.
8. Basu, Durga Das. 1962 *Commentary on the Constitution of India*. Calcutta : S.C. Sarkar & Sons Pvt. Ltd. Vol. II.
   Nayar, Baldev Raj. *op. cit.*, p. 144.
9. Appendix-II.
10. Bernstein, B.A. "Socio-linguistic Approach to Socialization." (cited by) Gumperz and Hymes. (1970) *Directions in Socio-Linguistics*. New York : Holt, Reinehart & Winston.
11. Chaturvedi and Mohale. *op. cit.*, p. 7.
12. Report of the Committee of Members of Parliament on Education. New Delhi : Govt. of India Press. 1967.
13. Pattnayak, D.P. *Language Policy and Programmes*. New Delhi : Ministry of Education, Govt. of India Press. 1970 p. 3.
14. Pattnayak, D.P. *op. cit.*, p. 1
15. *Ibid.*
16. Taraporewala *op. cit.*
17. Thirtha, N.V. Babel *op. cit.*
18. *Ibid.*
19. Report of the Official Language Commission. 1956. p. 32.
20. Dalen and Meyer. *op. cit.*, p. 259.
21. Appendix-III.
22. Good and Scates. *op. cit.*, p. 637
23. Emerson, Rupert. *From Empire to Nation*. Cambridge: Harvard University Press. 1960
24. Resolution passed by the General Assembly of UNESCO. (cited by) Nair, Baldev Raj. *op. cit.*, pp. 13-14.
25. Report of the Official Language Commission 1956. pp. 26-38.
26. Report of the Kothari Commission 1964-66. p. XVII.

# 6 Findings, Conclusion and Recommendations

The data collected in different schools revealed that though the safeguards in the Indian Constitution are given to the linguistic minorities, yet in practice, in most of the linguistic minority schools of the Union Territory of Delhi very little provisions were made to give instruction in the mother tongues of the students even at the primary level. As 'education' is a 'State-subject', the curriculum is being moulded according to the needs and requirements of the State itself. Even the centrally sponsored schemes are altered accordingly. According to the policy of teaching languages in the schools, the students were supposed to be instructed in their respective mother tongues at the primary level of their school education. Thus, the rights of the linguistic minorities were to be safeguarded. The minority language schools in the Union Territory of Delhi were seen following varied pattern of language teaching even at the primary level. Either it was mother tongue or regional language (Hindi) or mother tongue and English with one of these languages as the medium of instruction.

Looking into the structure of the three language formula, it was perceived, that in some of the schools, the students had to learn two to three languages on compulsory basis, even at the primary level. One more language was added to the aforesaid quantum of three at the lower secondary level. Even at the secondary level of education, three languages instead of two were being taught. It is significant to note that while calculating the marks for promotion, one language was dropped at all the levels of school education.

Thus the importance of learning the additional language was not of any significance to the students. Even failing in Hindi in VII or VIII class did not stop any promotion to the next higher class. The Hindi mother tongue students learnt Sanskrit as their third language in many cases. In the second category of language/languages at the post-primary level is the official language or associate official language. In practice, it was noticed, that in these linguistic minority schools, English, the associate official language was being taught as a compulsory second language upto X and even upto XII. The majority language schools were seen teaching English from the primary classes, sometimes introducing English as a medium of instruction even. In most of the minority language schools English assumed great importance both as a subject as well as a medium of instruction. Besides in the public schools under observation two modern foreign languages (English + one more foreign language) were being taught simultaneously at the lower secondary level of school education.[1, 2, 3]

In the language study questionnaire administered to the student population, it was seen that the students in all the mother tongue groups learnt three languages at the lower secondary level of education. They felt that they had difficulties in acquiring the four linguistic skills simultaneously (understanding, speaking, reading and writing) in the three languages. One would appreciate the honest expression that the students made about their incompetence in acquiring language skills in such a short period. English as a language was difficult for them, but the mother tongue was neither too easy to learn and use, they said. Some of the non-Hindi speaking students opted for classical language — Sanskrit as the third language. It appeared to be a difficult language for them because of its limited use and more so in restricted environment for verbal communication. The familiarity with Sanskrit normally got limited to the skill of reading and writing only. In classical languages like Arabic and Persian, the Urdu mother tongue students were not sure if they had developed even these two skills. Another important feature of the findings was that in spite of its not being in use, the Sanskrit language had been opted by a number of science students and that the sample group opting for it did not find it more difficult than English —a language more in use. The other regional language learnt by the sample group was found to be Hindi and in one case Urdu but, the data revealed that all the four linguistic skills in these languages are acquired by the students rather satisfactorily. The students opting for French/Russian/German as the third language in lieu of regional language under the three language formula had stated that they could not develop all the four linguistic skills in any of these languages. The respondents had also mentioned that the French/Russian/German were the languages difficult to learn. Reading and writing of the language were not considered difficult although the students got hardly any opportunity to communicate in these foreign languages.

Thus, it was evident that unless a proper environment for learning the languages was provided in the schools in which the classical languages and the foreign languages were offered as the third languages the student would not develop all the skills to a certain level.

As far as the impact of the three language formula on the over all studies of the different subjects was concerned, out of a total 236 students (as 64 students out of a sample of 300, did not respond at all) who responded to this particular aspect, a majority (73%) had expressed their opinion that the learning of the three languages did not constitute a burden for the students, rather it helped them in their studies. A small percentage (10%) expressed the view that the study of three language did not affect the study of other subjects. In contrast a small percentage of the students (17%) found the three language formula to be a burden on them as in their opinion the study of three language diversely affected the study of other subjects. Thus it was encouraging to note that the students who were learning the three languages in the schools found such learning beneficial, as the study of the three languages helped them in their academic pursuits.

The intellecutals and the language teachers, rated the three language formula high as in their opinion the formula would raise academic standard, promote mobility, develop communication and promote national integration. In addition, they felt that it would also enhance occupational opportunities and broaden the outlook of the people. English would further open up the facts to higher education. Nearly all of them were in favour of retaining English because it would help in promoting international understanding and in developing international relations. Though the majority of teachers felt that the study of three languages would constitute a burden on the students yet there was the likelihood that such studies would interfere with the acquisition of linguistic skills in the three languages. However, the intellectuals expressed the opinion that all the aspects of the formula were not given due consideration for implementation in the proper spirit of the Constitutional provision although no definite suggestions were forthcoming from the intellectuals surveyed. Some of their observations were well worth recording.

In fact, the first, second and third languages were designed to be taught compulsorily for ten, six and three years respectively, and any two of the three languages studies earlier (upto X) could be further studied for two more years (XI, XII). But the question of 'which' language or languages should be taken up as first, second and third languages was left to a very liberal and flexible pattern of language curriculum. Nowhere any compulsion was felt except that a pattern of three languages should be prescribed for the school course for the Indian children and this was by and large found being implemented. The states must provide not only one regional language say the mother tongue, for all residing and pursuing education with respective ones, but, should provide more than one regional language/mother tongue. Secondly, if English, the associate official language (under the Official Language Act, 1963, English shall continue for an indefinite period of time) appeared as the second chosen language, Hindi/Sanskrit was normally relegated to the third language position. Under such a scheme Hindi might not be studied at all. In Hindi speaking areas both Hindi and Sanskrit or Hindi preferably would be studied. In non-Hindi speaking areas no provision guaranteed the learning of Hindi in schools. Rather either Hindi or Sanskrit would fulfil the condition of the third language.

A cross-section of the society consisting of academics, journalists, doctors, engineers, businessmen, government officers, judiciary, religious heads, politicians and many others were surveyed and an overwhelming majority (more than 90%) of the sample strongly favoured the 3 language formula. Nearly all (98%) of the people thought that learning of mother tongue would be in the interest of individual because unless a person develops all the linguistic skills in the mother tongue he/she would not be able to identify himself/herself with the community of vast majority, 99% believed that the learning of Hindi would be in the interest of the society as this would help in creating a feeling that a person belonged not only to a particular community or region but to the whole of nation. An equally large number (94%) opined, that learning of English was essential keeping the larger interest of the nation in mind, as the interests of the nation were not confined to the geographical boundary but extended to the whole world. In fact, English was the language of the world population.

On the whole it was concluded that a majority of students was in favour of the three languages as they did not consider the language learning as an impediment in their studies. The public opinion was in favour of the formula as the benefit of the three languages would enhance the scope of the individual's role as an individual; his role in whole. However, in conclusion there was clear evidence that the study of three languages had left a permanent impact on the mind of everyone.

**Recommendations and Suggestions**

It is widely acknowledged that any study on the language policy and its implementation is beset with intricate complexity. The Government policy statements in the Constitution and through reports of different committees and commissions appointed by the Governments from time to time to study the language policy had been quite liberal, democratic and in keeping with the variegated nature of this multilingual country. There had been very broad guidelines stated as –

a) The Union of India prescribed Hindi in Devanagari script for all official purposes ;
b) English should continue indefinitely as an associate official language; and
c) The Indian states should enjoy full freedom to choose any language or languages used in the region as their official language.

Deducing from the constitutional provisions regarding the language policy, the educational implications are framed. Thereafter the placement of languages for learning at the school stage are decided upon. Such provisions are found differing in schools under Central administration and those under State administration. Further, differences in language studies are seen in Hindi and non-Hindi speaking states. Besides complications arise in deciding about the position of languages, as first, second and third language in different states and accordingly the duration of teaching of these, so as to enable the learners to acquire relative competence in them. Under the general provisions of three languages 'compulsorily' to be learnt in Indian schools, the three 'compulsory' languages do not figure in. This flexibility in a federal state seems just reasonable but it creates lot of controversy and rightly so, in a democracy. The Indian states have chosen their state/regional languages for state official purposes. Delhi, the Union Territory, as well as the seat of the Central Government, follows Hindi as an official medium and hence schools, by and large follow Hindi as medium of instruction.

It is not proper to generalise on the status of language in the country on the basis of such a small study. Still some fruitful understanding had emerged on the study which was planted on a Hindi speaking belt and which involved linguistic minority schools. The linguistic minorities are non-Hindi mother tongue people. There could be two reasons for encouraging the learning of the regional mother tongues — (a) primary education should best be given in the mother tongue, and (b) this first language was supposed to be taught for ten years and preferably be the medium of high school education.

Just contrary findings were available from the present study were in the practice of mother tongue as the language for primary education was but an apology and not a reality. Parallel arrangements were made to introduce English and Hindi in the primary grades as these languages appeared to offer better prospects than dependence on the mother tongue would do. This trend appeared growing fast with all minority language groups (Delhi has 51 linguistic minority schools) unchecked, except in Sindhi, Bengali and Urdu medium schools where frail attempt to continue these languages upto the lower secondary level was visible. Therefore, outside the region/state the respective languages show a moribund existence and it is none of the constitutional flaws.

An encouraging feature emerging from this study, was non-resistant and eager learning of Hindi, the language of the Union Territory and of the environment. So Hindi received a wider publicity and use amongst the school population in this Hindi belt, for all purposes. A happy state of affairs indeed.

In respect of one language, i.e. Marathi, although going by the school population, it should have been introduced as a language in the Nutan Marathi Senior Secondary School, New Delhi but it was not so. This linguistic minority school, never had Marathi to learn or teach and went on with Hindi as a strong language. This deviation from practising mother tongue at the primary level, therefore, was a denial *per se* to a section of the primary level students, although the school retained the three language teaching-learning, in true fairness of the constitutional provision. There might not have been a clamour from the minority i.e. the Marathi children, to learn Marathi. No intervention was necessary, no compulsion was asked for the introduction of the minority mother tongue (Marathi) but the three languages, viz. Hindi, English and Sanskrit, were compulsorily learnt by the school. Should a recommendation be enlisted that the minority languages in the Hindi belt should receive proper attention ?

Hindi received a wide publicity and use amongst the school population in Delhi. It was seen that the minority language groups learnt Hindi with eagerness. It is recommended that this happy state of affairs should continue. But there had not been any uniformity about the stage or level, as when Hindi was introduced in these schools and what had been the duration of teaching Hindi in such schools. This system was also not violative of the Constitution rather it was quite in keeping with the liberal design of the Government which upheld rightly the learning of three languages compulsorily in any case. Learning Hindi, in these linguistic minority schools was then a matter of great convenience for the children, than observance of the constitutional provision.

Turning to English, one could say that this language was seen occupying the position of the compulsory second language in Delhi as much as in places outside Delhi. Schools do hesitate to continue the mother tongue/regional language as the medium of instruction, but seldom hesitate to resort to using English as the medium of education even from the primary stage. Irrespective of the fact whether the children learn the skills confidently or not, the students and behind them the parents and guardians find learning English as indispensable. Could there be a stage that discontinuance of English would set in as a voluntary measure? Or, should the government reap much benefit by discontinuing it when no special provision appear in sight that two rather than three languages would have a place in the Constitution ? The country ensures progress by broadening the scope of its functioning — national and international. By no means, learning a language less, can a country guarantee any advancement. Hence, by way of suggestion, one would say that better technique of teaching languages in lesser time should be adopted as soon as possible. Intensive in-service teacher training on a compulsory basis after certain minimum requirements are set, should form a part of teacher education departments in the country.

Sanskrit came out in the study to be the third language offered in non-Muslim schools, as Arabic/Persian in Muslim institutions. There prevails a notion amongst the adult members of the community that the link with the classical language should at all costs be maintained. Even in the Bengali school, Sanskrit was learnt as a fourth language and it was there. It was not the compulsion of the curriculum except for those offering the humanities group. But Sanskrit was seen as a language learnt by science students, strange indeed. For the Hindi medium and Hindi mother tongue groups Sanskrit invariably was found to be the third language in use.

In this language matrix, one knows very well that using one language and the knowledge of it, would very much cripple the person's activity, mobility and mental development. Knowing two languages could have been the option of an individual much to the disadvantage of the person concerned, because limitations would be with regard to communication. A minimum of three languages as proclaimed by the Government, offers a flexibility for intellectual, commercial and professional inter-communication. The chances for progress are not curbed by the democratic government but chances are enhanced at the level of individual learner's own effort and initiative. After all, every bit of life's experiences are not learnt in the schools but outside. There is no dearth of people in our country knowing even twelve to thirteen languages without even a mild murmur. Individual initiative should be exploited by teachers and others in encouraging pupil at young age to learn as many languages as possible. Some languages are for reading, writing, speaking and understanding. Some are for understanding and speaking, some are again for reading and writing. The present study showed that at least two-thirds of the student population found the learning of three languages as beneficial to their general acquisition and achievement. It might be, as one educationist, said, a difficulty of the adult community projected as a problem of the children.

In fact the three language formula has been accepted by the nation, by and large. The states that are making available the opportunities of learning only two languages, would soon be found revising their decisions. It is a common knowledge that for better prospects within the country the national official language must be picked up, learnt and used. The adoption of use of Hindi is seen as obligatory to carry on with national jobs and extending one's communication range. Even this small study had shown how widely Hindi was understood by 100% of the children in the Hindi belt. It takes time to acquire facility in the use of a language. The Indian Government, through the constitutional provision had shown a singularly unique and wise decision in arriving at the three-language formula and in allowing time to implement it slowly and steadily by acquiring the concurrence of the people of the great Republic and not by bulldozing any part of it on the people of the nation. A nation grows richer by adopting more languages than by dropping a few. Children of the future generation must not be deprived of learning more language than three in this muitilingual country.

Moreover, as far as the development of Indian languages and literature are concerned, there had not happened any instance to lament on the cultivation and development of such rich heritage of languages in the country.

For the use of languages for the greater mass of people in the country the consciousness should be roused to pick up as many languages in as best manner as possible.

## Notes and References

1 Chaturvedi and Mohale. *op. cit.*, p. 31.
2 Directorate of Education. Delhi ; Old Secretariat.
3 Ḍelhi Public School, Mathura Road, New Delhi.

# *BIBLIOGRAPHY*

**Books**


Ahmad, Z.A. *National Language for India*. Kitabistan Series-1. Allahabad, 1941.

Altekar, A.S. *Education in Ancient India*. Ed. 5. Varanasi : Nand Kishore & Brothers, 1957.

Allen, W.S. *Ancient Ideas on the Origin and Development of Languages*. Translation of the Philological Society. London, 1980.

Anandvardhan. *Dhuanyalankar*. Delhi : Motilal Banarsi Dass, 1981

Anderson, William L. and Stagberg, Norman G. *Introductory Reading on Language*. New York : Holt, Rinchart & Winstor, 1967.

*Atharv Veda Samhita*. Delhi : Munshi Ram Manohar Lal, 1982.

Ballal, *Bhoj Prabandh*. Varanasi : Chaukhamba Vidyabhawan, 1970.

Ballard, P.B. *Thought and Language*. London : London Press, 1973.

Bannerji. Nikunja Behari. *Language, Meaning and Persons*. London : George Allen & Unwin Ltd., 1963.

Barber, C.L. *The Story of Language Aids to English*. London : The English Language Book Society & Pan Book Ltd., 1964.

Basu, Aparna. *The Growth of Education and Political Development in India 1898-1920*. Delhi : Oxford University Press, 1974.

Basu, Durga Das. *Commentary on the Constitution of India*. Vol. 2. Calcutta : S.C. Sarkar & Sons (Pvt) Ltd., 1950.

Ben, G. Blount. *Language Culture and Society*. U.S.A. ; Winthrop Publications, 1974.

Bernard, Berelson and Morris Jansuritz (Ed). *Public Opinion and Communication*. Illinois : The Free Press, 1950.

Bernier Francis. *Travels in Mughal Empire*. Delhi : S. Chand & Co., 1972.

Best, John W. *Research in Education*. New Delhi : Prentice Hall of India Pvt., Ltd., 1977

Bhamah. *Kavyalankar*. Bombay : Nirnaya Sagar, 1928.

Bharat Muni. *Natya Shastra*. Varanasi : Chaukhamba Sanskrit Prakashan, 1978.

Bhoj. *Saraswati Kanthavaran*. Varanasi Chaukhamba Orientalia, 1976.

Bhoj. *Shringar Prakash*. (Ed. by Josyer G.R. and G. Sriniwasan). Mysore : Coronation Press, 1955.

*Bibliography of Doctoral Dissertations 1979-1985*. New Delhi : Social Sciences and Humanities. Association of Indian Universities, 1987.

Bloomfield, Leonard. *Language*. New York : Henry Halt & Co., 1934.

Boyle, D.G. *Language and Thinking in Human Development*. London: Hutchinson University Library, 1971.

Bright, William (Ed). *Sociolinguistics*. The Hague : Mouton & Co., 1966.

*Britannica Encyclopaedia of Education*. Chicago, 1929.

Burn, Sir Richard (Ed). *The Cambridge History of India*. Vol. IV. Delhi: S. Chand & Co., 1971.

Butch, M. L. *Survey of Research in Education*. 2 Vol. Baroda : The Centre of Advanced Study in Education, Maharaja Sayajirao University of Baroda, 1978.

Carrol, John B. *The Study of Language*. Cambridge : Harvard University Press, 1963.

Chagla, M.C. *Education and the Nation*. Bombay : Allied Publishers, 1970.

Chaitnya Krishna. *A new History of Sanskrit Literature*. Bombay : Asia Publishing House, 1962.

*Chambers Encyclopaedia of Education*. London, 1950.

*Chandogya Upanishad*. Gorakhpur : Geeta Press, 1976.

Chao, Yuen Ren. *Language and Symbolic Systems*. Cambridge : Cambridge University Press, 1968.

Charles, Barber. *The Flux of Language*. London : George Allen and Unwin Ltd., 1964.

Chatterji, Chinmoy. *Vedanta Education*. Lucknow : British Book Depot., 1957.

Chatterjee Kalyan K. *English Education in India : Issues and Opinions*. Delhi : The Macmillan Co. of India Ltd., 1976.

Chatterji, Suniti Kumar. *Languages and Literatures of Modern India*. Calcutta : Bengal Publishers Pvt. Ltd., 1968.

Chatterji Suniti Kumar. *Some Aspects of Indo-Iranian Literary and Cultural Tradition*. Calcutta : Bengal Publishers Pvt. Ltd., 1977.

Chatterjee, Suniti Kumar. *Language and Linguistic Problem*. Ed.3. Madras : Oxford University Press, 1945.

Chatterjee, Suniti Kumar. *Select Writings*. Vol.I. New Delhi : Vikas Publishing House Pvt. Ltd., 1948.

Chatterjee, Suniti Kumar (Ed). *The Cultural Heritage of India*. Vol.5. Calcutta : The Rama Krishna Mission Institute of Culture, 1978.

Chatterjee, Suniti Kumar. *Indo-Aryan and Hindi*. Calcutta : K.L. Mukhopadhyay and Sons., 1969.

Chaturvedi, M.C. and B.V. Mohale. *Position of Languages in School Curriculum in India*. New Delhi : National Council of Educational Research and Training, 1976.

Chaudhri, Rai Harendra Nath. *Our Language Problem*. Calcutta, 1978.

Chinappa, S. Paul. *British System of Education in India*. Bangalore : Bangalore South Institute, 1915.

Coldwell. R, J.L. Wyatt and T. Ramakrishna Pillai. *Comparative Grammar of the South Indian Family of Languages*. U.S.A. : Telegraph Book, 1980.

Cooper, D.E. *Knowledge of Language*. London : Prism Press, 1975.

Dalen and Meyer. *Understanding Educational Research*. New York : McGrew Hill Book Company Inc., 1962.

Dandin, *Dashkumar Charitam*. Bombay : Sanskrit and Prakrit Series, 1919.

Dandin. *Kavyadarsha*. Delhi : Mehar Chand Lachman Das, 1973.

Das, Durga. *India from Curzon to Nehru and After*. London : Collins, 1969.

Das, S.K. *Educational System of Ancient Hindus*. Calcutta : Mitra Press, 1936.

Das, Seth Govind. *Raj Bhasha Hindi*. Prayag Hindi Sahitya Sammelan, 1965.

DeLaguna, C.A. *Speech*. New Haven : Yale University Press, 1927.

Dell, Hynes A. (ed). *Language Culture and Society*. Harper International Edn., 1966.

Desai, M.P. *The Problem of English*. Ahmedabad : Navjivan Publishing House, 1964.

Diamond, A.S. *The History and Origin of Language*. London : Methuen & Co. Ltd., 1959.

Dinkar, Ramdhari Singh. *Sanskriti Ke Char Adhyaya*. Delhi : Rajpal & Sons., 1956.

Durrani, F.K. Khan. *A Plan of Muslim Educational Reform*. Lahore : Sheikh Ghulam Ali & Sons., 1942.

Dutt, N.K. *Aryanization in India*. Calcutta : Mukhopadhyay & Sons., 1970.

Edmund J. King. *Education & Social Change*. U.K. : Pergamon Press, 1966.

Elphinstone. *Ancient India*. Calcutta : Sushil Gupta (India) Ltd., 1953.

Emerson, Rupart. *From Empire to Nation*. Cambridge : Harvard University Press, 1960.

*Encyclopaedia of Modern Education*. New York, 1943.

*Encyclopaedia of Social Sciences*, 1937.

Entwistle William J. *Aspects of Language*. London : Faber & Faber.

Fishman, Ferguson Charles A. and Jyotindra Dass Gupta (Ed). *Language Problems of Developing Nations*. New York : John Wiley, 1968.

Fishman, Joshua (Ed). *Readings in the Sociology of Languages*. Paris: Mouton Hauge, 1968.

Fishman, Joshua (Ed). *Advances in the Sociology of Language*. Paris: Mouton, 1971.

Fraenkal Gerd. *Language*. Boston : Ginn and Co., 1965.

Francis, John. *Nationalism and Language Reform in China*. Princeton : Princeton University Press, 1950.

Garratt, G.T. (Ed). *The Legacy of India*. Oxford : Clarendon Press, 1937.

Garrett, Henry E. *Statistics in Psychology and Education*. N.Y.: Longmans Green & Co., 1953.

Ghosh, Shankar. *Socialism, Democracy and Nationalism in India*. Bombay : Allied Publishers, 1973.

Gokak, V.K. *Education in India — Its Present and Future*. Bombay : Asia Publishing House, 1964.

Good and Scates. *Methods of Research*. New York : Appleton Century Crafts, 1954.

Good, Barr and Scates. *The Methods of Educational Research*. New York : Appleton Century Crafts, Inc., 1941.

Gray Louis A. *Foundation of Language*. New York : Macmillan Co., 1939.

Gulistan J. Kerawalla. *Language Problems and Policies in India and the U.S.S.R.* New Delhi : National Council of Educational Research and Training, 1979.

Gumperz, John T. *Language in Social Groups*. Stanford, California : Stanford University Press, 1971.

Gumperz, John T. and Hymes Dell (Ed). *Directions in Sociolinguistics*. New York : Holt Reinehart & Winston Inc., 1972.

Gunchandra. *Natyadarpana*. Baroda : M.S. University, 1929.

Gune, P.D. *An Introduction to Comparative Philology*. Poona : Oriental Book House, 1950.

Gupta, Jyotindra Das. *Language, Conflict and National Development. Group Politics and National Language Policy in India*. Berkeley : University of California Press, 1970.

Handa, R.L. *Missing Links in Link Language*. New Delhi : Sterling Publishers Pvt. Ltd., 1983.

Harney H. Smith et al. *Area Hand Book for Afghanistan*. Historical Setting. Washington : U.S. Govt. Printing Office, 1973.

Haughan, E.I. *Language Conflicts and Language Planning*. Cambridge: Harvard University Press, 1966.

Henry, M. Hoenigswald. *Language Change and Linguistic Reconstruction*. The University of Chicago Press, 1960.

Hockett, Charles F. *A Course in Modern Linguistics*. New York: The Macmillan Co., 1958.

Hussain, Yusuf. *Glimpses of Medieval Indian Culture*. Bombay : Asia Publishing House, 1957.

Ikram, S.H. *Muslim Civilization in India*. New York : Columbia University Press, 1964.

Jaffar, S.M. *Education in Muslim India* (Education during the Muslim Period of Indian History) (1000-1800 A.D.) Delhi : Idarah-I Adabiyat-I, 1936.

Jain, Jagdish Chandra. *History of Prakrit Literature* (From B.C. 500 to 1800 A.D.)(Hindi). Varanasi : Choukhamba Vidya Bhawan, 1961.

Jerrold J. Kotz. *The Philosophy of Lanaguage*. New York : Harper and Row Publishers, 1968.

Jesperson Otto. *Mankind, Nation and Individual*. London : George Allen & Unwin Ltd., 1922.

Jesperson Otto. *Language-Its Nature, Development and Origin*. London : George Allen & Unwin Ltd., 1922.

John, V.V. *Education and Language Policy*. Bombay : Nachiketa Publications, 1969.

Jorome Bruner et al. *A Study of Thinking*. New York : John Wiley and Sons Inc., London Chapman Hall Ltd., 1956.

Jules Block. *Indo-Aryan-From the Vedas to Modern Times*. Paris : 11, Rue Saint Sulpice, 1956.

Kaul, Onkar N. *Language in Education*. Patiala : Indian Institute of Language Studies, 1983.

Kaushik, Jagdish Prasad. *Bhartiya Arya Bhashaon Ka Itihas*. Jaipur : Apollo Prakashan, 1970.

Keay, F.E. *Indian Education in Ancient and Later Times*. Geoffrey Cambridge : Oxford Univ. Press, 1938.

Keay, F.E. *A History of Education in India and Pakistan* (Education since 1947-48). Oxford Univ. Press, 1949.

Keith, A.B. *History of Sanskrit Literature*. London : Oxford University Press, 1920.

Kellog, S.H. *A Grammar of Hindi Language*. London : Routledge and Kegan Paul Ltd., 1875.

Kodesia, K. *The Problems of Linguistic States in India*. Delhi: Sterling Publishers Pvt. Ltd., 1969.

Krishnamachari, M. *History of Classical Sanskrit Literature*. Delhi: Motilal Banarsi Dass, 1974.

Kuppuswamy, B. *Educational Reconstruction*. Mysore : Sri Kantha Business Syndicate, 1949.

Kumaramangalam, Mohan. *India's Language Crisis*. Madras : New Century Book House, 1965.

Langacker Ronald W. *Language and its Structure*. New York : Harcourt Brace and World Inc., 1968.

Law, N.N. *Promotion of Learning in India — During Mohammadan Rule*. Delhi : Idarah-I Abadiyat-I 1973.

Leona Jakoboviti and Murraya S. Miron (Ed). *Readings in the Psychology of Language*. New Jersey : Englewood Cliffs: Prentice Hall, Inc., 1967.

Leonard George B. *Education and Ecstasy*. New York : Del Publishing Co. Inc., 1968.

Lewis, M.M. *Infant Speech*. London : Kegan Paul, 1936.

Macdonell Arthur A. *A History of Sanskrit Literature*. Delhi : Motilal Banarsi Dass, 1962.

Majumdar, R.C. *An Advanced History of India*. London : Macmillan & Co. Ltd., 1948.

Majumdar, R.C. (Ed). *The History and Culture of the Indian People*. Vol. III, IV, V, VI, VIII. Bombay : Bhartiya Vidya Bhawan Series, 1974.

Malvia, Kanhaiyalal and Bheru Lal M.P. *Hindi. The National Language*. New Delhi : Malvia Prakashan, 1958.

Mammat. *Kavya Prakash*. Banaras : Chaukhamba Vidyabhavan, 1955.

Mathur, Y.B. *Muslims and Changing India*. New Delhi : Trimurti Publications, 1972.

Mathur Y.B. *Growth of Muslim Politics in India*. Delhi : Pragati Publications, 1979.

Max Black (Ed). *The Importance of Language*. London : Carnell University Press, 1962.

Max Muller F. *A History of Ancient Sanskrit Literature*. Varanasi : Chowkhamba Sanskrit Series. Office, 1968.

Mayhew, A. *The Education of India 1835-1920*. London : Faber & Faber.

Mishra, Satya Swaroop. *A Comparative Grammar of Sanskrit*, Goeck and Hittite. Calcutta : The World Press Pvt. Ltd., 1968.

Mitra, Veda. *Education in Ancient India*. New Delhi : India Book Depot, 1964.

Mookerji, Radha Kumud. *Ancient Indian Education*. London : Macmillan & Co. Ltd., 1951.

Moser, C.A. *Survey Methods in Social Investigation*. The English Long Book Society and Heinemann Educational Books Ltd., 1958.

Mujeeb. *Islamic Influence of Indian Society*. Delhi : Meenakshi Prakashan, 1972.

Mukerjee, L. *History of India*. *Modern Period*. Ed.7. Calcutta : Mandal Brothers.

Munshi, K.M. *Gujarat and Its Literature From Early Times*. 1852. Bombay : Bhartiya Vidya Bhawan, 1976.

Murrey, B. Emeneau Delb Hynew and others (ed). *India as a Linguistic Area in Language,* Culture and Society. International Edition, 1966.

Naik, J.P. *Policy and Performance in Indian Education* (1947-74) Delhi : Sangam Books, 1979.

Nayar, Baldev Raj. *National Communication and Language Policy in India*. New York : Frederick A Praeger, 1969.

Nurullah and Naik. *A Student's History of Education in India* (1800-1947). Bombay : Macmillan and Co. Ltd., 1956.

Ogden, C.K. and Richards, I.A. *The Meaning of Meaning*. London : Routledge and Kegan Paul Ltd., 1949.

Oppenheim, A.N. *Questionnaire - Design and Attitude Measurement*. London : Heinemann, 1973.

Pal, Susan. *Language, Shift*. New York : Academic Press, 1979.

Pandit, P.B. *Lectures*. Delhi : Deptt. of Linguistics, Delhi University.

Parsons, C.J. *Thesis and Project Work*. London : George Allen & Unwin Ltd., 1973-76.

Patanjali. *Mahabhashya*. Poona : Bhandarkar Oriental Research Institute, 1972.

Pattnayak, D.P. *Language, Policy and Programme*. New Delhi : Ministry of Education and Youth Services. Govt. of India Press, 1970.

Pattnayak, D.P. *Aspects and Applied Linguistics*. Bombay : Asia Publishing House, 1931.

Pattnayak, D.P. *Multilingualism and Mother tongue Education*. Delhi: Oxford University Press, 1981.

Patel. *The Educational Philosophy of Mahatma Gandhi*. Allahabad : Navjivan Publishing House, 1953.

Percival Spear. *India — A Medieval History*. The University of Michigan Press, 1961.

Percival Spear. *India — A Modern History*. The University of Michigan Press, 1961.

Prasad, N.K. *The Language Issue in India*. Delhi : Leela Devi Publications, 1979.

Pride, J. B. and Holmes Janet (Ed) *Sociolinguistics*. England : Penguin Books Ltd., 1972.

Raghavan, V, *The Indian Heritage: An Anthology of Sanskrit Literature*. Bangalore : The Indian Instiute of Culture, 1956.

Raja C. Kanhan. *Survey of Sanskrit Literature*. Bombay : Bhartiya Vidya Bhawan, 1962.

Rajshekhar., *Kavya Mimansa*. Varanasi : Chaukhamba Vidya Bhawan, 1982.

Ramanathan, G.R. *Educational Planning and National Integration*. Bombay : Asia Publishing House, 1965.

Ramgopal. *Linguistic Affairs of India*. Bombay : Asia Publishing House, 1966.

Rao, P. Kodanna., *Rational Language Policy for India*. Bangalore : Bangalore Committee for English, 1965.

Reddy, Sundra G. (Ed) *The Language Problem in India*. Delhi : National Publishing House, 1973.

*Rkveda Samhita*. Delhi : Motilal Banarsidas, 1977.

Richard Diebold J.P. *Psycholinguistics*. Bloomington : Indiana University Press. 1965.

Ryburn, W.M. *The Teaching of the Mother Tongue*. Geoffrey Cumberleg : Oxford University Press, 1954.

Sabarwal, Satish (Ed)., *Towards a Cultural Policy*. Delhi : Vikas Publishing House Pvt. Ltd., 1975.

Sachau, E.C. *Alberuni's India* 1914. London : Brodway House, 1914.

Sapir, Edward. *Language: A harvest Book*. Nerw York ; Hercourt,Brace & World Inc., 1921.

Sarkar, Amal. *Hand Book of Languages and Dialects of India*. Calcutta, 1964.

Seth, Govind Das. *Raj Bhasha Hindi*. Prayag : Hindi Sahitya Sammelan, 1965.

Shah, A.B. *The Great Debate. Language Controversy and University Education*. Bombay : Lalvani Publishing House, 1968.

Sharp, H. *Educational Records*. Bureau of Education India, 1926.

Shastri, Vasudev Lakshmana. *Brahm Sutra Shankarbhasya*. Bombay: Nirpaya Sagar Prasad, 1934.

Shrivastava, A.L. *The Mughal Empire* (1526-1803 A.D.). Agra : Shiv Lal Agarwal & Co., 1953.

Shrivastava, A.L. *Medieval Indian Culture*. Agra : Shiv Lal Agarwal & Co., 1964.

Shrivastava, Bhagwan Dayal. *The Development of Modern Indian Education*. Bombay : Orient Longmans Ltd., 1955.

Shriwastva, G.P. *A Study In Administrative Personnel*. Delhi : S. Chand and Co., 1965.

Shriwastva, Gopinath. *The Language Controversy and the Minorities*. Delhi : Atma Ram and Sons., 1976.

Sitarammayya, Pattabhi. *The History of the Indian National Congress* (1885-1935). Bombay : Padma Publications Ltd., 1935.

Slobin Dan I. *Psycholinguistics*. London : Scott, Foresman,& Co., 1971.

Spencer, J.E. *Asia East by South: A Cultural Geography*. New York: John Willey & Sons. Inc., 1954.

Stanley Lane Poole. *Baber*. Delhi : S. Chand & Co., 1957.

Stanley Lane Poole, *Mediaeval India Under Mohammadan Rule* (A.D.712-1764). Delhi : Universal Publication, 1963.

Stuart, E.H. *Linguistic Change*. Chicago : University of Chicago Press, 1917.

Tara Chand. *Impact of Western Culture*. Allahabad : The Indian Press Publications Ltd., 1967.

Taraporewala. *Elements of the Science of Language*. Calcutta : Calcutta University, 1962.

Thirtha. *Babel*. Madras : M. Seshachalam & Co., 1962.

Tiwari, Bhola Nath. *Bhasha Vigyan*. Allahabad : Kitab Mahal Pvt. Ltd., 1965.

Tripathi, R.P. *Rise and Fall of Mughal Empire*. Allahabad : Central Book Depot., 1956.

Vakil and Natrajan. *Education in India*. Bombay : Allied Publishers, 1948.

Varma, Satyakama. *Vakyapadiya*. Delhi : Bhartiya Prakashan, 1968.

Varma, Shiv Raj. *Hindi ka Rashtrabhasa ke Roop men Vikas*. New Delhi: Atma Ram & Sons., 1970.

Vendryes, J. *Language*. London : Routledge & Kegan Paul Ltd., 1924.

Venkateswara, S. V. *Indian Culture Through the Ages*. New York : Longman Green, 1928.

Verma, Baidya Nath. *Contemporary India*. Bombay : Asia Publishing House, 1964.

Vidomee Verboj. *Multilingualism*. Leyden : A.W.Sytheff., 1963.

Virginia R.Clark: Eschholz A. Paul and Elfred F. Rosae. (Ed). *Language*. New York : St. Martin Press, 1977.

Vishwanath. *Sahityadarpana*. Varanasi : Chaukhamba Vidyabhawan, 1957.

Vyas, Bhola Shankar. *The Sanskrit Language*. Varanasi : Chaukhamba Vidya Bhawan, 1965.

Weinreineh, U. *Language in Contact*. New York : New York: Linguistic Society, 1953.

Whitney, Fredrich L. *The Elements of Research*. New York : Prentice Hall Inc., 1937.

Wilson, H.H. *Rgveda Samhita*. Delhi : Nag Publishers, 1977.

Winternitz, M. *A History of Indian Literature*. Vol.I. Calcutta : University of Calcutta, 1927.

*World Book Encyclopaedia*, Chicago, 1962.

Yaskmuni. Niruktam (Nighantu). Calcutta : 5 Clive Row. 1952.

**Reports etc.**

*All India Reporter*. Vol. 69. Nagpur : All India Reporter Ltd., 1982.

Chaturvedi, M.C. and Satvir Singh. Third All India Educational Survey, Languages and Media of Instruction Indian School N.C.E.R.T., 1981.

*Constitution of India*. New Delhi : Govt. of India Press, 1981.

*Debates of The Constituent Assembly — Lok Sabha*. New Delhi : Parliament House.

*Debates of the Constituent Assembly — Rajya Sabha*. New Delhi : Parliament House.

*Delhi Diary*. Speeches delivered in Delhi from 10.9.47 to 30.1.48). Ahmedabad : Navjeevan Publishing House, 1948.

*Delhi Gazetteer*. Delhi : Government of India, 1976.

*Education in India 1947-48*. Govt. of India Press, Ministry of Education, 1951.

*Educational Statistics 1981-82*. Delhi : Directorate of Education, Delhi Administration.

*Indian and Foreign Review*. New Delhi : Ministry of Information and Broadcasting, 1966.

Mitra, R.L. Indian "Schools in 1864." *Journal of Asiatic Society of Bengal*.

National Policy on Education 1968. New Delhi : Ministry of Education, 1968.

Pattnayak, D.P. Role of Language Radicalisation of Education. Presidential Address. 20-30 Dec. 1977. Muzaffarnagar.

Platten, C.J. The use of Vernacular Language. Regional Paper on Vernacular Languages. Paris. U.N.E.S.C.O.

Proceedings of the Convention on the Plan of English in Our Educational System 1967. Madras : Hall and Company. 1967.

Proceedings of a Seminar on Language and Society in India. Simla : Indian Institute of Advanced Studies, 1969.

*Punjab District Gazetteer*. Lahore; The Civil and Military Gazette Press, 1913.

Report of Kamal Yar Jung. Education Committee. New Delhi : Ministry of Education. 1942-45.

Report of the Committee of Dr. Tara Chand. New Delhi ; Ministry of Education, 1948.

The Report of the Radha Krishnan (Education Commission)1948-49. New Delhi : Govt. of India, Ministry of Education, 1950.

Report of the (Mudaliar) Secondary Education Commission. 1952-53. New Delhi : Ministry of Education, 1955.

Report of the Official Language Commission 1956. New Delhi : Govt. of India Press, 1957.

Report of the Sanskrit Commission 1956-57. New Delhi : Govt. of India Press, 1958.

Report of the Committee of Parliament on Official Language. 1958. New Delhi : Govt. of India Press, 1959.

Report of the Official Language Controversy. New Delhi : Bureau of Parliamentary Research. Congress Party in Parliament. Parliament House.

Report of Proceedings of Central Advisory Board of Education. Silver Jubilee Souvenir. New Delhi : Govt. of India. Ministry of Education, 1960.

Report of the University Grants Commission (Medium of Instruction) New Delhi : University Grants Commission.

Report of the Committee on Emotional Integration. New Delhi : Govt. of India Press, 1962.

Report of the Education Commission (Kothari Commission) 1964-1966. New Delhi : Govt. of India Press, 1967.
Report of the Committee of Members of Parliament on Education 1967. New Delhi : Govt. Of India Press, 1968.
Report of Census of India, 1971. Delhi : Govt. of India Press, 1971.
Report of the Seminar onNational Integration. New Delhi : University Grants Commission, 1978.
Report of Census of India. 1981. Delhi : Govt. of India Press, 1981.
A Review of Education in India 1947-61. Ist Year Book of Education. New Delhi : Ministry of Education, 1961.
Shrivastava, R.N. Societal Bilingualism and Language Teaching in India. *Indian Journal of Applied Linguistics*. VI, 2, 1980.
*Speeches of Maulana Azad 1947-55*. New Delhi : Publication Division, 1956.
System of Education. England : Longman, Green & Co., Ltd. 1929.
Third All India Educational Survey Educational Facilities and Enrolment (School Education) N.C.E.R.T. 1979.
Unesco Monographs and Fundamental Education. VIII. Paris. 1953

**APPENDIX- I**

## QUESTIONNAIRE

### INSTRUCTIONS

Please read the questions carefully and give your answer in front of each question.

1. Your Name :
2. School :
3. Class :
4. State/Union Territory to which you belong :
5. Your mother tongue :
6. Family Background :
   i) Father's name :
   ii) Father's education :
   iii) Father's occupation :
   iv) The language (s) your father generally speaks :
   v) Mother's education :
   vi) Mother's occupation :
   vii) The language (s) your mother generally speaks :
   viii) Approximate income : (Please tick mark ( ) in one of the columns in the table given below).

| Below Rs. 500/-p.m. | Between Rs. 500/- to Rs. 1500/-p.m. | Above Rs. 1500/-p.m. |
|---|---|---|
| | | |

1. Read the instructions first, then answer :-
   You may be taught certain subjects in certain language media. Now read the question below and write the languages taught and the languages used as media for teaching science and non-science subjects.

| Class | Languages learnt | Languages in which science and non-science subjects were taught |
|---|---|---|
| Class I to V | | |
| Class VI to VIII | | |
| Class IX to X | | |

2. Name the Languages you -

| Understand | Speak | Read | Write |
|---|---|---|---|
| | | | |

3.(a) Name the languages you find difficult to learn out of the three languages, you learn in the school.

(b) Do you face any difficulty in learning languages in school? If yes, mention your difficulties in the table given below.

| Linguistic skills | Mother tongue/ Regional language | Sanskrit/ Arabic/ Persian | English | Hindi |
|---|---|---|---|---|
| 1. In understanding the meaning | | | | |
| 2. In speaking the language | | | | |
| 3. In reading the script | | | | |
| 4. In writing fast | | | | |

4. Name the languages you use at home with your-
   i) Father-
   ii) Mother-
   iii) Brothers and sisters-
   iv) Grand-parents-
   v) Servants-
   vi) Neighbours-

vii) Teachers-
viii) Friends-

5. Name the languages you use in-
   i) Playground-
   ii) In conversation with people belonging to different linguistic groups.
   iii) In shopping-
   iv) In reading books other than textbooks-
   v) In reading newspapers-
   vi) In watching films.
   vii) In listening radio -
   viii) In saying prayer to god-
6. In which languages do you write your-
   i) Diary-
   ii) Poems-
   iii) Story/stories-
   iv) Letters to friends-
   v) Letters to relatives-
7. What do you think is the effect of learning three languages on the study of other subjects? Please give your opinion in not more than ten lines.

**APPENDIX-II**

## QUESTIONNAIRE

You are requested to fill in the following questionnaire. It is not necessary for you to disclose your name and address. These data will be treated as confidential and used only anonymously for research purposes, the intention, being, to highlight the public opinion regarding the 'three language formula' and its implementation.

1. Name:
2. Address:
3. Qualifications :
   a) Academic:
   b) Professional:
4. School/Organisation:
5. Designation i.e. Nature of work.
6. Teaching experience:
7. Your mother tongue:
8. The State you belong to:
9. The languages (s) you teach:

| Classes | Periods | Time Allotted | Language(s) | Media for teaching different language(s) |
|---|---|---|---|---|
| | | | | |

10. Knowledge of language teaching:
11. Preference of language teaching:

**INSTRUCTIONS :**

A five point scale ranging from 5 to 1 is given below. Please indicate as to what extent do you agree with them. Consider the statement.

"Teaching all the subjects through the medium of English language will deteriorate the standard of education".

You can record your view under anyone of the following category:

| 5 | 4 | 3 | 2 | 1 |
|---|---|---|---|---|
| Agree | Slightly agree | Neutral | Slightly disagree | Disagree |

If you put a cross (X) on 5, it would mean that you completely agree with the statement....

Similarly - 1 - Disagree
2 - Slightly disagree
3 - Neutral
4 - Slightly agree
5 - Agree

You are requested now to go through the following statements and record your views against each statement.

1. The three language formula would help in raising the overall academic standard.

| 5 | 4 | 3 | 2 | 1 |
|---|---|---|---|---|
| Agree | Slightly agree | Neutral | Slightly disagree | Disagree |

2. The implementation of the three language formula will help in promoting the mobility of the people.

| 5 | 4 | 3 | 2 | 1 |
|---|---|---|---|---|
| Agree | Slightly agree | Neutral | Slightly disagree | Disagree |

3. The said formula when implemented totally will help in developing communication among the people.

| 5 | 4 | 3 | 2 | 1 |
|---|---|---|---|---|
| Agree | Slightly agree | Neutral | Slightly disagree | Disagree |

4. The three language formula will promote national integration.

| 5 | 4 | 3 | 2 | 1 |
|---|---|---|---|---|
| Agree | Slightly agree | Neutral | Slightly disagree | Disagree |

5. The knowledge of three languages as described under the said formula, will enhance the occupational opportunities:

| 5 | 4 | 3 | 2 | 1 |
|---|---|---|---|---|
| Agree | Slightly agree | Neutral | Slightly disagree | Disagree |

6. The knowledge of regional language (s) under the three language formula will help in enriching the linguistic heritage of our country.

| 5 | 4 | 3 | 2 | 1 |
|---|---|---|---|---|
| Agree | Slightly agree | Neutral | Slightly disagree | Disagree |

7. The knowledge of three languages will be helpful in broadening the outlook and enriching the knowledge.

| 5 | 4 | 3 | 2 | 1 |
|---|---|---|---|---|
| Agree | Slightly agree | Neutral | Slightly disagree | Disagree |

8. The ıearning of English language under the three language formula will help in establishing international understanding and relations.

| 5 | 4 | 3 | 2 | 1 |
|---|---|---|---|---|
| Agree | Slightly agree | Neutral | Slightly disagree | Disagree |

9. There is no need to modify the three language formula.

| 5 | 4 | 3 | 2 | 1 |
|---|---|---|---|---|
| Agree | Slightly agree | Neutral | Slightly disagree | Disagree |

10. Learning the three languages does not constitute any burden for the children.

| 5 | 4 | 3 | 2 | 1 |
|---|---|---|---|---|
| Agree | Slightly agree | Neutral | Slightly disagree | Disagree |

11. Learning more than two languages at the same time does not clash with the acquisition of different language skills in different languages.

| 5 | 4 | 3 | 2 | 1 |
|---|---|---|---|---|
| Agree | Slightly agree | Neutral | Slightly disagree | Disagree |
| X | X | X | X | X |

Would you like any modification, alteration or addition in the three language formula? If yes, express your opinion(s) in not more than 20 lines.

**APPENDIX-III**

## INTERVIEW SCHEDULE

1. Non-Hindi states, especially Tamil Nadu is doing without adopting three language formula i.e. Mother tongue, Hindi and English. They are teaching only two languages i.e. Tamil and English. What measures should the Centre adopt so that the non-Hindi speaking states willingly/compulsorily introduce Hindi the official language of the country in their school-curricula?
2. The school authorities are shifting to English medium after 5th standard, when there is no such policy or education. How would Hindi or other regional languages be in a position to replace English.
3. English is in demand everywhere and at every level of school education. If it continues like this, how would Hindi/regional languages be promoted as the medium of instruction at higher level and get their due place.
4. What languages should be taught to the students in their own (personal) interest and in the interest of society and nation?

**Annexure - I**

## SCHOOLS HAVING MINORITY LANGUAGE AS MEDIUM OF INSTRUCTION [1]

| S.No. | Languages/Schools | Class. |
|---|---|---|
| | **Punjabi as Medium** | |
| 1. | Maharaja Ranjit Singh Co-Edn. Middle School, Ranjit Nagar, New Delhi. | Primary Stage |
| 2. | Guru Nanak Girls School, Subzi Mandi. | I to VIII |
| 3. | S.G.T.B. Khalsa Girls Sr. Sec. School, Ali Ganj. | II, IV & V to XII |
| 4. | S.G.T.B. Khalsa Girls Sr. Sec. School, Sis Ganj. | I to XII |
| 5. | Bhai Joga Singh Girls Sr. Sec. School, East Patel Nagar. | III to VIII |
| 6. | S.G.T.B. Girls S.S. School, Dev Nagar. | I to XII |
| 7. | S.G.T.B. Boys S.S. School, Dev Nagar. | I To VIII |
| | **Urdu Medium** | |
| 1. | G.G.M.S. Kala Mahal. | VI to VIII |
| 2. | G.G.M.S. Haweli Azam Khan. | V to VIII |
| 3. | G.G.M.S. Lal Kuan. | VI to VIII |
| 4. | G.G.M.S. Bulbuli Khana. | VI to VIII |
| 5. | G.B.M.S. Matia Mahal. | VI to VIII |
| 6. | G.B.M.S., Okhla. | VI to VIII |
| 7. | G.G.S. School, Jafrabad. | VI to X |
| 8. | G.B.S. School, Jafrabad. | VI to X |
| 9. | G.B.S. School, Trilok Puri. | VI to VIII |
| 10. | G.B.S.S., Pataudi House. | VI to X |
| 11. | G.B.S.S, New Friends Colony. | IX to X |
| 12. | G.B.S.S., Jama Masjid No. 2. | IX to X |
| 13. | G.B.S.S.S., Jama Masjid. | VI to XII |
| 14. | G.G.S.S. School, Chasma Building. | VI to XII |
| 15. | G.G.S.S. School Bulbuli Khana. | VI to XII |
| 16. | G.G.S.S. School Zeenat Mahal No. 2. | VI to XII |
| | **Aided Schools** | |
| 1. | Fatehpuri Muslim S.S. School. | VI to XII |

1. Educational Statistics 1981-82 : Directorate of Education, Delhi Administration. Table No. XVII-3, pp. 27-28.

* Enhanced 2 more minority schools. Information gathered from the Directorate of Education, Delhi : Old Secretariat. 1987.

| | |
|---|---|
| 2. Shafiq Memorial S.S. School. | I to XII |
| 3. Anglo-Arabic S.S. School. | VI to XII |
| 4. Majurul Islam Sec. School. | I to X |
| 5. Quami Boys S.S. School. | I to X |
| **Bengali Medium** | |
| 1. Bengali Boys S.S. School, Alipur Road. | I to XII |
| 2. Raisina Bengali S.S. School, Reading Road. | I to VIII |
| 3. Union Academy, Raja Bazar, New Delhi. | I to V |
| 4. V.N. Bengali S.S. School, Sarojini Nagar. | I to XII |
| 5. Bidhan Chandra (Co-ed.) S.S. School, Moti Bagh. | I to X |
| 6. Lady Irwin, Canning Road, New Delhi. | I to VIII |
| 7. Shyama Prasad (Co-edn.) Vidyalaya, Lodhi Estate. | I to X |
| 8. Vidya Bhawan Girls S.S. School, New Rajinder Nagar. | I to XII |
| **Tamil Medium** | |
| 1. D.T.E.A.,Mandir Marg | I to V |
| 2. D.T.E.A.,Lodhi Estate | I to V |
| 3. D.T.E.A. Laxmi Bai Nagar | I to V |
| 4. D.T.E.A., R.K. Puram. | I to V |
| 5. D.T.E.A., Moti Bagh. | I to V |
| 6. D.T.E.A., Pusa Road. | I to V |
| 7. D.T.E.A., Janak Puri. | I to IV |
| **Sindhi Medium** | |
| 1. S.E.S. Baba Neh Raj (Co-edn.) S.S School Lajpat Nagar, New Delhi. | I to VIII |
| 2. G.B.M.S. Bara Hindu Rao, Delhi. | I to V |
| **Gujarati Medium** | |
| 1. S.S.L.T. Gujrati, Raj Niwas Marg, Delhi. | I to V |
| **Telugu Medium** | |
| 1. Andhra Education Society (Co-edn.) Rouse Avenue, New Delhi. | I to V |
| 2. Telugu School, Sector-II, R.K. Puram, New Delhi. | I to V |
| 3. Andhra Edn. Society, Middle School, Prasad Nagar, | I to V |
| **Malayalam Medium** | |
| 1. Kerala Education Society (Co-edn.) Sr. Sec. School Canning Road, New Delhi. | I to V |
| 2. Kerala Public Middle School, Janak Puri. | I to V |

**Raisina Bengali Senior Secondary School**

**Table (a) The mother tongues of the students, the regions they belonged to and the languages generally used by their parents**

| *Mother tongue of the students* | *Bengali* | *English* | *Bengali + Hindi* | *Ben. + English* | *Hindi + English* | *Ben. + Hindi + Engish* | *Total* | *Hindi speak-ing areas* | *Non-Hindi speaking areas* |
|---|---|---|---|---|---|---|---|---|---|
| Bengali | 38=76% | 1=2% | 3=6% | 2=4% | 1=2% | 4=8% | 49 | 28=56% | 22=44% |
| 50 | (32)=(64%) | (5)=(10%) | -- | (6)=(12%) | (1)=(2%) | (6)=(12%) | (50) | | |

N.B. : The figures within parentheses are for fathers and the figures outside are for mothers.

**Table (b) Parents' education and occupation**

| *Education/ Occupation* | | *Illiterate* | *Lower-secondary upto VIII class* | *Higher secondary i.e. till XII class* | *Graduate* | *Post-graduate* | *Total* |
|---|---|---|---|---|---|---|---|
| Business | M | – | – | – | – | – | – |
| | F | – | – | – | 2=4% | – | 2=4% |

contd....

| | | | | | | | |
|---|---|---|---|---|---|---|---|
| Service | M | -- | -- | 1=2% | -- | 2=4% | 3=6% |
| | F | -- | -- | 14=28% | 15=30% | 14=28% | 43=86% |
| Not in service | M | 3=6% | 12=24% | 8=16% | 18=36% | 5=10% | 46=92% |
| | F | -- | -- | -- | 5=10% | -- | 5=10% |
| Total | M | 3=6% | 12=24% | 9=18% | 18=36% | 7=14% | 49=98% |
| | F | -- | -- | 14=28% | 22=44% | 14=28% | 50=100% |

N.B. M stands for mother and F stands for Father.

**Table (c) Financial Background of the families of the students**

| *Below Rs. 500/- per month* | *Between Rs. 500/- to Rs. 1500/- per month* | *Above Rs. 1500/- per month* |
|---|---|---|
| 9 = 18% | 23 = 46% | 18 = 36% |

**Table (d) Languages learnt and languages used as media of instruction at different levels of school education**

| Languages learnt/ mother tongue | Class 1 to 5 | | | Class 6 to 8 | | Class 9 to 10 | | |
|---|---|---|---|---|---|---|---|---|
| | *Ben. + H + + Eng.* | *Bengali* | *English* | *Ben. + Hindi + + Eng. + Skt.* | *Bengali* | *Ben + Eng.* | *Hindi + Eng.* | *English* |
| Bengali | 50=100% | -- | -- | 50=100% | -- | 35=70% | 15=30% | -- |
| 50 | -- | (25)=(50%) | (25)=(50%) | -- | (50)=(100%) | -- | -- | (50)=(100%) |

N.B. The figures within parentheses show the languages used as media of instruction and the figures outside are for the languages learnt at different levels of school education.

**Table (e) Language attainment and four language skills**

| *(i) Understand only* | | | *(ii) Learn and speak only* | | *(iii) Learn, read and write* | | *(iv) Understand, speak, read and write* | | | | |
|---|---|---|---|---|---|---|---|---|---|---|---|
| *Language/ Mother tongue* | *Punjabi* | *Assamese* | *Language/ Mother Tongue* | *Sanskrit* | *Lan. M.T.* | *Skt.* | *Lan. M.T.* | *Ben.* | *Hindi* | *Eng.* | *Skt.* |
| Bengali 50 | 12=24% | 20=40% | Bengali 50 | 5=10% | Beng. 50 | 40=80% | Beng. 50 | 50 100% | 50 100% | 50 100% | 10 20% |

**Table (f) (i) Languages difficult to learn**

| *Mother Tongue* | *Bengali* | *Hindi* | *English* | *Sanskrit* | *Bengali + English* |
|---|---|---|---|---|---|
| Bengali 50 | 50=100% | 50=100% | 50=100% | 50=100% | -- |
| | (1)=(2%) | -- | (3)=(6%) | (14)=28%) | (1)=(2%) |

N.B. Figures within parentheses show the languages difficult to learn and the figures outside the parentheses show the language learnt.

**Table (f) (ii) Languages difficult to learn in terms of skills**

| *Mother* | *Mother tongue* | | | | *Classical Language* | | | | *English* | | | | *Hindi* | | | |
|---|---|---|---|---|---|---|---|---|---|---|---|---|---|---|---|---|
| tongue | U | S | R | W | U | S | R | W | U | S | R | W | U | S | R | W |
| Bengali 50 | 9 | 5 | 4 | 8 | 24 | 27 | 24 | 27 | 3 | 3 | 3 | 4 | 5 | 3 | 3 | 4 |

N.B. U = Understand, S= Speak, R= Read, W = Write.

**Table (g) Language students spoke to various persons**

| *Mother tongue* | *To speak to/ languages used* | *Father* | *Mother* | *Brothers/ sisters* | *Grand-parents* | *Servant* | *Neighbour* | *Teachers* | *Friends* |
|---|---|---|---|---|---|---|---|---|---|
| Bengali | B | 23=46% | 36=72% | 16=32% | 25=50% | 7=14% | 1=2% | 9=18% | 2=4% |
| 50 | H | -- | -- | -- | -- | 40=80% | 3=6% | -- | -- |
| | E | 5=10% | -- | 3=6% | -- | -- | 2=4% | 11=22% | 1=2% |
| | B+H | -- | 1=2% | -- | -- | 1=2% | 15=30% | -- | 2=4% |
| | B+E | 18=36% | 10=20% | 17=34% | 5=10% | | | 21=42% | 11=22% |
| | H+E | -- | -- | -- | -- | -- | 12=24% | -- | 1=2% |
| | H+Pu | -- | -- | -- | -- | 2=4% | -- | -- | -- |
| | B+H+E | 4=8% | 3=6% | 4=8% | 1=2% | -- | 12=24% | 9=18% | 32=64% |
| | H+E+Pu | -- | -- | -- | -- | -- | 2=4% | -- | -- |
| | B+H+Pu | -- | -- | -- | -- | -- | 2=4% | -- | -- |
| | B+H+E+Pu | -- | -- | 1=2% | -- | -- | 1=2% | -- | 1=2% |
| | | 50=100% | 50=100% | 41=82% | 31=62% | 50=100% | 50=100% | 50=100% | 50=100% |

**Table (h) The languages used in various situations**

| *Mother Tongue* | *Languages used* | *Play-ground* | *Conversation with different language people* | *Shopping* | *Reading books other than text-books* | *Reading News-papers* | *Watching films* | *Listen-ing to radio* | *Saying prayers to God* |
|---|---|---|---|---|---|---|---|---|---|
| Bengali | B | 13=26% | -- | -- | 6=12% | -- | 2=4% | 2=4% | 41=82% |
| 50 | H | 3=6% | 10=20% | 21=42% | -- | -- | 2=4% | 6=12% | -- |
| | E | -- | 19=38% | 3=6% | 9=18% | 32=64% | 2=4% | 1=2% | -- |
| | Skt. | -- | -- | -- | -- | -- | -- | -- | 5=10% |
| | B+H | 11=22% | 2=4% | 2=4% | 1=2% | -- | 1=2% | 2=4% | -- |
| | B+E | 4=8% | -- | -- | 17=34% | 8=16% | 2=4% | 1=2% | -- |
| | B+Skt. | -- | -- | -- | -- | -- | -- | -- | 4=8% |
| | H+E | 4=8% | 14=28% | 22=44% | 6=12% | 2=4% | 12=24% | 27=54% | -- |
| | E+Pu | -- | -- | 1=2% | -- | -- | -- | -- | -- |
| | B+H+E | 15=30% | 5=10% | 1=2% | 10=20% | 8=16% | 29=58% | 11=22% | -- |
| | | 50=100% | 50=100% | 50=100% | 49=98% | 50=100% | 50=100% | 50=100% | 50=100% |

**Table (i) Languages used for writing for different purposes**

| *Mother tongue* | *Language used in writing* | *Diary* | *Literary articles* | *Letters to friends* | *Letters to relatives* |
|---|---|---|---|---|---|
| Bengali 50 | Bengali | 18=36% | 7=14% | 4=8% | 23=46% |
| | English | 14=28% | 12=24% | 24=48% | 5=10% |
| | B+E | 12=24% | 13=26% | 15=30% | 19=38% |
| | H+E | 1=2% | – | 2=4% | 1=2% |
| | B+H+E | 5=10% | 12=24% | 5=10% | 2=4% |
| | | 50=100% | 44=88% (6) (12%) | 50=100% | 50=100% |

N.B. Figure in parentheses shows 'no' response.

**Table (j) Students' opinion regarding the effect of learning three languages on other subjects**

| *Opinion of students Mothertongue* | *Helped in studies* | *Adverse effect on studies* | *No effect* | *No response* | *Total* |
|---|---|---|---|---|---|
| Bengali 50 | 23=46% | 9=18% | 7=14% | 11=22% | 50=100% |

# Index

C